Holy

Volume II

The Gospels and Acts
Undistorted by Faith

❖

Robert M. Price

Mindvendor

❖ Authors Note ❖

What is the role of tradition in biblical scholarship? There are two ways to view it. If, as G.K. Chesterton said, tradition is a "democracy of the dead," giving the scholars of the past a vote in our deliberations, tradition becomes the dead hand of the past, always outvoting new ideas and theories. But there is also a very real tradition of discovery and innovation, which refuses to acquiesce to the ghosts of the past and their orthodoxies.

If we decide to throw off that yoke, even while learning all we can from our scholarly forbears, we will be free to do what they did: discover all-new paradigms to allow new discoveries. If we dare to do that, we can accelerate the progress of biblical research. It is in that spirit that *Holy Fable*, volume II is offered. Reading it, you will find it is a fair trade: if we declare independence from tradition we will find ourselves more than rewarded by new horizons of understanding.

Who really wrote the gospels? When and why? Could they have been products of the second century rather than the first? Do they give us information about a man named Jesus? Or "only" about the various groups whose figurehead he was? Does the Book of Acts chronicle the history of early Christianity, or is it a piece of institutional propaganda? Is there a single coherent message in the New Testament?

Is it possible to arrive at firm answers to such questions, or must we learn to be satisfied with mere possibilities? And can we understand the text better if we set faith aside?

Titles by Robert M. Price

Beyond Born Again: Toward Evangelical Maturity
Inerrant the Wind: The Evangelical Crisis of Biblical Authority
Deconstructing Jesus: How Reliable is the Gospel Tradition?
The Widow Traditions in Luke-Acts: A Feminist-Critical Scrutiny
The DaVinci Fraud: Why the Truth Is Stranger than Fiction
The Paperback Apocalypse: How the Christian Church Was Left Behind
The Pre-Nicene New Testament: 54 Formative Texts
Jesus Is Dead
Atheism and Faitheism
Evolving out of Eden: Christian Responses to Evolution (with Edwin Suominen)
The Reason-Driven Life: What Am I Here on Earth for?
Moses and Minimalism: Form Criticism versus Fiction in the Pentateuch
The Christ Myth Theory and Its Problems
The Case Against "The Case for Christ": A New Testament Scholar Refutes the Reverend Lee Strobel
The Tommentary: Interpreting the Gospel of Thomas
The Needletoe Letters: A Parody of "The Screwtape Letters"
Top Secret: The Truth Behind Today's Pop Mysticisms
The Politically Correct Bible
Jesus Christ Superstar: The Making of a Modern Gospel
Biblical Buddhism: Tales and Sermons of Saint Iodasaph
Bart Ehrman Interpreted: How One Radical New Testament Scholar Understands Another
Latter-day Scripture: Studies in the Book of Mormon
The Sage of Aquarius: A Centennial Study of "The Aquarian Gospel of Jesus the Christ"
The Amazing Colossal Apostle: The Search for the Historical Paul
Night of the Living Savior
Blaming Jesus for Jehovah: Rethinking the Righteousness of Christianity
The Human Bible New Testament
Secret Scrolls: Revelations from the Lost Gospel Novels
Killing History: Jesus in the No-Spin Zone
The Historical Bejeezus: What a Long, Strange Quest it's Been
Preaching Deconstruction

For John Lowe,
who loves the Bible as much as I do.

CONTENTS TO VOL. II

INTRODUCTION

Having read the first volume of *Holy Fable*, you know that my goal is to provide broader access to a viable but generally neglected (or unknown) approach to biblical criticism. It is a variety of "the Higher Criticism," a term little heard these days because it represents a more daring, less "safe" approach to the study of the Bible. The history of biblical scholarship is one of those "one step forward, two steps back" things. Trying to make progress in this field is like one of those dreams in which you need to be running, but you seem to be struggling against a miasma that sucks at your feet and makes it almost impossible to get anywhere.

And this retardation/retrenchment results in a two-front war for the forward-looking critic. On the one hand, the aspiring scholar must fend off sophistical damage-control efforts and attempts at obfuscation by religious apologists whose only interest in genuine criticism is to refute it, playing a role equivalent to Al Pacino's character as an undercover cop seeking to infiltrate the homosexual underground in the movie *Cruising*. It's the last place he wants to be, but it's a dirty job somebody has to do.

On the other hand, the radical critic has to free himself from the inertia of "consensus scholarship," the Magisterium of the mainstream which by its very nature seeks safety in numbers. Venturesome hypotheses are heresy there, because they are, again by nature, breaking the conventional rules for playing the game. If you want to win the pennant, you can't change the number of bases, or of players on a team. The true Higher Critic might convince enough colleagues to start a new game or even a new league, but that is not the goal. Far be it from him to compete in a popularity contest. The history of scientific revolutions[1] proves that paradigms are glacially

10

slow to shift. But really, who cares if they ever do? The radical critic takes a lesson from Nietzsche: he repudiates the safe and comfortable collectivity of "those who seek glory from one another" and is instead happy enough to go it alone, his only goal to pursue his burning questions as far as they will go. Paul Feyerabend knew this: "The only principle that does not inhibit progress is *anything goes.*"[2] Like Nietzsche's mad prophet, the critic must realize again and again that

> I have come too early. My time is not yet. This tremendous event is still on its way, still wandering; it has not yet reached the ears of men. Lightning and thunder require time; the light of the stars requires time; deeds, though done, still require time to be seen and heard. This deed is still more distant from them than the most distant stars.

The first volume of *Holy Fable* covered the Old Testament, seeking to supply the interested reader with unflinchingly radical perspectives on the sacred text, some of these being novel speculations of my own, others the forgotten contributions of earlier generations buried by timid subsequent generations. This New Testament volume does the same. And like its predecessor, this book is in no way intended as an attack on the Bible. To the contrary, my goal is to *defend* the Bible, which I love, against those who would attempt to suffocate it in the mummy wrappings of dogma and apologetics, like Boris Karloff in *The Mummy.* I love and study the Bible for its own sake, not for the sake of something else, e.g., a supposedly infallible answer book to save me the trouble of thinking for myself. Not as proof for a miraculous Savior to issue me a ticket to heaven. No, as always, one must "act without the fruits of action."[3]

---

[1] Thomas S. Kuhn, *The Structure of Scientific Revolutions* Chicago: University of Chicago Press, 1962).

[2] Paul Feyerabend, *Against Method* (New York: Verso. Rev. ed. 1988), p. 14.

[3] Franklin Edgerton, trans., *The Bhagavad Gita* (New York: Harper Torchbooks. Harper & Row, 1964), pp. 159-161; Mircea Eliade, *Yoga: Immortality and Freedom.* Trans. Willard R. Trask. Bollingen Series LVI (Princeton: Princeton University Press, 1969), p. 39, n. 70.

Finally, let me reiterate that, as always, I am not trying to win anyone over. Rather, my purpose is merely to provide information and perspectives that may be new to the reader. Do with them what you will. All independent thinkers are continually engaged in forming (and reforming) their own syntheses, revising them as they take new data and opinions into account. We will never really finish. Our quests will be rudely suspended when the Grim Reaper taps us on the shoulder. I am reminded of an anecdote[4] concerning the great New Testament scholar Ernst Käsemann who one day warned his students under no circumstances to exceed the assigned page limit on a paper. He told them they would be so proud of their work that they would say to themselves, "This is so great, Herr Käsemann won't mind if I go on a bit longer!" But *no*, they must *not*! So, naturally, one student is so enthusiastic about his paper that he goes over the limit anyhow. He is eager to get the graded paper back from the professor but is shocked to see the extra pages have been torn off! At the bottom of the last remaining page, Käsemann had written, "You were doing so well, but you finished so abruptly!" That's what's going to happen to your scholarly quest and to mine. Only it won't be Käsemann.

What the hell?, you say. *Then why bother in the first place?* Because it's the chase. It's the hunt. It's acting without the fruits of action. You needn't be bitter about it, like the fellow who wrote Ecclesiastes 2:21, "sometimes a man who has toiled with wisdom and knowledge and skill must leave all to be enjoyed by a man who did not toil for it. This also is vanity and a great evil." No, it isn't! Better that someone pick up where you left off! Pass the torch! Doing your part is all you can do, and that should be satisfaction enough. It is for me.

---

[4] I have this hadith from David M. Scholer.

INTRODUCTION

Robert M. Price
November 19, 2017

10

The Gospel According to Mark
This Was the Son of God

Mark my Words

There is some reason (though that's as strongly as I would put it) to think the Gospel of Mark was written in Rome. For one thing, it uses a number of Latin loan-words (like "praetorium" in 15:16 and "centurion" in 15:39).[5] For another, a Roman origin would explain the continued copying and preservation of Mark in view of the fact that both Matthew and Luke incorporated almost the whole text of Mark into their own gospels. Why keep making copies of an obsolete, redundant gospel? After all, Matthew and Luke also both used the Q source, a collection of sayings, most without narrative contexts, and this is probably why scribes did not bother to continue copying Q (with the result that we don't have Q anymore and have to reconstruct it from Matthew and Luke). If, however, Mark had the prestige of being the gospel of the Roman Church, no one was going to let it lapse.

Papias, mid-second century bishop of Hierapolis, is quoted by Church Fathers Irenaeus and Eusebius as describing Mark as a transcription of the preaching of Peter to the congregation in Rome. But there is no reason to accept that claim. First, Papias provides other tidbits of alleged apostolic information that are obviously legendary and spurious, e.g., that before Judas Iscariot died (Acts 1:18), popping like a tick, he swelled up to the proportions of a parade balloon and urinated maggots. Second, like the rest of the gospels, Mark is just not written in the form of memoirs.[6] If Papias

---

[5] Benjamin W. Bacon, *Is Mark a Roman Gospel?* Harvard Theological Studies VII (Cambridge: Harvard University Press, 1919), pp. 53-59.
[6] Dennis E. Nineham, *Explorations in Theology1* (London: SCM Press, 1977), Chapter

was right, we should expect to read something like Boswell's *Johnson*,[7] or like the "Preaching of John," a section of the second-century Acts of John in which the aged apostle recounts his memories of his Lord: "I remember how Jesus used to..."[8]

Can we locate Mark amid the competing factions of early Christians, each attached to a different apostle or authority group (1 Cor. 1:12; Gal. 1:6-9; 2:6; Matt. 7:21-23; 16:17-19; Mark 9:38-39; James 2:20)? Quite likely we can. We can certainly eliminate any allegiance to Peter and the Twelve in view of Mark's unrelentingly negative portrayal of these men as uncomprehending clods and self-aggrandizing schemers.[9] Mark is equally severe in his treatment of the Holy Family of Jesus (called in the early church the Heirs and the *Desposunoi*, "those with the Lord"). Mark 3:21, in which his relatives try to take custody of Jesus, thinking him insane, is damning in this respect.[10] Nor does Mark carry a torch for the women disciples of Jesus, notably Mary Magdalene, as he pointedly tells us they *disobeyed* the charge of the young man at the tomb to tell Peter and his colleagues to go back to Galilee to rejoin the risen Jesus. Who is left? The best conjecture, if only by process of elimination, would seem to be Paul,[11] who appears in Mark 9:38-39 as the "strange exorcist" who

---

2, "Eye-witness Testimony and the Gospel Tradition I," pp. 24-37; Chapter 3, "Eye-witness Testimony and the Gospel Tradition II," pp. 38-48; Chapter 4, "Eye-witness Testimony and the Gospel Tradition III," pp. 49-60.

[7] C.S. Lewis makes the fantastic, credibility-shattering claim that the Gospel of John(!) represents a precursor to Boswell's *Johnson* in its on-scene reportage of its subject's words and behavior. Lewis, "Modern Theology and Biblical Criticism," in Walter Hooper, ed., *Christian Reflections* (Grand Rapids: Eerdmans, 1980), pp. 155.

[8] This is not to say the Acts of John preserves historically authentic material (it doesn't), just that the author *did* understand what eyewitness recollections would sound like.

[9] Bacon, *Roman Gospel*, Chapter III, "The Internal Evidence," Section E., "Attitude toward Jewish-Christian Leaders," pp. 75-80; Theodore J. Weeden, *Mark: Traditions in Conflict* (Philadelphia: Fortress Press, 1971).

[10] Burton L. Mack, *A Myth of Innocence: Mark and Christian Origins* (Philadelphia: Fortress Press, 1988), pp. 90-91.

[11] Bacon, *Roman Gospel*, Chapter III, "The Internal Evidence," Section D, "The 'Paulinism' of Mark," pp. 66-75; Ralph P. Martin, *Mark: Evangelist and Theologian*. Contemporary Evangelical Perspectives (Grand Rapids: Zondervan, 1973), pp. 161-162; Tom Dykstra, *Mark, Canonizer of Paul: A New Look at Intertextuality in Mark's Gospel* (St. Paul: OCABS Press, 2012).

invoked the name of Jesus but did not belong to the circle of the Twelve.

When was it written? Mainstream scholars and Christian apologists (when there's a difference) chant as if it's a creed (and, come to think of it, it *is*) a date of 70 C.E. for the writing of Mark's gospel. Why? They gravitate toward the earliest semi-plausible date in order to shorten the span between a historical Jesus and the earliest known gospel.[12] And of course the point of that is to minimize the likelihood of distortion, embellishment, and fabrication of the Jesus tradition, even though the forty year interval is easily enough time for these processes to prevail. At any rate, there are at least two factors militating against so early a date. First, Mark 13, the Olivet Discourse, is very likely based on an apocalyptic tract written to reassure Christians of a bright future after the Roman suppression of the messianic revolt of Simon bar Kochba in 136 C.E.[13] Second, we can detect concentric "tree rings" here and there in Mark, each betokening a new delay of the Parousia (Second Coming) of Christ. We have to allow a fair amount of time for the failure of each predicted deadline to be acknowledged and reckoned with. Thus a whole series of them demand a pretty late date for Mark, somewhere about the mid-second century. (I'll have more to say on these "tree rings" as we get to each one.)

To what extent was Mark based on oral tradition, as form critics supposed?[14] Or was it mainly free composition?[15] Or was it

---

[12] Mack, *Myth of Innocence*, p. 318.

[13] Hermann Detering, "The Synoptic Apocalypse (Mark 13 par): a Document from the Time of Bar Kochba." Trans. Michael Conley and Darrell J. Doughty, *Journal of Higher Criticism*. Fall 2000 (7/2), pp. 161-210.

[14] Rudolf Bultmann, *The History of the Synoptic Tradition*. Trans. John Marsh (New York: Harper & Row, 1968), pp. 339-351; Martin Dibelius, *From Tradition to Gospel* (New York: Scribners, n.d.,) Chapter I, "Formgeschichte, or the Criticism of Literary Form," pp. 1-8; Vincent Taylor, *The Formation of the Gospel Tradition: Eight Lectures* (London: Macmillan, 1957), Chapter II, "The Formative Process in the Primitive Communities," pp. 22-43; D.E. Nineham, *Saint Mark*. Pelican New Testament Commentaries (Baltimore: Penguin Books, 1969).

[15] Bruno Bauer, *Christ and the Caesars: The Origin of Christianity from Romanized Greek Culture*. Trans. Frank E. Schacht (Charleston: Alexander Davidonis, 1998), pp. 316-331; Albert Schweitzer, *The Quest of the Historical Jesus: A Critical Study of its Progress*

both? Had the evangelist (gospel writer) rewritten Old Testament stories from the Greek Septuagint?[16] Or were such rewrites themselves the products of many anonymous story-tellers who not only read the Old Testament stories as anticipating or predicting Jesus but went on to recast them as fulfillments of such predictions/expectations?[17] These may have reached Mark via oral transmission, and he organized them, editing here and there.

Do we possess Mark's gospel in its original form? There is a long-standing debate over the ending. Did the author really intend his gospel to conclude with 16:8? Most scholars think so today, but it has not always been so. Others have thought Mark wrote more but that anything following 16:8 has been accidentally lost.[18] Others have suggested Mark left the gospel unfinished at his untimely death. Still other theories have it that various pieces of our Markan text do not belong there but are subsequent interpolations, and that some authentic passages have been misplaced.

And then there is Secret Mark, a longer, gnosticizing version of the text which has supposedly been bowdlerized to give us canonical Mark. Morton Smith[19] claimed to have discovered a copied text of part of a letter from the second-century theologian Clement of Alexandria in which he quoted a passage existing only in this longer version of Mark, access to which was available only to the

---

from *Reimarus to Wrede*. Trans. W. Montgomery (New York: Macmillan, 1961), Chapter XI, "Bruno Bauer: The First Sceptical Life of Jesus," pp. 137-160; Randel Helms, *Gospel Fictions* (Buffalo: Prometheus Books, 1989), p. 11; Mack, *Myth of Innocence*, pp. 322-323; Robert M. Fowler, *Let the Reader Understand: Reader-Response Criticism and the Gospel of Mark* (Minneapolis: Fortress Press, 1991).

[16] Helms, *Gospel Fictions*, pp. 20-21, etc.

[17] David Friedrich Strauss, *The Life of Jesus Critically Examined*. Trans. George Eliot (Mary Ann Evans). Lives of Jesus Series (Philadelphia: Fortress Press, 1972), p. 84.

[18] N. Clayton Croy, *The Mutilation of Mark's Gospel* (Nashville: Abingdon Press, 2003) revives this theory as well as the kindred proposal that the beginning of the text has been lost, too, accounting for the abruptness of Mark 1:1.

[19] Morton Smith, *The Secret Gospel: The Discovery and Interpretation of the Secret Gospel According to Mark* (New York: Harper & Row, 1973); Smith, *Clement of Alexandria and a Secret Gospel of Mark* (Cambridge: Harvard University Press, 1973).

illuminati. The debate on this matter is particularly vociferous, some experts alleging that Smith produced the text as an elaborate hoax,[20] while others take the Secret Gospel of Mark to be in fact the original.[21] I am in the odd position of thinking the text is a modern hoax yet hoping it is not! As Stephan Hermann Huller[22] has suggested, certain features of Secret Mark may imply that the document was the same as the so-called Gospel according to the Egyptians mentioned by ancient heresiologists. That gospel was said to have been the work of the Gnostic Basilides. You see what this would add up to: the Gospel of Mark might be the work of Basilides! As we will see, Mark's Christology shows interesting parallels with that of Cerinthus as well.[23]

Christology brings up a major theme in Mark's Gospel, that of the Messianic Secret.[24] William Wrede sought to explain the glaring incongruity of Jesus performing miracles and exorcisms, plainly manifesting his supernatural messianic identity, even as he

---

[20] Stephen C. Carlson, *The Gospel Hoax: Morton Smith's Invention of* Secret Mark (Waco: Baylor University Press, 2005); Peter Jeffery, *The Secret Gospel of Mark Unveiled: Imagined Rituals of Sex, Death, and Madness in a Biblical Forgery* (New Haven: Yale University Press, 2007); Robert M. Price, "Second Thoughts on the Secret Gospel" *Bulletin of Biblical Research* 14/1 (Spring 2004), pp. 127-132.

[21] John Dominic Crossan, *The Historical Jesus: The Life of a Mediterranean Jewish Peasant* (New York: HarperOne, 1993), p. 329; Scott G. Brown, *Mark's Other Gospel: Rethinking Morton Smith's Controversial Discovery*. Studies in Christianity and Judaism 15 (Waterloo: Wilfred Laurier University Press, 2005); Robert Conner, *The Secret Gospel of Mark: Morton Smith, Clement of Alexandria and Four Decades of Academic Burlesque* (Oxford: Mandrake of Oxford, 2015). Helmut Koester, *Ancient Christian Gospels: Their History and Development* (Harrisburg: Trinity Press International, 1990), pp. 293-303, argues that our snippets from the Secret Gospel would make a lot of sense as part of the same redactional layer that adds several bits here and there to Mark that were not found in the earlier edition of Mark that Matthew and Luke had..

[22] Stephan Hermann Huller, *Against Polycarp*, unpublished manuscript.

[23] Michael Goulder, *St. Paul versus St. Peter: A Tale of Two Missions* (Louisville: Westminster/John Knox Press, 1995), pp. 108-113.

[24] William Wrede, *The Messianic Secret*. Trans. J.C.G. Greig (Cambridge: James Clarke, 1971); James L. Blevins, *The Messianic Secret in Markan Research, 1901-1976* (Washington, D.C.: University Press of America, 1981); Christopher Tuckett, ed., *The Messianic Secret*. Issues in Religion and Theology 1 (Philadelphia: Fortress Press / London: SPCK Press, 1983); Heikki Räisänen, *The 'Messianic Secret' in Mark's Gospel*. Trans. Christopher Tuckett. Studies of the New Testament and its World (Edinburgh: T&T Clark, 1990).

repeatedly silenced the beneficiaries of those miracles. It can't just be stupid incoherence, because it is obviously a juxtaposition of clashing *patterns*. Wrede discerned a theological harmonization underlying the Gospel of Mark. Among his reading public there must have been one faction who believed Jesus had become the messianic Son of God as of his resurrection, and they anticipated his soon return in apocalyptic glory. But as the years went by with no messianic advent of Jesus, some began to rethink their expectations. This latter faction redefined the messianic role ("job description") in order to conform it to what Jesus had actually done during his earthly life: healings, exorcisms, dying and rising. This way they could view Jesus' historical ministry as already being a messianic advent. So, on this understanding, when would Jesus have become the Messiah? Why, at his baptism, of course, the beginning of his mission. How was Mark (or an immediate predecessor) to harmonize the two conceptions? He rewrote the gospel story on the premise that, while Jesus had indeed become the messianic Son at his baptism, he kept it a secret until his resurrection. (Why? Of course, to make this harmonization work!) Those who held the earlier belief that Jesus was elevated to messianic honors on Easter were not exactly wrong, certainly no heretics. Since Jesus had kept it a secret until Easter (Mark 9:9), it was quite natural for most people to infer that it was only then that he *became* the Messiah. I find Wrede's theory completely convincing.[25]

Let us not miss a neglected implication of Jesus' repeated warnings to his beneficiaries to keep mum. He does not want to further spread his fame, as he is already swamped wherever he goes. But even Jesus cannot staunch the spread of news and gossip. The reason this is noteworthy is that apologists for the historical accuracy of the gospels constantly assure us that the apostles would have suppressed the growth of rumors and legends about Jesus.[26] But this story and others like it demonstrate that such an attempt would have been hopeless even had the disciples/apologists/ evangelists had some reason to try it. If Jesus himself could not prevent the

---

[25] Robert M. Price, *The Historical Bejeezus: What a Long, Strange Quest It's Been* (Cranford, NJ: American Atheist Press, 2013), pp. 175-180.
[26] F.F. Bruce, *The New Testament Documents: Are They Reliable?* (Grand Rapids: Eerdmans, 1960), pp. 45-46; E. Basil Redlich, *Form Criticism: Its Value and Limitations.* Duckworth's Theology Series (London: Duckworth, 1939), pp. 60-61; Stanley N. Gundry, "A Critique of the Fundamental Assumption of Form Criticism, Part I," *Bibiotheca Sacra* (April, 1966) No. 489, pp.35-36.

circulation of stories about him, why would the apostles have better luck?

Mark was one of the two basic sources used by both Matthew and Luke in writing their own gospels. Matthew's was a greatly expanded edition of Mark, while Luke's was an attempt to do a better job than Mark (and others) had done. The other common source of Matthew and Luke was the Q Document, a collection of sayings ascribed to Jesus, possibly Cynic in origin.

There are other theories of Synoptic relationships. ("Synoptic" means, "from a single viewpoint," referring to the great amount of material common to Matthew, Mark, and Luke.) Some think Matthew used Mark and added more material from somewhere else; then Luke used both Mark and Matthew. Others say Luke used Mark plus material from somewhere else; then Matthew used both Mark and Luke. Still others picture Mark harmonizing both Luke and Matthew, eliminating much of the material where Matthew and Luke contradict one another. The goal of all such theories seems to be to simplify Synoptic relationships by eliminating the hypothetical Q source. But to do this, these scholars must posit still *other* hypothetical sources to explain where Matthew and Luke derived all their extra material. So we get rid of Q but have to replace it with large tracts of "M" and "L" material whose origin we can explain as little as we could Q.

Right from the Start (1:1)

The first verse ("The beginning of the gospel of Jesus Christ the Son of God") appears to be intended as the title of the book. Of course, we (think we) know what a gospel is, but what would this phrase have meant to the original readers? They probably wouldn't have been too confused, because the terminology was already in use. A first-century B.C.E. monument set up by the Provincial Assembly in Asia Minor reads: "Whereas... Providence... has... brought our life to the peak of perfection in giving us Augustus Caesar... who, being sent to us and to our descendants as a savior..., and whereas... the birthday of the god has been for the whole world *the beginning of the gospel concerning him*, let all reckon a new era beginning from the date of his birth."[27]

Mark 1:2-3 quotes Isaiah 40:3, an announcement of the impending return from Babylon. The prophetic voice summons its hearers to pave the way for the Lord's people through the wilderness they must cross between Babylon and Israel. But Mark makes it sound as if the voice itself (as if John the Baptist's) is located in the wilderness.

When John Did his Baptism Thing (1:4-8)

John is depicted as conducting a revival movement complete with a new way of salvation, "preaching a baptism of repentance." I think of Black Elk[28] preaching to his fellow Oglala Sioux that if they would only don a particular ceremonial garment shown to him in a vision, they could gain the power of the ancestors to reclaim their lands. A closer parallel would be the angelic revelation to Hermas that God was now allowing a second (i.e., post-baptismal) opportunity to have sins forgiven before the End Times Tribulation (Shepherd of Hermas, Mandates 3:1-6). Obviously, Judaism traditionally taught that one could be cleansed of ceremonial uncleanness through periodic sacrifices of greater or lesser gravity, and that, as far as moral guilt before God was concerned, God always stood ready to welcome any sinner who repented. But John's baptismal rite is conceived as an emergency measure on the eve of the End. If you confessed your sins to John, he would immerse you, and the holy waters (like those of the Ganges) would wash away your guilt. "Who can endure the day of his coming, and who can [remain] stand[ing] when he appears?" (Mal. 3:2). Those baptized, tagged, by John, that's who.

John's manner of dress implies he thought he was the fulfillment of the prophecy of Elijah's return at the End of Days (Mal.4:5-6), though the ascetic's hair shirt might simply have been

---

[27] Helms, Gospel Fictions, p. 24.

[28] John G. Neihardt, Black Elk Speaks: Being the Life Story of a Holy Man of the Oglala Sioux (Lincoln: University of Nebraska Press, 1988).

the typical garb of a prophet (Zech. 13:4). John acts as a herald for the Coming One, who may be intended as the Messiah, the angelic Melchizedek, or God himself. He is greater than John at least insofar as his baptism will be greater: an inundation of the Holy Spirit

Jesus Goes Under (1:9-11)

Jesus gets in line to be baptized, presumably confessing his sins. Later evangelists did not like this development and tried to diminish its impact. Jesus? A sinner? Uh-oh! Look carefully at what Mark says happened next: Jesus emerges dripping from the waters, looks heavenward, and sees what no one else sees, the rolling back of the heavens (like the Red Sea at Moses' command) to clear a path for the Spirit to descend to earth in the visible (but not material) likeness of a dove. It then, Mark says "entered *into* him," something else the subsequent evangelists did not like, for they all changed it to have the Spirit settling *upon* him (Matt. 3:16; Luke 3:22; John 1:32).[29] This would seem to imply something like the Christology of the Ebionites, the Cerinthians, the Valentinian Gnostics, etc., who believed Jesus became the channeler for the Christ Spirit at his baptism.[30]

The utterance seems to draw upon three Old Testament texts. "Beloved Son" probably comes from Genesis 22:2 (especially the Greek Septuagint version, "Take your son, the beloved one, whom you have loved"), where Abraham is told to offer his son Isaac as a sacrifice. This passage has always been associated typologically with the atonement of Jesus, as if God planned it as a charade pointing to the future atonement brought by Jesus' sacrifice. "My

---

[29] Fowler, *Let the Reader Understand*, p. 16.

[30] Stevan L. Davies, *Spirit Possession and the Origin of Christianity* (Dublin: Bardic Press, 2014), pp. 52-56, revives this kind of Christology but from a non-supernatural viewpoint, relying upon anthropology and psychology. Also, there is an interesting parallel in Vaishnava Hinduism in the notion of the *Avesha*, a "partial incarnation of a temporary nature." Parashurama was one of these. "He finished his mission long before his life came to an end. Soon after he finished his mission, he handed over his own divine powers to Ramacandra and retired to the mountains" (Shakti M. Gupta, *Vishnu and his Incarnations* [Bombay: Somaiya Publications, 1974], p. 11).

Son" surely reflects Psalm 2:7, God's endorsement of the new king of Judah. "In whom I am well pleased" seems to derive from Isaiah 42:1, "Behold my servant, whom I uphold, my beloved in whom my soul delights." Look at the context: "I have put my Spirit upon him," suggesting the Spirit's descent at the Jordan. The sounding forth of the divine voice at the baptism is an impressive piece of narrative theology. Great artistry has gone into it, and to great effect. Oddly, though, it becomes problematical if one insists on straining the text through the filter of inerrancy, because artistry is not history. I can imagine a learned scribe comparing and conflating relevant portions of this and that classic Old Testament text in order to compose something for God to say that sounds like something God would say! Like Joseph Smith writing the Book of Mormon, the gospel writer paraphrases and excerpts bits and pieces from the Bible to make the heavenly voice sound like God. What I cannot imagine, not without laughing, is God himself sitting down, putting together the lines he will speak by looking at old material he has used in the past. "Let's see... I want this *to sound biblical...*"

Historical Jesus scholars almost unanimously declare the baptism scene one of the indisputably authentic events in the gospels. And indeed it might have happened in one form or another. But we mustn't close our critical eye to a very significant parallel from Zoroastrianism, a neighboring faith which had long been an important influence on Judaism at several points. According to Zoroastrian scripture, the founder was the son of a Vedic priest. One day Zoroaster, having immersed himself in a river for ritual purification, comes up from the water only to behold the archangel Vohu Mana offering him a cup to drink. He then commissions him to preach the unity and supremacy of the Wise Lord Ahura Mazda. At once who should appear but the evil anti-God Ahriman? He tries to persuade Zoroaster to abandon this path, though he spurns the offer. Let's see: a cleansing rite in the river, the appearance of a heavenly messenger, a call to ministry, temptation by a devil, and the prophet's successful resistance. Is there an echo in here?

William R. Stegner[31] notes additional parallels to a

Targumic version of the *Akedah* Isaac (=Binding of Isaac) from Genesis. In it Isaac, once tied to the altar, gazes into heaven and sees the sky opened, revealing the angels and the Shekinah Glory of God. He hears a voice proclaiming, "Behold, two chosen ones," etc. The Targum (an Aramaic paraphrase of the Hebrew text embellished with scribal interpretations) notes that the lad's mere willingness to be sacrificed, even though it didn't actually wind up happening, may serve as an atonement for the sins of Israel.[32] Did Mark know of this tradition?

Another striking parallel is that between John the Baptist and his successor, Jesus, on the one hand and Elijah and Elisha on the other. Dale Miller[33] sees Jesus' Jordan baptism as a replay of 2 Kings 2, where, near the Jordan, Elisha receives a double dose of his master's miracle-working spirit. Henceforth, Elisha plays the role of successor and superior to Elijah, exactly as the Spirit-endowed Jesus does to the Baptizer. Coincidence? Not likely. It seems more probable that the gospel story has been rewritten as a New Testament version of the Elijah-Elisha original.

Frank R. Zindler[34]argues that Mark 1:2-14a is an early interpolation and that Mark 614-29 is another, attempting to explain the reference to John's imprisonment back in 1:14a. If this is true, there would have been no reference in Mark to a place called "Nazareth." "Jesus the Nazorean" would then denote "Jesus the

---

[31] William R. Stegner, "The Baptism of Jesus: A Story Modeled on the Binding of Isaac." In Herschel Shanks (ed.), *Abraham & Family: New Insights into the Patriarchal Narratives* (Washington, D.C.: Biblical Archaeology Society, 2001), pp. 57-66.

[32] Shalom Spiegel, *The Last Trial: On the Legends and Lore of the Command to Abraham to Offer Isaac as a Sacrifice: The Akedah.* Trans. Judah Goldin. A Jewish Lights Classic Reprint (Woodstock, VT: Jewish Lights, 1993), pp. 42-43; Solomon Schechter, *Some Aspects of Rabbinic Theology* (New York: Macmillan, 1910), p. 175.

[33] Dale Miller, *The Gospel of Mark as Midrash on Earlier Jewish and New Testament Literature.* Studies in the Bible and Early Christianity 21 Lewiston/ Queenston/ Lampeter: Edwin Mellen Press, 1990), p. 48.

[34] Frank R. Zindler, "Mark's 'Jesus from Nazareth in the Galilee,'" in Zindler and Robert M. Price, eds., *Bart Ehrman and the Quest of the Historical Jesus of Nazareth* (Cranford: American Atheist Press, 2013), pp. 377-378.

adherent of the Nazarene sect" (cf., Act 24:5).

Dust Devil (1:12-13)

The first thing the Spirit indwelling Jesus does is to impel him into the wilderness to be tested: is he worthy to perform his ordained mission? Is he a fit vessel for the Spirit that now motivates him? For the moment, forget about Matthew and Luke (John has no Temptation narrative). Read Mark for himself. Then you'll see that, not only does Mark not have Jesus rebutting three suggestions of Satan, he doesn't even say Jesus was fasting the whole time, or, for that matter, *any* of the time. Instead, he says the opposite: the angels "ministered to him," which cannot mean anything but *feeding* him, just as the angels brought food to Elijah during his forty day retreat to the wilderness (1 Kings 19:5-7). Presumably, Mark is pretty much copying that very story.[35]

Then again, you have to think, too, that Mark was making Jesus recapitulate Moses' desert sojourn of forty years in Midian before embarking on his own mission.[36]

Jesus Begins (1:14-15)

For some unknown period Jesus remains inactive, cooling his heels until the news comes that the Baptizer has been thrown in jail, as if Jesus had expected it. Once John is off stage, Jesus picks up the fallen banner and wanders the roads of Galilee preaching "the gospel of God," namely, "The time is fulfilled; the kingdom of God is at hand. Repent and believe the gospel." We can see how this "beginning of the gospel" echoes the language of that Asia Minor monument, where "the beginning of the gospel" denoted the new age of peace and justice that commenced with the reign of Caesar Augustus. The kingdom of God being "at hand" cannot mean, here anyway, that it is always present to anyone with the spiritual faculty to sense it (Thom. 3, 113). To preface "the kingdom of God" with "the time is fulfilled," means that the hands of the prophetic clock are near to midnight. Something new but long expected is around the next corner!

---

[35] Miller, *Mark as Midrash*, p. 48.
[36] John Bowman, *The Gospel of Mark: The New Christian Jewish Passover Haggadah*. Studia Post-Biblica 8 (Leiden: E.J. Brill, 1965), p. 109.

In Greek, Jesus' proclamation is in indirect discourse, not a direct quote. It is a summation of what Mark supposed Jesus was preaching. This fact is one of the clues that have led many scholars (certainly not all[37]) to suspect that Jesus was not in fact an apocalyptic preacher,[38] but that this element belongs to a later stratum of the developing gospel tradition, making him the mouthpiece for Christian prophets of imminent doom.

Drop Everything (1:16-20; 2:13-17)

These stories of recruitment are properly dramatic, depicting the existential crisis with which the hearer of the gospel is confronted. To this end, it is fundamentally important that Andrew, Peter, James, John, and Levi are not previously acquainted with Jesus and perhaps have never even heard of him. When he summons them they recognize the never-to-be-repeated call of destiny, and they do not turn a deaf ear. Up till this moment they have lived a comfortably mundane life, enjoying the anesthesia of the routine and the robotic. They have lived like Bilbo Baggins in his hobbit hole in the Shire. But now Gandalf knocks on the door and presses him into service on a quest in a faraway land, among alien companions, bereft of familiar security, but alive and awake as never before. They leave the dead to bury their dead, for they have now been raised from a death they did not know had befallen them. Of course, these potent, brief tales are designed as discipleship paradigms, so many challenging recruitment invitations aimed at the readers. Albert Schweitzer explains perfectly the purpose of the discipleship paradigms of Mark.[39]

> He comes to us as One unknown, without a name, as of old, by the lake-side, He came to those men who knew Him not. He speaks to us the same word: "Follow thou Me!" and sets us to the tasks which He has to fulfil for our time. He commands. And to those who obey Him, whether they be wise or simple, He will reveal Himself in the toils, the conflicts, the sufferings which they shall pass through in His

---

[37] Bart D. Ehrman, *Jesus: Apocalyptic Prophet of the New Millennium* (New York: Oxford University Press, 1999), is an able proponent of the apocalyptic Jesus model.

[38] Mack, *Myth of Innocence*, pp. 59, 61, 70-71, 166-167, 328.

[39] Schweitzer, *Quest*, p. 403.

fellowship, and, as an ineffable mystery, they shall learn in their own experience Who He is.

These episodes were probably aimed at those "itinerant radicals," "wandering charismatics," prophets and apostles who criss-crossed Palestine and eventually the Mediterranean, spreading the gospel as personal representatives, almost *avatars*[40] or *tulkus*,[41] of the Son of Man.[42]

The purpose of these anecdotes is one thing; their origin is another. It seems plain that they are one and all based on the story of Elijah recruiting Elisha in 1 Kings 19:19-21. Like Elisha, the sons of Zebedee, Peter and Andrew, and Levi summarily abandon family and livelihood to follow the master.

The Levi episode has an extra function: it provides the transition to the famous controversy over Jesus' fellowship with despised "tax-collectors and sinners." Jesus garners trouble among his critics by entertaining many of Levi's colleagues. Some Pharisees see this and warn (at least I *think* this is the point) that Jesus will ruin his status as a prophet by thus risking contagion from these impious companions (cf., Luke 7:39; 1 Cor. 5:9; 15:33). Was such openness to sinners unique to Jesus? Was it anathema to pious Jews? To some, yes, as with all religious communities. But the policy of Jesus was also authentically Jewish.

> When [Aaron] would walk along the road and meet an evil or wicked man, he would greet him. On the morrow if that man sought to commit a transgression, he would think: "Woe unto me! how shall I lift my eyes afterward and look upon Aaron? I should be ashamed before him, for he

---

[40] Gupta, *passim.*; Geoffrey Parrinder, *Avatar and Incarnation*. Wilde Lectures in Natural and Comparative Religion in the University of Oxford (London: Faber & Faber, 1970); Daniel E. Bassuk, *Incarnation in Hinduism and Christianity: The Myth of the God-Man* (London: Macmillan, 1987).

[41] Alexandra David-Neel, *Magic and Mystery in Tibet* (Baltimore: Penguin Books, 1971), pp. 113-130.

[42] Gerd Theissen, "The Wandering Radicals: Light Shed by the Sociology of Literature on the Early Transmission of Jesus Sayings," in Theissen, *Social Reality and the Early Christians: Theology, Ethics, and the New Testament*. Trans. Margaret Kohl (Minneapolis: Fortress Press, 1992), pp. 33-59, Stevan L. Davies, *The Revolt of the Widows: The Social World of the Apocryphal Acts* (Carbondale: University of Southern Illinois Press, 1980), pp. 29-32.

greeted me." And thus that man would refrain from transgression. (*Fathers according to Rabbi Nathan* 12)

In the neighbourhood of R. Zera there lived some lawless men. He nevertheless showed them friendship in order to lead them to repent; but the Rabbis were annoyed [at his action]. When R. Zera's soul went to rest, they said: "Until now we had the burnt man with the dwarfed legs to implore Divine mercy for us; who will do so now?" Thereupon they felt remorse in their hearts and repented. (*Sanhedrin* 37 a)[43]

Get the Hell out of Here! (1:21-28)

Why did Mark bother to locate Jesus' initial teaching and exorcism in the town called Capernaum ("Village of Nahum")? Probably because he wanted to allude to *Nahum* 1:15a, which is the only passage outside of Isaiah to use the word *euanggelizomenou* in a specifically religious sense. "Behold upon the mountains the feet of him that brings glad tidings and publishes peace!" Nahum is referring to "anyone who brings such good news," but Mark naturally supposes Nahum was predicting one individual in particular. Guess who? And the natural choice for his debut must be a place named for the prophet Nahum, right?[44]

Like a drunk in a nightclub, the local demoniac begins heckling Jesus: "What have we to do with you, Jesus of Nazareth? Have you come to destroy us? I know who you are ~ the Holy One of God!" Mark must have borrowed this exclamation from the defensive alarm of the widow of Zarephath in 1 Kings 17:18: "What have you against me, O man of God? You have come to me to bring my sin to remembrance, and to cause the death of my son!"[45]

An interesting parallel occurs in Buddhist scripture, where Mara the Tempter "assumes the form of a peasant and disturbs Buddha's preaching. He tries to distract the audience by making a

---

[43] Judah Goldin, ed. and trans., *The Fathers according to Rabbi Nathan*. Yale Judaica Series Vol. X (New Haven: Yale University Press, 1955), p. 64. Schechter, *Some Aspects*, p. 321.

[44] Miller, *Mark as Midrash*, p. 58.
[45] Miller, *Mark as Midrash*, p. 76.

terrific noise. Such half-comic exploits end in his discomfiture, as it appears that he is nonplussed and rendered harmless, if his identity is discovered."[46] Seeing that Mark 1:21-28 thus belongs to a *category*, a sub-type of miracle stories, form-criticism bids us ask after the story's special function in the early church, and it is not far to seek. Just as various healing and exorcism stories were preserved as "how-to" paradigms for aspiring healers and exorcists, so this one may have taught a Christian preacher how to deal with hecklers in the audience. Similar rejoinders are found in the Koran (6:25-27; 10:77-78; 11:7-8; 14:10-11; 16:101-102; 25:4-9; 27:67-69; 34:43-46; 46:7-9; 52:33-34; 68:15-16; 69:38-43; 81:15-26), not to mention Acts 16:16-18.[47]

Mark's larger goal here is not merely to show how great Jesus was, but, beyond this, to drive home the *authority of his teaching*, because that is the logically erroneous inference of the synagogue congregation. His authority is verified for them by the fact that he can perform exorcisms. Here is a prime case of what Dostoyevsky warned against: mystery, miracle, and authority. A con job, though perhaps not intentionally. The supposed miracle-worker may draw the same conclusion himself: "Wow! If I can do *this*, I must be privy to the truth of God!" But obviously *not*, right? Would Superman necessarily be infallible *ex cathedra*? Would his super-strength, invulnerability, super-speed, and X-ray vision verify his opinion, if he had one, about Anselm's Ontological Argument? It's like when Jerry Seinfeld was trying to convince George Costanza that Superman must have a super sense of humor if everything else about him was super. It's like thinking some actor or rock star's political opinions should be taken seriously.

To the Kitchen, Woman! (1:29-39)

---

[46] Har Dayal, *The Bodhisattva Doctrine in Buddhist Sanskrit Literature* (Dehli: Motilal Banarsidass, 1978), p. 307.

[47] My favorite inspired comeback is one used by Holy Hubert Lindsey, a campus soapbox preacher at Berkeley. Some kid called out, "Hey Hubert! It takes an idiot to be a Christian!" Hubert's reply? "*You qualify!*" See Hubert Lindsey, with Howard G. Earl, *Bless Your Dirty Heart* (Plainfield, NJ: Logos International, 1972), p. 17; also, Chapter 8, "Silencing the Hecklers," pp. 94-106.

Why does no one seem to discern the humor at the root of this anecdote? Jesus exorcises a fever that is consuming Simon Peter's mother-in-law (a funnier character-type than Pete's mother would have been), and why? So she'll be able to cook dinner for Jesus and his disciples! "Now *that's* better!" The story is the reverse of that of Mary and Martha (Luke 10:38-42), where Jesus defends Mary's shirking the kitchen chores so she can dine on his teaching instead.

Where did Mark get this story? It is another Elijah retread, this time from 1 Kings 17:8-16, in which the prophet saves the widow of Zarephath and her son from imminent starvation. In gratitude, she serves the man of God. In the parallel Elisha story (already a retread of the same story?) in 2 Kings 4, Elisha resurrects the dead son of the Shunammite woman, who also had served him. Mark reshuffles these elements with the result that now it is the old woman herself who is raised up from her illness, not her son, even though he (Peter) is still important to the story, and, sure enough, she winds up serving the man of God, in this case Jesus.[48]

Alms for an Ex-Leper (1:40-45)[49]

Jesus heals a leper. I don't want to rationalize or demythologize this miracle like John Dominic Crossan[50] and Barbara Thiering[51] do. They say Jesus did not actually heal a damn thing; he only "declared" the poor guy "clean" in a fictive sense, meaning that, for all Jesus had to say about it, the man, still festering, should no longer be an "unclean" pariah shunned by the public. But somehow the fact that *Jesus* was willing to invite him over for pizza doesn't seem like it would make any difference to anybody *else*, brought up as they were on the Torah restrictions (Lev. chapter 14) that said one must not approach lepers. (Some people want Jesus to have been a first-century

---

[48] Miller, *Mark as Midrash*, p. 79.

[49] Graham Chapman, John Cleese, Terry Gilliam, Eric Idle, Terry Jones, and Michael Palin, *Monty Python's The Life of Brian (of Nazareth)* (New York: Ace Books, 1979), cf., p. 26, "Spare a talent for an old ex-leper, sir?"

[50] Crossan, *Historical Jesus*, pp. 336-337; Crossan, *Jesus: A Revolutionary Biography* (San Francisco: HarperSanFrancisco, 1994), p. 82.

[51] Barbara Thiering, *Jesus the Man: A New Interpretation from the Dead Sea Scrolls* (London: Corgi Books, 1993), p. 34.

Gandhi, crusading for the social acceptance of the Untouchables, but that's just liberal proof-texting.) By the way, Wrede[52] shot this exegetical clay pigeon down a century before Thiering and Crossan sent it up: if Jesus was merely "declaring" him clean, why would he tell the man to go get declared clean by a priest—who wouldn't have done it anyway if the man was still showing leprosy because Jesus hadn't actually healed him of it?

But I *will* note that the gospel writers do not use the word "leprosy" the way we do today, referring to Hansen's Disease, where your nose falls off into your soup bowl.[53] In the New Testament the reference is to eczema and psoriasis,[54] not quite so dire, but still enough to quarantine a guy.

Bowman[55] observes that this story of the leper occurs so early in the gospel because it is based on Exodus 4:6-7, recalling the credential miracle which God gave Moses to impress Pharaoh by temporarily(!) turning his hand leprous white. Moses gave himself leprosy then removed it; even so, God had given this nameless sufferer leprosy, and Jesus removes it.

Through the Roof! (2:1-12)

Wolfgang Roth[56] proposes that the famous story of a paralyzed man carried by friends on a stretcher to Jesus and tearing the thatch off a roof to lower him amid the gathered crowd derives from an Elijah story in 2 Kings 1:2-17a: King Ahaziah wastes away in bed after crashing through the roof lattice. Mark's paralytic is already afflicted when he descends through the roof on his bed (pallet). He gets up from his bed because whatever sin of his had earned him God's punishment, paralysis, is now forgiven as the reward for the faith of

---

[52] Wrede, *Messianic Secret*, p. 50.

[53] Edward Conze, *Buddhism: Its Essence and Development*. Harper Colophon Books (New York: Harper & Row, 1975), p. 62: "In order that he should have no attachment to food, [a monk] is bidden to eat everything and anything which is thrown into his [begging] bowl [cf., Luke 10:8]; and the Venerable Pindola has been held up to the reverence of posterity for calmly eating a leper's thumb which had fallen into his bowl."

[54] Or possibly melanoma, as Chaim Trachtman, "Tzaraat as Cancer," *The Torah.com: A historical and contextual approach*. http://thetorah.com/tzaraat-as-cancer/ Thanks to the learned Robert Kraut for drawing my attention to this.

[55] Bowman, *Gospel of Mark*, p. 113.

[56] Wolfgang Roth, *Hebrew Gospel: Cracking the Code of Mark* (Oak Park: Meyer-Stone Books, 1988), p. 56.

his friends—not his own, if he had any! By contrast, King Ahaziah seeks healing but in vain because of his own *lack* of faith, faith in the God of Israel. Azariah had snubbed Yahweh by sending a messenger to the priests of the Philistine oracle god Baalzebub to inquire as to his prospects. Elijah intercepted the king's envoy to save him the trip: Go back to Ahaziah and tell him he's doomed because of his unbelief. Mark reverses this dismal situation by having Jesus grant forgiveness and salvation because of faith. What about the business with the false god Baalzebub? Don't worry: Mark has kept it in reserve for use in a later story (3:22).

Is Jesus invoking his authority as the messianic Son of Man to pull rank and settle the dispute? That would seem pretty superfluous given that he has just sought to establish his point by scriptural argumentation. Plus, it ill-fits the notion, prevalent throughout the gospel, of the Messianic Secret. The answer is simple. This is one of several instances in the gospels where the phrase "son of man" simply denotes "humanity" or "human being," as in Ezekiel 2:1, 3, 6, 8;6, etc.; Psalm 8:4; 144:3; Daniel 7:13; 8:17. As Matthew (9:8) knew, Mark's "the son of man has authority on earth to forgive sins" referred to "men" in general, not to any special prerogative of Jesus Christ.

Not So Fast (2:18-22)

There is a conflict between 2:19-20 and verses 21-22. The former passage argues that fasting is not appropriate in all circumstances but that its time will come around again, while the second argues that fasting is an outmoded practice, preparatory to the kingdom of God which has already arrived, if one has eyes to see it. These sayings stem from Christian groups and/or prophets who had very different opinions on whether Christians should fast. Contrast also Matthew 6:16-18, where it is simply taken for granted that Jesus' disciples *do* fast.

On a different matter, it is worth noting that verses 19-20 have no obvious or necessary reference, as is often suggested, to the Messianic Banquet as anticipated in Jesus' meals with disciples and friends, or to Jesus leaving them on Good Friday. We mustn't over-theologize the comparison. Is the bridegroom supposed to be Jesus? Or just a bridegroom? Isn't the point that there is a time for fasting and a time for feasting? It's not the one or the other all the time

(Eccl.3:4). Why be a party-pooper by interrupting a dinner with, "Hey, everybody! What say let's stop all this eating and fast for world hunger?" Imagine a "socially conscious" parent making her child spend Christmas, not opening presents, but morbidly meditating on those kids whose parents cannot afford presents or Christmas dinner (I bet it happens). What would Jesus do? Not that.

Not Too Shabbas! (2:23-28)

What is it that Jesus has his disciples doing one Sabbath that so offends the pious Pharisees? Jesus' men are not stealing the grain, only gleaning it as prescribed for the poor and homeless in Leviticus 19:9-10. The problem was that they were doing it on the Sabbath. Why couldn't Jesus' boys have just stolen, er, gleaned a double portion the day before and saved it in a Glad bag (cf., Exod. 16:23)? Is Jesus shown here as flouting the Torah commandment to rest from all work on the Sabbath day? Not exactly, since his justification for the act is to answer with a counter argument *from scripture*: the "legal precedent" of David satisfying his famished men with the reserved sacrament of the showbread, and with the high priest's permission (1 Sam. 21:1-6). By the way, Jesus (actually Mark, if that makes you feel better) has forgotten which priest was in office at the time. It was not Abiathar but rather Ahimelech. Big deal, unless you happen to be an inerrantist, neurotically straining out gnats and swallowing camels.

Is Mark 2:28 a self-aggrandizing invocation of Jesus' supposed messianic authority to settle the question? Again, no: he has already rested his defense with a scriptural argument, the only kind that even might stand a chance of convincing his opponents. "So the son of man is lord even of the Sabbath" is nothing but a continuation of the thought expressed in the previous verse: "the Sabbath was made for man, not man for the Sabbath." It is by no means a Christological assertion.

The Sound of One Hand Withering (3:1-6)

Jesus spots a cripple in the synagogue audience. One hand is shriveled, a useless club. Jesus knows there are detractors present just looking to catch him in the act of breaking the Sabbath. So he poses a Socratic question, "Is it lawful to do good on the Sabbath, or to do evil, to save life or to kill?" Well, obviously, it isn't legal to do evil or to kill on the Sabbath. But in which general direction does the Torah point? The reasoning is much the same as in Mark 2:37, "The Sabbath was made for man, not man for the Sabbath." In both passages, Jesus is setting coordinates for use in charting whether certain acts actually *are* Sabbath violations. And these (healing and gleaning on the Sabbath) are *not*. Of course, Jesus is not trying to win his critics' agreement, much less permission; he is just appealing to the rest of the congregation's common sense and explaining why he acts as he does.

The scene is neither a historical memory nor cut from whole cloth. Mark has rewritten the story of the Judean prophet in 1 Kings 13:1-7ff.[57] The unnamed prophet confronts King Jeroboam in the temple he has had built in Bethel and predicts that the Judean King Josiah will destroy this counterfeit of the one true Temple in Jerusalem. Jeroboam considers this blasphemous and orders the prophet arrested. The results are surprising: "the king stretched forth his hand from the altar, saying, 'Take hold of him!' and his hand which he stretched forth against him withered." In Mark, the man is just some bystander, but the authorities are nonetheless present in the house of worship (this time a synagogue, not a temple), waiting to pounce. The man's hand is already withered when Jesus puts the spotlight on him. "'Stretch out your hand!' He stretched it out , and his hand was restored" (Mark 3:5). In the same way, the anonymous prophet of 1 Kings heals the sufferer: "And King Jeroboam said to the man of God, 'Entreat the Lord your God, and let my hand be restored to me.' And the man of God entreated the Lord, and he restored the king's hand to him, and it became as before" (1 Kings 13:6 LXX). The withering and the healing were both the aftermath of the villain's attempt to nab the prophet in 1 Kings, but Mark changes it so it is the healing of the withered hand which makes the villains plot to arrest him: "The Pharisees went out and immediately took council with the Herodians against him, how to destroy him" (3:6).

Some Summary! (3:7-12)

---

[57] Helms, *Gospel Fictions*, pp. 90-91.

Mark's occasional summaries appear to imply that he had plenty more such miracle stories (1:39; 3:7-12; 6:56) and parables (4:2, 33-34) and that he has chosen a few at random to share with readers (cf., John 20:30-31; 21:25). Better to leave 'em wanting more than making the audience wish you'd stopped sooner than you did. "Yeah, yeah—I *get* it!" But the truth is that Mark is generalizing from the very few miracle stories and parables he does have. Compare Mark 7:13b, "And many such things you do." In fact, he had at his disposal even fewer than might first appear, since he (if not some subsequent redactor) has included two versions of a linked sequence of miracles and sayings.[58] The first version consists of Mark 4:35-41 (Stilling the Storm), 5:1-20 (Gadarene Demoniac), 5:21-43 (Woman with a Hemorrhage combined with Jairus' Daughter), and 6:34-44 (Feeding the 5,000). The second miracle-chain is made up of Mark 6:45-51 (Walking on Water), 7:24-31 (The Syro-Phoenician Woman), 7:32-37 (Healing the Deaf-Mute), 8:1-10 (Feeding the 4,000), and 8:22-26 (Healing the Blind Man). The order is not precisely parallel, but that could be the result of variation during transmission or of Markan redaction. But it is plain that, first, there is a pair of sea miracles; second, a pair of exorcisms; third, a pair of pairs of healing miracles; fourth, a pair of miraculous feedings. If both sequences appeared in Mark's initially published gospel, we ought to conclude that Mark knew both versions, each already sacred tradition, and did not feel at liberty to leave out either one; *or* that he felt the need to pad out his gospel, like a college student trying to beef up his term paper.

Would Mark's summaries count as "pseudo-iteration"?[59] Gérard Genette refers to "scenes presented, particularly by their wording in the imperfect, as iterative, whereas their richness and precision of detail ensure that no reader can seriously believe they occur and reoccur in that manner, several times, without any variation." To use

---

[58] Paul J. Achtemeier, *Jesus and the Miracle Tradition* (Eugene, OR: Cascade Books, 2008), Chapter 4, "Toward the Isolation of Pre-Markan Miracle Catenae," pp. 55-86; Chapter 5, "The Origin and Function of the Pre-Markan Catenae," pp. 87-116. I noticed this back in 1976 in my preparation for a Bible study group in my church. I say this, not to pat myself on the back (which, needless to say, would be pathetic), but rather to show that the sequences are not a piece of subjective optical illusion, which no two observers would agree upon. It is there to be seen.

[59] Gérard Genette, *Narrative Discourse: An Essay in Method.* Trans. Jane E. Lewin (Ithaca: Cornell University Press, 1980), p. 121.

a less highfalutin example than Genette uses, I think of the scene in
A *Christmas Story* in which Ralphie's mom is laboring to mummify
his younger brother Randy in the cocoon of a hugely padded
snowsuit, and we are offered this as a typical morning's routine of
getting ready for school. But Randy's frightened protests and his
mother's irritated resignation make it plain that neither has
experienced such difficulty before. Okay, I guess Mark's summaries
are not exactly pseudo-iteration, but they do seem related: making
unique or rare events ("We never saw anything like this!" Mark 2:12)
into an almost routine occurrence. It's kind of like the suspicious
character of the Passion predictions; if Jesus kept predicting his arrest
and execution, how could the disciples have been so flabbergasted
when they came to pass? "We never heard of something like this!"
Oh yeah? Well, in the same way, if Jesus exorcised demoniacs and
healed the blind and the deaf on every street corner, wouldn't people
get *used* to it, just as people today no longer marvel at once-new
technological advances?

Getting No Respect (3:13-35)

Exodus chapter 18 features a story pretending to show how Moses
got the idea for establishing a system of lowers courts applying the
laws he had received from God while in a trance state. What the
story is actually doing is to invoke (fictively) Moses to legitimate a
court system in a later day. In that story Moses is kept busy all day
hearing cases brought before him by average Israelites (as Solomon
does in 1 Kings 3:16-28). His father-in-law, the Midianite priest
Jethro, brings Moses' wife and sons to rejoin him. Upon arriving at
the Israelite camp, he finds Moses thus occupied. Seeing that Moses
is hard at it all day, Jethro proposes that his son-in-law appoint
subordinates. Moses sees his point and does as Jethro advises.

Somewhere along the line, some Jewish Christian, a partisan
of the Twelve *and* of the Heirs (once the rivalry between the two
factions had been resolved[60]), rewrote the Exodus 18 story for

---

[60] Adolf Harnack, "Die Verklärungsgeschichte Jesu, der Bericht des Paulus I Kor 15,
3 ff. und die beiden Christusvision des Petrus" (*Sitzungsberichte der Berliner Akademie
der Wissenschaften*, Phil.-hist. Klasse, 1922), pp. 62-80. Harnack proposed that the list
of resurrection appearances in 1 Corinthians 15:5-8 grew from an initial
juxtaposition of two equivalent but rival Jewish Christian factional slogans on behalf
of their respective figureheads, Cephas, leader of the Twelve (verse5) and James the
Just, seen as the real leader of the same or another group of apostles (verse 7). The

Christian use (perhaps as a means of reinforcing the rapprochement between the "Twelvers"[61] and the Holy Family faction). The Christian rewrite had Jesus' relatives learning that he was swamped all day, every day, with healing and teaching, not even taking a lunch break. They think he must have been driven to distraction, so they decide to go and suggest that he, like Moses, appoint attendants to share the burden. In this initial Christian version, Jesus would have welcomed his family, as Moses had welcomed his, including Jethro, and heeded their advice. Thus Jesus picked out his best dozen to assist him, and it was all the idea of the Holy Family. And everyone lived happily ever after.

But that's not how it reads now. Mark, a member of a Gentile faction and no fan of either the Twelve or the Heirs, has split the story in two and reversed the order of the two halves. The idea for choosing the Twelve is no longer credited to the Heirs, but to Jesus himself, and he appoints these disciples before his relatives even get there. So what is the reason for their coming to see him? The originally innocent concern for his possible "burn-out" has now, separated from its natural context, become simply thinking Jesus is crazy! Yeah, that's just what you expect from the "Holy" Family. And when they get there, Jesus won't even see them! The disciples, who come in for several drubbings elsewhere in the gospel, come off unscathed in this particular scene, while the Heirs take it on the collective chin.

Mark's Jesus, however, does not, like Moses, choose *seventy* to assist him, but Luke will restore this number in Luke 10:1. Mark has Jesus choose twelve, based on the choice of the twelve spies in Deuteronomy 1:23.[62]

It no doubt seems strange at first, seeing, sandwiched into the middle of this material, an entirely different mini-episode (3:20-27) recounting a controversy between Jesus and certain interloping

---

joining together of the two slogans denoted that the two groups' rivalry had ended in a united Judeo-Christian (Ebionite) front. This passage in Mark presupposes the same late retrospective.

[61] Sorry, I just can't resist borrowing this nomenclature from the major Shi'ite faction which expects the apocalyptic return of the Mahdi, the *twelfth* Imam. Oddly enough, the rival Jewish-Christian group, the Heirs of Jesus, share the honorific, "the Pillars" (Gal. 2:9), with the blood relatives of the Prophet Muhammad who were so dubbed because the Islamic Holy Family was the legitimating source of the *hadith* considered binding upon Shi'ites.

[62] Miller, *Mark as Midrash*, p. 117.

scribes (Torah experts).[63] Seeing Jesus perform exorcisms, these critics warn the crowds not to be bamboozled: Jesus is just a two-bit conjurer. He performs his exorcisms, they claim to know, only by virtue of being in cahoots with Beelzebul. Some manuscripts have "Beelzebub," our old fiend from 2 Kings 1:2, 3, the forbidden oracle-god of Philistine Ekron. "Beelzebul" means "Lord of the House," i.e., of the world, a mighty patron of exorcists, while "Beelzebub" means "Lord of the Flies," since his oracle priests would listen for a buzzing noise, the voices of spirits telling the desired fortune.

Jesus' reply to the charge seems to come from Isaiah 49:24,[64] "Can the prey be taken from the mighty, or the captives of a tyrant be rescued? Surely thus says [Yahweh]: 'Even the captives of the mighty shall be taken, and the prey of the tyrant be rescued, for I will contend with those who contend with you, and I will save your children,'" and from 1 Samuel 2:25, "If a man sins against a man, God will mediate for him; but if a man sins against [Yahweh], who can intercede for him?"[65] the latter becoming the saying of Jesus in Mark 3:28-29.

Why would Mark sandwich the Beelzebul Controversy (as it is known) smack dab in the middle of the visit of Jesus' nuisance relatives? Because the relatives think Jesus to be insane, while the scribes may be claiming Jesus is demon-possessed, kind of the same thing. Plus, the Beelzebul rejoinder uses the metaphor of a house divided asunder and about to collapse, and Mark wants us to see there a warning that the "royal house" of Jesus with their constituency, in rivalry with the Twelvers, will bring down the house of Jewish Christianity like the House of Ussher.

Matthew and Luke (hence the Q source) make an interesting addition to Jesus' response to the scribes. Luke's, as usual, is probably closer to the Q original: "If I by Beel-zebul cast out demons, by whom do your sons cast them out? Consequently, they shall be

---

[63] One cannot but wonder if, in these "scribes who came down from Jerusalem" (Mark 3:22) to check out the rumors about Jesus, there is perhaps some reflection of the circumcision advocates who "came down from Judea" to interfere with Paul's congregants in Antioch, demanding that they get circumcised (Acts 15:1) and the "false brethren" (Gal. 2:4) of "the circumcision party" (Gal. 2:12) who came to Antioch "from James" in Jerusalem (Gal. 2:12).

[64] Rikki E. Watts, *Isaiah's New Exodus and Mark*. Wissenschaftliche Untersuchungen zum Neuen Testament 2. Reihe 88 (Tübingen: Mohr Siebeck, 1997), pp. 148-149.

[65] Miller, *Mark as Midrash*, p. 136.

your judges. But if I cast out demons by the finger of God, then the kingdom of God has come upon you" (Luke 11:19-20). Compressed into these verses is an unmistakable midrash upon the Exodus story of Moses' miracle contest with the magicians of Pharaoh. Initially able to match Moses feat for feat, they prove incapable of copying the miracle of the gnats and warn Pharaoh to give in, since "This is the finger of God" and no mere sorcery like theirs (Exodus 8:19). The "sons" of the scribes correspond to the Egyptian magicians and can dispel the scribes' charge against Jesus if they would.

Parabolic Puzzles (4:1-34)

Jesus caps off his parables with the tag line, "Whoever has ears, let him hear." This might mean no more than, "If the shoe fits, wear it," but it seems rather to refer to an implicit esoteric meaning within these superficially humble, mundane stories, which is all Charles W. Hedrick[66] thinks they are. While it is possible, though I think extremely unlikely, that he is right about how they ultimately originated, it seems clear that at least Mark regarded the parables as nuts to be cracked. "Whoever has ears, let him hear," even if Mark has added it, is equivalent to "insider" winks to the reader like Mark 13:14 ("Let the reader understand") and Revelation 13:18 ("This calls for wisdom: let him who has understanding reckon the number of the Beast, for it is the number of a man; his number is 666"). And Christian scholars have certainly not been shy about proposing interpretations! Augustine took the parables to be theological allegories. Adolf Jülicher understood them to be simple moral examples or wise lessons, rather like Aesop's Fables.[67] C.H. Dodd[68] agreed the parables were (mostly) not allegories, but he denied they were supposed to be homespun lessons about life. Instead, he proposed that the parables, many of which begin, "The kingdom of God is like...," were announcements that the great Messianic Age had fully arrived with its herald Jesus, and that one should not take the old prophecies literally.[69] Dodd saw Jesus as preaching "realized

---

[66] Charles W. Hedrick, *Parables as Poetic Fictions: The Creative Voice of Jesus* (Peabody: Hendrickson Publishers, 1994), p. 3.

[67] Adolf Jülicher, *Die Gleichnisreden Jesu* (Tübingen, 1899).

[68] C.H. Dodd, *The Parables of the Kingdom* (New York: Scribners, 1961).

[69] Hussein Ali, before he declared himself the Manifestation of God and took the name Bahá'u'lláh ("Glory of God"), had been a disciple of Ali Muhammad, the Bab ("Gate"), who claimed to be the predicted Mahdi or Hidden Imam, and he wrote a

eschatology," a la Luke 17:20-21 and John 5:25; 11:23-26. The threats of judgment referred not to some Technicolor Armageddon but to a looming defeat by Rome unless Israel should repent.

Joachim Jeremias[70] was a great fan of Dodd's understanding of the parables, both their lack of multi-point allegory and their focus on the coming of the kingdom of God, but with one key difference. As Bultmann's "ecclesiastical redactor" tried to restore futuristic eschatology to the gnosticizing Gospel of John, so did Jeremias seek to adjust Dodd's reading of the parables by positing that Jesus in his parables preached an eschatology newly inaugurated but not yet consummated. There would be a future coming of the kingdom "with power" (Mark 9:1), but, as of Jesus' ministry, it became possible to "taste the powers of the age to come" (Heb. 6:5). Jeremias also, like his predecessor A.T. Cadoux,[71] viewed many of the parables as apologias for Jesus' controversial ministry to backsliders and outcasts. A great many New Testament scholars jumped on the Dodd-Jeremias bandwagon, including Archibald M. Hunter,[72] Oscar Cullmann,[73] Norman Perrin,[74] and George Eldon Ladd.[75]

The first parable, that of the Sower (or the Soils), seems to urge hearers to examine themselves, to ask themselves whether their response to Jesus' gospel is genuine or only skin-deep. But the point may be more Gnostic: are you one of the *sarkics*, carnal ones who wallow in ignorance and apathy, more interested in Reality TV than in spiritual enlightenment? Or are you perhaps one of the *psuchikoi*, a "natural man" who "does not receive the gifts of the Spirit of God, for they are folly to him" (1 Cor. 2:14)? These are the "pew

---

treatise defending his master's realized eschatology and criticizing the literalism of contemporary Muslims who failed to understand what was happening. See Bahá'u'lláh, *The Kitáb-I-Iqán: The Book of Certitude.* Trans. Shoghi Effendi (Wilmette, IL: 1950). Too bad for Dodd that Jesus didn't write something like this!

[70] Joachim Jeremias, *The Parables of Jesus.* Trans. S.H. Hooke (New York: Scribners, 1972).

[71] A.T. Cadoux, *Parables of Jesus: Their Art and Use* (London: James Clark, 1931), pp. 120-123, 138-141, 228-232.

[72] Archibald M. Hunter, *Interpreting the Parables* (Philadelphia: Westminster Press, 1960).

[73] Oscar Cullmann, *Salvation in History.* Trans. Sidney G. Sowers (New York: Harper & Row, 1967).

[74] Norman Perrin, *The Kingdom of God in the Teaching of Jesus* (London: SCM Press, 1963).

[75] George Eldon Ladd, *The Presence of the Future: The Eschatology of Biblical Realism* (Grand Rapids: Eerdmans, 1974).

potatoes," conventionally religious like Babbitt in *Elmer Gantry*. Or might you be ripe ground, the intended recipients of the teaching of Jesus, "not taught by human wisdom but taught by the Spirit, interpreting spiritual truths to those who possess the Spirit" (1 Cor. 2:13)? It is no accident that this parable leads immediately, interrupting the flow, to the exchange between Jesus and the disciples on the meaning of the parables. Jesus congratulates his inner circle on their privilege of access to the inner meaning, even while rebuking them for their seeming inability to utilize it! It is very parallel to 1 Corinthians 2:9-3:3. Jesus even confesses that, though he could simply teach in plain words, his teaching is not to be profaned by blurting it out to the unworthy ("Do not cast your pearls before swine," Matt. 7:6),[76] but reserved only to the elite; hence his use of parables to reveal the truth to those attuned to it and to hide it from those who just can't pick up that wavelength. "This calls for wisdom..." The Sufi mystics of Islam, being Gnostics in their own right, had the same policy: "In addressing you we speak according to the measure of your understanding, since what is meat for Gnostics is poison to the uninitiated, and the highest mysteries ought to be jealously guarded from profane ears."[77]

But Jeremias,[78] Hunter[79] and others just don't want to see Mark's Jesus this way, so they are forced to posit some mistranslation from the hypothetical Aramaic original words of Jesus.

Is Mark 4:21-25 a parable of the kingdom? It seems to be more Gnostic in color, equivalent to Thomas 24: "His disciples say, 'Show us the place where you are, for it is needful for us to seek it.' He says to them, 'Whoever has ears to hear, let him hear! Within a man of light there is light, and he illuminates the whole world. When he fails to shine, there is darkness.'" Where is the Living Jesus? He is the spark of the divine light within, not just within anybody or even any Christian, but within the pneumatic Gnostic, "a man of light." And the Gnostic must work on that light to make it brighter so he can

---

[76] Cadoux, *Parables of Jesus*, p. 142.Cf. Edward J. Thomas, *The History of Buddhist Thought* (London: Routledge & Kegan Paul, 1951), p. 181: "The sutra is not to be recited to foolish people, but only to those who are striving for complete enlightenment."

[77] Summation by Reynold A. Nicholson in his *The Mystics of Islam* (London: Routledge and Kegan Paul, 1963), p. 94.

[78] Jeremias, *Parables of Jesus*, Appendix 1, "The Problem of Mark 4:11-13," pp. 110-112.

[79] Hunter, *Interpreting the Parables*, pp. 17-18.

share it with others who possess the spark but have not yet awakened to it.

So I can't really see how these parables fit naturally into Jeremias's framework. Maybe we'll have better luck with the parable of the Seed Growing Secretly (4:26-29). It would make sense as referring to the coming of the kingdom. But even then, it's not really clear. Should we take it as parallel in meaning to James 5:7-8?

> Be patient, therefore, brethren, until the coming of the Lord. Behold, the farmer waits for the precious fruit of the earth, being patient over it until it receives the early and the late rain. You also be patient. Establish your hearts, for the coming of the Lord is at hand. Do not grumble, brethren, against one another, that you may not be judged; behold, the Judge is standing at the doors.

Or is it closer in meaning to Revelation 14:14-16?

> Then I looked, and lo, a white cloud, and seated on the cloud one like a son of man, with a golden crown on his head, and a sharp sickle in his hand. And another angel came out of the temple, calling with a loud voice to him who sat upon the cloud, "Put in your sickle, and reap, for the hour to reap has come, for the harvest of the earth is fully ripe." So he who sat upon the cloud swung his sickle on the earth, and the earth was reaped.

In the first case, Mark 4:26-29 would counsel us to "hang in there" in the face of trying circumstances. It can't be long now! Does this imply Christians are getting tired of waiting? Is this a parable, like some of Matthew's, that already takes into account a considerable delay of the Second Coming? I suspect so, in light of a handful of other Markan delay texts, as we will see.

In the second case, a different note is struck: *This is it!* As in 1 John 2:18, "It is the last hour!"[80] Time to get your white robe out of the closet and get up on the roof! Yes, both texts say that the End is near, but there is a real difference. James 5:7-8 sounds a little lame, offering cold comfort. "Yeah, we've heard that before." But in

---

[80] "It's *happening*, Reg!" Chapman, Cleese, Gilliam, Idle, Jones, and Palin, *Life of Brian*, p. 138.

Revelation 14:14-16 the fire alarm has sounded! Get moving! You could take the parable of the Seed Growing Secretly either way. It's like one of those equivocal utterances of the Delphic Oracle, or your newspaper horoscope. Do you have ears to hear? I think of the time when, as a kid, my eardrum crumbled and I heard double.

Mark 4:30-32, the Parable of the Mustard Seed, is beset with the same difficulty. Is the point that Jesus' disciples need not be afraid that they are what they look like, a small gaggle of deluded fanatics? "Yeah, *we're* gonna judge fallen angels! I'm getting measured for my crown next week! You don't wanna miss out, man." No, Jesus reassures his hearers, "Fear not, little flock, for it is your Father's good pleasure to give you the kingdom" (Luke 12:32). No, really, it may look pretty pitiful right now, but don't give up: before you know it, this thing's going to expand beyond anything you can even imagine! Or is the idea that, as the Puritan post-millennialists thought, and today's Dominionists still think, the world will, inch by inch, someday become the kingdom of God? H. Richard Niebuhr called it the "Christ the Transformer of Culture" model.[81] But the difference is not really that great after all, since both readings imply a retrospective "scene of writing." You can easily picture Jesus giving the discouraged disciples such a pep talk, but it is fictive since it presupposes the reader (not the *hearer*, mind you) knows the kingdom has already expanded by the time he reads this parable. Either that, or the parable is yet another encouragement in light of the delay of the Parousia.

But the paradigm has once again shifted. Robert W. Funk,[82] Charles W. Hedrick,[83] John Dominic Crossan,[84] and Bernard Brandon Scott[85] have all discarded the eschatological element altogether. All view Jesus as a sage in the tradition of Diogenes, Antisthenes, and the Cynics. In their view, the "kingdom of God" denoted the providential governance of the world that ensures that

---

[81] H. Richard Niebuhr, *Christ and Culture*. Harper Torchlight Books (New York: Harper& Brothers, 1956), Chapter 6, "Christ the Transformer of Culture," pp. 190-229.

[82] Robert W. Funk, *Parables and Presence* (Philadelphia: Fortress Press, 1982).

[83] Hedrick, *Parables as Poetic Fictions*.

[84] John Dominic Crossan, *In Parables: The Challenge of the Historical Jesus*. Eagle Books (Santa Rosa: Polebridge Press, 1992); Crossan, *Cliffs of Fall: Paradox and Polyvalence in the Parables of Jesus* (Eugene, OR: Wipf & Stock, 2008).

[85] Bernard Brandon Scott, *Hear Then the Parable: A Commentary on the Parables of Jesus* (Philadelphia: Fortress Press, 1989).

the birds need not toil and the flowers need not spin or weave. Like the Cynics, Jesus would have wanted his contemporaries to live in accord with Nature by using reason. The idea of the in-breaking of an apocalyptic, supernatural Millennium would have been a subsequent overlay, fundamentally distorting the Jesus tradition.

I admit that, no matter how you picture Jesus, the parable interpretations generated by these scholars strike me as perverse and wholly anachronistic. Were Jesus' parables, in effect, Zen *koans*, "language events" propelling their hearers to see reality in a new perspective? I'm not sure Jesus would even understand what that means. Hedrick and Scott zero in on goofs and blunders in the parables' descriptions of agriculture, herding, and unlikely human behavior, and they take these as subtle signals that Jesus meant to entice his audience to up-end and subvert traditional assumptions about life and religion. (Why not just admit that the parables were the work of post-Jesus story-tellers not familiar with Palestinian practices?) To me, it all sounds like super-sophisticated hermeneutics whose echoes cannot escape the ivory towers of academia where they originated.

Finally, it seems worth asking: did Mark himself have any real idea of what the parables were supposed to mean? After all, sometimes people say So-and-so has some mysterious esoteric meaning and what they're really saying is that no surface meaning is evident. Suppose, for the sake of argument, that 4:30, "To what can we compare the kingdom of God? What parable shall we use for it?" was originally a saying by itself. Then it would sound like a rhetorical question, like the one in the hymn: "What language shall I borrow?" It would imply that *no* language, *no* parable, could be up to the task, because the reality of the kingdom is ineffable, as when the Buddha disappointed a disciple who asked him to describe Nirvana. He couldn't do it, he answered, because it would be like a frog asked by his tadpole son what life is like on dry land, breathing air. All the language the tadpole knew was conditioned by, predicated on, life under water. No words that made sense to him could begin to describe a world utterly alien to his concept-world. Does Jesus, then, mean to say the kingdom of God "passeth understanding" (Phil. 4:7), one of those "things that cannot be told, which man may not utter" (2 Cor. 12:4)? We would be back to a Gnostic Jesus.

Mark makes what first seems one more generalizing summary: "With many such parables he spoke the word to them, as they were able to hear it; he did not speak to them without a parable, but privately to his own disciples he explained everything" (4:33-34). But there is an interesting note here. Mark has no Sermon on the Mount. For him, Jesus taught the crowds exclusively in parables, not aphorisms or discourses. Sure, there are extended collections of sayings (like the Mission Charge, the Olivet Discourse), but all this material is shared only with the disciples and other "in-crowd" associates, the people to whom he would explain the parables backstage. This is a significantly different picture from that which we receive in the other gospels. But it is quite familiar from the various Gnostic gospels in which he holds back the gnosis for his inner circle. As with Gnostic, Sufi,[86] and Mahayana Buddhist[87] teaching, this is a way of undercutting conventional orthodoxy by claiming a venerable pedigree for one's own, more recent, "superior" teaching. "Yeah, I know it sounds unfamiliar. The reason you've never heard it before is that Jesus (or Buddha or Muhammad) didn't tell it to everyone, only to the elite, and now I think you're ready to hear it! Then I can be your guru, okay?" The handy text "He who hears you hears me" (Luke 10:16) really means, "He who hears me hears Jesus."

Little Lord Jesus, No Crying He Makes (4:35-41)

Helms[88] has no difficulty showing how the Stilling of the Storm story was rewritten from Jonah's fishy adventure, with embellishments from the Psalms. He finds the basis for the story in Jonah 1:4-6.

> But [Yahweh] hurled a great wind upon the sea, and there

---

[86] Nicholson, *Mystics of Islam*, p. 53: "most, if not all, mystical Traditions [*hadith*] ascribed to Mohammed were forged and fathered upon him by the Sufis, who represent themselves as the true interpreters of his esoteric teaching." Ignaz Goldziher, *Introduction to Islamic Theology and Law*. Trans. Andras and Ruth Hamori. Modern Classics in Near Eastern Studies (Princeton: Princeton University Press, 1981), p. 139: "In order to secure a legitimate and traditional Islamic point of departure for this esotericism, they borrowed from Shi'ism... the doctrine asserting that Muhammad entrusted to his mandatary, Ali, the secret meaning of the revelations. These teachings, transmitted only among the elect, are the kabbalah of Sufism."

[87] Edward J. Thomas, *History of Buddhist Thought* (London: Routledge & Kegan Paul, 1951), pp. 180-182; J. Edgar Bruns, *The Christian Buddhism of St. John: New Insights into the Fourth Gospel* (New York: Paulist Press, 1971), pp. 12-17.

[88] Helms, *Gospel Fictions*, pp. 76, 77.

was a mighty tempest on the sea, so that the ship threatened to break up. Then the mariners were afraid, and each cried to his god... But Jonah had gone down into the inner part of the ship and had lain down, and was fast asleep. So the captain came and said to him, "What do you mean, you sleeper? Arise, call upon your god! Perhaps the god will give a thought to us, that we do not perish."

Once Jonah turns out to be the guilty party, they throw him overboard, "and the sea ceased from its raging. The men feared [Yahweh] exceedingly" (1:15b-16a). Psalm 107:23-29 makes its own contribution to the gospel tale.

Some went down to the sea in ships, doing business on the great waters; they saw the deeds of [Yahweh], his wondrous works in the deep. For he commanded, and raised the stormy wind, which lifted up the waves of the sea. They mounted up to the heavens, they went down unto the depths; their courage melted away in their evil plight; they reeled and staggered like drunken men, and were at their wits' end. Then they cried to [Yahweh] in their trouble, and he delivered them from their distress; he made the storm be still, and the waves of the sea were hushed.

Jesus is unconcerned with the stormy weather (and a pretty deep sleeper!) and appears almost annoyed that the terrified disciples shook him awake. "What's the problem, guys? Surely you know God's not going to allow anything to happen to us?" Well, too bad nobody told that to those poor bastards whose blood Pilate spattered on their sacrifices, or those unlucky souls who happened to be lounging in the shade of the Tower of Siloam when it collapsed on them (Luke 13:1-5). Or does Jesus just mean that God would protect his elite team, not necessarily the rest of us commoners?

The Son of Jehovah versus the Cyclops (5:1-20)

The epic tale of the Gerasene Demoniac combines elements from scripture and from the *Odyssey*. I don't see how anyone can deny that, as per MacDonald,[89] the basis of the tale is *Odyssey* 9:101-565. Odysseus and his troops come ashore in the territory of the hulking Cyclopes. This becomes Jesus and his disciples arriving by boat in the land of the Gerasenes or, in some manuscripts, Gadarenes (or even "Gergesenes," supposedly the remnant of the ancient Girgashites, hence perhaps related to the mythical Anakim/Rephaim,[90] who were *giants*). Goats are peacefully grazing in Homer's landscape, pigs in Mark's. As soon as each group of men disembarks, they come upon a savage man-monster who lives in a cave. Mark says the Demoniac goes naked, just as Polyphemus was usually depicted nude in ancient art. The Cyclops demands to know whether Odysseus has come gunning for him, just as Mark's Demoniac pleads with Jesus not to torture him. Polyphemus asks Odysseus his name, and he replies "Noman," while Jesus asks the Demoniac his name, which turns out to be "Legion," reminiscent of the fact that Odysseus' men were soldiers. Jesus evicts the legion of demons, transferring them into the unsuspecting swine, recalling Circe's having changed Odysseus' troops into swine. Odysseus manages to stab the Cyclops' one eye. As Odysseus and his crew depart, the gloating Odysseus bids Polyphemus to tell others how he has blinded him; in the same way, Jesus tells the cured Demoniac to tell everyone how he has exorcised him. As Odysseus' boat recedes into the distance, Polyphemus demands he return, but he refuses. Similarly, as Jesus is about to leave, the ex-demoniac volunteers to join him, but Jesus refuses him. MacDonald argues that nothing but too-close copying from the source is the only explanation as to why Jesus should be shown rebuffing a would-be disciple. On the other hand, however, it is not difficult to understand Jesus as commissioning the man as his missionary to the Gentile region of the Decapolis.[91]

---

[89]Dennis R. MacDonald, *The Homeric Epics and the Gospel of Mark* (New Haven: Yale University Press, 2000), pp. 65, 73, 173.

[90] J. Duncan M. Derrett, *The Making of Mark: The Scriptural Bases of the Earliest Gospel*. Volumes 1 and 2 (Shipston-on-Stour, Warwickshire: P. Drinkwater, 1985), p. 102.

[91] Is it possible that the Gadarene Demoniac is a garbled version of *Paul*, the exorcism representing his conversion from darkness to light, resulting in Jesus sending him as his Apostle to the Gentiles? Stranger (though admittedly not *much*

Mark also seems to have lifted details from Psalm 107, the same source he used in the Stilling of the Storm. The Demoniac having been chained up would come from the psalm's mention of "prisoners in irons" (v. 10), who "wandered in desert wastes" (v. 4) and "cried to [Yahweh] in their trouble" (v. 6), and who "broke their chains asunder" (v. 14). Mark may even have been thinking of the drowning of the Egyptian legions in the Red Sea.

Twelve Year Old Sandwich (5:21-43)

Mark has once again intercalated two separate stories to indicate that they somehow interpret one another. But let's take them one by one. First, the story of Jairus' Daughter. It retells the tale of Elisha and the Shunammite woman (2 Kings 4). Mark replaces the Shunammite, a mother, with a father. His name, "Jairus," means "he will awaken," a dead giveaway as to the fictive character of the tale. Jairus, like his Shunammite prototype, approaches the prophet, in this case Jesus, humbly asking for help. In both stories, the prophet resolves to make a house call. He intends to raise up the child even though he is told the child is dead already. Once he gets there, he seeks privacy (relative or absolute: Elisha excludes everyone, Jesus only the neighbors). Then he touches and addresses the dead child, who gets right up. The reaction of the parents is verbally almost verbatim the same. The Shunammite is "ecstatic with all this ecstasy" (2 Kings 4:31 LXX), while Mr. and Mrs. Jairus are "ecstatic with great ecstasy" (Mark 5:42).[92]

The story must have functioned as a narrative incantation for the use of early Christian healers; otherwise, why preserve the Aramaic *Talitha cumi?*[93]

Ever wonder what Jesus had in mind when he ordered the parents not to tell anyone about the miracle? What were they supposed to do? Place their daughter under house arrest, put up a fake gravestone, and pretend to the outside world that she died? This is an arbitrary, even jolting, redaction of a miracle story that must originally have concluded with the standard acclamation of the

stranger) things have happened.

[92] Helms, *Gospel Fictions*, p. 66.

[93] Davies, *Revolt of the Widows*, pp. 23-28.

crowd (in this case, the very same ones who, a moment before, had been deriding Jesus for claiming she was only asleep). Mark (or a predecessor) has substituted this gag order in the interest of the Messianic Secret motif.[94]

Now what about the woman with the hemorrhage? She is the Shunammite again! Jesus heals her of a reproductive problem just as Elisha had miraculously made it possible for the Shunammite to conceive. The woman had suffered from the bleeding for *twelve years*, exactly the age of Jairus' daughter, the symbolic implication being that she was the daughter the bleeding woman had never been able to have, now, so to speak, restored to her.

Why did Mark break up the story of Jairus' daughter and insert the old woman's story right in the middle? Simple: he wanted to provide narrative suspense, just as in the 2 Kings original, where we have to join the Shunammite on her journey to Elisha and then endure the failed attempt of Gehazi to raise her son. As we will see, Mark liked this element of a disciple's failure, but instead of using it here, which would have made the story even more like its prototype, he has reserved it for use in 9:18, 28.

Local Boy Makes Good, er, Bad (6:1-6)

Miller[95] spots 1 Samuel 10:1-27 as the probable source of Mark's episode of Jesus getting the cold shoulder from his own townsfolk. Saul, newly crowned king of Israel, is possessed by the prophetic spirit and commences speaking in tongues ("prophesying," v. 10). But "all who knew him previously" begin to mock him: "What has come over the son of Kish? Is Saul, too, among the prophets?" "Who is their father?" (v. 11). And this, we are told, is the origin of "a proverb, 'Is Saul, too, among the prophets?'" (v. 12).[96] This is just like Mark, where the people, to whom Jesus had long been a familiar face, find themselves affronted to hear that he now supposedly possesses the gravitas of a prophet. "Look – there's God coming

---

[94] Wrede, *Messianic Secret*, pp. 50-51; Nineham, *Saint Mark*, p. 162.

[95] Miller, *Mark as Midrash*, p. 167.

[96] Somebody please tell me what this "proverb" might mean? What circumstance would invite its application?

outta the men's room."[97] They cannot believe it and raise the issue of Jesus' too-familiar family connections: a prophet must come from out of nowhere, not someone like us (cf. John 7:27-28, "'When the Christ appears, no one will know where he comes from.' ...'You know me and you know where I come from, but I have not come of my own accord'"). Jesus is no more than the son of Mary and the brother of James, Joses, Simon and Judas, just as Saul is merely Kish's son. There is even a matching proverb in the case of Jesus: "A prophet is not without honor except in his home town and among his relatives and in his household."

If 1 Samuel 10:1-27 is the prototype, how was the Markan version composed? It was not simply a paraphrase. Mark appears to have had at hand two pieces of tradition (or two written scraps), one a story of Jesus' winning the acclaim of his old neighbors, the other a floating proverb that had somewhere along the line been ascribed to Jesus. First we read, "He went away from there and came to his own country; and his disciples followed him. And on the Sabbath he began to teach in the synagogue; and many who heard him were astonished, saying, "Where did this man get all this? What is the wisdom given to him? What mighty works are wrought by his hands! Is not this the carpenter, the son of Mary and brother of James and Joses and Judas and Simon, and are not his sisters here with us?" Here we must imagine Jesus' old acquaintances looking at one another with proud smiles. And then we hear the screech of brakes as Mark shifts into reverse: "and they took offense at him." Huh? What *happened*? Luke (4:23-27) saw the problem and added narrative motivation for the crowd turning ugly: out of left field Jesus gratuitously insulted them. What gives?

Apparently Mark, like all ancient "scissors-and-paste" historians,[98] felt obliged to include his other item involving Jesus and the hometown crowd—even though it diametrically contradicted the previous story.[99] The only transition he could think of was the stop-on-a-dime "and they took offense at him." This is just what he does following the Transfiguration when he juxtaposes two grossly inconsistent responses to the problem of the prophet Elijah not having appeared as Jesus' messianic herald. One: Elijah *did* come, but

---

[97] Woody Allen, "Annie Hall," in Allen, *Four Films of Woody Allen: Annie Hall, Interiors, Manhattan, Stardust Memories* (New York: Random House, 1982), p. 66.

[98] R.G. Collingwood, *The Idea of History*. A Galaxy Book (New York: Oxford University Press, 1956), pp. 257-261.

[99] Bultmann, *History of the Synoptic Tradition*, p. 31.

only figuratively, in the person of John the Baptist. Two: Elijah appeared in person, with Moses, atop the Mount of Transfiguration.[100] So, okay, Jesus was welcomed with open arms ~ until the wind shifted and they repudiated him. This took place in order that the proverb might be fulfilled in him.

But there is another item on Mark's agenda in this passage: sectarian politics. Why is there a list of Jesus' brothers? Why not leave it at "his brothers," just as Mark speaks only generically of "his sisters," *period*. It is reminiscent of the list of apostles given in Mark 3:16-19, and that is no coincidence, for this is a roster of the Pillars (Gal. 2:8): James the Just, Simon bar-Cleophas, and Judas Thomas.[101] My guess is that "Joses" (= Joseph) has slipped, via copying error, from its original position in front of "the carpenter" earlier in the sentence. And I think that the triumvirate of "James, John, and Simon Peter" elsewhere in Mark represent a confusion of similarly named characters.[102]

Marching Orders (6:7-11)

These instructions reflect the practices of Cynic preachers, who were so like the early Christian itinerants that outsiders often could not tell the difference.[103] Christian missionaries are expressly told not to

---

[100] Strauss, *Life of Jesus*, pp. 542-543.

[101] Robert Eisenman, *James the Brother of Jesus: The Key to Unlocking the Secrets of Early Christianity and the Dead Sea Scrolls* (New York: Viking Press, 1997); Robert M. Price, "Eisenman's Gospel of James the Just: A Review," in Bruce Chilton and Jacob Neusner, eds., *The Brother of Jesus: James the Just and his Mission* (Louisville: Westminster John Knox Press, 2001), Section: "The Name Game," pp. 188-189.

[102] But weren't the Pillars supposed to be James, Cephas, and *John*? I am persuaded that there must originally have been *four* pillars, given the very nature of the metaphor, as in "the foursquare gospel," and that the original fourth brother of Jesus, before the misplaced "Joses" replaced him, was named John. This identification is reflected in Luke 1:36, where Mary and Elizabeth are made cousins, thus making their sons cousins. As we have seen, there was a tendency in the evolution of the tradition to make Jesus' brothers into cousins to protect the perpetual virginity of Mary. I think making John the Baptist into Jesus' cousin is part of the same trajectory, and it implies that someone named John had first been known as Jesus' brother. This John may not originally have been understood as the Baptist, but John the brother of the Lord (as he is still known in Chrysostom's *Encomium on John the Baptist*) still occurs in Galatians 2:9. He is not referred to there as John son of Zebedee.

[103] F. Gerald Downing, *Cynics and Christian Origins* (Edinburgh: T&T Clark, 1992),

take with them a pouch, a hallmark of the Cynics, though they are allowed, like their Cynic competitors, to carry a staff, something otherwise so obvious for a traveler that even to mention it implies it was a point at issue.

But the Mission Charge owes even more of a debt to the Elisha stories. Did Jesus forbid the missioners to "take along money [or] two cloaks"? Or isn't Mark warning missioners in his day not to repeat the fatal error of Elisha's wayward disciple Gehazi, who enriched himself at the expense of his master's clients? Falsely claiming he'd been authorized by Elisha to do it, Gehazi exacted from the healed Naaman "a talent of silver and two cloaks" (2 Kings 5:22).[104] Mark sends them out with a staff (6:8), because of what Elisha told Gehazi when he sent him to raise up the Shunammite's son: "take my staff in your hand and go" (2 Kings 4:29a). Luke went back to the same text for content for his own Mission Charge to the Seventy (Luke 10:4b). When Luke's Jesus tells these missionaries to "salute no one on the road," he gets it straight from Elisha's command to Gehazi in 2 Kings 4:29b, "If you meet anyone, do not salute him, and if anyone salutes you, do not reply."

The Haunting of Herod (6:12-29)

Herod Antipas hears reports (how accurate?) about Jesus' miracles, apparently because the disciples whom Jesus sent out spread stories about him. But Herod thinks this "Jesus" is an alias for a resurrected John the Baptist. It is his guilt talking to him, since it is *his* fault John is, or *was*, dead. Mark sees fit to fill in for his readers just what happened to John. By the way, this one verse, Mark 6:14, explodes the oft-heard claim of ax-grinding apologists (sorry for the redundancy!) that no Jew had ever entertained the thought that a man could rise from the dead "in power" before the general resurrection. Jairus' daughter, Lazarus, and the Widow of Nain's son were all, apologists say, mere cases of operating-table resuscitations, temporary reprieves from death, not true resurrections like Jesus'. But Herod concludes, because of the reported miracles, that John has been raised from the dead with miraculous powers. John the Baptist, Herod thought, must be "the first-fruits of the resurrection."

Chapter 5, "Christians and Cynics in the 50's: The Q Document," pp. 115-142.

[104] Roth, *Hebrew Gospel*, p. 50; Miller, *Mark as Midrash*, p. 175.

Virtually all scholars believe there is a solid basis of historical fact underlying the tale of the Baptizer's death despite certain difficulties harmonizing Mark with Josephus. But everyone will admit some embellishment borrowed from the Old Testament. Obviously, Herod Antipas' words to his step-daughter, "Whatever you ask of me I will give it to you, up to half my kingdom," come from Esther 5:3. When Herodias maneuvers her husband into ordering the beheading of his pet prophet, it looks a lot like the story of King Darius getting manipulated into condemning Daniel (Dan. 6:6-15).[105]

But maybe we should go a lot farther. As MacDonald[106] argues, the whole thing would make a lot of sense as a rewrite of the *Odyssey*'s story of the murder of Agamemnon (3:254-308; 4:512-547; 11:404-434). Both episodes are even presented as flashbacks. Herodias, like her twin Queen Clytemnestra, deserted her original husband, liking his cousin better. Antipas was the boy-toy in the one case, Aegisthus in the other. When Agamemnon returned from ten long years of the Trojan War, a chagrinned Clytemnestra decided to plot her husband's death. Herodias, publicly denounced for her adultery by John, decides to protect her marriage to Herod Antipas by killing the Baptist. Aegisthus put on a banquet to celebrate Agamemnon's return, and Antipas hosted a feast for his own birthday (the same date *every month*). During the banquet Agamemnon is assassinated, sprawling face-down among the dinner platters, while the Baptizer is decapitated and his head is displayed on a serving platter. The big difference is that, in Mark, the role of Agamemnon has been divided between two characters, Herodias' rightful husband (Philip according to Mark; another brother named Herod in Josephus, *Antiquities* II.3.5) and John the Baptizer. So what? Well, to err is human, but to inspire inerrantly is divine.

All You Can Eat Special (6:30-44)

Both of Mark's miraculous feeding stories are transparently taken from the tale of Elisha multiplying twenty barley loaves for a hundred men in 2 Kings 4:42-44. In all three stories we find the initial inventory of how much food is available, the prophet's

[105] Miller, *Mark as Midrash*, p. 178.
[106] MacDonald, *Homeric Epics*, pp. 80-81, 176.

instruction to divide it among a hopelessly large number of people, the skeptical objection of the bystanders, then puzzled obedience, and finally the wonder that not only are all fed, but there were leftovers!

Would you rather believe that the story has a basis in fact and was merely garnished with details from the Elisha story? I've got news for you: without the Elisha "details," *there is no story here!* Or would you prefer to think it's history repeating itself? Well, ask yourself what is more probable: that Jesus miraculously multiplied food, or that somebody rewrote a well-known story about a man multiplying food?

I Was Walking on the Sea One Day (6:45-52)

Mark's story of Jesus walking on water owes some features to Psalm 107 (= LXX: 106): 23-30 and Job 9:8b ("who... trampled the waves of the sea"), referring originally to the primordial victory of Yahweh over Yamm, the personified Sea. But MacDonald traces the story as a whole to the *Iliad* 24:332, 340-341, 345-346, 351-352.[107] Old King Priam has undertaken a difficult journey to the camp of the Greeks to beg the body of his son, Hector. Zeus looks down from Olympus and observes the king's slow progress, then sends Hermes, guide to travelers, to help him along. "Under his feet he fastened the supple sandals, never-fading gold, that wing him over the waves and boundless earth with the rush of gusting winds... [Hermes] flew, the mighty giant-killer, touching down on Troy and the Hellespont in no time and from there he went on foot." Hermes approaches Priam and his servant, who think he is a robber intending to kill them. But he hastens to assure them he wants only to aid them, whereupon he takes the reins of their mule cart. Now they reach Achilles' beached ship in no time flat. Only then does he reveal his identity: "Old man, I am a god come down to you. I am immortal Hermes - my Father sent me here to be your escort, but now I will hasten back." That is passably close to Mark's story, in which the disciples are making poor headway against the storm when all at once they see Jesus approaching across the surface of the lake, a sight inspiring terror, albeit for different reasons. Jesus walking on the waves echoes Hermes "winging... over the waves... with the rush of gusting winds."

---

[107] MacDonald, *Homeric Epics*, pp. 148-153.

Once the divine visitor, whether Hermes or Jesus, calms them down, announcing "I am...,", he joins them in their vehicle, and they arrive at once at their destination.

How about the obtuse reaction of the disciples (Mark 6:52)? What does their incomprehension on this occasion have to do with missing the point of the feeding miracles? Bowman[108] explains it from Exodus, where the children of Israel see a pair of miracles, one involving walking through the (Red) Sea, the other a miraculous provision of bread from heaven. Despite seeing these wonders, the people remain stubborn in their unbelief. Ditto the disciples of Jesus after bread and sea miracles. "Their hearts were hardened," just like Pharaoh's. The point is underscored in 8:14-21.[109]

Washing the Hand That Slaps (7:1-23)

This dramatic scene of confrontation over hand-washing and the Corban provision (15:1-9) brims with problems. First, Jesus commits the *Tu Quo Que* fallacy.[110] He deflects a good question by making a counter-charge: "Well, look who's talking!" That is no explanation, not even an answer. Second, the quote from Isaiah 29:13 comes from the Greek Septuagint. The wording of the original does not lend itself so well to the point at issue, saying only that the worship of hypocrites is a charade, not specifically that they promulgate their own home-made commandments. We simply cannot imagine Jesus debating Palestinian Jewish Pharisees by proof-texting the Greek Bible! Their ancestors had greeted the publication of the Septuagint with mock funerals! Third, the passage appears to caricature the Pharisees. As it happens, this very issue comes up several times in the Mishnah, which records the traditions of the scribes and rabbis, and in every case the Jewish sages take the very same position Jesus does here. These Pharisees shown here are B-movie villains, not historical depictions.

Mark 7:14, if you look closely, contains an interesting reference to Elijah. Jesus shouts, "Listen to me, all of you, and understand." This is a reflection of 1 Kings 18: 30, "Then Elijah said to all the

---

[108] Bowman, *Gospel of Mark*, p. 159.

[109] Bowman, *Gospel of Mark*, p. 180.

[110] S. Morris Engel, *With Good Reason: An Introduction to Informal Fallacies* (New York: St. Martin's, 5th ed., 1994), pp. 204-206.

people, 'Come near to me;' and all the people came near to him."
Elijah then rebuilt the neglected altar of Yahweh and prepared for
the miracle which would win the people back from idolatrous
compromise with Baalism. Mark deems the Judaism of the scribes as
pretty much the same as Baal idolatry, a false religion to be
repudiated by consistent Christians. *Ouch.*

The Bitch Is Back (7:24-30)

Why does Jesus, trying to travel incognito through the region of Tyre
and Sidon, treat the Syro-Phoenician woman so harshly? There are
two reasons. First, in terms of narrative motivation (it has to make
sense as a story, no matter what lesson it may be trying to teach),
Jesus is testing the woman's resolve by a Socratic pose of
indifference.[111] Is this all it will take to discourage her? She passes the
test. Once the woman proves her worthiness, he relents and
transcends the original refusal. Second, the story seems to be
anachronistic for Jesus and to reflect the debates of the early church.
The woman stands for Gentiles in general. The healing of her
daughter at a distance combines time and space metaphors for the
Gentile Mission, still in the future, just as the daughter is a member
of the next generation. And Jesus heals her without being in close
proximity, as he will one day do from heaven as Gentles come to
faith. A wonderful piece of theological artistry—but that means it
never happened. It is a didactic allegory.

Where did Mark get the raw material for the story? Evidently he
derived it from 1 Kings 17:8-16, where Elijah encounters the widow
of Sidonian Zarephath. Before Elijah performs the miracle on her
boy's behalf, there is a tense interchange between the prophet and
the woman, as Elijah raises the bar to gauge the woman's faith. He
tells her to make him supper with the pitiful crumbs she was about
to use as her and her son's last meal. She might have been forgiven
had she told him to go take a flying leap into Sheol, but she decides
instead to obey him, proving her faith (cf., Heb. 11:17-19),
whereupon the meal is multiplied.[112] Likewise, the Syro-Phoenician

---

[111] Usually it is the other way around: the story uses the bystanders' skepticism to
create a hurdle for the miracle-worker to jump, but this time it is Jesus who raises
the bar for the supplicating woman to jump. (Joshua 24:19-21 is similar.) Gerd
Theissen, *The Miracle Stories of the Early Christian Tradition*. Trans. Francis McDonagh
(Philadelphia: Fortress Press, 1983), p. 254.

parries Jesus' initial dismissal with a clever comeback which indicates she still has faith in Jesus to help her.

Why does Jesus call the poor mother and her daughter, by implication, dogs? Mark has borrowed it from 2 Kings 8:7-15, which has Elisha tell Hazael (a Syrian, like the woman in Mark), that he will replace Ben-Hadad on the throne. He replies, "What is your servant, the dog, that he should accomplish this great thing?" In Mark, what's at stake is whether the great deed shall be done *for* the "dog."[113]

Abba Cadabra (7:31-37)

Bowman[114] understands Mark 7:31-38 as a midrash upon Isaiah 29:18 ("In that day the deaf shall hear the words of a book, and out of their gloom and darkness the eyes of the blind shall see") plus Isaiah 35:5-6 ("Then the eyes of the blind shall be opened and the ears of the deaf *unstopped*; then shall the lame man leap like a hart, and the tongue of the mute sing for joy"). We probably ought to include the stories of the blind man of Bethsaida (8:22-26) and of Bar-Timaeus (10:46-52), who leaped up to follow Jesus, as based on the same Isaiah passages.

Why does Jesus tell the newly-sighted man not to return to the town but to find another? Most likely we are to understand Jesus as trying to avoid unwanted publicity (cf., Mark 1:27-28, 45; 2:1-2; 3:7-12; 5:43; 6:32-33; 53-56; 7:24). If the blind man went back home, where everyone knew him, there's no way the news of his healing at Jesus' hands would not spread like wildfire. Look what happens in a similar case in John chapter 9.

Uh, what's with the spit and polish? Sticking fingers in ears, etc.? These were ancient methods used by magicians (or, if you prefer, faith healers).[115] Applying spittle to the eyes of the blind was imitative magic, as if washing away an obscuring substance (cf., John 9:6-7; Acts 9:18). Applying saliva to the tongue of the "tongue-tied" mute was intended to loosen its "knot." Plugging, then unplugging,

---

112 Roth, *Hebrew Gospel*, pp. 51-52; Miller, *Mark as Midrash*, pp. 196-197.

113 Roth, *Hebrew Gospel*, p. 44.

114 Bowman, *Gospel of Mark*, p. 172.

115 John M. Hull, *Hellenistic Magic and the Synoptic Tradition*. Studies in Biblical Theology. Second Series 28 (Naperville: Alec R. Allenson, 1974), Chapter V, "Mark," pp. 73-86; Morton Smith, *Jesus the Magician* (San Francisco: Harper & Row, 1978).

the deaf man's ears modeled the deafness clogging the man's ears, and its extraction, like having ear wax removed. The Aramaic word *Ephphatha* has been retained in the Greek text of Mark because healing stories like this one were used as healing formulae by aspiring healers in the early church (1 Cor. 12:9; Mark 16:18), and the exotic foreign word made for a nice-sounding incantation.[116]

Treebeard Sighting (8:22-26)

Scholars have long scratched their heads over why on earth Mark would depict Jesus not quite healing a blind man on the first try and having another go. It is possible the point is to illustrate a two-stage recovery from spiritual blindness, but what is that supposed to mean? I suspect the solution is simpler: again, the story functions as a narrative healing formula, one reserved especially for difficult cases, precisely parallel to Mark 9:28-29, where the amateur exorcist is warned that deaf-mute epileptic cases require extra fortification. "This kind does not come out by anything but prayer," to which some manuscripts add "and fasting," in case even the added prayer doesn't prove adequate. It is striking that, though they both gobbled up by far most of the text of Mark, Matthew and Luke both saw fit to leave out these two Markan healing pericopes (7:31-37 and 8:22-26). Why? Because these two post-Markan evangelists were embarrassed to depict Jesus having to resort to magic tricks. That would really be no better than having him whip out a stethoscope and a hypodermic needle. He's the Son of God, after all! He simply says the word and it's done (Matt. 8:8; Luke 7:7). And no more would Matthew and Luke appreciate a portrayal of Jesus along the lines of an "all too human" faith-healer, ironically, a portrayal resulting from the original shaping of the story to make it useful to blundering mortal healers.

Miracle of Mitosis (8:1-10)

Here's the second version of the multiplication of loaves and fish. This time, the miracle is not that Jesus can produce great quantities of food from the equivalent of a few dinner rolls and some sardines,

---

[116] Davies, *Revolt of the Widows*, pp. 23-28.

but rather that the disciples, having been in exactly the same situation before, remain obtuse as to how to solve the problem of feeding the multitude! We simply have two slightly different versions of the same story, and our evangelist did not feel entitled to cut either version, since each had its admirers and both were already deemed sacred tradition. The result, however, is an absurdity. It cannot have happened twice. No one is so stupid as the disciples are depicted here. It is very likely that both stories began as parts of early Christian Eucharistic liturgies (just like Luke 24:28-31). The greater plenitude of physical nourishment which Jesus expands from modest material food stands for the greater spiritual nourishment conveyed by the communion elements.

Do the Math (8:14-21)

This brief scene, however refreshingly humorous, with the mighty disciples caught out like ill-prepared schoolboys, cannot be historical. It is based on the editorial juxtaposition of the two redundant feeding stories. Originally there was only one, and so this passage is a subsequent redactional comment.

No Sign for You! (8:11-13)

This is really remarkable: challenged to provide a sign from God to authenticate his teaching, Jesus flatly refuses, retorting that only a religiously corrupt generation would even think of such a thing. It must have seemed a cheap dodge, but of course Mark's Jesus is entirely correct. As the Deuteronomist already knew, someone's impressive ability to perform (i.e., to fake) a miracle has no logical connection to the truth of what he may teach or believe. And this has nothing to do with whether miracles occur or *can* occur. But there is a startling element that, when they bother to notice it, sends conventional interpreters into a theological panic. Wait... isn't Jesus saying that he will do no miracle *during this generation*? Uh, what about all the miracles recounted in Mark's own gospel? Here come the contrived harmonizations: "Oh, Jesus only meant he would not do any miracles *on command.*" "Walk across my swimming pool!" Or "he was saying that it is faith that produces miracles, not miracles that produce faith." Well, why didn't he *say* that? Come off it. It isn't only modern skeptics that read the passage as presupposing that Jesus never did any miracles. The Q version already tried to "correct" the statement by adding the qualifier, "except for the sign of Jonah" (Matt. 16:4 / Luke 11:29). And what's *that?* The very ambiguity of the phrase shows it has no meaning except to negate the "no miracles" statement.

Matthew 12:38-40 supplies a definite referent, namely the resurrection. And speaking of the resurrection, what we have here is an exact analogy to the way Matthew and Luke supplement the unacceptably abrupt ending of Mark's Empty Tomb story, adding angels and personal appearances of the risen Christ. It was the same kind of embarrassment, dealt with in the same way: multiple and inconsistent.

Why *did* Mark have Jesus deny he would do miracles when he also shows him doing plenty? Again, he is a "scissors-and-paste historian" who hates to discard any precious bit of "information" about the past. Just as he juxtaposed mutually contradictory excuses for Elijah's no-show and jammed together a story of Jesus' hometown welcome and a proverb about prophets being *personae non grata*. He must have inherited the "no sign" pericope from an earlier time when Jesus was not even supposed to be a miracle-worker (cf., 1 Cor. 1:22-23) and felt compelled to make room for it.

But doesn't the polemical nature of the saying actually presuppose someone's belief that he *did* them? No, it presupposes only that some "seek signs" (1 Cor. 1:22), and that Jesus was believed to have disappointed them and had to make virtue of necessity (precisely as in 1 Corinthians 1:23). We see exactly the same thing in the Koran 13:7: "Those who disbelieve say: 'If only some portent were sent down upon him by his Lord!' Thou art a warner only, and for every folk a guide.'"[117]

Mistaken Identity (8:27-38)

Many consider this passage the great turning point of Mark's gospel, and with good reason. In it the rather dim-witted disciples finally

---

[117] Mohammed Marmaduke Pickthall, trans., *The Meaning of the Glorious Koran: An Explanatory Translation.* A Mentor Book (New York: New American Library, n.d.), p. 183.

reach a plateau of understanding where they can see more of the divine (and authorial) plan.

Why does Mark tell us the scene is set in the region of Caesarea Philippi, one of the Hellenistic cities established by Herod the Great? It might be because the viewpoints he is about to discredit were held by some Christians in that area in his own day. Not bad. But it may be a hint that this passage is derived from that in Mark 6:12-29, which begins with the guilty musings of another Herod, Antipas, son of Herod the Great. Both passages summarize popular theories of Jesus' identity: John the Baptist, Elijah, or another biblical prophet returned. Gerd Theissen has shown that, while 6:12-29 might possibly be based on some tradition, 8:27-38 cannot be. It is a matter of grammar and what Mark C. Goodacre calls "editorial fatigue," leaving loose ends, as every author or editor bemoans once he or she sees the finished work in print—with hitherto-undetected goofs jumping out.[118] In the earlier passage, the three options are put in indirect discourse, as secondhand reports, and issue in accusatives. In the Caesarea Philippi version, Mark purports to offer direct quotes from the disciples, introduced with the conjunction *hoti* ("that") and issuing in nominatives—in the first and second options. But the third one is introduced the same way (and should be direct discourse) but has the accusative instead of the nominative. It looks like Mark just forgot to change the third option consistently. And you see what this means, right? The Caesarea Philippi scene is completely a Markan creation.[119]

What was he getting at? The Messianic Secret, that's what. If, as evangelical apologists love to insist, Jesus had been "claiming" to be the Messiah, how can it be that *none* of his fans thinks that's what he is? Plainly, Mark's Jesus has been leaving it to the imagination of the crowd. They are free to draw their own conclusions. That is how one faction happens to think Jesus is the resurrected John the Baptist, another believes they are following the returned Elijah, while a third thinks they are listening to, say, Jeremiah[120] or Isaiah, maybe Ezekiel.[121] Jesus does not even seem to expect any particular estimate

---

[118] For instance, I remember looking through the published version of an article I had proofed at least two or three times after writing it, only to cringe upon seeing that I had written "detonation" when I meant "denotation"! Hoo boy.

[119] Theissen, *Miracle Stories*, pp. 170-171.

[120] I wonder, had you been able to take a poll, would we have heard cries of "I am of John! "I am of Elijah!" "I am of Jeremiah!" What, is Christ divided?

[121] I'm guessing nobody thought he was Obadiah or Habakkuk.

from his fans. When none of the disciples agrees with the crowd about Jesus, and Peter ventures, "You are the Christ," Jesus tells him to keep it under his turban. It is not even clear that Jesus accepts Peter's declaration, unlike Matthew's version. I'd say this is what you'd call the Messianic Secret.

One thing Jesus *is* clear about: he is going to be arrested, tormented, crucified, and resurrected. Is this supposed to be a clarification of Jesus' messiahship? Or a *denial* of it? Six-six-six of one, half a dozen of the other. How many times have you heard it piously said that Jesus *did* think himself the Messiah but completely *redefined* it. Uh, you mean, in other words, he *didn't* think he was the Messiah? Because that's like saying, "Yes, I'm a Socialist, but of course I mean that in the sense that I believe in free markets and private ownership of the means of production. Are you with me, comrades?" Because if you define "Messiah" as a savior who surrenders to death on a Roman cross, rises again, and gets enthroned invisibly in heaven—you're not talking about the Jewish Messiah anymore. Unless you're the Cheshire Cat.

Poor Peter, who expected a pat on the head, instead gets a punch in the mouth: "Out of my sight, Satan! You are thinking as men think, not as God thinks!" Peter is unwittingly speaking for Satan, tempting Jesus to shun the cross. How striking that here in Mark 8:33 and again in Matthew, Satan would dissuade Jesus from his destiny on Golgotha, while in Luke 22:3-4 and John 6:70-71; 13:27 it is Satan's scheme to deliver him to his killers! For Luke and John, Satan is like the Archons, the cosmic rulers of 1 Corinthians 2:7-8, who engineered Jesus' death, not knowing they were signing their own death warrant in the process. In Matthew and Mark, by contrast, Satan knows better and wants to prevent the atoning sacrifice.

Go Transfigure! (1:2-8)

When Jesus climbs the mountain to be transfigured, we are reading Mark's rewrite of Moses going up Mount Sinai to receive the stone tablets engraved with the Ten Commandments in Exodus 24:18-24 and 34:29. As Bowman notes,[122] Mark's beginning, "And six days later" (9:2), has to be a nod to the Exodus story. Moses takes Joshua with him (24:13). Then the glory cloud covers the summit for *six days*

---

[122] Bowman, *Gospel of Mark*, p. 190.

(verse 16). On the seventh day, God calls to Moses from inside the cloud. Mark has only foreshortened the process.

The glowing apparition of Jesus is rewritten from that of Moses in Exodus 34:29, but as Derrett[123] points out, Mark is also working from Malachi 3:2, especially since Elijah, too, appears: "But who can endure the day of his coming, and who can stand when he appears? For he is like a refiner's fire and like fuller's soap." So this must be the predicted return of Elijah, and Jesus' clothing gleams white "like no fuller on earth could have bleached them" (Mark 9:3).

Jesus appears *like* Moses, yet *with* Moses (cf., John 1:1). Jesus is the expected "prophet like Moses" predicted in Deuteronomy 18:15: "[Yahweh] your God will raise up for you a prophet like me from among you, from your brothers. Him you shall heed." Then the heavenly voice reiterates this commandment in Mark 9:7, "This is my beloved son; listen to him."[124]

The sharp-eyed Derrett[125] traces Jesus' command to hush up the vision till the Son of Man be raised from the dead (9:9) to similar instructions in Daniel 12:4a ("But you, Daniel, shut up the words, and seal the book, until the time of the end.") and Zephaniah 3:8a, LXX ("Therefore wait upon me, saith the Lord, *until the day when I rise up* as a witness").

Apocalyptic as a genre is heavily dependent upon the conceit that long-concealed knowledge (of the future, of the heavens, etc.) is now being revealed. Gnosticism is related to Apocalyptic in this and other ways.[126] Gnostic gospels and revelations make regular use of the device, pretending to share, not new teachings, but old ones only now disclosed that Jesus revealed to none but the most advanced disciples, who passed it on to their chosen elite until "now it can be told!" We see the same thing here (as well as in chapter 13). Jesus could have just as easily brought all twelve with him, but he left three quarters of them down below, minding the store. And who are the lucky trio? Bartholomew, Thaddaeus, and Matthew? Um, Simon Zelotes, Judas not Iscariot, and Lebbaeus? No, Peter, James, and John, the gospel counterparts to the three Pillars of the Jerusalem church, are the ones privileged to behold the true form of the Son of

---

[123] Derrett, *Making of Mark*, p. 159.

[124] Bowman, *Gospel of Mark*, p. 193.

[125] Derrett, *Making of Mark*, p. 155.

[126] Walter Schmithals, *The Apocalyptic Movement: Introduction and Interpretation.* Trans. John E. Steely (New York: Abingdon Press, 1975), Chapter 5, "Apocalyptic and Gnosis," pp. 89-110.

God.

It is just like Buddhism, where the Buddha appears to most people as one of themselves, but a very few spiritually sensitive adepts can see through that guise to his radiant, celestial form beneath. No wonder he tells them not to say a word about it to the rest, the "weaker brethren." The situation is exactly like that in the Gospel of Thomas, saying 13:

> Jesus says to his disciples, "Compare me and tell me what I am like." Simon Peter says to him, "You are like a righteous angel." Matthew says to him, "You are like a philosopher possessed of understanding." Thomas says to him, "Master, my mouth can scarcely frame the words of what you are like!" Jesus says, "I am not your master, because you have drunk, you have become filled, from the bubbling spring which I have measured out." He took him aside privately and said three things to him. So when Thomas rejoined his companions, they pressed him, saying, "What did Jesus say to you?" Thomas said to them, "If I tell you even one of the things he said to me, you will pick up stones and hurl them at me~and fire will erupt from the stones and consume you!"

Finally, we have to call attention to, first, the Messianic Secrecy motif ("Tell the vision to no one till the son of man is risen from the dead") and, second, the *delay* motif. As we will see, Mark 13:30 sets a deadline for the Parousia, the coming of the kingdom of God and the Son of Man: the generation of Jesus' contemporaries will live to see it (though, given the attendant tribulations, they might wish they *hadn't!*). But no such luck. Back to the drawing board. While there were still a few left alive after the war with Rome, the scope of the promise was narrowed considerably: "There are *some* standing here who will not taste death before they see the kingdom of God coming with power." But time went by, and that promise failed, too. Mark 13 adds a couple of temporal buffers to retard the building speed of the eschatological denouement: "when you hear of wars and rumors of wars, do not be alarmed; this must take place, but the end is not yet" (verse 7). "The gospel must first be preached to all nations" (verse 10). Well, *that* ought to give us some time! The logic here is exactly that of the cold-water-throwing passage 2 Thessalonians 2:1-3.

But even these temporizing tactics proved insufficient, so finally Mark makes the prediction refer, however implausibly, to the Transfiguration. He has cut loose future expectation and searched around for some usable event that could have come and gone already in "this generation." The Transfiguration seemed a likely candidate... but in that case, couldn't *all* those standing there have seen it? Um, well, what if Jesus *excluded some of them* from seeing the newly redefined "coming with power"? Sure, *that* works; why *not*?[127]

Kettle Logic

Freud spoke of the "logic of the kettle"[128] whereby one arms oneself with an arsenal of excuses, little caring if they are consistent with one another, so long as they are all aimed in the same direction. "I never borrowed your kettle! And besides, I returned it last month in perfect condition! And it already had that crack in it when you loaned it to me!" It is the same way here. What answer to give to skeptical scribes who allege Jesus cannot have been the Messiah since Elijah had not appeared as his herald? Answer one: he *did* appear, but *figuratively*: John the Baptist. This answer went over like a lead balloon. Second answer: he did appear, he *himself*, but he appeared only to a handful of people. The objector replies, "Is that so? Why did we never hear that until now?" The Christian response: "Jesus told us to keep it secret, uh, till now." Mark was only concerned to include all the old tradition, heedless that these puzzle pieces did not fit together.[129]

Passionate Predictions (8:31, 9:12-13; 30-32; 10:32-34; 14:27-28)

---

[127] But why, some rascal may ask, did Mark not simply *cut* passages like Mark 9:1 and 13:30? The texts, the sayings, were already venerated as sacred. Thus ancient redactors tended to add new material designed to mitigate the older, now troublesome texts, which they were not at liberty to omit. Look at the grief Tertullian gave Marcion for (as Tertullian believed) cutting out verses from Luke.

[128] Sigmund Freud, *The Interpretation of Dreams* in the Standard Edition of the Complete Psychological Works of Sigmund Freud. Trans. A. A. Brill, 4:119-120; Freud, *Jokes and Their Relation to the Unconscious* in Standard Edition 13:62 and 206.

[129] Strauss, *Life of Jesus*, pp. 542-543.

How can Jesus have so explicitly predicted his coming arrest and death and yet his disciples are taken completely by surprise when it happens? Peter here certainly seems to understand the prediction, and he doesn't like what he hears! Why is he so flabbergasted when it happens? Is the Christ to be ignored on such a point? It seems more likely that this prediction of the Passion, like those to follow in the next chapters, is really aimed over the heads of the characters in the scene, directly at the readers,[130] to assure them that things are progressing according to the plan of God. But Jesus did not actually say such words; otherwise the disciples must not have been so surprised in the event. Besides, as Erhardt Güttgemanns[131] pointed out, there is just no viable way to posit a process of oral tradition by which these sentences, with the specific wording by which they differ slightly from one another, might have made the journey from Jesus' lips through the hands of tradition repeaters to Mark's ears and then onto the pages of his gospel. Even if one retreats to positing that a single basic Passion prediction made it through the chain of transmission and that Mark reworded it slightly for use and reuse, one is over halfway to declaring the Passion predictions as literary, not historical, in origin. If you admit Mark had that much of a role in providing these sentences, there is no good reason remaining to assume he did not invent them *de novo*.

Complaint Department (9:14-29)

This episode is the direct sequel to the Transfiguration, not intrinsically, mind you, but by way of Mark's redactional juxtaposition. This story of the deaf-mute epileptic requires Jesus to have been absent temporarily, allowing us to observe the helpless ineptitude of the disciples without him. It belongs to a particular sub-category of miracle stories which glorify the hero by showing that even his apprentices cannot match his power. The story (2 Kings 4:31) of Gehazi's failure to heal the Shunammite woman's son, even using Elisha's miracle-working staff (magic wand), is another.

But by placing this tale immediately after the

---

[130] Fowler, *Let the Reader Understand*, p. 21.
[131] Erhardt Güttgemanns, *Candid Questions Concerning Gospel Form Criticism: A Methodological Sketch of the Fundamental Problematics of Form and Redaction Criticism.* Trans. William Guy Doty. Pittsburgh Theological Monograph Series # 26 (Pittsburgh: Pickwick Press, 1979), p. 327.

Transfiguration, Mark makes it an analogue to the Golden Calf incident in Exodus 32.[132] In that one, Moses is off with Joshua, leaving Aaron in charge. Upon his return, Moses finds that Aaron has lost all control of the situation, caving in to the people's demand that he fashion an idol for them to worship, like a baby-sitter letting the kids get away with murder. Mark has, so to speak, converted Aaron's Golden Calf into a stubborn demon, not far-fetched given the Jewish belief that "what pagans sacrifice they offer to demons and not to God" (1 Cor. 10:20a). Now Jesus and his three musketeers return from their own mountain to discover the rest of the disciples amid the jeers of the crowd and his enemies, unable to get rid of the damn demon.

One might observe that the most poignant and profound thing said about faith in the whole Bible occurs right here. "I believe; help my unbelief!" And who says it: an apostle? A prophet? A saint? No, just *some guy*.

Whether you want to call it "Christology" or not, there is a revealing statement by Jesus, exasperated by his disciples' failure: "O faithless generation! How long am I to be with you? How long must I bear with you?" Here is the irritated chagrin of a god marooned for a while among stupid human beings: "What fools these mortals be!" Imagine the lunatic megalomania of someone saying this in real life! That's how you know you are reading mythic fiction instead of actual history. Imagine somebody sitting down next to you on the bus, remarking, "Yeah, I just got done slaying the Nemean Lion." I'm pretty sure you'd get up and look for another seat.

Jockeying for Position (9:33-37; 10:45)

These stories of the disciples arguing over who is the greatest (or perhaps, as Albert Schweitzer[133] thought, who would be first in line to replace Jesus as his caliph when he was gone) are based on similar disputes in the Pentateuch between Moses on the one hand and

---

[132] Bowman, *Gospel of Mark*, p. 199; Miller, *Mark as Midrash*, p. 232.

[133] Albert Schweitzer, *The Mystery of the Kingdom of God: The Secret of Jesus' Messiahship and Passion*. Trans. Walter Lowrie (New York: Schocken Books, 1964), pp. 78-79. Cf., Thomas 12: "The disciples say to Jesus, 'We know that you will depart from us. Who is it who will be great over us?' Jesus says to them, 'Wherever you have come from [i.e., on your missionary journeys] you will go report to James the Just, for whom heaven and earth were prepared.'"

Aaron and Miriam on the other (Num. 12), or perhaps Dathan and Abiram (Num. 16).[134] These ambitious climbers covet Moses' privileged position with Yahweh and gripe about it until God himself steps in to decide the matter in favor of Moses. Jesus similarly intervenes here, albeit less spectacularly. Ever wondered why God picked Moses to lead his people in the first place? Wasn't it precisely because Moses did *not* seek power? He "was very meek, more than all the men that were on the face of the earth" (Num. 12:3),[135] the same qualification Jesus requires here for anyone who might aim to be a leader among his flock (Mark 9:35).

Working our Side of the Street (9:38-39)

Mark isn't done with this portion of the Book of Numbers yet. The episode of the free-lance exorcist, who so distresses poor John, comes directly from that of Eldad and Medad, members of the seventy elders who were stranded on the toilet when the rest accompanied Moses to the Tent of Meeting to receive prophetic inspiration (Num. 11:24-30). John son of Zebedee is a renamed Joshua who protested that "Eldad and Medad are prophesying in the camp," i.e., "not following us" (Mark 9:38). Jesus is depicted as being just as broad-minded as Moses was, glad to acknowledge the work of God where ever he hears of it.[136] Even though the "name" is prominent in the story, the larger point reminds me of what Paul Tillich said about the work of God "which is always going on in history, even where the name of Jesus is not known but where the power of the New Being, which is his [Jesus'] being, is present."[137]

Isn't it interesting that Acts 19:13-16 takes a very different attitude toward this "unlicensed" use of the name of Jesus? That seems to result from Acts' agenda of portraying the Jerusalem-centered Church, of which it treats Paul as a mere functionary, as the exclusive institutional provider of salvation. The "Ghostbusters"

---

[134]Bowman, *Gospel of Mark*, p. 205.

[135] Miller, *Mark as Midrash*, p. 239.

[136] Bowman, *Gospel of Mark*, p. 206; Miller, *Mark as Midrash*, p. 242.

[137] Paul Tillich, *Systematic Theology Volume II: Existence and the Christ* (Chicago: University of Chicago Press, 1957), p. 164.

team of the priestly Sons of Sceva, Jews not Christians, simply *cannot* be other than charlatans. Things haven't changed much.[138]

Word Association (9:40-50)

You will look in vain for any connective train of logic running through the next few verses. Lacking one, Mark saw nothing amiss in stringing these sayings together by means of fortuitous "catchwords" and common topics. The sayings were originally independent and without context, so why not just, essentially, well, *list* them? It's the redactional equivalent, I guess, to *synchronicity*, "an acausal principal of connection."[139]

"For he that is not against us is for us" (Mark 9:40) does fit thematically with the preceding story of the "strange exorcist," though I suspect it is an add-on, especially since we find a Q version of it in different contexts in both Luke 11:23 and Matt. 12:30.

"For truly, I say to you, whoever gives you a cup of water to drink *because you bear the name of Christ*, will by no means lose his reward" (Mark 9:41) continues the idea that all it takes is the most basic allegiance to Christ or claiming the name "Christian." Not much of a creedal shibboleth there.

"Whoever *causes* one of *these little ones who believe in me to sin*, it would be better for him if a great millstone were hung round his neck and he were thrown into the sea" (Mark 9:42). The "little ones who believe in me" (recalling "the least of these my brethren" in Matthew 25:40) are new converts, those whose initial adoption of the name of Christ is all they have so far, "mere Christians," though in a slightly different sense than in verses 40-41. (This almost-but-not-quite-continuity is just what we expect in this kind of linkage.)

"And if your hand *causes you to sin*, cut it off; it is better for you to enter life maimed than with two hands to go to hell, to the unquenchable *fire*. And if your foot *causes you to sin*, cut it off; it is better for you to enter life lame than with two feet to be thrown into hell. And if your eye *causes you to sin*, pluck it out; it is better for you

---

[138] Once, many years ago, I bristled at hearing a fellow Gordon-Conwell student "explain" that when drug addicted thugs' lives were reclaimed and renewed when they joined the Nation of Islam (the Elijah Muhammad sect), it was a "Satanic counterfeit." Of course, such examples could be endlessly multiplied.

[139] Carl Jung, *Synchronicity: An Acausal Connecting Principle*. Trans. R.F.C. Hull. Bollingen Series (Princeton: Princeton University Press, 1973).

to enter the kingdom of God with one eye than with two eyes to be thrown into hell, where their worm does not die, and the *fire* is not quenched" (Mark 9:45-48). "Causing to sin" happens to occur in both 9:42 and 9:45-48. "Fire" is common to this sequence and to verse 49: "For every one will be *salted* with *fire*" (Mark 9:49), and "salt" pops up again in the verse after that: "*Salt* is good; but if the salt has lost its saltness, how will you season it?" (Mark 9:50a). More salt gets sprinkled in the second half of verse 50: "Have *salt* in yourselves, and be at peace with one another." And what on earth does the weird-sounding verse 49 mean? This is one of those places where it would sure come in handy if we could sniff out an underlying Aramaic original, mistranslated into Greek, that would make more sense. And Charles Cutler Torrey[140] found one: "Anything spoiling is salted." (At least that's *slightly* less baffling, I guess.)[141] And the warnings of impending hellfire (verses 43-48) come word for word from Isaiah 66:24.

The Great Amendment (10:1-12)

Some seek Jesus' opinion concerning the lively scribal debate over divorce. The House of Hillel believed in "divorce for every cause," for instance (and they chose this example purposely because of its trivial character), if the missus burns the soup, out she goes! The stricter House of Shammai believed that only adultery counted as a legitimate pretext for divorce. So Jesus is being asked which side he supports. In the Markan original (Mark 10:2-12), preserved also by Luke (16:18), Jesus undercuts the debate by saying divorce had never been the will of God in the first place. He allowed it only as a concession to human nature back when the Torah was given. What he means to imply is unclear. Human nature has not changed appreciably, so why should the "Plan B" of divorce change? But divorce only compounds tragedy, since a divorced woman cannot be blamed for marrying again, yet, since God does not really countenance divorce at all, she will be technically committing

---

[140] Charles Cutler Torrey, *Our Translated Gospels: Some of the Evidence* (New York: Harper & Brothers, 1936), pp. 11, 13.

[141] Might it originally have been connected to the saying "You are the salt of the earth," preserved in Matthew 5:13, with which it shares contextual material?

adultery. It is her divorcing husband's fault. Stumbling blocks to sin must sooner or later come, but woe to him, the husband in this case, by whom they come!

But perhaps Jesus *is* to be taken as forbidding divorce among his followers, the usual interpretation, because of the imperative in verse 6: "Let no one divide them asunder." If this is the case, given the terrible abuse from which death and divorce are the only escapes, we would have to consider those trapped in abusive marriages by their commitment to the Bible as martyrs for the doctrine of biblical inerrancy.

"Don't shove that baby in the Saviour's face!"[142] *(10:13-16)*

Jesus once again rolls his eyes in self-reproach: "Why the heaven did I ever choose such morons? I guess Marcion is right!" Their latest blunder is forgetting that the greatest among you is supposed to be your servant. Jesus, they imagine, shares their sense of petty self-importance and surely can't be bothered to lay his hands on small children to say a blessing over them. "Security!" "Get away, kid! Ya bother me!" It's a great scene. It was probably based on a previous great scene in 2 Kings 4, once again, the now-familiar story of Elisha and the Shunammite. "And when she came to the mountain, to the man of God, she caught hold of his feet. And Gehazi came to thrust her away. But the man of God said, 'Let her alone, for she is in bitter distress, and [Yahweh] has hidden it from me and has not told me'" (v. 27). What is she so upset about? Merely the death of her son, which is why she wants Elisha's divine blessing to restore him to life. Mark has lowered the stakes; the kids are in no danger, but their parents are asking Jesus for his blessing, and the thick-headed disciples shoo them away and get rebuked for it.

But what's the point of Mark's version? Oscar Cullmann[143] realized that it must have been a piece of a liturgy for infant baptism. New Testament baptism stories often include a rhetorical question like, "Who can hinder these people being baptized?" as in Acts 8:36; 10:47; 11:17; Matt. 3:13-15. It's equivalent to the question asked at

---

[142] Chapman, Cleese, Gilliam, Idle, Jones, and Palin, *Life of Brian*, p. 124.

[143] Oscar Cullmann, *Baptism in the New Testament.* Trans. J.K.S. Reid. Studies in Biblical Theology No. 1 (London: SCM Press, 1951), Appendix: "Traces of an Ancient Baptismal Formula in the New Testament," pp. 71-80.

weddings, "If anyone present knows of any reason these two should not be joined in matrimony, let him speak now or forever hold his peace." You never hear anyone pipe up. "Now just a darn minute!"

This scene has all the marks of a Vacation Bible School poster, lacking only the catcher's mitt and the model airplane.

Sorry You Asked? (10:17-31)

Here is the granddaddy of all discipleship paradigms: the story of the Rich Young Ruler. If you *really* want to follow Jesus, you must accept that conventional religiosity, even the sincere kind, is by no means sufficient. A *real* disciple, a cross-bearing one, would cash in all his possessions, disperse the proceeds to the poor (whose ranks you will now have joined), and walk the roads from town to town preaching the gospel. Evangelicals and fundamentalists, who claim to take everything short of the Book of Revelation literally, are quick to make an exception of this passage. All other texts they take as a letter from Jesus directly to themselves. Not this one. "No, heh-heh, Jesus doesn't mean *me*! No, he just happened to know that, for *this* guy, wealth was an idol preventing him from giving all to God. Or at least Jesus wanted to test whether or *not* it was by seeing if he'd be willing it to give it all away. Yeah, *that's* the ticket!" Did you notice? This very way of dealing with the unsettling passage prevents subsequent readers of it from posing the same challenge to themselves, since they think they have bracketed it by making it refer *only to this one man*.

But it is only the fundamentalist approach to the Bible that creates the bad conscience I am describing. The historical-critical approach allows us to recognize that the many and varied kinds of biblical materials are not written for the benefit of any old readers. It is the function of form criticism to discern *what* was written to *whom*. And it seems pretty clear that this recruitment paradigm was part of the stock-in-trade of the itinerant charismatics (3 John 5-8) for whom the Mission Charges (Mark 6:7-13; Matt. 10:5-23; Luke 9:1-6; 10:1-16) were composed. As Theissen[144] asks, who would have kept these verses alive in oral transmission but individuals who had actually *met* the challenge and pointed to such sayings as credentials (bragging rights)? In fact, 1 Corinthians chapter 9 and 2 Corinthians 11:5-15

---

[144] Gerd Theissen, *Sociology of Early Palestinian Christianity*. Trans. John Bowden (Philadelphia: Fortress Press, 1978), p. 10.

imply that some of these itinerant apostles did not so much use stories like that of the Rich Young Ruler to recruit new colleagues but rather to magnify their own clout against rivals who did *not* go on the road lacking all worldly resources.[145]

Though one always hears that the Rich Young Ruler turned his back on Jesus, refusing his demands, the text says no such thing. Jesus told him to "go" and sell everything, and he goes! Sure, he is downcast, but that doesn't mean he is reluctantly rejecting Jesus' council; after all, Jesus immediately comments how *hard* it is for a rich man to enter the kingdom of God, implying that this is just what the Ruler is doing! (But of course Mark does not explicitly *say* what the Ruler's decision was because the whole point is to leave it for the reader/hearer to decide how *he* is going to respond to the sobering challenge. Thus no "happily ever after.")

Jesus' striking comparison, "It is easier for a camel to go through a needle's eye, than for a rich man to enter into the kingdom of God," has sometimes been taken for another mistranslation from the Aramaic. The word rendered "camel" (*gamla*) could just as well be translated "cable" or "rope."[146] That might be a better comparison to the implied "thread." But there is no need to resort to this since we have a close parallel in rabbinic lore using animal imagery: "Are you from Pombeditha [= Fantasyland], where they can drive an elephant through the eye of a needle?" (*Baba* Mezia, 38, 2).

The Request of James and John (10:32-45)

This comical episode sure makes the sons of Zebedee look like a couple of self-seeking jerks, and of course that's Mark's point. He has rewritten the 2 Kings 2:9-10 story of Elisha's request of Elijah just before his ascension, only where the Deuteronomist's intent was to authorize Elisha as Elijah's official successor, Mark means to

---

[145] Gerd Theissen, *The Social Setting of Pauline Christianity: Essays on Corinth.* Trans. John Schütz (Philadelphia: Fortress Press, 1982), pp. 40-49; Dieter Georgi, *The Opponents of Paul in Second Corinthians.* Trans. Harold Attridge, Isabel and Thomas Best, Bernadette Brooten, Ron Cameron, Frank Fallon, Stephen Gero, Renate Rose, Herman Waetjen, and Michael Williams (Philadelphia: Fortress Press, 1986), pp. 238-241.

[146] George M. Lamsa, *Gospel Light: Comments from the Aramaic and Unchanged Eastern Customs on the Teachings of Jesus* (Philadelphia: A.J. Holman, 1939), pp. 115-116.

discredit James and John (whether he envisioned them as members of the Twelve or of the Pillars). The structure of the two stories is the same.[147] Jesus has just announced for the third time his impending death and resurrection, which prompts the brothers to shove their way to the head of the line: "Teacher, we want you to do for us whatever we may ask of you... Grant that we may sit, one at your right, one at your left, in your glory" (Mark 10:35, 37). It is an echo of 2 Kings 2:9, "Ask what I shall do for you before I am taken from you." Hearing the request, Elijah pauses a moment and replies, "You have asked a hard thing" (v. 10). Elisha seems to have underestimated the gravity of his petition, as have James and John, to whom Jesus replies, "You do not know what you are asking for."

What can we take away from this passage? First, since Jesus basically tells Jimmy and Johnny, "Sorry, boys, I'm afraid it's out of my nail-scarred hands," this opens the way for the ascendancy of other apostolic figureheads, as when the Marcionites claimed that Paul sat down at Jesus' right hand in heaven. And of course the point is not really that of a celestial seating chart, but rather of competing authority claims down on earth.

Second, Mark appears to have modified an original saying about Christian martyrdom, transforming it into a liturgical formula for Christian initiation. The officiator would ask the candidates, "Are you able to drink the cup that I drink?" The candidates would reply, "We can." Again he asks, "Are you able to be baptized with the baptism I am baptized with?" Again, "We can," whereupon the new recruits would be baptized, then take First Communion.

Secret Mark (between 10:34 and 35)

Let's try the Secret Gospel text on for size.

> And they come into Bethany [Mark 11:11-12]. And a certain woman whose brother had died [John 11:21] was there. And, coming, she prostrated herself before Jesus [Luke 17:16] and says to him, "Son of David, have mercy on me." [Mark 10:48] But the disciples rebuked her. [Mark 10:13]

---

[147] Miller, *Mark as Midrash*, p. 253.

And Jesus, being angered [Mark 3:5], went off with her into the garden where the tomb was [John 19:41], and straightway a great cry was heard from the tomb. And going near, Jesus rolled away the stone from the door of the tomb. [Matt. 28:2] And straightway, going in where the youth was, he stretched forth his hand and raised him, seizing his hand. [Mark 5:41] But the youth, looking upon him, loved him [Mark 10:21] and began to beseech him that he might be with him. [Mark 5:18] And going out of the tomb they came into the house of the youth, for he was rich. [Mark 10:22] And after six days [Mark 9:2] Jesus told him what to do and in the evening the youth comes to him [Mark 6:48], wearing a linen cloth over his naked body. [Mark 14:51-52] And he remained with him that night,[naked man with naked man,] for Jesus taught him the mystery of the kingdom of God. [Mark 4:11] And thence, arising, he returned to the other side of the Jordan.

This sure sounds like Mark all right, in fact maybe a bit *too much* like Mark. Look up the verse references in brackets and thou shalt see what I mean. If we didn't know better (and we don't), we might be tempted to think someone (ancient or modern) merely pasted together a bunch of Markan sentences gathered from elsewhere in the gospel, plus a couple from other gospels. Skeptics have suggested that the Clement letter to Theodore containing the Secret Mark text sounds too much like Clement, a too-dense concentration of characteristic and favorite Clementine words and idioms, implying a forger (or pasticheur) trying too hard. The same might be said of the Secret Gospel pericope itself: too much "Markishness."

Clement tells Theodore that the sneaky Carpocratian Gnostics interpolated the phrase "naked man with naked man" into their copies of Secret Mark, but, if it is an ancient document, I should think it is the squeamish Clement who was doing B.B. Warfield-style textual emendation: it *couldn't* have said that, so it *didn't* say it. Clement would have been scandalized by what the libertine Carpocratians made of it: the basis for a ritual of homosexual initiation. But we know that early Christians often baptized with the officiator as well as the baptismal candidate in the buff, symbolizing rebirth ("Naked I came from my mother's womb and naked shall I return," Job 1:21). The linen sheet was also common in baptism. If the passage did come from Mark, it was very likely a bit of liturgy accompanying water baptism.

At Mark 10:46, Secret Mark adds, "And the sister of the youth whom Jesus loved and his mother and Salome were there, and Jesus did not receive them." This looks like it was based on Jesus' refusal to welcome his mother and other relatives in Mark 3:31-35.

Blind Man's Bluff (10:46-52)

Isaiah 35:5-6, 8a says "Then the eyes of the blind shall be opened... then shall the lame man leap like a hart... And a highway shall be there, and it shall be called the holy way."[148] This passage probably provided Mark (or some Jesus fictioneer before him) with the elements for the story of Bartimaeus. The blind beggar *leaps up*, his *eyes are opened*, and he follows Jesus *on the way*. His occupation as a beggar may have been an inference from his name, which may come, as Derrett[149] decodes it, from the Aramaic *Bar-teymah*, "son of poverty." But then we would have to suspect that the name is given the character based on his function as a mere stage prop for the story.[150]

Intertextual Errands (11:1-6; 14:12-16)

The Passion Narrative contains two stories that almost sound like two versions of the same original episode, and evidently they were. What was that original? I should say it was 1 Samuel chapter 9,[151] where Kish sends two men, namely his son Saul and a servant (1 Sam. 9:3), on an errand. In both Markan stories Jesus also dispatches two men on each of two missions (Mark 11:1; 14:13). Saul and his companion were supposed to track down some runaway asses[152] (9:3), and Jesus' disciples are told to look for a particular ass's colt (11:2). Saul and his servant approach the city hoping to secure the

---

[148] Miller, *Mark as Midrash*, pp. 263-264.

[149] Derrett, *Making of Mark*, p. 185.

[150] Tzvetan Todorov, *The Poetics of Prose*. Trans. Richard Howard (Ithaca: Cornell University Press, 1977), Chapter 5, "Narrative-Men," pp. 66-79.

[151] Miller, *Mark as Midrash*; p. 325; Derrett, *Making of Mark*, p. 187.

[152] But someone will say, "Why didn't they just look behind them?"

help of a circuit-riding shaman and are met by young women coming out to draw water (9:11), while Jesus has told the disciples to look for a man carrying water (14:13). Saul and his companion (let's call him Kramer) are told they will find the man they seek, the prophet Samuel, as soon as they enter the city (9:13). Likewise, Jesus tells his men they will find the colt tied as soon as they enter the city (11:2). All transpires as they were told (9:6; 11:4; 14:16). Saul asks "Where is the house of the seer?" (9:18). Jesus tells the disciples to ask, "Where is my guest room?" (14:14). In 1 Samuel 9:20 Saul is told the missing animals have been located, and in Mark 11:6 Jesus says to assure the owner that his borrowed colt will be returned with a full tank of gas. In 9:19 Samuel oversees the preparation of a feast, and in 14:16 the disciples prepare the Passover.

The upper room, which Jesus has apparently rented beforehand, harks back to the second-story rooms provided for Elijah (1 Kings 17:19) and Elisha (2 Kings 4:10) by benefactors,[153] one of whom Elijah first met when he requested a drink of water from a woman who God told him would provide for him (1 Kings 17:9,10). He met her at the city gate, just as Jesus tells the disciples they will meet a man carrying water in a vessel as soon as they enter the city.

Now Entering Jerusalem (11:7-11)

The famous scene of Jesus entering the holy city riding the donkey fleshes out Zechariah 9:9. The responses of the crowd come straight from Psalm 118:26-27, "Blessed is he who enters in the name of [Yahweh]! ... Bind the festal procession with branches..." "Hosanna in the highest" comes from the Hebrew or Aramaic of "Save now!" in Psalm 118:25 and from Psalm 148 LXX: "Praise him in the highest!"[154] Of course the psalm offers its blessings on any and all pilgrims to the holy city, not to one individual. Even in Mark the fulfillment of Zechariah's prophecy is not explicit, nor do the exclamations of the crowd necessarily apply to Jesus in particular. Passover was always an occasion for magnifying hopes that the kingdom of God would soon arrive, so naturally the crowd is shouting slogans about it. But, in light of his Messianic Secret theme, there is no way Mark meant his readers to understand this scene as

---

[153] Miller, *Mark as Midrash*, p. 331.
[154] Helms, *Gospel Fictions*, p. 104.

the people's messianic acclamation of Jesus. (They do not, as they do in the other gospels, apply royal epithets to Jesus.) Of course, Mark assumes the reader knows what the depicted crowd does *not*: this *is* Zechariah's messianic king.

That Damned Fig Tree (11:12-14, 20)

As anyone can see from the sandwiching of this story with that of the Temple Cleansing, the ill-fated fig tree is made to symbolize unrepentant Jerusalem, and the tree episode can then be seen[155] to come from Psalm 37:35-36, "I have seen a wicked man overbearing, and towering like a cedar of Lebanon. Again I passed by, and, lo, he was no more; though I sought him, he could not be found." This is the inspiration for Jesus *seeking* figs on the *tree* but *finding none*, as well as the note that it was in *passing the spot again* that they discovered the tree blasted.

The blasting of the tree, by itself, looks like a pre-existent miracle story, perhaps originally depicting the boy Jesus petulantly zapping it when he found he should have to seek his lunch elsewhere that day. This pericope would have been fished out of the same stream of silliness that was eventually collected in the hilarious Apocryphal Infancy Gospels, what Gordon Fee used to call, collectively, "the Gospel of the Divine Brat." Verses 22-26 have been tacked on in an attempt to redeem the embarrassing fig tree debacle by making it into a lesson of faith. Nice try.

Throbbing Temple (11:11-26)

Jesus suddenly disrupts the Temple service, stampeding the sacrificial animals and (somehow) turning away Levitical functionaries trying to carry sacrificial vessels up to the altar. Let's face it: the story is historically impossible as it stands. The area in question is vast; for Jesus to commandeer it like this would require an armed occupation. As we now read it, it sounds as if some nut burst into a church basement rummage sale and overturned card tables with stacks of old Readers Digest books. If there was a real event underlying the tale, something much bigger must have happened, something which has been either forgotten and misunderstood or censored. S.G.F. Brandon[156] makes a powerful case that Jesus actually led an armed

---

[155] Miller, *Mark as Midrash*, pp. 274-275.

raid on the Temple treasury, and that the account was sanitized by Mark in order to suppress the revolutionary activity of Jesus which almost immediately resulted in his crucifixion by the Romans for sedition. By the time Mark wrote, Christians were seeking to live at peace with the Roman government and realized the story of Jesus had to be depoliticized. So in Mark's version it is not Rome but the Jews who wanted Jesus dead. The fact of the crucifixion, a Roman penalty, was too well known to be denied, so the best Mark could do was to redefine the whole thing as a frame-up. Pontius Pilate was a notorious Jew-hater eventually recalled by Rome for his atrocities, and thus a safe target. Mark's caricature of Pilate as a coward depicted him having Jesus executed despite his obvious innocence, because he let himself be bullied by a courtyard full of ruffians and idlers.

The alternative is that proposed by Burton Mack,[157] that the story of the Temple Cleansing is simply a piece of fiction cobbled together from various Old Testament fragments and that, once these are bracketed, there's not much story left. The whole notion of the "cleansing" would come from Malachi's messenger of the covenant who will purify the sons of Levi (Mal. 3:1-3). Jesus' expulsion of the Temple merchants and money changers would be derived from Zechariah 14:21b, "And there shall no longer be a trader in the house of [Yahweh Sabaoth] on that day." All Jesus says in the scene is no more than a conflation of Isaiah 56:7 ("My house shall be called a house of prayer for all the nations") and Jeremiah 7:11 ("Has this house, which is called by my name, become a den of robbers in your eyes?"). The priests and scribes react to this disturbance by plotting to destroy Jesus, just as the priests, prophets, and people grab Jeremiah and shout at him, "You shall die!" when he likewise predicts the destruction of the city and the Temple (26:8).[158]

I suspect that the Temple Cleansing episode reflects that of the entry of Simon bar-Gioras into the Temple to *clean out* the *robbers* of John of Gischala on the eve of the Temple's destruction. Simon was a would-be King of the Jews and leader of a rival sect of Jewish

[156] S.G.F. Brandon, *The Fall of Jerusalem and the Christian Church: A Study of the Effects of the Jewish Overthrow of A.D. 70 on Christianity* (London: SPCK, 1951), Chapter Ten, "The Markan Reaction to A.D. 70," pp. 185-205; Brandon, *Jesus and the Zealots: A Study of the Political Factor in Primitive Christianity* (New York: Scribners, 1967), Chapter 5, "The Markan Gospel an *Apologia ad Christianos Romanos*," pp. 221-282.
[157] Mack, *Myth of Innocence*, pp. 291-292; Nineham, *Saint Mark*, p. 301.
[158] Miller, *Mark as Midrash*, p. 274.

revolutionaries. He had made a pact with the Temple elders to uproot the *lestai* ("robbers") led by John, and the Temple elders hailed his entry into the Temple grounds with waving palm branches. He soon joined forces with John against the besieging Romans, but they were finally unsuccessful. Simon fled into a network of underground passages but, facing starvation, he eventually burst through to the surface, dressed in a white sheet, right in front of the stunned Roman soldiers. He was executed in Rome (Josephus, *Wars of the Jews*, vii. 2, § 1; vii. 5, § 6; 8, § 1). Do the parallels with the gospels lend plausibility to the gospel account by virtue of historical analogy? "Yes, this sort of thing did happen, and Jesus' Triumphal Entry looks like another instance of it." Could be. On the other hand, Christians who knew about these events may have sought to fill out their bare outline of Jesus' Passion with details borrowed from these events.

Or, as Lena Einhorn[159] argues, the Jesus story may be accurate in its basics, but the events actually occurred during the revolutionary period leading up to the fall of Jerusalem. Out of their desire to mollify Roman suspicions that Christians still harbored seditious aims, the New Testament writers retrojected the Temple clash, the arrest, and the crucifixion some thirty to forty years earlier, stripping them of political significance by placing Jesus safely in a relatively calm period for Roman Palestine.

Can't Have One without the Other (11:27-33)

Good question: where does Jesus get the authority (the right) to pull a stunt like the wholesale disruption of the Temple? That's what the Temple elders would like to know. Jesus' reply is so evasive, we can't even be sure he's *being* evasive! He promises to give them the answer if they'll agree to answer his question first: "John's baptismal ministry: was it authorized by heaven (i.e., God) or was it just his own idea?" The question is not quite so straightforward as you might

---

[159] Lena Einhorn, *A Shift in Time: How Historical Documents Reveal the Surprising Truth about Jesus* (New York: Yucca Publishing, 2016).

think. In a sense, John's activity must have been at least "of God," since, even if it *was* just his idea, look, the man was persuading huge masses of people to repent and renounce their sins. What could be wrong with that? Does it really matter whether an angel prodded him awake, as Moroni did Joseph Smith, and told him to put on that burlap tunic and get down to the river? Maybe the issue is the validity of John's prediction of imminent catastrophe. Maybe he was predicating repentance on a pipe dream. When it failed to happen (as it did!), people who had repented would become disillusioned and say, "Ah, to Gehenna with it. I'm going back to drinking."

Jesus knows these priestly bureaucrats, whose default mode is to play it safe, will hedge. They won't want to take a stand. He knows they dismissed the Baptizer (cf., Luke 7:29-30) as a crank, a precursor to Harold Camping. But Jesus also knows *they* know the crowds revere John as a real prophet and, better yet, a martyred saint. If the elders give their real opinion in the hearing of the crowd, they will be revealing themselves as accessories after the fact in his murder (cf., Matt. 23:29-31). So what do they come up with as they emerge from their whispering huddle? "Ah, we're still working on that one. We'll let you know when we come to a decision," as if they're some sort of Vatican committee plodding through an investigation of a new apparition of Mary floating above the bar in Club Bada Bing. The mills of God's self-appointed representatives grind slow.

Jesus' reply to this ("Why am I not surprised?") seems to imply that they already have their answer. He is no different from John the Baptizer: the only way to recognize either one as a genuine prophet is to consult one's heart. "If any man's will is to do his will, he shall know whether the teaching is from God or whether I am speaking on my own authority" (John 7:17). Jesus is throwing ball back into their court.

Jeremias[160] proposes a different understanding of Jesus' counter-question: Jesus means to appeal to John's authority (or lack of it). "Whatever you believe about John's authorization goes double for me, since he ordained me" (cf., 1 Cor. 9:2). This logic would work better if we were talking about Matthew or John, where Jesus does receive the endorsement of the Baptist, but he doesn't in Mark.

Shifty Sharecroppers (12:1-12)

---

[160] Joachim Jeremias, *New Testament Theology, Part One: The Proclamation of Jesus.* Trans. John Bowden (London: SCM Press, 1971), pp. 55-56.

Mark has Jesus borrow Isaiah 5:1-7 for the beginning of this parable. But the rest of it, as Dennis MacDonald[161] demonstrates to my satisfaction, is based on Homer's *Odyssey*. In fact, the *Odyssey* looks to be the origin of all the gospel parables depicting an absentee landlord or head of a large estate leaving his servants minding the store while he is away on a long trip. In these stories, Jesus' warning that, if the servants behave like mice in the absence of the housecat, they will be in for quite the unpleasant surprise when the boss gets home ahead of schedule! But in the *Odyssey*'s episode of Penelope's Suitors, it is not the servants who are wicked, but rather the suitors. They are the men, lesser nobles of Greece, who figure Odysseus, ten years absent after the Trojan War, must be dead. Each opportunist hopes to woo Queen Penelope and so to take her husband's place as king of Ithaca. And none is willing to give up. So Penelope is stuck playing hostess to these parasites, who are consuming the resources of the palace like a locust plague of freeloading moochers. But they realize that Prince Telemachus will soon reach maturity and will not delay to throw them all out on their rosy behinds, so they plot against him. If they manage to kill him, there will be no obstacle to (one of) them replacing Odysseus on the throne (and in Penelope's bed). But Telemachus detects their scheme and eludes them. The tenants working the vineyard are the gospel version of the suitors. The landlord (= Odysseus) remains long away, and when he sends his son to collect his share of the grape harvest, the tenants (really squatters) figure their chance has come. If they can murder the son, there will be no legal heir, so they will inherit the vineyard by right of occupation. Just an oddity? Or the *Odyssey*?

In the *Odyssey*, the suitors had to tread lightly lest their brazenness finally push the people of Ithaca, Odysseus' subjects, too far and provoke them to rise up. This is where Mark gets the caution of the Jewish leaders in the face of the veiled threat of Jesus' parable. For the evil tenants, of course, represent them.

Mark returned to his recently-used Psalm 118 for the quotation from verses 22-23 in Mark 12:10-11.

Mark 12:8 has the son, obviously Jesus, killed, then thrown out; Matthew has the villains *first* cast him out, *then* kill him, no doubt trying to make the parable reflect even more closely Jesus' fate. He was led *out of the city* to Golgotha. And Mark 12:9 has Jesus ask, rhetorically, then answer, his own question, whereas the Jewish

---

[161] MacDonald, *Homeric Epics*, p. 37.

authorities answer it in Matthew.

Caesar's Cut (12:13-17)

Mark makes clear just what Jesus' opponents are up to: they want to corner him so that, whatever he answers, he will earn the wrath of one group or the other. Is it scripturally licit for Jews to pay taxes to the Roman Caesar? In recent centuries Jews had certainly paid tax and tribute to foreign rulers. That was not controversial. But ever since Herod's kingdom ceased to be a formally independent client state of the Roman Empire and came under direct Roman rule, taxation had been a hot potato. Judas of Galilee had led a violent revolution in 6 C.E.[162] (Acts 5:37), outraged at the prospect of paying taxes to Rome for the first time. If Jesus took the accommodationist position of the Jewish hierarchy who did not want to rock the boat, Zealot sympathizers would write him off as a Quisling compromiser. But if he agreed with them that paying tribute to Caesar amounted to idolatry, he could give the authorities, both Roman and Jewish, solid grounds to take action against him.

So what do we make of Jesus' answer? It is not evasive. Rather, it cuts the Gordian Knot and solves the problem in one swift stroke. One cannot "render unto God" the Roman *denarius* because, bearing Caesar's image, these coins were considered technically idolatrous. No one worried about using them in everyday commerce, but when it came to paying the Temple taxes or buying sacrificial animals in the Temple, one had to take *denarii* to the exchange tables, changing the heathen coins for Jewish and Phoenician coinage which lacked images of living things, forbidden in Exodus 20:4. These they could "render unto God." So what about Jews paying Roman taxes? Simple: God doesn't want the filthy lucre of idolatrous pagan coins, so why not give 'em back to the idolatrous pagans who minted 'em? Where's the religious compromise in that? That is some damn fine *halakha*!

---

[162] I just can't buy the ingenious but, I think, far-fetched theory of Richard A. Horsley that Judas of Galilee was a nonviolent first-century Gandhi. (Horsley, *Jesus and the Spiral of Violence: Popular Jewish Resistance in Roman Palestine* [Minneapolis: Fortress Press, 1993], pp. 77-89). I can't square it with the fact that various subsequent violent revolutionaries were Judas' descendants and saw themselves as carrying on his legacy.

Dead Husbands Society (12:18-27)

Jesus' response to the trick question of the Sadducees is creative but draconian, disappointing generations of widows and widowers who hoped they would one day be reunited with their spouses in heaven. When he goes on the offensive, however, trying to provide Pentateuchal evidence for the end-time resurrection, he stumbles into absurdity. He seems to want to rest the whole weight of the doctrine upon the present tense of a single verb. Had God said, "I *was* the God of Abraham, Isaac, and Jacob," that would serve to identify him as the ancient Hebrew deity, if that's all he meant. Then why does it say, "I *am* the God," etc.? It "must" be to affirm that the patriarchs are still alive and socializing with their divine Patron. Not only is the inference a wild one; it also implies a heavenly afterlife going on right now, not a *future* resurrection when the patriarchs would *again* join Jehovah in fellowship. Yes, yes, this is typical ancient reasoning, not modern, but *why* is it "ancient," i.e., relegated to the museum of the past? Because it is *bad* reasoning.

Winner and Runner-Up (12:28-34)

Jewish sages used to kill time by speculating on the question Jesus gets asked here: which commandment of the Torah is most important? The point was not a triage list, enabling one to pick and choose, but rather an attempt to discern a center of gravity for the Torah as a whole. What's it generally getting at? Which commandment should be interpreted in light of which other commandment?[163] Sort of like what Jesus is doing in his run-ins with the scribes: "The Sabbath was made for man, not the other way around."

Anyway, Jesus nominates the Shema: "Hear, O Israel: Yahweh your God is one," and you shall love him with all you've got (Deut. 6:4), as the top commandment. But evidently Jesus had trouble

---

[163] Norman Geisler does a fine job of applying this approach systematically to Christian ethics in formulating his model of "hierarchical ethics" (*Ethics: Alternatives and Issues* [Grand Rapids: Zondervan, 1971]) or "graded absolutism" (*Christian Ethics: Options and Issues* [Grand Rapids: Baker Academic, 1989]) as an alternative to Joseph Fletcher's notorious *Situation Ethics: The New Morality* (Philadelphia: Westminster Press, 1966).

choosing his favorite, so he adds a runner-up, "And you shall love your neighbor as yourself" (Lev. 19:18).[164] Actually, by rating them in this way, Jesus clarifies the point of the whole exercise: one's first duty is to his Creator, but right up there with it is the duty to other people. Neither is to be sacrificed to the other even though devotion to God takes priority. Humanism does not really take a back seat, since it is the fact of God creating humans in his image that necessitates our according them dignity, respect, and love.

David's Sons Need Not Apply (12:35-37)

This passage plainly denies the Davidic descent of the Messiah. It must be a fossil of the apologetics of an early Christian sect which believed Jesus was the Messiah but was not of Davidic lineage. Very likely they were Galileans, contemporary heirs of the old northern kingdom of Israel, who had centuries earlier repudiated the Davidic monarchy (1 Kings 12:16). Such arguments had been made before, on behalf of the Hasmonean (Maccabean) rulers, who were Levitical, not Davidic. Mark (like Matthew) appears to have included the story, prizing it as an example of Jesus' rhetorical prowess, but oblivious of the Christological implications.

The Olivet Discourse (Chapter 13)

Timotheé Colani[165] was the first to notice that this checklist of apocalyptic signs didn't exactly match the teaching elsewhere in the gospels, where Jesus seems to urge constant readiness, as if the coming of the Son of Man (whether Jesus or someone else) might break in upon an unsuspecting humanity busy with trivia and sin (Mark 13:33-37; Luke 12:35-40).[166] Mark 13:5-31

---

[164] You see? There is something good in Leviticus. Set your alarm next time you're reading through Leviticus so you don't miss it.

[165] Timotheé Colani, "The Little Apocalypse of Mark 13." An excerpt from Colani, *Jesus-Christ et les croyances messianiques de son temps*, 1864, pp. 201-214. Trans. Nancy Wilson. *Journal of Higher Criticism* (10/1) Spring 2003, pp. 41-47.

blatantly contradicts what Jesus says in Luke 17:20-21: "The kingdom of God is not coming with signs to be observed, nor will they say, 'Lo, here!' or 'There!' For the kingdom of God is within you." And is the discourse about the coming destruction of the Jerusalem Temple, or about the eschatological Parousia? Colani hypothesized that originally the disciples asked simply about the former (13:3-4), since Jesus had just made a startling quip about the Temple buildings: "Take a good look while you can, boys, because it won't be long before this place will be as flat as a parking lot!" And Jesus' answer was short and sweet: "Of that day, or that hour, no one knows, not even the angels in heaven, nor the Son, but only the Father" (Mark 13:32). All the intervening material had a different, pre-Markan origin.

Eusebius (*Ecclesiastical History* Book III, 5:4) tells us that, just before the Roman siege clamped down, Jerusalem Christians were circulating copies of an apocalyptic flier warning them to run for the hills while the getting was still good. They took it seriously and fled to Pella. Colani suggested that this pamphlet eventually became the body of Chapter 13 of Mark's gospel. Yes, this tract does eventually get around to the ruination of Jerusalem and the Abomination of Desolation, but, Colani asks, is the cavalier attitude of Jesus toward the Temple (implied in the crack that prompted the disciples' question) really consistent with the mortified gravity of the reference to the Abomination of Desolation? Rather, good riddance, wouldn't you think? Besides, when "Jesus" says, "Let the reader understand," we know we are not dealing with a transcript of what anyone *said*, but rather something that originated as a *written text*.

Colani pinpointed a date for this pre-Markan apocalypse the same way scholars determine the dates of any other future-telling apocalypses: you look for the point where "predicted" events stop being accurately portrayed and the prediction suddenly veers off track. For instance, the Book of Daniel is strikingly accurate in its "predictions" of Antiochus Epiphanes and Judah Maccabee and the

---

[166] This is the key point of contention between two competing camps of fundamentalists, Pre-Tribulationists and Post-Tribulationists. The first point to the "any moment vigilance" texts as demanding that, if the Tribulation were to precede the Rapture, the latter must be at least seven years in the future at any given moment as long as the Tribulation has not yet begun.

triumph of the Hasmoneans over the Seleucids. But it drops off the edge when it predicts the imminent advent of the eschatological kingdom of the saints of the Most High. Bingo! Daniel was written in 163 B.C.E. Similarly, the Little Apocalypse expects the End of the World to follow immediately upon the destruction of Jerusalem, so it is a safe bet it was written, as Eusebius' account would also imply, on the eve of the Fall of Jerusalem in 70 C.E.

Most scholars tend to date Mark's gospel as a whole to ca. 70, but if you think Mark incorporated the Little Apocalypse into his work, the date of the Little Apocalypse says nothing about the date of the whole gospel. Matthew used Mark as a source; you don't date Matthew by evidence from Mark. Of course, it might be that the rest of Mark's gospel was written *earlier* than the Little Apocalypse, and that a subsequent redactor added it in. But there are too many other signs of a later date for Mark.

Hermann Detering[167] reopened the question of the date of the Little Apocalypse underlying Mark 13. He argues that Mark modified the original text, which is independently preserved in Matthew 24. Matthew of course had access to Mark, but the original was still available as well, and he preferred that one. And Matthew's version corresponds more closely to the circumstances of the second-century revolt of Bar Kochba and its suppression by Rome (132-135 C.E.). Since this version is prior to Mark's version, this dates Mark to somewhere around 140-150, and Matthew even later.

But there are other possibilities. For one, it might be that Mark reproduced the Little Apocalypse in its original form, and that Matthew, in his wide-ranging redaction/amplification of Mark, altered Mark 13, updating the historical references in order to keep the predictions current. Another possibility is that Matthew's copy of Mark did not yet contain the Little Apocalypse, and that it was Matthew who inserted it. And only then did some copyist of Mark's gospel decide to insert a version of the Little Apocalypse (doctored as Detering suggests). This last option appears less likely to me in light of Matthew 24:3b, "Tell us, when will this be, *and what will be the sign of your coming and of the end of the age?*" This longer version of the question explicitly asks, not just about the Temple's demolition, but about Jesus' Parousia and the "consummation of the age," a favorite

---

[167] Hermann Detering, "The Synoptic Apocalypse (Mark 13 par): a Document from the Time of Bar Kochba." Trans. Michael Conley and Darrell J. Doughty. *Journal of Higher Criticism* (7/2) Fall 2000, pp. 161-210.

Matthean phrase usually denoting Matthean redaction. It looks like an attempt by Matthew to harmonize the Little Apocalypse with the Markan context. If the hypothetical post-Markan redactor borrowed Matthew's version of the Little Apocalypse, why would he cut off the longer continuation of the disciples' question when Mark's gospel would seem to need the harmonization as much as Matthew's? In Detering's reckoning, there are three passages (13:10, 18, 26) in which Mark appears to have cut a bit too much from the version of the Little Apocalypse preserved in Matthew because, in these verses, Mark's version is unintelligible apart from Matthew's. Perhaps most striking of all is the fact that Matthew 24:29 says that the Parousia will occur "immediately" after the desolation of the Temple, while the troublesome word is absent from the corresponding Mark 13:24. Mark absolutely loves the word "immediately," so it seems strange not to find it here, while it does appear in Matthew. This kind of difference, Detering points out, usually denotes a later writer trimming an earlier text in order to minimize the scandal of the delay of the Parousia. In this instance that would mean Mark was sanitizing the Little Apocalypse, which Matthew preserved intact. Granted, the matter is complicated, but this suggestion does not seem contrived in my opinion.

The apocalyptic tract is much like the Secret Gospel pericope, a tissue of biblical phrases sewn together in order to make it sound properly "scriptural," a gimmick familiar to anyone who has heard "prophecies" in Pentecostal and Charismatic meetings. Mark 13:7 comes from Daniel 2:28 ("there is a God in heaven who reveals mysteries, and he has made known to King Nebuchadnezzar what will be in the latter days. Your dream and the visions of your head as you lay in bed are these"). Mark 13:8 comes from Isaiah 19:2 ("And I will stir up Egyptians against Egyptians, and they will fight, every man against his brother and every man against his neighbor, city against city, kingdom against kingdom") and/or 2 Chronicles 15:6 ("They were broken in pieces, nation against nation and city against city, for God troubled them with every sort of distress").

Mark 13:12 is derived from Micah 7:6 ("the son treats the father with contempt, the daughter rises up against her mother, the daughter-in-law against her mother-in-law; a man's enemies are the men of his own house"). Mark 13:14 comes from Daniel 9:27 ("And he shall make a strong covenant with many for one week; and for half of the week he shall cause sacrifice and offering to cease; and upon the wing of abominations shall come one who makes desolate, until the decreed end is poured out on the desolator"), Daniel 12:11 ("And from the time that the continual burnt offering is taken away, and the abomination that makes desolate is set up, there shall be a thousand two hundred and ninety days"), and Genesis 19:17 ("And when they had brought them forth, they said, 'Flee for your life; do not look back or stop anywhere in the valley; flee to the hills, lest you be consumed'").

Mark 13:19 is derived from Daniel 12:1 ("At that time shall arise Michael, the great prince who has charge of your people. And there shall be a time of trouble, such as never has been since there was a nation till that time; but at that time your people shall be delivered, every one whose name shall be found written in the book"). Mark 13:22 is based on Deuteronomy 13:2-3 ("and [if] the sign or wonder which he tells you comes to pass, and if he says, 'Let us go after other gods,' which you have not known, 'and let us serve them,' you shall not listen to the words of that prophet or to that dreamer of dreams; for [Yahweh] your God is testing you, to know whether you love [Yahweh] your God with all your heart and with all your soul'"). Mark 13:24 is from Isaiah 13:10 ("For the stars of the heavens and their constellations will not give their light; the sun will be dark at its rising and the moon will not shed its light"). Mark 13:25 comes from Isaiah 34:4 ("All the host of heaven shall rot away, and the skies roll up like a scroll. All their host shall fall, as leaves fall from the vine, like leaves falling from the fig tree").

Mark 13:26 derives from Daniel 7:13 ("I saw in the night visions, and behold, with the clouds of heaven there came one like a son of man, and he came to the Ancient of Days and was presented before him") and Mark 13:27 from Zechariah 2:10 ("Sing and rejoice, O daughter of Zion; for lo, I come and I will dwell in the midst of you, says [Yahweh]") and Deuteronomy 30:4 ("If your outcasts are in the uttermost parts of heaven, from there [Yahweh] your God will gather you, and from there he will fetch you").[168]

One final note: the fact that Mark 13:3 restricts the hearers of the Olivet Discourse to the inner circle (the "pre-Pillars") plus Andrew is reminiscent of Gnostic revelation discourses, as is the location of the discourse in a remote place, a hilltop, away from the others. As so often, this seems to imply that Mark knew the content would sound strange and unfamiliar to his intended readers. "No wonder, brethren; it's been a closely guarded secret until now" (cf.,

---

[168] Bowman, *Gospel of Mark*, pp. 241-242, Miller, *Mark as Midrash*, pp. 300-301.

Daniel 12:4).

Nabbing the Nazarene (14:1-2, 10-11)

Some see a contradiction between Mark 14:1-2 and verses 43-50. In the first set of verses, the scheming Sanhedrin resolve to eliminate Jesus, but they decide not to attempt a public arrest during the Passover feast when the city is crowded and Jesus' admirers are thick on the ground. And yet in the second group of verses they do have him apprehended during the feast. What gives? I have to admit I do not see a problem. Verses 10-11 explain the change of plans: with the unanticipated help of a man on the inside, Judas Iscariot, they see a way to arrest Jesus during the feast after all, just not publicly. And they do.

That Greasy Kid Stuff (14:3-9)

Helms[169] is certainly right: John's version of the Bethany anointing (John 12:1-8) does little to hide the story's ultimate origin in the mythology of the Egyptian god Osiris. Mary and Martha are just renamed versions of Isis and Nephthys, sisters and consorts of Osiris. Lazarus is not even renamed, for that name is just a shorter form of "Eleazar," Hebrew for "God is my help," but chosen for this character because it sounds like "El-Osiris" ("God Osiris"). The name of the site of the anointing, "Bethany," equals "Beth-Annu" ("House of the Sun," cf., Beth-Shemesh in Judg. 6:12). This in turn is synonymous with the Egyptian city Heliopolis. It is evident that the story even as Mark knew it was already derived from Osiris. Just as Isis restored the slain Osiris to life by anointing his body, the reference here to the unnamed woman anointing Jesus for the day of his death and burial must originally have been set on that day, the day when she raised him from the dead.

In all probability, the anointing woman was Mary Magdalene, and her name has been omitted. How could Mark have promised her worldwide fame *without giving her name*? But who omitted it? A post-Markan copyist or Mark himself, editing a prior source?

---

[169] Helms, *Gospel Fictions*, pp. 98-100.

Jesus Dionysus (14:12-25)

The Christian Eucharist, or Lord's Supper, introduced here, is in no sense represented as a reinterpretation of the Jewish Passover. Its major features, symbolically eating human flesh and drinking blood, are abominable in Judaism but fit perfectly into the contexts of other ancient religions with which we know Jews had long been familiar. The juice of the grape was the blood of Dionysus, beer that of Osiris. Bread was the body of the grain gods Dionysus and Osiris. Osiris offered his disciples a sacramental meal of bread and beer. Traditional conservatives see the problem; they just don't like the solution: early Christianity was syncretistic, drawing upon various ancient religions.

Scriptural references garnish the story in order to graft it into a Jewish, biblical context. Chief among them is Psalm 41:9, "Even my bosom friend, in whom I trusted, who ate my bread, has lifted his heel against me." Frank Kermode[170] traces the process of transformation of an original, entirely and abstractly theological claim that Jesus had been "delivered up" (*paradothē*, Romans 4:25) into a narrative of betrayal. God having "handed over" his son for our sins grew into the idea of a human agent "betraying" him (same Greek word). This character needed a name, so, in accordance with anti-Jewish polemic, he was named "Judas." His epithet "Iscariot" seems to denote either *Ish-karya* (Aramaic for "the false one)"[171] or a pun on Issachar, "hireling,"[172] the one paid to hand Jesus over to the authorities. So much of the Last Supper story is taken up with this matter because of the mention of the betrayer eating with his victim in Psalm 41.

All this almost renders the bread and cup secondary. They have been heavily reinterpreted in scriptural disguise as a covenant renewal. The connection with Exodus 24:8, "Behold the blood of the covenant which [Yahweh] has made with you in accordance with

---

[170] Frank Kermode, *The Genesis of Secrecy: On the Interpretation of Narrative*. Charles Eliot Norton Lectures 1977, 1978 (Cambridge: Harvard University Press, 1979), pp. 84-85.

[171] Bertil Gärtner, *Iscariot*. Trans. Victor I. Gruhn. Facet Books, Biblical Series - 29 (Philadelphia: Fortress Press, 1971).

[172] Miller, *Mark as Midrash*, p. 65.

these words" is hard to miss.

Verse 27's quotation of Zechariah 13:7, "I will strike down the shepherd, and the sheep will be scattered," looks like it has simply been rewritten into the following scene where Jesus' disciples flee from the arresting party.

But Peter swears up and down that, danger be damned, he will not forsake Jesus. This feature likely comes from Elisha's three avowals that he will not leave Elijah's side, in 2 Kings 2:2, 4, 6: "As [Yahweh] lives, and as you yourself live, I will not leave you." Roth[173] ventures that Mark has given Peter one such pledge and three betrayals of it. On the other hand, Mark may have been thinking of Ittai's pledge of loyalty to David, "Wherever my lord the king shall be, whether for death or for life, there also will your servant be" (1 Sam. 15:21).[174]

Rumble at the Garden (14:26-52)

This whole sequence is based on 2 Samuel chapters 15-16,[175] where a weeping David finds himself on the run from his usurping son Absalom (a Judas figure). David ascends the Mount of Olives and sends three of his allies (Sadoc, Achimaas and Jonathan, 15:27 LXX), back to Jerusalem. In the same way, Jesus goes up the Mount of Olives to the Garden of Gethsemane, where he will be overcome with morose sorrow. He, too, leaves three disciples behind as he retreats deeper into the garden. Jesus is moving simultaneously with his betrayer, but, unlike David, he plans to converge with him, not to avoid him.

David is mocked and harassed by a man named Shimei, a loyalist to Saul's dynasty. Shimei curses the fleeing king, whereupon David's man Abishai offers to chop the mocker's head off. David, however, forbids him. He figures he deserves the insults. As David's party slinks along in silence, Shimei follows them, beaning them with well-aimed rocks. Abishai is the prototype of the anonymous disciple (whom John's gospel later decides must have been Peter) who attempts to behead one of the arresting party. Shimei, his name another form of Shimeon or Simon, is the prototype for Simon who

---

[173] Roth, *Hebrew Gospel*, p. 17.

[174] Miller, *Mark as Midrash*, p. 33.

[175] Miller, *Mark as Midrash*, p. 332.

denies Jesus repeatedly, his stony missiles suggesting "Peter" ("rock") as well. Mark has turned God's assigning Shimei to curse David into Jesus' prediction of Peter's denials, as well as of Peter's calling down curses on himself (or on Jesus) in the high priest's courtyard (14:71).

What about Jesus' prayer? Mark is creating, not reporting. He has removed from the stage anyone who might have overheard it. And he took the contents of the prayer from one of the traditional Passover hymns, which he has had Jesus sing at the close of the supper, Psalm 116:10-15, "My distress was bitter. In panic I cried, 'How faithless all men are!'... I will take in my hand the cup of salvation and invoke [Yahweh] by name... A precious thing in [Yahweh's] eyes is the death of those who die faithful to him."[176]

Mark got the idea for Judas' kiss of betrayal (14:44-45) from 2 Samuel 20:7-10, where Joab, backed up by armed men, greets Amasa as a brother, kisses him, then stabs him.[177] This connection must have been evident to Luke since he modeled his version of Judas' miserable death (Acts 1:18) upon that of Amasa.[178] Second Samuel 20:10 LXX tells us that Amasa's "bowels poured out upon the ground," exactly as Acts tells us that when Judas died, "he burst open, so that his entrails poured out."

What about the young man who just manages to elude capture, leaving his linen cloth in the soldier's fist, which forces him to escape naked (Mark 14:51)? Why is it even part of the Gethsemane episode? Probably because Mark noticed the code phrase (as he viewed it) "that day" in Amos 2:16, "And he who is stout of heart among the mighty shall flee away naked in that day." [179] "That day" sounded like a *pesher* reference to the momentous day of Jesus' Passion.

Trials & Denials (14:53-72)

Yes, it is theoretically possible that Mark knew what had transpired at the trial of Jesus before the Sanhedrin because Joseph of Arimathea, present at the event, later filled the disciples in. But we need not seriously entertain the possibility since the very idea of a Sanhedrin trial on Passover Eve is nonsensical. This would be like the Pope skipping Christmas Eve High Mass in order to attend some meeting of a disciplinary committee called on account of a child-

---

[176] Helms, *Gospel Fictions*, p. 111.
[177] Miller, *Mark as Midrash*, p. 337.
[178] Helms, *Gospel Fictions*, p.117.
[179] Derrett, *Making of Mark*, p. 252.

molesting priest. He'd never do it, and such a meeting would never be scheduled for such a holy day.

Mark borrowed from Daniel 6:4 LXX the crossfire of false accusations:[180] "The governors and satraps sought to find occasion against Daniel, but they found against him no accusation." Mark's rewrite goes like this: "The chief priests and the whole council sought testimony against Jesus in order to kill him, but they found none" (14:55).

Mark dismisses "We heard him say, 'I will destroy this temple which is made with hands and in three days I will build another, not made with hands,'" as a groundless absurdity. Where did the statement come from? It must have originated as a prophecy, whether from the ascended Christ in the early church or from some Zadokite sectarian who believed the Jerusalem Temple had been so thoroughly corrupted by the official priesthood that God would wash his hands of it and replace it with a heavenly Temple (like that in Ezekiel chapters 40-43) to descend from the sky.

Does Jesus give a straight answer to the point-blank question whether he (thinks he) is the Christ (14:61)? Most manuscripts have him reply with a ringing "I am" (14:62). But there is something suspicious here. If this was what Mark had written, why would both Matthew and Luke, working from Mark, change this to the equivocal "You have said so" (Matt. 26:64) and "You say that I am" (Luke 22:70)? Why take a clear affirmative and make it into a cagey equivocation? I think it far more likely that those very few manuscripts of Mark which have Jesus reply, "You say" preserve the original reading, which subsequent copyists found disappointing and changed. Matthew and Luke paraphrased the altered reading but did not change the idea: Jesus equivocated: "If you say so!" Oh, I know that apologists like to reassure their fans that, according to ancient idiom, "You have said it," etc., actually *is* a clear affirmative. But there is no evidence for that.[181]

Every reader flinches at Mark 14:65, where Jesus gets punched out and ridiculed as a false prophet. That scene comes from 1 Kings 22:24: "Then Zedekiah the son of Chenaanah came near and struck Micaiah on the cheek, and said, 'How did the spirit of [Yahweh] go from me to speak to you?' And Micaiah said, 'Behold, you shall see on that day when you go into an inner chamber to hide yourself.'"[182]

---

[180] Helms, *Gospel Fictions*, p. 118.

[181] Dodd, *Historical Tradition*, p. 99, note 1.

Furthermore, Mark has used Micaiah's retort, "Behold, you shall see...," as the model for Jesus' retort that his accusers/attackers will one day behold him enthroned as the Son of Man from Daniel 7:13-14. Is it thinkable that the doctrine of the second coming of Christ sprang full-blown from Mark's reversal of order between the Son of Man's coming with the clouds, *then* sitting on the throne in Daniel 7?

Jesus' silence at both trials before the Sanhedrin and Pilate (14:60-61; 15:4-5) comes from Isaiah 50:7; 53:7.[183] So it wasn't a friendly Sanhedrinist who told Mark what happened at the trial; it was the Bible.

Pompous Pilate (15:1-20)

After Jesus' condemnation by the Sanhedrin, he is perp-walked to the judgment seat of the Procurator Pontius Pilate, who figures it is a question of sedition. The Jewish elders want to prove they are trustworthy allies of Rome cooperating (collaborating?) in the maintenance of social order by nipping the possible threat of a would-be king in the bud. Hearing this accusation, Pilate asks the prisoner, "*Are* you the king of the Jews?" If Jesus fearlessly claims he is, then it will be a very simple matter. But he doesn't. Jesus equivocates: "You have said so." I take that to amount to "If you say so." Certainly Pilate must take it that way, since, after hearing further accusations (perhaps that Jesus had threatened to demolish the Temple, as in 14:58), Pilate asks Jesus, "Have you no answer to make?" Would he have said this had Jesus given him a positive answer in verse 2?

Reluctant to condemn to death a man who will mount no defense but who seems harmless, Pilate suddenly thinks of an alternative. Mark says there is a long-standing custom whereby Rome shows its clemency by releasing any one prisoner whom the crowd chooses, so Pilate nominates Jesus. Apparently, from the flurry of accusations against Jesus as a rabble-rouser, Pilate must realize how popular Jesus is. Perhaps the crowd will relieve him of a decision he doesn't want to make. But he has miscalculated, for the Jewish elders

[182] Miller, *Mark as Midrash*, p. 350.

[183] John Dominic Crossan, *The Cross That Spoke: The Origins of the Passion Narrative* (San Francisco: Harper & Row, Publishers, 1988) p. 168.

manage to whip up the crowd to call for the setting free of the revolutionary killer Barabbas instead. Having thus painted himself into a corner, Pilate has no choice but to free Barabbas and send Jesus to the cross.

Just about everything is wrong with this picture. The historical Pilate would never have been intimidated by a relatively small crowd of nobodies. Nor can we possibly imagine he would release an anti-Roman terrorist and execute a harmless eccentric. Furthermore, there is no evidence for such a custom as is described here.

The mock veneration of Jesus as a king is so similar to the treatment of a half-witted derelict named Carabbas by a mob in Alexandria, as related by Philo, that we must suspect Mark borrowed the mocking sequence from that source[184] (and don't tell me the early Christians were not reading Philo).[185]

> Gaius Caesar gave Agrippa, the grandson of Herod the king, the third part of his paternal inheritance as a sovereignty, which Philip the tetrarch, who was his uncle on his father's side, had previously enjoyed. And when he was about to set out to take possession of his kingdom, Gaius advised him to avoid the voyage from Brundusium to Syria, which was a long and troublesome one, and rather to take the shorter one by Alexandria...There was a certain madman named Carabbas, afflicted not with a wild, savage, and dangerous madness (for that comes on in fits without being expected either by the patient or by bystanders), but with an intermittent and more gentle kind; this man spent all this days and nights naked in the roads, minding neither cold nor heat, the sport of idle children and wanton youths; and they, driving the poor wretch as far as the public gymnasium, and setting him up there on high that he might be seen by everybody, flattened out a leaf of papyrus and put it on his head instead of a diadem, and clothed the rest of his body

---

[184] Crossan, *Cross That Spoke*, pp. 142, 154. What an amazingly fascinating book!

[185] C.H. Dodd, *The Interpretation of the Fourth Gospel* (Cambridge at the University Press, 1951), Chapter 3, "Hellenistic Judaism: Philo of Alexandria," pp. 54-73; Sidney G. Sowers, *The Hermeneutics of Philo and Hebrews: A Comparison of the Interpretation of the Old Testament in Philo Judaeus and the Epistle to the Hebrews*. Basel Studies of Theology No. 1 (Zürich: EVZ-Verlag/Richmond: John Knox Press, 1965), Chapter V, "The Alexandrian Jewish Background to the Epistle to the Hebrews," pp. 64-74.

with a common door mat instead of a cloak, and instead of a scepter they put in his hand a small stick of the native papyrus which they found lying by the way side and gave to him; and when, like actors in theatrical spectacles, he had received all the insignia of royal authority, and had been dressed and adorned like a king, the young men bearing sticks on their shoulders stood on each side of him instead of spear-bearers, in imitation of the body-guards of the king, and then others came up, some as if to salute him, and others making as though they wished to plead their causes before him, and others pretending to wish to consult with him about the affairs of the state. Then from the multitude of those who were standing around there arose a wonderful shout of men calling out Maris; and this is the name by which it is said that they call the kings among the Syrians; for they knew that Agrippa was by birth a Syrian, and also that he was possessed of a great district of Syria of which he was the sovereign. (Philo, *Against Flaccus*, V, VI.[186]

The mob means to mock the visiting Jewish King Agrippa by using Carabbas as a living caricature of him. Mark has the Romans mocking Jesus, whom Mark knows is the real King of the Jews, by making King Jesus into a cruel caricature of himself.

A Face in the Crowd (15:21)

For some unspecified reason, Jesus is not forced to carry the crossbeam to Golgotha, the crucifixion site, so the Roman soldiers randomly choose a bystander, one Simon (a Diaspora Jew who had relocated to Jerusalem), and order him to hoist the heavy beam on his shoulder. Please note: Mark does *not* say Jesus began carrying it but then buckled under the weight, whereupon Simon was pressed into service, as we usually hear. That is a lame attempt to harmonize the Synoptics with John 19:17, which has Jesus simply carry the cross all by his lonesome.

---

[186] *The Works of Philo.* Trans. C.D. Yonge (Peabody: Hendrickson Publishers, 1993), p. 728.

Why even give Simon a name, much less identify him as the father of two other unknowns, Alexander and Rufus? The assigning of names to bit players makes characters of them, a stage in the legendary embellishment of narratives.[187] I cannot help thinking that the brief notice of Simon of Cyrene is the tip of an iceberg, and that Simon of Cyrene is identical with Simon Magus, a Gnostic Messiah of whom Irenaeus reports that he "taught that he himself was the one who appeared among the Jews as Son, came down in Samaria as Father, and arrived among the other nations as Holy Spirit... He was thought to suffer in Judaea, though he did not suffer" (*Against Heresies*, Book I, 23.1, 3).[188] The Gnostic Basilides taught that Jesus "did not suffer, but a certain Simon of Cyrene was impressed into service and carried his cross for him, and he was crucified by ignorance and error, transfigured by him so that he was supposed to be Jesus. As for Jesus himself, he assumed the appearance of Simon and stood by to deride the archons" (*Against Heresies*, Book I, 24, 4).[189] What Basilides noticed was that the last proper name before "they crucified *him*" (Mark 15:24) is not Jesus but *Simon of Cyrene*. Simon of Cyrene is easily identified with/as Simon Magus. The latter was also called "Simon of Gitta." Gitta (= Gath) was one of the five Philistine city states. The Philistines and Phoenicians were the "Sea Peoples," the *Kittim*, which equates to "Gitta." North African Cyrene was a Phoenician city. It all comes to the same thing. So I think Mark 15:21's snippet about Simon is a sanitized version of the story told by "heretics" that Simon Magus was crucified in the place and semblance of the Son. Guess what, folks? It's not a piece of history.

What is the significance of the names "Alexander and Rufus"? Apologists say these were two then-famous sons of Simon, implying all three had become notable Christian converts and leaders. In itself, that is plausible enough, but once we have discerned the mytho-theological background of the Simon-crucifixion, we might seek an alternative explanation of the names. Christian Lindtner[190] has supplied one that is suitably exotic. Lindtner sees the Jesus epic and even the individual gospels as Buddhist in origin. A major

---

[187] Bultmann, *History of the Synoptic Tradition*, pp. 68, 241, 269, 283, 310.

[188] Trans. Robert M. Grant. In Grant, *Irenaeus of Lyons. The Early Church Fathers* (London and New York: Rutledge, 1997), pp. 88, 89.

[189] Grant, *Irenaeus*, p. 91.

[190] Christian Lindtner, "Two Drops of Water with Blood," in Michael Lockwood, ed., *Buddhism's Relation to Christianity: A Miscellaneous Anthology with Occasional Comment* (Tabaram, Chennai: Tabaram Research Associates, 2010), p. 265.

Buddhist source for the Passion Narrative would be the *Mula-Sarvastivada-Vinaya*, which recounts the impalement of the innocent Gautama (an ancestor of Gautama Buddha) for the murder of a prostitute named Bhadra, whose actual killer had slipped away in the crowd. As Gautama is dying slowly in agony, his teacher approaches, and the two have a last talk. Gautama is dismayed that he will leave no sons behind. It begins to rain, and the water (identified with semen) mixes with Gautama's dripping blood as it falls to the ground. The story presupposes ancient Indian embryology, pre-scientific by our standards, so that we read that a pair of eggs developed from the mixed drops, and the shells broke, eventually growing into two posthumous sons for Gautama. His old mentor adopts them.

We have, then, a "crucified" martyr. The impalement stake takes the place of both Jesus' cross and the centurion's stabbing spear in John 19:34. The mixing of Gautama's blood with the rain water corresponds to the water and the blood draining from the ribs of Jesus in John 19:34. Gautama is dying in the place of an actual criminal, a killer, just as Jesus dies in the killer Barabbas' place. The word used for the "shells" (*kapalani*)[191] of the embryonic eggs is also used for "skulls," which brings to mind Golgotha, "the place of skulls." But the capper is that the Sanskrit phrase for "two-water-drops-with-blood" is *dvau sukra-bindu sa-rudhire*. Why? Sanskrit and Greek are, of course, cognate languages. The word *sa-rudhire* becomes the Greek *kai Rouphou*, "and red." "Rufus" means "red." The name "Alexander" (actually taking a genitive ending here, hence *Alexandrou*) is transliterated from the Sanskrit *sukra-bindu*. Thus *dvau sukra-bindu sa-rudhire* transliterates to *Alexandrou kai Rouphou*.

Cross a Fiction (15:22-39)

The crucifixion scene in Mark 15 is essentially a narrative fleshing out of Psalm 22. All the major "bullet-points" come from that psalm, though Mark never calls attention to his source. He says nothing to imply these "events" are fulfillments of some prediction encoded in Psalm 22. The piercing of Jesus' extremities (Mark 15: 24) reflects Psalm 22:16b. The parceling out of his garments and throwing dice

---

[191] Also, think of the cosmic container shells of Kabbalistic cosmogony, called *Kelipoth*.

for them (Mark 15:24) derives from Psalm 22:18. The "wagging heads" of the mockers (Mark 15:29) are from Psalm 22:7. And the keynote cry of abandonment, "My God, my God, why have you forsaken me?" (Mark 15:34) is a direct quotation of Psalm 22:1, not that Mark expects or wants you to recognize it as such (most readers today seem oblivious). Matthew adds another quote, "He trusts in God. Let God deliver him now if he desires him" (Matt. 27:43 from Psalm 22:8), as well as a strong allusion ("for he said, 'I am the son of God,'" Matthew 27:43b) to Wisdom of Solomon 2:12-20, which underlies the whole story anyway.[192] As for other details, Crossan[193] points out that the darkness at noon is borrowed from Amos 8:9, while the vinegar and gall come from Psalm 69:21.

Aftermath & Arimathea (15:40-47)

Joseph of Arimathea looks like a combination of King Priam, who takes a great risk by coming to Achilles' camp to beg the body of his son Hector, killed by Achilles,[194] and the Patriarch Joseph who asked Pharaoh's permission to bury the body of Jacob in the cave-tomb Jacob had hewn for himself back beyond the Sinai (Gen. 50:4-5).[195] Later legends made Joseph of Arimathea Jesus' uncle, and you have to wonder if this was a result of the same process that made Jesus' brothers into cousins so as to safeguard the perpetual virginity of Mary. In other words, could Joseph of Arimathea originally have been Joseph of Nazareth? In that case, the Priam parallel is all the stronger.

Running on Empty (16:1-8)

Both Crossan[196] and Miller[197] make the startling claim that the Empty Tomb narrative requires no source beyond the tenth chapter of Joshua (=Jesus, remember!). The five kings whom Joshua routed

---

192 Miller, *Mark as Midrash*, p. 362.
193 Crossan, *Cross That Spoke*, p. 198.
194 MacDonald, *Homeric Epics*, p. 159.
195 Miller, *Mark as Midrash*, p. 373.
196 Crossan, *Cross That Spoke*, p. 274.
197 Miller, *Mark as Midrash*, pp. 219, 377.

hide in the cave at Makkedah. When Joshua's scouts locate them, he has his men "Roll great stones against the mouth of the cave and set men by it to guard them" (10:18). Once the kings' troops are all mopped up, Joshua directs: "Open the mouth of the cave, and bring those five kings out to me from the cave" (10:22).

> And afterward Joshua smote them and put them to death, and he hung them on five trees. And they hung upon the trees until evening; but at the time of the going down of the sun, Joshua commanded, and they took them down from the trees, and threw them into the cave where they had hidden themselves, and they set great stones against the mouth of the cave, which remain to this very day. (Josh. 10:26-27).

Here "Jesus" (Joshua) plays the role of Pilate, and Mark simply reverses the order of the main events of the story. In Joshua, first, the stone is rolled away and the kings emerge alive. Second, the kings die. Third, the (corpses of the) kings are crucified until sundown. In Mark, Jesus, King of the Jews, is crucified, where his body will hang till sundown. Second, he dies. Third, he emerges alive (Mark implies) from the tomb once the stone is rolled away. None of this means the resurrection of Jesus is a product of cleverly running the film of Joshua 10 backwards. It just suggests how early Christians may have spun out a narrative version of what was originally a concise, formulaic proclamation,[198] "Christ is risen!" "God raised Jesus from the dead!" Granted, this *kerygma* may have been a piece of myth-based liturgy, as in the Attis religion: "Rejoice, you of the mystery! For your god is saved!"

Similarly, the vigil of Mary Magdalene and her sisters reflects the women's mourning cults devoted to the dying and rising gods, long practiced in Israel (Ezekiel 8:14, "Behold, there sat women weeping for Tammuz;" Zechariah 12:11, "On that day the mourning in Jerusalem will be as great as the mourning for Hadad-Rimmon in the plain of Megiddo;" Canticles 3:1-4, "I sought him whom my soul loves; I sought him but found him not; I called him but he gave no answer," etc.).

---

[198] Werner Kramer, *Christ, Lord, Son of God*. Trans. Brian Hardy. Studies in Biblical Theology No. 50 (London: SCM Press, 1966), Part One, I, A, 3: "The resurrection as a statement in the *pistis*-formula," pp. 20-25.

That the Empty Tomb story is Mark's own creation is evident from the fact that he knows about the young man, his message, *and the women's refusal to tell anyone about this encounter*. If they told no one, how does Mark know? He is "the omniscient narrator"—of fiction!

There is no real resurrection episode in Mark. The encounter with the white-clad youth sitting in the tomb should be seen as the conclusion of the Empty Tomb story as well as the conclusion of the gospel. Scribes and scholars have for many centuries recoiled from this realization. They have long insisted that Mark did go on to depict the reunion of the risen Jesus with his disciples in Galilee as anticipated in Mark 14:28 and 16:7 but that the last page got lost or utilized to line a birdcage before any copies could be made. Or perhaps Mark keeled over dead before he could pen the final chapter. This theory reminds me of the scene in *Monty Python and the Holy Grail*, in which Arthur and his knights discover an inscribed wall that is supposed to reveal the location of the Grail. They eagerly read on till the end, which trails off as the scribe suffered a heart attack.

> MAYNARD: It reads, "Here may be found the last words of Joseph of Arimathea. He who is valiant and pure of spirit may find the Holy Grail in the Castle of uuggggggh."
> ARTHUR: What?
> MAYNARD: "... the Castle of uuggggggh."
> BEDEMIR: What is that?
> MAYNARD: He must have died while carving it.
> LAUNCELOT: Oh, come on!
> MAYNARD: Well, that's what it says.
> ARTHUR: Look, if he was dying, he wouldn't bother to carve "aaggggh." He'd just say it!
> MAYNARD: Well, that's what's carved in the rock!
> GALAHAD: Perhaps he was dictating.
> ARTHUR: Oh, shut up. Well, does it say anything else?
> MAYNARD: No. Just, "uuggggggh."
> LAUNCELOT: Aauuggghhh.
> KNIGHT: Aaauggh.

It seems to me that both theories are ruled out by the simple fact that the book *does* have a rounded-off ending: the holy women pointedly disobey the young man's directive to communicate his message to the disciples. They don't do it. Thus, no reunion in Galilee. It's not as if Mark 16 ends with "And the women..." (or with "uugggggh..."). I regard both approaches, the loss of Mark's ending as well as a heart attack curtailing his writing, as pathetic attempts at harmonization. "Mark *must* agree with the other gospels; therefore it *does*, or at least it *did*!"

It is by no means far-fetched to imagine Mark putting Mary Magdalene and the others in a very bad light, given the rough treatment he accords to Peter and the Twelve and the Heirs. Some in the early church venerated the holy women as apostolic teachers, as in numerous Gnostic texts. As I mentioned earlier, it looks as if Mark has omitted her name from the Bethany anointing story, depriving her of the fame the story has promised her.

But it may be simpler than that. Mark may just have wanted to cover the novelty of the Empty Tomb story, which no one had previously heard.[199] "It's only come to light now!" And how did *that* happen? Of course, this is the same gimmick we saw in Mark 9:9, where Jesus tells Peter, James, and John to keep mum about the Transfiguration till the resurrection. Only Mark 16:8 gives no statute of limitations, but that's only because the women are not obeying but *dis*obeying someone's command.

Would it have made sense for a gospel to end without a resurrection appearance? Sure it would. Charles H. Talbert[200] gives examples of several ancient Hellenistic "apotheosis narratives" in which this or that hero or philosopher disappeared, was sought but never found, not even a bone or a stitch of clothing, but was announced by a divine voice to have ascended into heaven to dwell among the immortals. There might be a postmortem appearance but there might not. The absence of Jesus' body from the tomb and the news that "He is risen" would have satisfied ancient Hellenistic readers.

And there is still another possibility. My teacher, the late Darrell J. Doughty, once suggested[201] that Mark's gospel has a circular structure. You get to the last verse of chapter 16 and go back to chapter one. On a second reading, you realize that when Jesus

---

[199] Reginald H. Fuller, *The Formation of the Resurrection Narratives* (New York: Macmillan, 1971), p. 51.

[200] Charles H. Talbert, *What Is a Gospel? The Genre of the Canonical Gospels* (Philadelphia: Fortress Press, 1977).

[201] He set forth this theory in a now-untraceable article or set of notes.

appears unexpectedly on the shore to summon James and John, Peter and Andrew, this *is* the Galilean reunion of the disciples with their risen master. They have resignedly returned to their old occupation after the death of Jesus but rejoin him once they see him returned to life—precisely as in the Johannine Appendix (John chapter 21). And thus we are to understand the whole ministry of the "historical Jesus" as really that of the risen Jesus retrojected into the past, which is pretty much the unspoken implication of form criticism anyway, right? It is all the work of the "creative community."

Any way you look at this, though, it is plain that early readers of Mark did not care for the abrupt ending. The other three evangelists added their own endings, sometimes copying from one another. There is an important point here: Matthew, Luke, and John understood there was no place to go from Mark 16:8. They could not just continue what Mark had written. If there was to be more story, they had first to *undo and change* Mark's ending, *then* start adding. If Mark 16:8 was perceived as a broken-off non-ending, they could have figured out what might have come next, as in a modern Round-Robin tale written serially by several authors, each of whom takes off from the corner his predecessor painted him into.

Subsequent scribes who were just as disappointed with 16:8 did not have the luxury of erasing any Markan text to make it easier to "fix" it. By their time, the text, no matter how puzzling, was too sacrosanct. Here's what they came up with.

Apocryphal Appearances (19:9-20)

The Longer Ending [plus the Freer Logion]:

> Now when he rose early on the first day of the week, he appeared first to Mary Magdalene, from whom he had cast out seven demons. She went out and told those who had been with him, as they mourned and wept. But when they heard that he was alive and had been seen by her, they would not believe it. After this he appeared in another form to two of them, as they were walking into the country. And they went back and told the rest, but they did not believe them. Afterward he appeared to the eleven themselves as they sat at table; and he upbraided them for their unbelief and hardness of heart, because they had not believed those

who saw him after he had risen. [And they excused themselves, saying, "This age of lawlessness and unbelief is under Satan, who does not allow the truth and power of God to prevail over the unclean things of the spirits. Therefore reveal thy righteousness now"~thus they spoke to Christ. And Christ replied to them, "The term of years for Satan's power has been fulfilled, but other terrible things draw near. And for those who have sinned I was delivered over to death, that they may return to the truth and sin no more; that they may inherit the spiritual and incorruptible glory of Righteousness which is in heaven."] And he said to them, "Go into all the world and preach the gospel to the whole creation. He who believes and is baptized will be saved; but he who does not believe will be condemned. And these signs will accompany those who believe: in my name they will cast out demons; they will speak in new tongues; they will pick up serpents, and if they drink any deadly thing, it will not hurt them; they will lay their hands on the sick, and they will recover." So then the Lord Jesus, after he had spoken to them, was taken up into heaven, and sat down at the right hand of God. And they went forth and preached everywhere, while the Lord worked with them and confirmed the message by the signs that attended it. Amen.

The Shorter Ending:

But they reported briefly to Peter and those with him all that they had been told. And after this, Jesus himself sent out by means of them, from east to west, the sacred and imperishable proclamation of eternal salvation.

11

The Gospel According to Matthew
A Scribe Trained for the Kingdom of Heaven

The Gospel of the Disciple

This was the most popular of the gospels in the ancient church, at least if old gospel collections are any clue. When all four gospels were bound together, their order could vary—except that Matthew was almost always in the first place. This is no surprise given the shape and apparent purpose of this gospel as a manual of instruction for Gentile mission churches started by Jewish Torah-Christians, envisioned in the Great Commission at the close of the book (28:19-20), where the apostles (who stand for the subsequent Antiochene missionaries to the nations, cf., Acts 13:1-3) are given their marching orders.

Why Antioch? It looks like the Gospel of Matthew was written there, not only because of that church's missionary interests, but also because its author was conversant in Hebrew, Syriac, and Greek, since he quotes from all three versions of the Bible as needed. This implies his community was ethnically and linguistically mixed, and Antioch sure was. It was also theologically diverse, as witness the tussles over open table fellowship (or the avoidance of it) between Jewish and Gentile Christians[202] in Galatians 2:11-17. It is probably

---

[202] James D.G. Dunn, *Jesus, Paul and the Law: Studies in Mark and Galatians* (Louisville: Westminster/John Knox Press, 1990), Chapter 6, "The Incident in Antioch (Gal. 2.11-18)," pp. 129-181.

not reading too much into the Galatians 2 scenario to posit the sometimes uneasy co-existence of three major factions. There were apparently (as in Corinth, 1 Corinthians 1:12-13) both Paul and Peter (or Cephas, if there's a difference) parties, the one celebrating the fall of ritual barriers designed to segregate Jew from Gentile, the other taking a more restrictive stance. A third faction, begun or reinforced by James the Just through his representatives from the Home Office in Jerusalem (Gal. 2:12), took a hard line, demanding that Jewish and Gentile Christians not eat together so that the former could more easily stick to the old kosher laws. They may even have insisted that Gentile Christians submit to circumcision (cf., Acts 15:1).

This is germane to Matthew's gospel because it would appear to be a compromise document containing bits and pieces representing all three factions.[203] This is the best explanation, I think, of certain contradictory passages in the gospel. Also, this would explain the odd way the character of Peter is portrayed, as he is lifted up with one hand, slapped down with the other, and in rapid succession.[204] It looks as if the composite nature of the document results from the sedimentary accretion of new strata as scribes from each faction made their own "adjustments" to the text.

Our author, or the final redactor, would have belonged to the James faction, as he has the risen Jesus (his ventriloquist dummy, to put it bluntly) command that converts from "the nations" (Gentiles) be instructed to keep even the fine-print commandments of the Torah (Matthew 28:19-20 in light of 5:17-19). That he was a Jewish scribe is evident from Matthew 13:52: "every scribe who has been

---

[203] Robert M. Price, "Antioch's Aftershocks: Rereading Galatians and Matthew after Saldarini." In Alan J. Avery-Peck, Daniel Harrington, and Jacob Neusner, eds., *When Judaism and Christianity Began: Essays in Memory of Anthony J. Saldarini. Volume Two: Judaism and Christianity in the Beginning.* Supplements to the Journal for the Study of Judaism. Volume 85 (Leiden: Brill, 2004), Vol. 1, pp. 231-250.

[204] Arlo J. Nau, *Peter in Matthew: Discipleship, Diplomacy, and Dispraise... with an Assessment of Power and Privilege in the Petrine Office.* Good News Studies Volume 36. A Michael Glazier Book (Collegeville: Liturgical Press, 1992).

trained for the kingdom of heaven is like a householder who brings out of his treasure what is new and what is old." He knows the traditional Jewish interpretations of scripture but now views it through the lens of Christian faith, which discloses new meanings aplenty.

In fact, he has organized his gospel according to a fivefold plan, resulting in a new Jesus-Pentateuch supplementing the ancient Moses Pentateuch. The gospel organizes the teaching ascribed to Jesus into five major blocks, each capped off with a similar statement. First is the Sermon on the Mount: chapters 5-7, concluding with 7:28, "And when Jesus finished these sayings, the crowds were astonished at his teaching," etc. The second is the Mission Charge: chapter 10, ending with 11:1, "And when Jesus had finished instructing his twelve disciples," etc. The third is the Parable Chapter (13), finishing up with 13:53, "And when Jesus had finished these parables, he went away from there." The fourth is the Church Discipline section, chapter 18, which concludes with 19:1, "Now when Jesus had finished these sayings, he went away from Galilee," etc. The fifth is the Denunciation of the Pharisees *plus* the Olivet Discourse (chapters 23-25), which ends as of 26:1, "When Jesus had finished all these sayings, he said to his disciples," etc. The otherwise strange cramming together of the anti-Pharisee tirade with the prophetic Olivet Discourse underlines Matthew's determination to get everything into five "books," come hell or high water. Otherwise, we would have chapter 23 ending with something like "When Jesus had finished this nasty mud-slinging, he made a quick exit," followed by some narrative filler before making the Olivet Discourse a *sixth* book.

This gospel cannot have been written by the disciple Matthew (assuming there *was* one). For one thing, it is way too late for that. It is pretty much a massive overhaul of Mark's gospel, and that in successive stages. I place Mark around 140-150 C.E., and we must allow some years for Mark's gospel to have become outdated for Mathew's congregation, and more time for each stage of revision. The title (which does not occur in the text but is a traditional scribal convention) looks like a pun on the Greek word for "disciple" (*mathetēs*), a favorite term (as both noun and verb) of this evangelist.

The Root of David (1:1-17)

The Matthean genealogy presents several problems. Our evangelist seems to have made a few copyist errors in compiling his genealogy. In 1:7 Matthew has erroneously substituted "Asaph," the name of a notable Psalmist, for King Asa (1 Chron. 3:10). In 1:7-8 he has omitted Ahaziah, Jehoash, and Amaziah, who should have come after Joram and before Uzziah. Finally, in 1:10 Matthew has "Amos" when it should be King Amon. All these are quite natural scribal errors. It is always possible that some early copyist of Matthew's gospel made the errors, not the evangelist himself, but there is no manuscript evidence to suggest it. Of course, it is only inerrancy apologists who suggest it since this would salvage Matthew's accuracy. Let us note two important phenomena that will recur throughout inerrantists' handling of the Bible.

First, to decide that the error cannot have been Matthew's own is a clear case, as minor as it seems, of interpreting the text in light of one's prior theology, instead of the other way around as Protestants claim we must do. It is to straightjacket the text of the Bible according to the dictates of inerrancy theology. A historian free of this burden would simply note that it is theoretically possible for some post-Matthean scribe to have made the errors and leave it at that. Second, such a retreat to an imagined purer autograph manuscript opens a theological Pandora's Box. Benjamin B. Warfield was the most famous exponent of this strategy: with one's back against the wall, having no other escape at hand, the inerrantist should deduce that, with or without manuscript evidence, the original autograph copy, which does not survive, had a different reading, a factually correct one that would not embarrass inerrantism.[205] As brilliant as Warfield was, he seems somehow not

---

[205] Archibald A. Hodge and Benjamin B. Warfield, *Inspiration* (Grand Rapids: Baker Book House, 1979), p. 36.

to have noticed what an abyss he was opening up beneath the feet of his theological heirs: Warfield drove a wedge between the Bible we have, which might be erroneous at any and every point for all we can know, and the theoretical "original autographs" to which alone the doctrine of inerrancy may rightly apply. It is too bad we do not have that Bible!

Another difficulty is that Matthew (1:11) traces the descent through King Coniah/Jeconiah, none of whose sons were ever to take the throne according to Jeremiah 22:30.

As is well known, Matthew's genealogy cannot be made to agree with Luke's (Luke 3:23-38). They follow two altogether different lines of descent from David, Matthew through King Solomon, Luke through Nathan (Luke 3:31), another son of David. Many apologists adopt the speculation of Annius of Viterbo (ca. 1500),[206] that the Lukan genealogy is somehow that of Mary (though it, too, culminates in Joseph!). This is a bald-faced tactic of desperation: "according to Jewish usage Mary's name, being a woman['s], could not appear in the genealogy, males alone forming the line. So Joseph's name is introduced instead of Mary's, he being Mary's husband" (R.A. Torrey).[207] Torrey offers no source for the alleged Jewish custom, and Jacob Neusner, the world's greatest authority on Judaism, its history, documents, and customs, knows of no such practice as Torrey describes: "Sounds to me as if they're making it up as they go along."[208] It does sound absurd to me, not least because Torrey's claim implies that, in effect, there simply *were* no genealogies for women, something odd in a culture where Jewish identity is traced through one's mother. Besides, Matthew does not hesitate to include the names of women in his genealogy. And even if Torrey is right, look what he is doing: he is telling us *not to believe the plain statement of the*

---

[206] The theory was first revived in modern times by J.M. Heer, *Die Stammbäumme Jesu nach Mattäus und Lukas*, 1910, and P. Vogt, *Der Stammbaum bei den heiligen Evangelisten Matthäus*, 1907.

[207] Reuben Archer Torrey, *Difficulties in the Bible: Alleged Errors and Contradictions* (Chicago: Moody Press, nd.), p. 102.

[208] E-mail to Robert M. Price, November 27, 2007.

text to the effect that Joseph is the son of Heli. Like the very "Modernist" critics he despised, Torrey in the end brought to bear on the text some extra-textual piece of alleged background lore which dismisses the literal reading as an optical illusion. Is that not the essence of the Higher-Critical approach? Cultural idiom (e.g., myth) trumps simple narrative assertion. It is a very odd way to defend inerrancy.

Why, then, *are* there two different genealogies? They are two attempts by well-meaning Christian scribes to *prove* what began as a matter of *faith*. If Jesus was Messiah, and Messiah was the son of David, there had to be some way to demonstrate the connection. Just as modern genealogists find themselves forced, lacking complete evidence, to fill in gaps by speculating, so would early Christians as they connected the dots hypothetically, the best they could. No wonder they differed. As we so often find, the errors and contradictions in the Bible can be explained quite reasonably and naturally, with no aspersions cast on the biblical writers—as long as one discards the artificial rubric of inerrancy. It is inerrantism, not biblical criticism, that makes the Bible look silly.

Why are there *any genealogies at all*, given the belief that Jesus' conception was a miracle of the Holy Spirit, with no human father? The virginal conception doctrine and the Davidic descent doctrine are incompatible, and their very presence, side-by-side, in either Matthew or Luke, is already an attempt to harmonize the two doctrines. We may be sure that whoever compiled each genealogy originally wrote "and Joseph begat Jesus" (or, in Luke's source, "Jesus was the son of Joseph"). The Sinaitic Syriac version of Matthew actually has "Joseph, who was betrothed to the Virgin Mary, begat Jesus." Either Matthew and Luke changed the text to read, circuitously, "Joseph, the husband of Mary, of whom Jesus was

---

[209] Raymond E. Brown, *The Birth of the Messiah: A Commentary on the Infancy Narratives in Matthew and Luke* (Garden City: Doubleday, 1977), pp. 64, 89, 132, 138-139, 142, 150-152, 155, 511.

born, who is called Christ" (Matt. 1:16); "Jesus being the son, as was supposed, of Joseph" (Luke 3:23), or early copyists of their gospels did, in either case to resolve the contradiction. But it does not work. Raymond E. Brown[209] tries to combine the two approaches by saying that Joseph's marriage to Mary furnishes (the virgin-born) Jesus a legal claim to the throne that a literal heir of Joseph, and David, would have had naturally. But no one would have accepted a non-literal set of credentials in which the supposed Scion of the House of David was merely patched in by a formality. That would have been the lamest kind of attempt to see to the fulfillment of prophecy by means of one's own scheming, as when Abraham seeks the promised heir, not through the divinely appointed Sarah, but through the stop-gap surrogate Hagar.

Finally, note that Matthew 1:17 neatly apportions the generations of Jesus' descent into three symmetrical periods: from Abraham the Patriarch to King David; from David to the Babylonian Exile; and from the beginning of the Exile to the birth of Jesus. He finds great significance (without telling us exactly what it is) in the "fact" that each period contained fourteen generations (much as Mark appears to find some importance in the fact that Jairus' daughter was twelve years old and the woman with the issue of blood had suffered for twelve years, Mark 5:21-43). Only he is wrong: according to his own list of names, there are thirteen between Abraham and David, fourteen between David and Babylon, and another thirteen between Babylon and Jesus. He miscounted.

Beyond this, Matthew has grossly underestimated the historical durations involved. Fourteen generations would amount to about 350 years, but there is a span of 750 years between Abraham and David, 400 years between David and the Exile, and another 600 years between the Exile and Jesus.[210] How bizarre to truncate and hack the genealogies in order to create the false impression of a miraculous Providence which apparently expresses itself chiefly in repeating cycles of the same number of years—which the author has

---

[210] Brown, *Birth*, pp. 74-75.

created in the first place! Let me remind any reader who is considering whether perhaps an inspired writer might be entitled, even led, to play thus fast and loose with the data: even if there were a good reason to do it, would the result have anything at all to do with "factual inerrancy"?

Welcome News for Joseph (1:18-25)

Matthew jumps the gun: despite 1:18, Joseph does not "find" Mary's pregnancy to be of the Spirit till later, via his dream.

It is certainly not difficult to believe that a man might have had a meaningful dream which resolved an agonizing dilemma for him. Nor is there anything untoward in a man dreaming of an angel. This happens quite frequently even today. By the principle of analogy, the historian is perfectly free to allow that a man named Joseph *might* have had such a dream. The historian is, however, not obliged to believe the incident described here actually *did* happen. There are dreams, and there are fictive stories about dreams. Both are pretty common, and we would need more evidence than we have to push this one from the category of "possible" to that of "probable." Some protest indignantly that one is obliged to believe the story as a factual account until evidence proves otherwise. The story is "innocent until proven guilty." But is that appropriate? Whence derives such an automatic disposition to give historicity the benefit of the doubt? I think it is lurking inerrantism, masquerading as historical method. "Believing the Bible" has become the default mode for the fundamentalist, even if he is trying his best to be a genuine historian.[211]

Please note, by the way, that insofar as the historian may accept the angel-annunciation episode as even possibly historical, apologetics for biblical literalism has won a Pyrrhic victory: the story is plausible only insofar as it does not exceed the limits of familiar,

---

[211] James Barr, *Fundamentalism* (Philadelphia: Westminster Press, 1978), pp. 85-89.

even if unusual, experience. To admit the occurrence of meaningful dreams is not to admit the occurrence of miracles.

The real difficulty in the Matthean annunciation story is the assertion in 1:22-23 that an ancient prediction of the prophet Isaiah has been fulfilled in the miraculous conception of Jesus. To put it bluntly, there is simply no way that Matthew has correctly described the intention of Isaiah and his prophecy. It is easy to show what Isaiah was talking about, and that it had not a thing to do with any event to transpire seven centuries after his time, much less with the coming of a Messiah, less still with Jesus the Nazarene.

First, let me dispense with a red herring that has dominated the discussion of Matthew and Isaiah for much too long: the use of the words *almah* and *parthenos*, the former Hebrew from Isaiah 7:14, the latter Greek in Matthew 1:23. King James Version zealots greeted the publication of the Revised Standard Version in 1952 with public book burnings because the translators had rendered Isaiah's *almah* as "young woman," not "virgin" as in the King James Version. There is a separate word for "intact virgin" (*bethulah*), but Isaiah did not use it. He used the ambiguous *almah* instead. How did this make the RSV a good candidate for kindling? Literalists, it seems, were reading the text in a less than literal manner. They figured that, since Matthew plainly uses the word *parthenos*, meaning "intact virgin," and the conception of Jesus was the goal of Isaiah's prediction, then Isaiah must have meant "virgin," too, and so it should have been translated that way in both texts. The RSV translation committee (led by the saintly Bruce M. Metzger) was vilified as a bunch of "God-hating, Christ-denying liberals"[212] trying to undermine their readers' faith in prophecy. The trouble was that these zealots were interested only in what Matthew was saying, not what Isaiah had said.

More of that in a moment. First the moot point. It has become apparent that both *almah* and *parthenos* had become ambiguous in meaning by the time either was used in the Bible. Isaiah's *almah* could mean "virgin" but doesn't have to. Now it turns

---

[212] I actually saw this phrase in an old anti-RSV pamphlet.

out that *parthenos* needn't have specified technical virginity, either. How do we know? Simply because there is no reason to suppose the Septuagint translators were inept or ignorant on such a basic point, and, if they translated *almah* with *parthenos*, it must be because, by their time, the words had come to mean the same thing. And then we may infer that Matthew might have thought *parthenos* meant merely "maiden," too. By itself, neither word tells the tale. The punch line is that we cannot know for sure whether either Isaiah or Matthew meant to refer to a maiden who was technically a virgin. We would need to find other clues in the narratives.[213] So that should no longer be a problem.

But there *is* a problem. What is Isaiah 7:14 about? Anyone can see that the context features an exasperated Isaiah trying to awaken some faith in the weak-kneed King Ahaz on the eve of a feared invasion. Aram and Israel to the north have conspired to drive Ahaz from the throne of Judah and to set up Pekah as their puppet king in his stead. Isaiah insists the king has nothing to fear, for God will not abandon the city that houses his Temple. Then he accords Ahaz a great privilege: name any portent for Yahweh to perform as a sign that he will keep his promise to deliver Judah. If he does the one in the short run, he will surely do the other in the long run. That ought to build your shaky confidence, your Majesty! But Ahaz piously hides behind a protest that to request a sign would be presumptuous. In fact, he has no faith. And at this, Isaiah's patience snaps. "What? It isn't enough for you to wear out human beings? You have to exasperate the Almighty, too? All right, since you won't choose a sign, God will choose one *for* you. And when it happens, you'll remember I said this, and you'll see God's deliverance. Behold the *almah* shall conceive and have a son, and you shall call his name 'Immanuel,' and before the child is old enough to choose the food he likes from the food he doesn't, these two paper tigers you so fear, Israel and Aram, will have been wiped off the map!" (my paraphrase).

---

[213] Jane Schaberg, *The Illegitimacy of Jesus: A Feminist Theological Interpretation of the Infancy Narratives* (New York: Harper & Row, 1987), pp. 2-3.

There is a strict statute of limitations on this prophecy: it is something the king will shortly see for himself. Indeed, that is the whole point. Thus Isaiah cannot have meant to predict something to happen many centuries in the future. He was predicting the imminent devouring of those two big fish, the king's foes, by a much bigger fish: Assyria. And this would happen in a couple of short years, as measured by the birth of a certain baby some nine months hence. Who is the child?

If you look at the very next chapter, you will see that it was Isaiah's peculiar practice to name his own expected children after his prophecies, so that people, seeing his grown children, would be unable to forget or to deny he had predicted correctly. In chapter 8:1-8:

> Then [Yahweh] said to me, "Take a large tablet and write upon it in common characters, 'Belonging to Maher-shalal-hashbaz.'" [= "The plunder speeds; the prey hastens."] And I got reliable witnesses, Uriah the priest and Zechariah the son of Jeberechiah, to attest for me. And I went to the prophetess, and she conceived and bore a son. Then [Yahweh] said to me, "Call his name Maher-shalal-hashbaz; for before the child knows how to cry 'My father' or 'My mother,' the wealth of Damascus and the spoil of Samaria will be carried away before the king of Assyria."

> [Yahweh] spoke to me again: "Because this people have refused the waters of Shiloah that flow gently, and melt in fear before Rezin and the son of Remaliah; therefore, behold, [Adonai] is bringing up against them the waters of the River, mighty and many, the king of Assyria and all his glory; and it will rise over all its channels and go over all its banks; and it will sweep on into Judah, it will overflow and pass on, reaching even to the neck; and its outspread wings will fill the breadth of your land, O Immanuel."

Another baby, same prophecy! It becomes clear that the *almah* of 7:14 was Isaiah's young wife, here called "the prophetess." And since God speaks partially to Immanuel, this prediction must have been made a year or two after the one in chapter 7.

All this is obvious, or it ought to be, to a reader who professes to take the text literally. The reason, I think, that many or most fundamentalists have no clue as to Isaiah's actual intent is that they don't care *what* Isaiah said for his own generation. They won't linger long enough to study the Old Testament passages in their ancient contexts because they can't wait to get to Jesus. Jesus is where all the action is, and they are interested in Isaiah only as a clairvoyant whose alleged predictions of Jesus they may use to convert unbelievers.

But what about the evangelist Matthew? Can he have completely failed to grasp Isaiah's point? No, he wasn't stupid. The gospel shows, as we will see later, that he was trilingual, able to read Hebrew, Aramaic, and Greek. He must have known good and well what Isaiah was talking about. And that Isaiah hadn't a clue about Jesus. So what was he doing claiming that Isaiah predicted Jesus in Isaiah 7:14?

Matthew shared the ancient view that, because the Bible is an inspired book, none of it could become irrelevant. Irrelevancy is just as bad as errancy if you expect the Bible to be an oracle of divine truth speaking to you no matter when and where in the historical time line you happen to be. And the defeat of Israel and Aram by Assyria, though the prediction came true, was long in the past. The old text had to be made to speak again to a new generation. And the way the ancients did that was to assume that the inspiring Spirit had built in esoteric meanings, available only by esoteric means of interpretation. There were deeper levels of prediction in the old texts, prophecies of things which had not yet happened. The hitch was that they were no real help *as* predictions before the fact. One could only recognize that a text *was* a prediction of some event *after* it had come true. Then in hindsight it looked pretty impressive.

Esoteric reading always ignored the original, contextual meaning and quoted words and phrases out of context. The later Kabbalah made an elaborate science out of this, though the result was nothing any Protestant reader of the Bible could countenance as exegesis. The Dead Sea Scrolls writers used similar methods of interpretation, seeing Isaiah, Habakkuk, and other ancient scriptures as brim-full of predictions of the foundation of their sect, its persecution by the Temple authorities, the coming of the interpreter *par excellence*, the Teacher of Righteousness, his betrayal at the hands of someone called "the Wicked Priest," etc. They didn't know to expect any of these things before they happened. No, it was only afterwards that they stumbled upon certain puns, turns of phrase, wording of verses taken out of context, etc., that looked like secret predictions once you knew in retrospect what they "must have" been talking about. It was kind of like the notorious "Bible Code" books today. Such interpretation was called *pesher*, or "puzzle solution."

There are a few more of these "formula quotations" in Matthew[214] and all make sense understood in this way. We will take them in turn as they come up. But we must pause to note a serious irony at this point. An earlier generation of biblical critics (e.g., the hostile Joseph Wheless),[215] writing as they did before the discovery of the Dead Sea Scrolls, could as yet know nothing about the ancient Jewish esoteric interpretation. Thus it seemed to them that Matthew was guilty of the worst kind of opportunistic, really fraudulent, text-twisting, quoting texts out of context, as if they had been overtly depicting Jesus, predicting Messiah, and that Matthew must have just hoped no ancient reader would chance to look up the Old Testament texts and find out what mincemeat Matthew had made of them. Most ancient readers did not have private copies to consult, after all. Knowing about the so-called *pesher* technique, we are able to vindicate Matthew (and his New Testament colleagues) from such

---

[214] Krister Stendahl, *The School of St. Matthew and Its Use of the Old Testament.* (Philadelphia: Fortress Press, 1968).

[215] Joseph Wheless, *Is It God's Word?* (New York: Alfred A. Knopf, 1929), Chapter XIII, "The 'Prophecies' of Jesus Christ," pp. 273-304.

allegations.

But not so fast. For one thing, one must come to the sober realization that what Wheless and his allies charged Matthew with doing, most fundamentalists (e.g., "prophecy scholar" Hal Lindsey[216]) *are* in fact doing with the poor, much-abused text, and are proud of it. Their more educated predecessors (e.g., the erudite Arthur W. Pink) held a view much like that of the ancient Jewish esotericists: every Bible prophecy was susceptible to several different predictive interpretations, new ones coming to light with contemporary developments. Should they have felt comfortable saying this? We will return to their case momentarily. But Lindsey and company seem completely to disregard context. They proof-text in the most opportunistic manner when they claim that there were hundreds of messianic predictions that any Jew should have recognized as fulfilled in Jesus,[217] or that Ezekiel predicted the 1980 Soviet invasion of Afghanistan. To get Matthew off the hook, to vindicate him as not being such a fraud, one must be ready to admit that Lindsey and the others *are* in fact charlatans. It cuts both ways. And of course it means one cannot proof-text the Old Testament as Lindsey does.

Another irony is even more problematical. If one recognizes that the biblical author, believing in scriptural inspiration, thought he had the right to decipher hidden messages far removed from the original author's intent, then must/may the modern inerrantist, sharing the faith in inspiration, begin to treat scripture like a Ouija Board as Matthew and the Dead Sea Scrolls writers did? Evangelical scholars including Richard N. Longenecker[218] and Gordon D. Fee[219] think not. They are good Protestants and realize, as Martin Luther did, that if one departs from the straight and narrow of the grammatico-historical method, there will be no escape from

---

[216] Hal Lindsey with C.C. Carlson, *The Late Great Planet Earth* (New York: Bantam Books, 1973).

[217] Lindsey, *Late Great*, p. 21.

[218] Longenecker, *Biblical Exegesis*, pp. 218-219.

[219] Gordon D. Fee and Douglas Stuart, *How to Read the Bible for All It's Worth* (Grand Rapids: Zondervan, 2nd ed., 1993), p. 185.

Swedenborgian fantasies. *Urantia Book,* here we come. One can detect palpable embarrassment as these scholars allow that the New Testament authors were entitled, being inspired themselves, to treat the Bible in a way we must not. One feels that, to be consistent, they ought to jettison the New Testament *pesher* interpretations of the Old as part of the first-century cultural clothing. But they fear to do that, because then they would be left standing in mid-air, believing in doctrines taught by Matthew or James or Paul, yet without being able to assent to the exegetical reasonings that led those worthies to embrace their positions. So here is the irony: to vindicate the New Testament writers as being more than fraudulent proof-texters, one must credit (or blame) them with practicing what we consider superstitious Bibliomancy when practiced today. The critique of Matthew and his brethren is implicit but unmistakable. "It was all right for them to be superstitious, but not us. But since they were inspired, we can't call it superstition." Oh yes we can. We must if we are to be good, honest Protestants.

Any Major Magus Will Tell You (chapter 2)

Where do the Magi (Matt. 2:1-2) come from, and what are they doing in Jerusalem? Here is how I, and I think most scholars, make sense of the story. First, these men (no number or rank is specified, no "three kings") must be members of the ancient caste of "Chaldeans" or astrologers in the Parthian Empire, Rome's neighbor to the east. Their business was to study the stars and to chart earthly events on the basis of them. God had, they believed, established a celestial-terrestrial harmony: "As above, so below."[220] Isaiah 47:13-15 condemns astrology, but Matthew certainly has nothing against it (nor does Revelation, which derives most of its imagery from ancient astrology).[221] It is not precisely as if he is advertising astrology or recommending it here. It is more like the ancient Christian appeal to (forged) Sibylline Oracles as prophecies of Jesus, or the evangelistic

---

[220] Even though it usually turns out to be "as above, so baloney."

[221] Bruce J. Malina, *On the Genre and Message of the Book of Revelation: Star Visions and Sky Journeys* (Peabody: Hendrickon Publishers, 1995).

prophesying of the slave girl in Philippi (Acts 16:16-18). Or think of the confessions of the gospel demons who recognize the Son of God in their midst and do not hesitate to broadcast it. The point is that Christ's advent receives notice and acclamation from every source. "Every knee shall bow, in heaven and on earth and under the earth, and every tongue shall confess" (Phil. 2:10-11).

These Wise Men have seen some celestial phenomenon occurring in the constellation Pisces, allotted by them to the Jews. Every nation had its particular constellation, just as each was believed to have its own angel prince (Dan. 10:13), a natural correspondence, given that stars and angels were often equated. What did they see? It might have been, as is often suggested, an alignment of Jupiter, Saturn, and Mars, or a nova. Its occurrence in Pisces implied an event of moment for Jews, no doubt the birth of a new royal heir. The Wise Men are not led by a floating star to Jerusalem. The text does not say so. Rather, they naturally assume that a royal newborn, whom they wish to honor, will lie in a nursery in the royal palace of his father, presumably Herod the Great. When they ask Herod of the child's whereabouts, they do not want directions to another locality; they only want to be shown to the royal crib. The puzzled Herod understands all this as little as the ancient king of Israel understood the arrival and request of Naaman to see the man of God, Elisha, about a healing (2 Kings 5:7).

He senses something afoot and calls together his theological advisors. As no child has been born to him in these days, he wonders if it might be the predicted Messiah. And as far as Herod knows, he is nowhere on the premises. Where, then, to look for him? Bethlehem, they tell him, so he sends the (no doubt surprised) Magi there to look for him. When they arrive, now led by a low-flying star, they find the household of Joseph, kneel before the child (as old as two years, since the signal of his birth was two years previous, Matthew 2:7, 16), leave him expensive gifts, and return home without letting Herod know where they found him. Herod, of course, paranoid maniac that he is, fears some plot. He can easily imagine some peasant revolutionists wielding a newborn as a banner of revolt, acting as regents for the new "Messiah." These imagined conspiracies he must nip in the bud. But, thanks to another angelic visit, Joseph knows to flee into Egypt, evading Herod's butchers. The rest of the Bethlehem babies are not so lucky, tiny "sons of men" who are "lifted up" on spear points.

One suspects that Matthew has fiddled with an earlier story, adding the absurd business about the moving star behaving like Tinkerbelle. Surely the original story had the Wise Men simply find their way to Bethlehem and ask around till they found him, as the shepherds do in Luke's nativity. (Notice that there are no Lukan shepherds on the scene in Matthew. Further contrasts with Luke's version must wait till we get to that gospel.)

Ever since David Friedrich Strauss[222] it has been common for scholars to compare the slaughter of the innocents to numerous parallels in other sacred tales, where Abraham, Zoroaster, Moses, Krishna, Theseus, and others are persecuted as children but survive thanks to divine Providence. Why should this one be any less mythical? Apologists counter that such a bloodbath as Matthew recounts would be by no means out of character for the historical Herod the Great who freely assassinated numerous wives, sons, and daughters when he began to suspect they were plotting against him. That makes sense to me. It is the kind of thing this madman did. On the other hand, many atrocities of Herod have been catalogued by Josephus and others, and this one, a major assault on one of his own towns, is conspicuous by its absence anywhere else but Matthew. Even Luke knows nothing of it. What tips the balance for me is the fact that the whole story appears to have been based on Josephus's version of Moses' nativity in *Antiquities of the Jews* 9:2:2-4.

While the affairs of the Hebrews were in this condition, there was this occasion offered itself to the Egyptians, which

---

[222] David Friedrich Strauss, *The Life of Jesus Critically Examined*. Trans. George Eliot (Mary Ann Evans). Lives of Jesus Series (Philadelphia: Fortress Press, 1972), pp. 162-178.

made them more solicitous for the extinction of our nation. One of those sacred scribes, who are very sagacious in foretelling future events truly, told the king, that about this time there would a child be born to the Israelites, who, if he were reared, would bring the Egyptian dominion low, and would raise the Israelites; that he would excel all men in virtue, and obtain a glory that would be remembered through all ages. [In the same way, Herod's priestly scribes tell him where Messiah must be born, Matthew 2:5] Which thing was so feared by the king [Herod is likewise afraid at the news of the new king's birth, Matthew 2:3], that, according to this man's opinion, he commanded that they should cast every male child, which was born to the Israelites, into the river, and destroy it [Cf. Herod's order to butcher Bethlehem's babies in Matthew 2:16]; that besides this, the Egyptian midwives should watch the labors of the Hebrew women, and observe what is born, for those were the women who were enjoined to do the office of midwives to them; and by reason of their relation to the king, would not transgress his commands. He enjoined also, that if any parents should disobey him, and venture to save their male children alive, they and their families should be destroyed. This was a severe affliction indeed to those that suffered it, not only as they were deprived of their sons, and while they were the parents themselves, they were obliged to be subservient to the destruction of their own children, but as it was to be supposed to tend to the extirpation of their nation, while upon the destruction of their children, and their own gradual dissolution, the calamity would become very hard and inconsolable to them. And this was the ill state they were in. But no one can be too hard for the purpose of God, though he contrive ten thousand subtle devices for that end; for this child, whom the sacred scribe foretold, was brought up and concealed from the observers appointed by the king; and he that foretold him did not mistake in the consequences of his preservation, which were brought to pass after the manner following:

A man whose name was Amram, one of the nobler sort of the Hebrews [Just like the righteous Joseph in Matthew

1:19], was afraid for his whole nation, lest it should fail, by the want of young men to be brought up hereafter, and was very uneasy at it, his wife being then with child, and he knew not what to do [Just as Joseph is upset at the news of Mary's pregnancy]. Hereupon he betook himself to prayer to God; and entreated him to have compassion on those men who had nowise transgressed the laws of his worship, and to afford them deliverance from the miseries they at that time endured, and to render abortive their enemies' hopes of the destruction of their nation. Accordingly God had mercy on him, and was moved by his supplication. He stood by him in his sleep, and exhorted him not to despair of his future favors... Know therefore that I shall provide for you all in common what is for your good, and particularly for thyself what shall make thee famous; for that child, out of dread of whose nativity the Egyptians have doomed the Israelite children to destruction, shall be this child of thine, and shall be concealed from those who watch to destroy him: and when he is brought up in a surprising way, he shall deliver the Hebrew nation from the distress they are under from the Egyptians. His memory shall be famous while the world lasts; and this not only among the Hebrews, but foreigners also: - all which shall be the effect of my favor to thee, and to thy posterity. [Just so, an angel appears to Joseph in a dream to quiet his fears and to foretell the child's future deliverance of his people, Matthew 1:20-21.]

When the vision had informed him of these things, Amram awaked and told it to Jochebed who was his wife. [On waking, Joseph (Matt. 1:24) goes to his wife, reassured, just as Amram did.] And now the fear increased upon them on account of the prediction in Amram's dream; for they were under concern, not only for the child, but on account of the great happiness that was to come to him also.

The visit of the Wise Men, Parthian Magi, seems to derive from events surrounding the official visit of the Armenian King Tiridates to Nero's coronation. He came from the East, bringing with him the sons of three other Parthian rulers. According to Dio Cassius' *Roman History* 43:1-7, "Tiridates declared unto Nero, 'I have come to you, my god, to pay homage, as I do to Mithras.'" (Of course, the Matthean Magi are said to bow to worship the new king, too, in Matthew 2:2.) After this display, the Armenian king and his entourage (whom Pliny, in his *Natural History*, 30:6:16-17, called Magi), "did not return by the route he had followed in coming," instead sailing back a different way, just as Matthew's Magi from the East "departed into their own country another way" (2:12).[223]

The slaughter of the innocents raises a significant problem of theodicy (justifying the ways of God): why did God warn only Joseph and not the other Bethlehem families? An oversight? Why, yes. But not God's. It is Matthew's oversight. And that is a big clue that the story is a piece of fiction. All the author was concerned about was his story and the supposed scriptural proof-texts on which he built it. The proof-texts this time come from Micah, Hosea, and Jeremiah. Micah 5:2 reads:

> But you, O Bethlehem Ephrathah,
>   who are little to be among the clans of Judah,
> from you shall come forth for me
>   one who is to be ruler in Israel,
> whose origin is from of old,
>   from ancient days.

Matthew's quotation of it is a bit different:

> And you, O Bethlehem, in the land of Judah,
> are *by no means* least among the rulers of Judah;
> for from you shall come a ruler
> who will govern my people Israel.

I suppose it hardly matters, but Matthew has rewritten the quotation, which is not exactly what we mean by quotation! He has decided to honor Bethlehem by denying that it is small, as to significance, anyway. No one but an inerrantist is liable to lose any sleep over this,

---

[223] Brown, *Birth*, p. 174.

but an inerrantist *should* toss and turn! It is his doctrine, and nothing else, that makes a molehill into a mountain, that creates a major problem where there was none.

And is the Micah passage a stipulation that the Messiah, whoever that might turn out to be, had to be born in Bethlehem? Not necessarily. For one thing, this passage is probably part of a birth oracle, greeting the birth of a new king (and hence quite appropriate for Matthew's context), heaping divine honors upon him and his envisioned reign. It is pro forma: they said such things when any new prince was born. And the reference is probably metaphorical for the Davidic dynasty. "From David's town" is like saying, "from Jesse's root." Both are figures of speech for Davidic dynastic credentials.

Jeremiah 31:15 has "Rachel" (mother of Joseph, hero of the northern tribes) inconsolable with grief as if, centuries later, she could witness the deportation of Israelites to Assyria after the conquest of Samaria by that empire. The verse is claimed here as a prediction of the slaughter of the Bethlehem babies, but it might be more fitting to call it a literary allusion. (In the same way, many of Origen's supposed allegorizations of scripture strike me as mere allusions to coincidentally fitting biblical language.)

Hosea 11:1, on the other hand, is the clearest possible example of coded *pesher* exegesis because the original meaning is so obvious and obviously does not refer to Jesus. As anyone can see, Hosea depicts God reminiscing about the day he led his "son" Israel by a mighty hand out of Egypt and the house of bondage. That is what it means when it says, "Out of Egypt I have called my son," and the context makes that absolutely unmistakable. Matthew simply cannot have thought otherwise. Thus he is divining an extra and secret meaning. He infers, from the mere occurrence of "my son" in the verse, that it must contain a hidden reference to Jesus, and Matthew infers that Jesus must have had a visit to Egypt if God was to have an opportunity to summon him from there again. No wonder Luke knows nothing of such a sojourn; it never happened except in Matthew's imagination. Creative license? Yes. Historically true? Come on. You know better.

Originally this episode must have concluded with the angel intervening in a dream, as he constantly does in this gospel, telling Joseph that the coast is clear. Herod is dead, and the heat is off. And thus they returned to Israel. But then Matthew feels the need to justify, from scripture, the residence of the Holy Family in Galilee. Luke assumed Mary and Joseph lived in Nazareth from the start and went to Bethlehem for Jesus' birth, providentially, on the occasion of the census, then returned home. By contrast, Matthew imagined them living in Bethlehem and moving to Nazareth only after returning from Egypt, because of another angelic warning that the previous reassurance had been premature: Herod is dead all right, but his son Archelaeus has succeeded him, and, like Rehoboam, he is even worse than his father. This hiccup in the narrative sequence is another plain sign of fictive origin. Which is more likely, the angel jumps the gun, telling Mary and Joseph it is safe to go home, then calls right back to tell them to skip Bethlehem and head for the hills in Galilee? Or that Matthew has added a new episode, wanting to take the Holy Family to Nazareth? I find it easier for some reason to imagine Matthew rewriting his story than for the angels of an all-knowing God to make such a goof. (And besides, why were they still gunning for the Holy Infant? Why would Herod not have been satisfied his troops had succeeded? Why would Archelaus still have been on the war-path?)

And that's not the only goof. Matthew wants to make the Holy Family's residence in Nazareth a matter of prophecy, too, so he cites scripture as saying: "He shall be called a Nazarene." The trouble is, there is no such verse. He might have been thinking of Judges 13:5, where the angel instructs Mrs. Manoah concerning her son that "the boy shall be a Nazirite pledged to God from birth," but, if so, this is a pretty sloppy citation. Now we are not just talking about hidden meanings in old texts (as large a bite as that is to chew); we are talking about rewriting the "ancient" text to make it fit the "predicted" event. A "Nazirite" and a "Nazarene" are not the same thing, and Jesus' notorious wine-drinking (Matt. 11:19) alone eliminates the possibility that he was a perpetual Nazirite.

Some have speculated that Matthew is citing some unknown scripture. But we have a pretty good library of contemporary apocrypha and pseudepigrapha, and this phrase occurs in none of them. And besides, that would raise the issue of canon, a much bigger can of worms. Talk about the cure being worse than the disease! Unless the Bible is supposed to be supernaturally inerrant there is no reason to get upset about Matthew "quoting" a passage he felt sure was *somewhere* in scripture—but wasn't.

But the single biggest problem for inerrantism is the fact that there was in those days *no Nazareth for them to move to!* As Rene Salm[224] has shown in excruciating, exhaustive detail, Nazareth, though it had been inhabited for many centuries before Jesus, had been long deserted by the first century C.E. As far as any surviving evidence tells us, resettlement began only in the mid-first century C.E. This means that an inhabited Nazareth was not there in time for Jesus to have lived there, but it *was* there for the gospel writers to have known of it and to have supposed he *had* lived there.

"Jesus the Nazarene" or "Nazorean" must have originally denoted (as many scholars have suggested) membership in the attested Jewish sect of the Nazoreans,[225] possibly identical with the Mandaean Gnostics, who continue today, calling themselves "Nasoreans" and tracing their descent from John the Baptist's ministry of repentance. The thing was, Christians felt a bit uneasy with the notion that Jesus had been a member of a particular sect, as this might imply he was a mortal with mere "opinions" and who felt he had something to learn from others more mature in the faith than he.[226] The same "anxiety of influence," after all, had led

---

[224] Rene Salm, *The Myth of Nazareth: The Invented Town of Jesus* (Cranford: American Atheist Press, 2008)

[225] Robert Eisler, *The Messiah Jesus and John the Baptist According to Flavius Josephus' Recently Rediscovered 'Capture of Jerusalem' and the other Jewish and Christian Sources.* Trans. Alexander Haggerty Krappe (New York: Dial Press, 1931), pp. 232-235; Hugh J. Schonfield, *The Passover Plot: New Light on the History of Jesus* (New York: Bantam Books, 1967), Appendix 2, "North Palestinean [sic] Sectarians and Christian Origins," pp. 199-206.

[226] Strauss, *Life of Jesus*, p. 202: "it must have been the interest of the

Christians to be embarrassed at the fact of Jesus having applied to John for baptism. And thus it came as a relief to be able to reinterpret "Nazarene/Nazorean" (both forms occur in the gospels) as a place name reference. Of course, all such qualms are silly. Everybody except Christian Identity lunatics[227] believes Jesus belonged to the Jewish religion, right? If he did not shun that label, there is no reason to think he should have eschewed others. That's not the problem. The real problem is the unhistorical character of all the gospel statements that place Jesus in a non-existent Nazareth.

John's Reluctant Baptism (chapter 3)

Matthew 3:1-17 abounds in fascinating details, but almost every piece of the narrative can be questioned as authentically historical. In Matthew 3:14-16, John, embarrassed, tries to dissuade Jesus from being baptized: what need has he for the rite? He is no sinner, after all. Jesus' answer is far from clear; it doesn't *have* to be, since it is manifestly there only to reassure the reader that, despite appearances, nothing is wrong theologically. Why bother with this? There were members of rival sects who insisted that for Jesus to have been baptized by John made John the superior, Jesus the inferior. Here John is made to utter these doubts on the reader's behalf, only

---

Christian legend to represent Jesus as independent of human teachers." The Infancy Gospels even portray young Jesus as making fools of his would-be tutors, and even striking one of them dead after he hits Jesus with a ruler! Buddhists had the same problem with the traditional story of the Buddha's career which had him initially studying with one guru, then another, before striking out in his own direction (Edward J. Thomas, *The Life of Buddha as Legend and History*, History of Civilization [London: Routledge & Kegan Paul, 1927, 1975], p. 62). So, when they posited that a whole chain of previous and future Buddhas had/would repeat, step by step, the biography of Siddhartha, they conspicuously omitted this early period of tutelage (Har Dayal, *The Bodhisattva Doctrine in Buddhist Sanskrit Literature* [1932; rpt. Delhi: Motilal Banarsidass, 1978; rpt. New York: Samuel Weiser, n.d.], p. 306).

[227] Michael Barkun, *Religion and the Racist Right: The Origins of the Christian Identity Movement* (Chapel Hill: University of North Carolina Press, 1994).

to have Jesus quiet them. "It is necessary for us to fulfill all righteousness" probably does not mean "fulfill prophecy," since the evangelist provides no Old Testament text of which the baptism might be the fulfillment. Instead, the intent is probably "to embrace every pious practice" as an example to others. But all that really matters is that Jesus was *not* there to repent of any sins, God forbid. Apparently the problem had not occurred to Mark, who may not have had so high a Christology as Matthew.

But how do we know this didn't happen? For one thing, no other evangelist mentions it. Why shouldn't they? Such a story grows in the telling rather than shrinking, and, given wider Christian embarrassment over the Baptist connection, surely such a disavowal made by John would be told and retold, just like the business of John being unworthy to shine Jesus' shoes, which appears in all four gospels. For another, Matthew's version squarely contradicts John's (John 1:32-33):

> And John bore witness, "I saw the Spirit descend as a dove from heaven, and it remained on him. I myself did not know him; but he who sent me to baptize with water said to me, 'He on whom you see the Spirit descend and remain, this is he who baptizes with the Holy Spirit.'"

In Matthew John recognizes Jesus as soon as he sees him standing in line; only later does the Spirit descend on the baptized Jesus. But in John's gospel, John the Baptist pointedly did not know who Jesus was till he saw the Spirit descend upon him.

Second, the divine voice in verse 17 speaks to the crowd concerning Jesus: "*This is* my beloved Son, with whom I am well pleased," while Mark 1:11 has "*You are* my beloved Son, with whom I am well pleased." Which did God say? He can't have said *both*, and it matters. Mark has no Nativity story, so this would appear to be the first time Jesus hears the news of his divine Sonship. But, after the events of Matthew's Nativity, we cannot imagine Jesus not having already been instructed in what mighty angels and prophets had said of him when he was born; thus the heavenly voice speaks not to *him*, but rather to the bystanders (actually the readers). Which did God say? I submit he did not say both at the same time. Why bother saying "you are," since Jesus must be included in those who hear him say, "This is"? It is easily understandable as a redactional change, impossible to harmonize as a historical discrepancy.

Desert Ordeal (4:1-11)

Jesus embarks for the desert, where the devil appears and offers him three temptations, which he successfully resists. Did this really happen? Well, people sure have retreated to the desert on vision quests. People have had visions. People think they have seen the devil. So we are not reading about something that *couldn't* have happened. On the other hand, there are also a number of close parallels to this story from other religions. Abraham, the Buddha, and Zoroaster are all subjected to the same sort of temptations at the outset of their ministries, and all pull through with flying colors.[228] Those others, nobody doubts, are edifying legends. So the gospel Temptation story might be another of these legends. But one cannot prove it either way.

    This passage is, once again, artistry, not reportage. Sure, you can protest that the facts may be artfully rendered while still being facts, but what is that except to admit that the facts, *at best*, have been played up, polished, stylized, and *distorted*. Don't hide behind euphemisms. Specifically, what I have in mind is the clear theme of Jesus repeating the trials of Israel in the Sinai desert, but succeeding where Israel failed. In Matthew 4:4, Jesus is made to quote Deuteronomy 8:3, the moral of the story of Israel complaining of hunger all those years in the wilderness. Matthew 4:7 has Jesus quote Deuteronomy 6:16, referring to the trial at Massa, while Matthew 4:10 has him quote Deuteronomy 6:13, a warning to shun

---

[228] Strauss, *Life of Jesus*, p. 259-263; Robert M. Price, *The Incredible Shrinking Son of Man: How Reliable Is the Gospel Tradition?* (Amherst: Prometheus Books, 2003), pp 124-128.

Canaanite polytheism. The point is: Jesus is the New Israel, the True Israel, in whom is no guile, no stubbornness, no self-seeking or lack of faithful endurance. But we are reading a choreographed play (like a Christmas pageant): set in the wilderness, people playing ancient biblical characters, and with a new happy ending. Anyone who discerns the Deuteronomy parallel realizes at once the didactic, thus fictive, nature of the story.

Though most scholars think Matthew and Luke both derived the threefold Temptation from their common Q source (all the material they share with one another that they did not get from Mark), I believe it is all Matthew's expansion of Mark. Mark 1:13 had Jesus sojourning in the wilderness for forty days, fed ("served") by angels as Elijah was. Matthew has him fasting and introduces the dialogue with the devil. Matthew thus contributes the sequence of Deuteronomy quotes, concluding with Satan showing Jesus the panorama of counties he may rule if he will only bow the knee. This mountaintop scene must be derived from Deuteronomy 32:48-49, where, from atop Mount Nebo, Moses views all the kingdoms his people will conquer after his death. This scene, with slight changes, reappears in our version of Luke, but it was not present in the earlier version of Luke used by the Marcionites. Hence it was not part of Q.

In all this, a believer in inspiration and inerrancy might counter that I am holding the ancient text to alien standards of scientific modernity, that the ancients would not have considered something like this to be an error. That is the way Everett F. Harrison[229] argued the point in his oft-quoted essay, "Criteria of Biblical Inerrancy." But don't you see, if you argue this way, you are switching sides? This is the point of historical and literary criticism in a nutshell: it is not a case of "hoax or history." Ancient literature was subject to a thousand vicissitudes that make the absolutist abstraction of "inerrancy" an obstacle in the way of understanding the Bible. If you argue as Harrison argued, you have given up inerrancy. You are

---

[229] Everett F. Harrison, "Criteria of Biblical Inerrancy." In Frank E. Gaebelein, ed., Christianity Today (New York: Pyramid Books, 1968), pp. 86-90.

admitting that there are many good reasons (including genre conventions, ancient standards of veracity, etc.) that the Bible should be found frequently failing to line up with the straight yardstick of "inerrancy." If you say, "Close enough for ancient standards!" you are embracing, inch by inch, the Higher Criticism—as indeed you should.

Equivocal Kingdom (4:17)

Comparing Matthew's numerous mentions of "the kingdom of heaven" with their parallels in Luke and Mark, it becomes obvious that the sayings originally featured the wording "kingdom of God." The meaning is the same: the reign of God or the realm of God, depending on the saying. "Heaven" stands for God metonymically, as when we say "Washington," meaning "the Federal Government." Heaven is where God exercises his power, so the reign of God is the reign of heaven. It is obvious that Matthew has altered "kingdom of God" sayings into "Kingdom of heaven" sayings, motivated by a more acute sense of reverence. Jews had long since stopped using the holiest, most personal name of God, Yahweh or Jehovah, substituting for it the more generic Adonai ("Lord") or Elohim ("God"). In time, even these came to seem too sacred to utter, so pious Jews spoke of "Heaven," "the Power," or *HaShem* ("the Name"). Matthew prefers "Heaven." It is understandable, and nothing is lost. Except strict inerrancy, which, logically, is the only kind there is. Jesus said something according to the earlier record, but Matthew decided to change the words, technically making Jesus say words he did not actually say. This is no more a problem than when today some add inclusive language to liturgical readings of scripture. They don't mean to deceive the hearers into thinking Paul actually wrote "brothers *and sisters*." It is just to amend a present-day liturgical text. So with Matthew. He is adjusting a text, not fabricating pseudo-history. But this does involve producing a narrative in which, technically, Jesus is said to have said things he did not say.

And do not begin to say to yourselves, "Jesus might have used both idioms interchangeably, and the gospels happen to quote him using one or the other on different occasions." For I tell you it is the same occasion, e.g., when the disciples try to fend off parents bringing their babies for Jesus to kiss, and he says, in Matthew 19:14, "for to such belongs the kingdom of heaven," and in Mark 10:14, "for to such belongs the kingdom of God." What, did this happen twice with only this difference, like a director ordering a retake of a scene? *Deja vue* all over again?

Again, belief in inerrancy creates a problem where no one would see one otherwise. Remember, if you are willing to allow Matthew to have made such a redactional change, you have stepped across the border: you should soon realize that redaction, with the same motive and the same freedom, does not stop there. And if, like some today, you want to maintain that such an understanding of scripture is compatible with inerrancy, go ahead. You will soon have reduced the term to meaning absolutely nothing.

The Sermon on the Mount (chapters 5-7)

Three major issues will concern us throughout the Sermon on the Mount. First, is it possible to face squarely the ethical demands made here? If we try to whittle them down to something we *can* handle, then do we not quietly abandon the notion that scripture is infallible by admitting that it is unreasonable? Second, does the Sermon require Christian obedience to the Jewish Torah? If it does, we would have an intractable conflict between Jesus and Paul. And third, is the Sermon compatible with the atoning death of Christ, or does it teach a salvation plan based on good works?

One other point. Chapters 5-7 are a compilation of thematically related sayings, some related only by common words, as if fished out of a concordance. There are five more or less topical sections in Matthew, implying the role of Jesus as a new Moses giving a new Pentateuch. But this means the so-called Sermon on the Mount did not originate as a single sermon on one single occasion. Say what you will about "the marvelously retentive memory of the Oriental," no one can have heard a speech of this length and memorized it on the spot. I suppose someone might have if he were miraculously aided by the Holy Spirit, but that would be arbitrary to suggest and discontinuous with the historical and psychological processes all readers take for granted as producing the texts. And when you have to invoke "miracle" for your theory to work, it is a poor theory resting on the tactics of desperation.

It is hard to see how it matters that chapters 5-7 were not originally a single piece. For the sake of argument, let us allow that Jesus really did say every word attributed to him here, though perhaps not on one single occasion. The problem appears out of left field only when we recall that the text is supposed to be inerrant, because (for his own good purpose, already described) the evangelist says Jesus gave these sayings as a single speech one day, when in fact he didn't. Again, you may say I am nitpicking, and you would be exactly right! But is that not the whole point of biblical inerrancy?

Can't Beat Those Beatitudes (5:1-12)

Are these blessings to be taken as indicatives or imperatives? Much hangs on our answer. I believe that Hans Windisch[230] was correct: these are the requirements for entry into the blessed state of salvation. That seems obvious, I dare say, to most readers. "These are the character traits one must cultivate for divine approval." Lutherans including Joachim Jeremias,[231] as well as other Protestants like Anglican Archibald M. Hunter[232] and Pentecostal Gordon D.

---

[230] Hans Windisch, *The Meaning of the Sermon on the Mount: A Contribution to the Historical Understanding of the Gospels and to the Problem of Their True Exegesis.* Trans. S. MacLean Gilmour (Philadelphia: Westminster Press, 1951)

[231] Joachim Jeremias, *The Sermon on the Mount.* Trans. Norman Perrin. Facet Books. Biblical Series 2 (Philadelphia: Fortress Press, 1963); Archibald M. Hunter, *A Pattern for Life: An Exposition of the Sermon on the Mount* (Philadelphia: Westminster Press, 1953), Chapter V, "The Sermon and the Gospel," pp. 100-104.

[232] Hunter, *Pattern for Life,* pp. 30-31, 39.

Fee,[233] argue to the contrary: the text assumes the reader is already a regenerated believer in Jesus Christ, and that, by the sheerest grace of God, the reader already possesses all these traits, having received them as a package along with the Holy Spirit. The beatitudes are merely giving the thumbs-up sign to those lucky stiffs who possess God's grace as new creatures in Christ. I call this the Lutheran table-cloth trick: the individual beatitudes are like glasses and plates on the dinner table, and the Lutheran snatches away the understanding upon which the dinnerware first rested, leaving them resting upon a different surface instead. The original surface on which they lay was the belief that repentance and sincere attempts to produce its fruits would win God's favor. The new surface turns out to be Paulinist theology, though nothing in the Sermon on the Mount context seems to suggest it.

Or think of the parable of the Sower (Matt. 13:4-9, 18-23; Mark 4:39, 14-20). Jesus tells how the common seed falls into various types of soil, some rich and receptive, others not. The hearers are to understand that they correspond to one or another kind of soil. If they are the wrong kind and do not afford the gospel seed purchase and nourishment, or if they prove unable to prevent Satan's birds of ill-omen from snatching up the seed, they will be damned. What are they to do? Idly wonder which category they already belong to, as if they had bottles of Coke with a message under the cap, whether they had won the prize or not? No, surely the point is that it is up to them whether they will prove to be fruitful or unfruitful soil. It is not yet determined. They will determine their destiny by the choice Jesus now calls upon them to make. It must be the same with Matthew's beatitudes: do you belong to the class of people he blesses? Are you a peace-maker? Do you hunger and thirst to be righteous? Are you meek, merciful, persecuted for righteousness' sake? It is up to you so to aspire and so to inherit the kingdom of God, er, I mean, the kingdom of heaven.

Some cannot bring themselves to read the text this way, even if

---

[233] "Life of Jesus" class lectures, 1975.

their better exegetical judgment tells them the Lutheran view is strained and inherently implausible. It looks pretty good nonetheless to those who share Luther's terror of any God whose favor one must win (though I think in the gospel the point is rather to avoid forfeiting God's kind forgiveness by heedless sinning, not quite the same thing). So many New Testament readers would rather treat Jesus as a ventriloquist dummy from whose dead, wooden lips they are pleased to hear the projected voice of Paul, actually of Martin Luther.[234]

Matthew's Sermon on the Mount contains more and slightly different beatitudes from the list in Luke's gospel. Let's wait till we get to Luke to discuss the difference.

No Abolition Movement (5:17-48)

In Matthew 5:17-19 the Jesus/Paul conflict (pardon me for not using a harmonizing euphemism like "tension") comes fully into view. Note first that Jesus is made to address and rebut a rival *Christian* theory about the meaning of Jesus' saving mission. He is not merely rebutting slanders or misunderstandings put about by detractors in his own day. We can be sure of this from the specific wording: "Think not that *I have come to...*" That is, people hold competing views of Christian soteriology, some thinking that "Christ came to abolish the Law and the Prophets," or in other words, "Christ is the end of the Law unto righteousness to every one who believes" (Rom. 10:4). The representatives of such theology quite naturally abandon Torah observance and go about teaching that one may feel free to break or relax the commandments:

> They have been told about you that you teach all the Jews who are among the Gentiles to forsake Moses, telling them not to circumcise their children or observe the customs.

---

[234] Krister Stendahl, "Paul and the Introspective Conscience of the West." In Stendahl, *Paul among Jews and Gentiles* (Philadelphia: Fortress Press, 1976), pp. 78-108.

> What then is to be done? They will certainly hear that you
> have come. Do therefore what we tell you. We have four
> men who are under a vow; take these men and purify
> yourself along with them and pay their expenses, so that they
> may shave their heads. Thus all will know that there is
> nothing in what they have been told about you but that you
> yourself live in observance of the law. (Acts 21:21-24)

Matthew speaks through Jesus against a rival Christian mission, that
of Paul,[235] who has his own choice words for anyone who tells his
converts they must be circumcised and observe the Law:

> I am astonished that you are so quickly deserting him who
> called you in the grace of Christ and turning to a different
> gospel— not that there is another gospel, but there are some
> who trouble you and want to pervert the gospel of Christ.
> But even if we, or an angel from heaven, should preach to
> you a gospel contrary to that which we preached to you, let
> him be accursed. As we have said before, so now I say again,
> If any one is preaching to you a gospel contrary to that
> which you received, let him be accursed. (Gal. 1:6-9):

But someone will say, "Yet Matthew does not name Paul
specifically!" True! In fact, I suspect Matthew 5:19-19 represents the
work of the Ecclesiastical Redactor, trying to counter the teaching of
his contemporary Marcion. Whereas Paul held that the Torah (at
least its ceremonial portions) had become obsolete, the doctrine
condemned here is a rejection of *the Old Testament canon*: "the Law
and the Prophets." That's Marcionism. But Marcionism was radical
Paulinism.

Two things are clear from this: for Matthew, Christians must
keep even the least of the Torah commandments, say, not seething a

---

[235] Gerhard Barth, "Matthew's Understanding of the Law." In Günther
Bornkamm, Gerhard Barth, and Heinz Joachim Held, *Tradition and
Interpretation in Matthew*. Trans. Percy Scott. New Testament Library
(Philadelphia: Fortress Press, 1963), p. 161.

goat in goat's milk. Oh, I know what you're thinking: "But Jesus doesn't say the Torah remains binding on Christians. He says that it remains in force till he fulfils *all prophecy*, very soon now, on the cross." You mean he is only giving stop-gap instructions, an "interim ethic," for that brief period, no longer relevant even to Matthew's readers? That seems quite odd. Why would Matthew leave us to infer this? If this was the intention of the speaker, Matthew has taken it out of context in a drastic and misleading manner. And besides, this very passage says explicitly that the scope of prophecy far exceeds any imminent event such as the crucifixion, extending even unto the wiping away of heaven and earth! Is it not more natural to suppose Jesus (Matthew) means that the Torah remains in force till the end of history?

As one reads the "Matthean antitheses" in 5:21-48 it becomes evident that, far from being rescinded, the demands of the Torah are being made far more stringent by going right to the heart of the matter. Matthew's Jesus is, like contemporary rabbis, "erecting a fence around the Torah," trying to fend off sinners before they get within breaking distance of the commandments. There is nothing wrong with the commandments; they are not rescinded. Rather, by dealing with the issue of motivation, one protects the Law from violation. Is Jesus "setting aside" the commandments, as many contend? Hardly! No, the point is rather that the commandment against murder is in no danger of violation if we can purify the heart of rage. No one will think to require an oath of us if we are known to be trustworthy.[236] The adultery commandment is safe from violation if men will curb their lustful thoughts towards other men's wives. If he meant to set aside the commandments, we would be reading, "You have always heard it said, 'You shall not commit adultery,' but I say to you, don't worry about it: love the one you're with." Seventeenth-century Messiah Jacob Frank,[237] who believed the

---

[236] Henry Drummond: "That won't be necessary to swear him in." Matthew Harrison Brady: "Oh, I can make affirmation. I have no objection to swearing to God." Drummond: "No. I take it you will tell the truth." *Inherit the Wind* (1960), film script.

kingdom of God had arrived and annulled the Torah, taught exactly this and hosted liturgical orgies! Not Jesus. Not Matthew. If Jesus or Matthew had meant to set aside the commandment against murder, he would have said, "You have heard it said, 'Do not murder,' but I say to you, let every man watch his own back, and may the best man win!" Did he? Luckily not. "You have always heard: 'Keep the vows you make to God,' but I say, it's all just words, so who cares what you say?" The whole idea is ridiculous.

You can see, though, why some in the early church (apparently including Matthew) thought Paul taught such antinomianism. In Romans he even expects that someone first hearing his gospel of freedom from the Torah will conclude he is an antinomian: "What then? Are we to sin the more, so that grace may more abound? Never!" Paul avoided the implication, I think, because he knew from Jeremiah 30:31-36 that the New Covenant brought with it a new law, written upon the heart, from which righteousness would henceforth spontaneously arise, thanks to the Spirit. Matthew does not employ this conceptuality. He is closer to the rabbis who distinguished between "the law of goodness," the minimum requirement of the good man, and "the law of holiness," the spontaneous zeal of the one who acts solely to please the God whom he loves. He asks not, "What can I get away with?" but rather, "What else may I do?" The rabbis even use the same examples as Matthew: lust, wrath, vows.[238]

Even so, in verses 38-48, Jesus does not urge the abolition of the civil law against retaliation and restitution. Such laws in every society are enacted for the sake of the hard-hearted, as Jesus also says

---

[237] Gershom Scholem, "Redemption through Sin," trans. Hillel Halkin [Michael A. Meyer translated the rest of the book]. In Scholem, *The Messianic Idea in Judaism and Other Essays on Jewish Spirituality* (New York: Schocken Books, 1971), pp. 78-141.

[238] Solomon Schechter, *Some Aspects of Rabbinic Theology* (NY: Macmillan, 1910), Chapter XIII, "The Law of Holiness and the Law of Goodness," pp. 199-218.

re divorce. Such laws must remain in place to curb chaos, since there remain numerous tares among the wheat. But Jesus calls us (the wheat) up higher: why avail yourself of that law (cf., 1 Cor. 6:7)? God cannot be hurt by the sins of men. Why not try to be perfect in this sense, like him, rising above the injuries men would inflict? The air is rare upon that summit, and mundane life may not allow it, as Count Tolstoy found out the hard way, letting his property be despoiled, leaving his family destitute. And here is our question as to whether scripture can be infallible if it is unreasonable, for it is plain that ruin and conquest by the evil will follow if one does not resist the evil person. We admire the courage of pacifistic martyrs, but if their refusal to take up arms, their insistence on turning the other cheek, contributes to Hitler's conquest, we must curse them in the very next breath. They are pious fools, imagining themselves too pure to bloody their hands, not realizing their "nobility" helps the wicked enslave the children of the righteous. "The fathers have eaten sour grapes, but the children's teeth are set on edge." You have the right to yield only yourself up to martyrdom, not to make others suffer for your principles. Thus, perhaps, the evangelists, as they included demands that most readers could not be expected to follow, intended these teachings as "councils of perfection" relevant only to those who had "let goods and kindred go," through voluntary poverty. To these Jesus says, at least in Matthew's version (19:21), "If you would be perfect..." Similarly, celibacy, the best path according to both Matthew and Paul, is only for the elite (Matt. 19:12; 1 Cor. 7:7).

Evangelical hermeneutics prefers a "democratic" approach, making every text equally applicable to every reader's conscience. But they're willing to make the occasional exception: Evangelicals usually view Jesus' telling the Rich Young Ruler to give up his wealth (and his membership in the Christian Businessmen's Association) as an aberration irrelevant to everyone else. Jesus, a mind-reader, happened to know that, because of some weird quirk, this particular man was enslaved by his riches, unlike all other rich people, and that he alone, unlike wealthy readers, should renounce his property. By contrast, the Catholic reads the text as Matthew intended (I think): "The Rich Young Ruler is better than me: Jesus discerns that the man's conventional piety is not enough for him; he is a potential saint capable of much more." The Protestant sees the man as worse than him: "That guy was like Ebenezer Scrooge, a miser. But for me there is no conflict of interests, and so Jesus does not want me to renounce my wealth."

In verse 22 we get a glimpse of the Essene-like Matthean community: "But I say to you that every one who is angry with his brother shall be liable to judgment; whoever insults his brother shall be liable to the council, and whoever says, 'You fool!' shall be liable to the hell of fire." The implied model of community life in no way matches that of modern churches. But it sounds a lot like the monastic lifestyle of the Dead Sea Scrolls.

> If a man answer his neighbour defiantly or speak brusquely so as to undermine the composure of his fellow, and in so doing flout the orders of one who is registered as his superior, he is to be mulcted [a quarter of his food rations] for one year. If a man speaks in anger against one of the registered priests, he is to be mulcted for one year, placed in isolation, and regarded as outside the state of purity entailed in membership of the community. If, however, he spoke unintentionally, he is to be mulcted only for six months... If a man defames his neighbour unjustly, and does so deliberately, he is to be mulcted for one year and regarded as "outside"... If he harbor a grudge against his neighbor without legitimate cause, he is to be mulcted for one year. The same is to apply also to anyone who takes personal revenge on his neighbor in any respect... Anyone who indulges in indecent talk is to be mulcted for three months. (*Manual of Discipline*)

Jesus gives advice on sacrifice (Matt. 5:23-24): don't think of offering an animal to God as long as you are estranged from another person. We can easily imagine an Old Testament (Isa.1:10-17) or an ancient Jewish setting for this text, but it certainly does not seem to envision any future in which, in the plan of God, sacrifices have been suspended thanks to the atoning death of Jesus~or the fall of Jerusalem, supposedly anticipated by Jesus. The saying assumes an ongoing practice of sacrifices at the temple, and the only reform in view is that demanded by the prophets: do not imagine God will accept your offerings as long as you appear before him with some outstanding wrong on your conscience. So refrain from sacrifice till you can make restoration and be reconciled to your fellows. If Jesus is shown teaching an ethic for an ongoing Jewish dispensation, it sounds as if he does not expect it to end and to be replaced by the Christian religion. It is not as if the same sentiment could not be transposed into a new theological framework. In 1 Corinthians 11:27-29, it is. But that is Paul, not Jesus. We have to remind ourselves of what Adolf Harnack[239] said: are we to imagine that Jesus taught one way of piety and salvation, all the while knowing (*but not saying*) that it would shortly be replaced by something altogether different? Of course, the implication here, as elsewhere, is that the religion *about* Jesus was not Jesus' own religion (not part of the message he came to teach) but rather a creative adaptation to wholly new circumstances as history unfolded.

Matthew 5:25-26 is often taken to refer to settling accounts with the Almighty before the Day of Judgment arrives and it becomes too late. This interpretation is hardly certain; the saying may simply represent shrewd advice by Jesus, speaking as a sage: better settle out of court if you can! Amen to that. But it is not unnatural to refer the saying to Judgment Day in light of the immediately preceding talk of being sentenced to the Gehenna of fire. And in that case, we seem to have a contradiction to the picture of eternal torment found in Matthew 25:41, where the description of

[239] Adolf Harnack, *What Is Christianity?* Trans. Thomas Bailey Saunders. Harper Torchbooks (New York: Harper & Row, 1957), p. 143: "To contend that Jesus meant his whole message to be taken provisionally, and everything in it to receive a different interpretation after his death and resurrection, nay, parts of it to be put aside as of no account, is a desperate supposition."

the fire of hell as "everlasting" certainly implies unending suffering. Otherwise, what's the point of it never going out? If Matthew 5:26 does refer to eschatological judgment, it is not of eternal duration. One can pay one's debt and be set free. The model used, as in Matthew 18:23-35, is the debtor's prison, where one is incarcerated till his loved ones can come up with the money he owed, or perhaps till he can work off the debt. This is the way hell is viewed in Hinduism and Buddhism, as working off bad karma for a determined duration (though these faiths stipulate perverse torments beyond anything dreamt of by Dante!).[240]

More eschatological threats greet us in Matthew 5:29-30, along with a conception of the afterlife that ill accords with that in 1 Corinthians 15 with its "spiritual body" not composed of flesh and blood. For Matthew has Jesus advise sinners to cut their losses: amputate any body part that is going to addict you to sin, for that way leads to Gehenna. If one removes the offending member, and thus stops sinning, well, granted, one winds up maimed for eternity, but it's not so bad considering the alternative! Here we may think of the Johannine Jesus who still bears gaping flesh wounds in his resurrected body. But for Matthew, at any rate, unlike Paul, the saved will inhabit the same bodies they wore when they died. The non-inerrantist simply concludes from this that the Bible records various speculations and beliefs on the afterlife, as on so many other subjects, and he does not waste his time bemoaning that we lack an infallible answer book. The non-inerrantist humbly confesses with Paul, "Now we see in a glass darkly" and does not insist, like the Fallen Sophia of Gnostic myth, to know what only God can know.

---

[240] L. Austine Waddell, *Tibetan Buddhism with Its Mystic Cults, Symbolism and Mythology, and in its Relation to Indian Buddhism* (1895; rpt. New York: Dover, 1972), pp. 89-100. Also Daigan and Alicia Matsunaga, *The Buddhist Concept of Hell* (New York: Philosophical Library, 1972), Chapter IV, "Description and Analysis of the Eight Hells," pp. 75-106. Appendix, pp. 107-136. One is reminded of Robert E. Howard's poem, "From the Hells beneath the Hells."

We seem to have another dubious memory-quotation of scripture in 5:43: "You shall love your neighbor and hate your enemy." Of course the source text, Leviticus 19:18, which Jesus elsewhere (Matt. 22:39) ranks as the second greatest commandment, reads: "You shall not take vengeance, nor bear any grudge against the sons of your people; but you shall love your neighbor as yourself." My guess is that the saying reached Matthew, with an interpretive comment added, and that the evangelist did not realize the expansion was not actually part of the text of Leviticus. As it seems silly, not to mention redundant, to command one to hate someone already characterized as one's enemy, I take it to mean "You shall love your neighbor, reserving your hatred for the enemy." Or in other words, "Don't treat your friend as if he were your enemy." That way, Jesus' counterpoint makes even more sense: "But I say to you, treat your enemy like your friend." Inerrantists must find a problem here, since scripture does not actually read as Matthew says it does. But no one else has any difficulty: it is all explained very naturally.

The Perils of Piety (6:1-18)

Some might detect a contradiction between Matthew 6:1 and 5:16. After all, does not Jesus tell us to let the light of our good deeds be shed abroad? And does he not also tell us to avoid practicing our pious acts before others, hoping they will see them and think well of us? I see no contradiction here. Matthew 5:16 is telling you to be bold in well-doing, not to hide your light under a bushel basket. If you have help and guidance you would give to those who need it, then God wants you to do it. Be a faithful steward of the gifts and opportunities he has given you. As the parallel analogy with tangy salt implies, the point is "use it or lose it." If you let God's gifts lie fallow, no one is benefiting, and you are no different from the person with no gifts to put to use. And it will be your fault. Instead, live the kind of life that people will observe and say "Thank God for people like that!" God is getting the glory. It is not so in 6:1. The concern there is to resist the temptation to bask in the admiration of others; otherwise you will soon be doing your good deeds simply to receive the nodding approval of an audience. In addition, Matthew 6 seems more concerned with specifically pious, i.e., religious, actions, not about practical help to the poor and the sick, etc. And yet there is a problem with taking this section as inerrant and infallible moral teaching. The motivation all the way through, as Walter Kaufmann[241] pointed out, is "enlightened self-interest." The question Jesus poses is that of a shrewd calculus: whose approbation is worth more? Should I practice religion before other people whose admiration will stroke my ego in the short run? Or should I make that impossible by restricting my performance to a private venue, a command performance for God's eyes only? In that case, he will reward me, and to a much greater extent! It's not a tough choice! Closet, here I come!   Are   you   watching,   God?

Here we have a great example of what Kant called a hypothetical imperative versus a categorical imperative. In true piety, the soul seeks God for God's own sake, as the rabbis taught. It is the creature's duty to worship its creator. There can be no question of "reward;" to raise it is disgusting bad taste. Should I ask my wife to pay me for loving her? For Jesus or Matthew to suggest that it is a superior investment of one's time to do what will merit a heavenly reward reduces worship to a matter of financial management, investment strategy. It implies there is no absolute duty to serve God. But if one's goal is a heavenly reward, then worship might not be a bad strategy. None of this rises to the level of moral discourse. Fortunately, Jesus is elsewhere credited with a keen "Kantian" perspective, in Luke 17:7-10: one deserves no praise for merely doing what he should be blamed for *not* doing.

Verses 12, 14-15, propose a doctrine of forgiveness so radical that it cannot be reconciled with what we usually understand as Pauline soteriology. According to the latter, by faith one makes the transaction with God whereby Christ's atonement blots out one's sins. But here it is as easy as holding a grudge to forfeit salvation completely! This is an insecure ultra-Arminianism calculated to drive

---

[241] Walter Kaufmann, *The Faith of a Heretic* (Garden City: Doubleday Anchor, 1963), pp. 209-211.

the fearful soul to distraction. If God be for us, who can be against us? Who will bring charge against us? No one needs to, really; just get steamed at someone who did you wrong, and you have fallen from grace. That is some fragile salvation! Not that Paul says so; no, it is Matthew's Jesus who throws these scares into his flock, like a thunderclap causing the fearful sheep to bleat in terror.

The Lord's Prayer (or the Our Father) is offered as an example of simple, to-the-point prayer. Why chew the ear of the Almighty? "Your Father knows what you need before you ask" (6:8; cf., Rom. 8:27). But if the goal is to distinguish Christian prayer from formalistic synagogue prayers, the result is ironic. The Lord's Prayer is in fact quite close to a couple of those very prayers.

> Exalted and hallowed be his great name
> in the world which he created according to his will.
> May he rule his kingdom
> In your lifetime and in your days
> And in the lifetime of the whole house of Israel, speedily and soon.
> And to this, say: Amen.
>
> (The *Qaddish*)
>
> Lead me not into the power of transgression,
> And bring me not into the power of sin,
> And not into the power of iniquity,
> And not into the power of temptation,
> And not into the power of anything shameful.
>
> (an ancient evening prayer)[242]

Treasures of the Heart (6:19-34)

This passage urges that one not preoccupy oneself with worldly needs

---

[242] The text of both prayers comes from Joachim Jeremias, *The Lord's Prayer*. Trans. John Reuman. Facet Books, Biblical Series-8 (Philadelphia: Fortress Press, 1964), pp. 21, 30.

but instead focus on the work of God (piety? Moral living? Evangelism?). On the one hand, striving for worldly security can never provide it, since all is fleeting (an implicit parallel with the Buddhist doctrine of impermanence and suffering); on the other, God will take care of the one who is working for him to further heaven's ends. One might interpret the text very literally, as exhorting the reader to renounce secular employment. The popular (among scholars) Cynic hypothesis[243] understands the passage this way: the Cynics did renounce all social convention and lived as wandering mendicants, as Jesus is shown doing. But it is reasonable to read these verses as simply warning against worried preoccupation, the "cares of the world" (Matt. 13:22) that render the gospel seed barren. One may do one's work in the world the best one can, and leave it to God to see that there is enough.

Still, it seems impossible to evade the force of verses 19-21. We have tried our best to do so by pretending to ourselves that the text said, "Go ahead and heap up treasure on earth, so long as your heart is not tied to it."[244] But Jesus takes for granted the impossibility of thus dividing one's loyalties between God and Mammon, the Almighty Dollar. What he actually says is: *do not amass earthly treasures since your heart would inevitably be there.* Is there any Christian who admits this is the point and resolves to obey it and embrace voluntary poverty? Very few, I would guess. Nor do I blame them. It would be unreasonable to embrace voluntary poverty so long as one has dependants. Not greed but better judgment would compel us to "disobey" this call to gospel poverty. And in that case, is the text inerrant? Can we call it "sure and worthy of all acceptance" without

---

[243] F. Gerald Downing, *Cynics and Christian Origins* (Edinburgh: T&T Clark, 1992); Burton L. Mack, *A Myth of Innocence: Mark and Christian Origins* (Philadelphia: Fortress Press, 1988), pp. 67-69, 73-74; John Dominic Crossan, *The Historical Jesus: The Life of a Mediterranean Jewish Peasant* (New York: HarperOne, 1993) pp. 351, 421-422.

[244] Dietrich Bonhoeffer, *The Cost of Discipleship*. Trans. Reginald H. Fuller (New York: Macmillan, rev. ed., 1963), pp. 88-89.

whittling it down to what our non-inspired common sense tells us already?

Don't Knock Prayer (7:7-11)

Verses 7-9 make a promise. Is it a reliable one? Does every one who seeks good gifts from his heavenly Father receive them? Does every one who knocks gain admittance to his desired future? Does every single one who seeks eventually find? That is a pretty optimistic assurance. One's own experience, as well as one's casual observation of others' lives, easily provides enough counter-evidence to doubt these blithe assurances. If they are not borne out in experience, and they seem not to be, then one may rightly charge these verses with error, offering us erroneous teachings. The only alternative (the one uniformly taken) is obfuscation, redefining "find," "be opened," "receive," and "good things." The gospel reader defaults to Stoicism, a justification of God's seeming lack of fairness and justice, his neglect of prayers, by means of a "transvaluation of values" as Nietzsche called it. If the "good" does not happen to us, we back-pedal and say that the "good" is not to be measured by human standards. We may be consigned to Auschwitz and it will be an answer to our prayer for "good" to befall us because God wants to teach us some hard lessons "for our own good." (That is an extreme example, though a real one, as it did, after all, happen to plenty of pious people.) Ill fortune is face-savingly defined as "good fortune," a valuable opportunity to learn in the School of Hard Knocks, tuition-free. What matters is that God gets off the hook. God will answer your prayer, but, like the plastic Eight Ball, the answer may be "Ask again later." Or just "No." But that is certainly not what the confident urgings of verses 7-9 imply. We are willing to twist language beyond meaning to make these passages inerrant. Whatever it is they're saying, it's true!

Only a Few? (7:13-14)

In view of the billion-plus sincere Christians in the world today, what are we to make of Matthew 7:14? The more confident we are of our salvation, the less confidence can we have in this verse. It is like the initial projection of Jehovah's Witnesses back in the early period when they envisioned nothing like their eventual success; at first they said only 144, 000 would qualify for the heavenly paradise. Later they had to make special eschatological arrangements for the larger numbers. If this saying is infallible and inerrant, rather than a mere rhetorical ploy to prompt repentance, then an awful lot of good Christians are going to find that they were not introspective enough and somehow fell short of being the genuine article.

Wooden Nickels (7:15-23)

Verses 15-20 commit the genetic fallacy: you can spot false teachers by their failure to practice what they preach. Well, if all that means is that these prophets are "false" in the sense of not being true to their ideals, that's obvious to the point of superfluous redundancy. "You can spot a bachelor if he's unmarried." No kidding. Instead, the point would seem to be, "Feel free to reject what they say if they are hypocrites." But in fact there are very many cases of people teaching perfectly valid truths while personally they cannot seem to live up to them. If we are fans of such people we do not quote these verses. Rather we will quote Psalm 103:14, "He knoweth our frame, he remembereth that we are dust." And we may be right to do so. One may be a "false prophet" in the sense that he proves himself an unworthy vessel for the treasure he bears about. But it is simply not true that one who fails to live up to a good idea discredits that idea. I should say this text is in error.

I see Paulinist Christians between the lines of 7:22-23: they are eagerly standing in line at the Pearly Gates, sure that they will be admitted on the basis of their resumes of miracle-working and prophesying. But they are in for a nasty surprise when the bouncer tells them to get lost. Where did they go wrong? They had failed to obey the will of the Father because they neglected the least of these commandments; they are workers of *anomia*, "lawlessness." Thus the Sermon ends on the same note on which it began.

Uh, Weeping - and also Gnashing. Gnashing and Weeping.[245] *(8:5-13)*

Matthew commends the faith of a Roman centurion as superior to that of contemporary Jews. In view here is the rivalry between Matthew's (Syrian or Galilean) Jewish community and the Yavneh (Jamnia) Sanhedrin. These latter are the unbelieving Jews he has in mind, while the centurion stands for the Gentiles at whom the Great Commission aims (Matt. 28:19-20). Matthew's Jewish competitors will find themselves just as rudely surprised as the crestfallen Paulinists at the end of the Sermon. Both groups considered themselves entitled, which nobody is.

Luke's version of this Q passage depicts the anguish of those excluded from the heavenly banquet in their moment of realization in much the same terms: "There you will weep and gnash your teeth" (Luke 13:28). That was probably the original Q text. Matthew has altered it slightly but significantly: "the sons of the kingdom will be thrown into the outer darkness; there men will weep and gnash their teeth." Luke gives no hint of what happens to them next. Matthew has rephrased it so that the reprobate are consigned to a *place* characterized by "weeping and gnashing of teeth." Matthew decided he really liked this phrase and went on to insert it in several places, including parable interpretations. On this basis Matthew has introduced a good bit of hell-fire teaching into the gospel tradition.

Let It Rot (8:19-22)

This passage shows Jesus warning a would-be follower to reconsider his decision. The itinerant life is not an easy one: the son of man (i.e., humans), unlike birds and foxes, possesses no natural habitat

[245] Woody Allen, *Hannah and her Sisters*: "Yes, now - now that you mention it, uh, I-I-I have, uh, buzzing - and also ringing. Ringing and buzzing. Um, am I going deaf, or something?"

and wanders like Cain. Jesus throws cold water on the zeal of another who asks leave to see to his father's burial first. "Follow me, and let the dead bury their own dead." After we get past the initial thrill of Jesus saying something so radical, like a Zen slap, we are tempted to whittle the saying down to something tame that we can imagine obeying, but which no one would have bothered remembering Jesus saying. Or we may respect it enough not to eviscerate it, but then reject it as crazy. Consider the alternatives. In the former case, many harmonists have suggested that the would-be disciple means "I'll, er, be happy to follow you *someday*—after my father dies and is out of the way." Maybe years? Or perhaps he wants to wait till his father's body, already dead and laid out in a tomb, has decayed off the bones, which the son then wants to rebury in an ossuary, a formality not strictly required by Jewish custom. And then Jesus would be telling him not to waste time with such niceties but to get busy with something constructive for the living. Okay! Now that we've cut it down to size, and the saying presents no problem, we can say we believe it.

Otherwise, we see Jesus imperiously commanding the man to neglect the elementary social and familial duties of Judaism (see the Book of Tobit to see how important burial was). Now that's the thundering we might expect from a God-man! But do we think it would be right for us to do this? Not for a minute. We would not hesitate for a moment to brand a guru that said such a thing as a nefarious cult leader.

Looking at the substantial Cynic parallels,[246] we can understand that there was a context of meaning in which the saying could be understood. We can, then, believe our eyes. But then it becomes equally clear that whoever said this was no representative of the historic Jewish tradition.

Stilling the Storm (8:23-27)

Günther Bornkamm[247] uses the Stilling of the Storm passage to show the riches of the text which it becomes possible to discover once one

---

[246] For instance, a friend tactfully broached the question whether the old and ailing Diogenes had made any funeral plans, and the philosopher replied he had not. "The stench ought to get me buried quick enough!"

[247] Günther Bornkamm, "The Stilling of the Storm in Matthew." In

drops the blindfold of inerrantism and looks afresh at the text with lenses such as redaction criticism. Bornkamm calls attention to subtle editorial changes Matthew made in Mark. Notice that in Mark 4:38, the disciples (understandably) speak indignantly to Jesus, waking him up to help bail the boat: "Teacher, do you not care that we perish?" Matthew 8:25 has substituted the reverent language of Christian prayer: "Lord, save, we perish!" Mark 4:39 has Jesus stop the storm in its tracks, then ask rhetorically why the disciples were so upset. Didn't they trust a providential Father? Jesus did; hence he slept like a baby. But Matthew 8:26 has Jesus comment on their poor faith, *then* quiet the storm. Why? Apparently in order to make the story into a lesson about answered prayer. (We will see another example shortly.) In Mark the focus is on the divine power of Jesus. Matthew feels he can take that for granted, but he seeks to build the faith of his readers to venture confidently in prayer. But it didn't happen both ways. The disciples didn't say both "Don't you care? We're dying here!" and "Lord, save! We perish!" Jesus didn't rebuke their lack of faith, still the storm, and then repeat his rebuke of their faithlessness verbatim again afterward! Such is the preposterous "solution" inerrantism offers to the "problem" it created. We can imagine Jesus hearing this and asking, "What? Have you no common sense?"

Double the Demoniacs (8:28-34)

Matthew borrows the story of the Legion of demons from Mark. Too bad Gerasa is more than thirty miles away from the Sea of Galilee! Imagine the marathon pig race[248] to get there and drown! Some manuscripts read "Gadara" or "Gergesa," no doubt because various

---

Günther Bornkamm, Gerhard Barth, and Heinz Joachim Held, *Tradition and Interpretation in Matthew*. Trans. Percy Scott. New Testament Library (Philadelphia: Fortress Press, 1963), pp. 52-57.

[248] I used to live in Mount Olive, North Carolina. One year, attending the town's annual Pickle Festival, I watched a bunch of pigs racing round an enclosed track. Posted on the circular wall of the pig-o-drome were posterboards emblazoned with Bible verses. Were they intended to ward off demons who might have wanted to possess the piggies? I don't want to know!

scribes knew the geography and figured a previous scribe must have written the wrong name. But Gadara presents the same problem: it lies six miles from the Sea of Galilee. Gergesa is possibly to be identified with a ruined village called Kersa on the east coast of the sea, but this one lacks any precipice for the pigs to rush over.

Matthew has a peculiar propensity to double items that are single in Mark, Luke, and John. Matthew alone has Jesus heal, in effect, two Bartimaeuses and ride two donkeys into Jerusalem, and he has two men, not just one, walk on water, as we shall see. In the present case, Mark 5:2 and Luke 8:27 are both quite clear that a single demoniac met Jesus on shore. Why is it suddenly a *pair* of possessed men in Matthew? Is it possible he was working from Mark and somehow misconstrued Mark 5:10, "And he begged him not to send *them* out of the country," as if more than one demoniac (instead of more than one demon) was speaking? Who knows, but in any event, he certainly doubled the character. Some inerrantists swallow hard and say that it really happened this way, Matthew's way, with two demoniacs, and that Luke and Mark, knowing the same story, each zeroed in on his favorite demoniac, leaving the other aside.[249] Is this the best defense an inerrantist can offer?

Apostle Palsy (9:1-8)

The story of the healing of the paralytic serves in Mark 2:1-12 to impress the reader with the divine authority of Jesus. For Matthew, the issue is no longer whether Jesus had such authority, but whether the institution he founded (Matt. 16:18) has it. Mark 2:12 has the audience "amazed and [they] glorified God saying, 'We never saw anything like this!'" Matthew has changed it to, "they glorified God, who had given such authority *to men*," not just to Jesus. And not necessarily the authority to heal but to *forgive sins*. Here comes sacramental penance.

Identity Theft (9:9)

---

[249] Maybe Mark liked Legion better, while Luke had a greater affinity for Legion's sidekick, Beel-ze-Bill?

Mark 2:14 tells the story of a toll collector named Levi heeding Jesus' call to discipleship. Matthew's story is verbatim the same except for the name, Matthew. Notice that neither gospel, nor any other New Testament source, calls the character "Levi, surnamed Mathew" or "Levi who was also called Matthew." What we have is an editorial substitution of one name for another. Perhaps Matthew felt that a dramatic tale of discipleship like this should not be "wasted" on a minor character who did not wind up among the twelve. So much for the notion that the author of the present gospel was Matthew the tax-collector. Had the disciple Matthew (mentioned in Mark 3:18) authored the book, surely he would have known and told the story of his own call to discipleship rather than lifting another man's story from another gospel.

Twelve Times Two (9:18-26)

Mark combined two traditional healing stories, one about a woman with a menstrual problem of twelve years' duration, the other of the raising up of a comatose girl twelve years old. Heinz Joachim Held[250] shows how Matthew has made this double story, originally simply about the unbounded power of Jesus, into an encouragement to faithful prayer. In Mark 5:29 the old woman is healed as soon as she touches Jesus' prayer shawl. Jesus then congratulates her (5:34). But in Matthew 9:22, the healing comes *after* Jesus becomes telepathically aware of her faith and blesses her for it. Even so, Matthew avers, God answers the prayer of faith.

Two Blind Mice (9:27-31)

Matthew doubles the number of blind seekers in Mark 10:46-52. No one knows why. Could he possibly have read Mark's version and hastily concluded Mark was talking about two men: Bartimaeus *and* his father Timaeus?

---

[250] Heinz Joachim Held, "Matthew as Interpreter of the Miracle Stories." In Günther Bornkamm, Gerhard Barth, and Heinz Joachim Held, *Tradition and Interpretation in Matthew*. Trans. Percy Scott. New Testament Library (Philadelphia: Fortress Press, 1963) pp. 216, 240, 284-289.

Raised from the Deadline (10:1-23)

According to this mission charge, Christian missionaries are to avoid Gentiles and Samaritans. The commands here are clearly intended to govern Christian missionary practice for Matthew's readers/churches on a permanent basis, since it governs missionary practice up to the coming of the Son of Man (10:23).[251] And yet the Gospel of Matthew as a whole concludes with the Great Commission which commands a world mission, pointedly including "the nations," or Gentiles. Inerrantists seem reluctant to recognize the inconsistency for fear they would have to admit it denotes Matthean stupidity or ineptitude. Free of the hobgoblin of inerrancy, we can recognize a simple and natural explanation not available to the poor inerrantist. Chapter 10's mission charge stems from an earlier stage of the mission as the Matthean church defined it. Early on, they did not preach to Gentiles or Samaritans, perhaps expecting that God would miraculously bring them to faith in the Last Days (as per Isaiah 2:2-4; Micah 4:1-3).[252] They seem to have held the exclusivist policy of the Jerusalem elders (Acts 11:1-3) who reproached Peter for preaching to Gentiles.

But as policy changed to keep up with actual evangelistic practice, the Matthean community embraced the Gentile Mission and pictured the risen Jesus endorsing it (Matt. 28:19). The material in Chapter 10 was already sacred text, so, rather than rewrite it, Matthew allowed the Great Commission, placed at the end of the book (plus 24:14), to supersede and "update" it. Thus he made it look like the instructions in chapter 10 were intended only for a preliminary preaching junket to Jewish villages. This editorial move inadvertently created a glaring embarrassment, since it accidentally gives the impression Jesus thinks he will come in apocalyptic glory only a few weeks hence. It suggests the Second Coming would occur before the first was over!

---

[251] S.G.F. Brandon, *The Fall of Jerusalem and the Christian Church: A Study of the Effects of the Jewish Overthrow of A.D. 70 on Early Christianity* (London: SPCK, 1951), p. 175.

[252] Joachim Jeremias, *Jesus' Promise to the Nations*. Trans. S.H. Hooke. Franz Delitzsch Lectures for 1953. Studies in Biblical Theology No. 24 (London: SCM Press, 1967).

Hating and Loving Less (10:37)

Most scholars regard Matthew 10:37 as an amelioration of the shocking Q saying found in Luke 14:26: "Whoever comes to me and does not hate father and mother cannot be my disciple." I am inclined, however, to think that Matthew has correctly interpreted the original saying. It would be gratuitous and beside the point for Jesus to inculcate feelings of loathing and abomination toward one's family, especially if he also urged people to love their enemies. Surely the saying means to deal with the need for hard choices in a time of persecution; "hate" means exactly what its synonym does in Hebrews 12:2: "Looking to Jesus, the pioneer and perfecter of our faith, who for the joy that was set before him endured the cross, *despising* the shame, and is seated at the right hand of the throne of God."[253] Jesus did not exactly "hate" the treatment he was to endure, as if he cursed his fate every time he thought of it; rather, the writer to the Hebrews is saying that Jesus completely *disdained* the prospect of crucifixion, laughed in its face, would not let it frighten or dissuade him. In the second-century hagiography, *The Martyrdom of Perpetua and Felicitas*, a young mother (Perpetua) is condemned to the arena for the crime of being a Christian believer. On the eve of execution, her family visits her in jail with her newborn baby, begging her to recant and save her life, if only for her baby's sake. But she will not be moved and insists on going through with it. This is what Jesus is talking about. It is not that Perpetua had hostile feelings towards her family. ("Get the hell out of here, you bastards!") She just spurned their entreaties, focused on what seemed to her a higher goal. I am not sure that Matthew's rewriting the sentence ought to count as more than a translation choice, since he may have had an Aramaic original before him.

On Second Thought (11:2-19)

John languishes in Herod's fortress. Given the menu there, he probably looks back fondly to his old diet of roasted grasshoppers. One day his visiting disciples tell him of great miracles performed by

---

[253] See also 4 Macc. 1:9: "All of these, by despising sufferings that bring death, demonstrated that reason controls the emotions."

a man named Jesus. Some of the old light returns to John's red-rimmed eyes. His voice trembles. "Could this be the One? The One I predicted? Go ask him!" But wait a minute. Had not John already recognized and endorsed this man as the Coming One (Matt. 3:13-14)? The standard harmonization here is that John must first have been convinced of Jesus' messiahship and, in jail, he must have been counting the days till the Messiah Jesus should storm the walls of Herod's fortress and free his herald. But day after day passed, and John began to give up hope. A disillusioned Baptist lost faith in Jesus, despite the heavenly voice, etc. And now the news of his miracles reawakens hope.

But nowhere in the text is there the slightest hint of John's ever having previously had faith in Jesus, much less of it flagging, or of his faith in Jesus reawakening. Plainly the story here in chapter 11 does not presuppose the earlier baptism scene. We saw how Matthew appears to have rewritten the baptism episode to quiet the suspicions of those who found it troubling that John should have baptized Jesus at all. But Matthew simply did not think to alter this episode in order to make it consistent with the Jordan scene.[254]

Jesus gives a kind of eulogy in advance for the soon-to-be-slain John. "Truly, I say to you, among those born of women there has risen no one greater than John the Baptist; yet he who is least in the kingdom of heaven is greater than he" (11:11). I cannot help thinking this last clause was, already in the Q original, a subsequent "correction" to what went before it. Some nervous Christian realized that, if John were indeed the greatest of men, then he must be greater than Jesus himself, and that would not do. This was in fact the contention of the John the Baptist sect for decades afterward.

> And, behold, one of the disciples of John asserted that John was the Christ, and not Jesus, inasmuch as Jesus Himself declared that John was greater than all men and all prophets. "If then," said he, "he be greater than all, he must be held to be greater than Moses and than Jesus himself. But if he be the greatest of all, must he be the Christ." (Pseudo-Clementine *Recognitions*, Book I, 60:1-3)[255]

---

[254] Strauss, *Life of Jesus*, p. 222.
[255] Trans. Thomas Smith. Quoted in J. Louis Martyn, *The Gospel of John in Christian History: Essays for Interpreters* (Eugene: Wipf & Stock, 2004), p.

The wording of the Q saying makes sense only on such an understanding. The saying, without the "correction," must have originated among the sectarians of John the Baptist.

Another quizzical passage follows immediately: "From the days of John the Baptist until now the kingdom of heaven has suffered violence, and men of violence take it by force" (verse 12). For one thing, it seems to consider John a figure of the past, not of recent days.[256] For another, the notion of violent men trying to take the kingdom by force would seem to imply something like the exploits of revolutionary messiahs following the death of Herod the Great and during the war with Rome. What comment is being made about them? Not clear.[257]

Next comes another odd one: "For all the prophets and the law prophesied until John; and if you are willing to accept it, he is Elijah who is to come" (verses 13-14). John is made the goal of Old Testament prophecy, the fulfillment of Malachi 4:5-6, the very last prophecy in the Old Testament. This has nothing to do with any suspension or abrogation of the Torah, as if it applied only until his advent; rather, the point is that it all *pointed* to him,[258] a claim Christians would later make about Jesus. Thus the saying must have originated (like the one in the first half of verse 11) among the followers of the Baptist, a continuing rival to Christianity on into the second century (and quite possibly in the form of Mandaeanism still today).

Verses 18-19 ("For John came neither eating nor drinking, and they say, 'He has a demon. The Son of man came eating and drinking, and they say, 'Behold, a glutton and a drunkard, a friend of toll-collectors and sinners!'") might seem to belong better with Matthew 9:14 (or, earlier, in Mark 2:18, "Now John's disciples and

---

139.

[256] Eisler, *Messiah Jesus*, pp. 224, 258-259.

[257] S.G.F. Brandon, *Jesus and the Zealots: A Study of the Political Factor in Primitive Christianity* (New York: Scribners, 1967), pp. 78, 200, 300-301; Oscar Cullmann, *The State in the New Testament* (New York: Scribners, 1956), pp. 20-21; Cullmann, *Jesus and the Revolutionaries*. Trans. Gareth Putnam (New York: Harper & Row, 1970), pp. 35-36.

[258] Hugh J. Schonfield, *The Authentic New Testament*. A Mentor Religious Classic (New York: New American Library, 1958), p. 104.

the Pharisees were fasting; and people came and said to him, 'Why do John's disciples and the disciples of the Pharisees fast, but your disciples do not fast?'")

Anti-Intellectualism (11:25-26)

Jesus' words in verses 25-26, "I thank thee, Father, Lord of heaven and earth, that thou hast hidden these things from the wise and understanding and revealed them to babes; yes, Father, for such was thy gracious will," are closely parallel to 1 Corinthians 1:20-29 27. Both say that God was pleased with the irony of sharing the truth with the simple folk, concealing it from the "wise."

Verse 27a, "All things have been delivered to me by my Father: and no one knows the Son, except the Father," anticipates Jesus' (Matthew's) words following Peter's confession: "Blessed are you, Simon bar-Jona! For flesh and blood has not revealed it to you, but my Father who is in heaven" (Matt. 16:17).

He Seems to Be a Preacher of Foreign Divinities" (11:27)

"And no one knows the Father except the Son, and anyone to whom the Son chooses to reveal him" (verse 27b). This saying sounds more Marcionite than anything else. Moses didn't know God? Deuteronomy 34:10 sure gives the impression they were pals. Did Isaiah, Jeremiah, Abraham, and Job not know God? The Old Testament and Judaism believed they did. But Marcion taught that Jesus' Father was not the God of Israel, and that he remained unknown till Jesus came to reveal him. It doesn't really fit here, because it must be a contribution from the Paulinist faction.

Jesus Quotes Jesus (11:28-30)

Rest assured, however, we are back to Jewish scribalism in the very next verse. One of the favorite verses in the New Testament for devout meditation is Matthew 11:28-30: "Come to me, all who labor and are heavy-laden, and I will give you rest. Take my yoke upon you, and learn from me; for I am gentle and lowly in heart: and you will find rest for your souls. For my yoke is easy, and my burden is light." Here Matthew has appropriated a passage from The Wisdom of Jesus son of Sirach (Ecclesiasticus) and put it on the lips of Jesus Christ.

> Draw near to me, you who are untaught,
> and lodge in my school.
> Why do you say you are lacking in these things,
> and why are your souls very thirsty?
> I opened my mouth and said,
> "Get these things for yourselves without money.
>
> Put your neck under the yoke,
> and let your souls receive instruction;
> it is to be found close by.
>
> See with your eyes that I have labored little
> and found for myself much rest."
>
> (Sirach 51:23-27)

Gleaning Scripture (12:1-8)

These verses add to Mark's original a second scriptural precedent (Num. 28:9-10) for the disciples' right to glean grain on the Sabbath, as well as a quote from Hosea 6:6. The point (as already in Mark) is to show that Jesus' supposed indifference to the Torah is nothing of the kind. If he did not recognize the authority of scripture, he would not be offering counter-arguments from it.

Binding Beelzebul (12:22-32)

Matthew and Luke found the Beelzebul Controversy (Matt. 12:22-33, Luke 11:14-22) in the Q source. But there is also a Markan version (3:22-30). Both versions seem to have slightly elaborated a common (pre-Markan and pre-Q) original. Both Mark and Q have added rhetorical questions. Q (according to Matthew) adds "And if I cast out demons by Beelzebul, by whom do your sons cast them out? Therefore, they shall be your judges. But if it is by the Spirit of God that I cast out demons, then the kingdom of God has come upon you" (verses 27-28). Luke has "finger" instead of "Spirit," and Luke, as elsewhere, probably preserves Q's original wording. Mark adds "How can Satan cast out Satan?" (Mark 3:23). Both Q's and Mark's additions seek to "correct" an earlier version in which Jesus did not refute and mock the notion of using Satan's power to cast out demons but rather *affirmed and defended* the practice. How can you ransack a strong man's house unless you tie him up securely first? Once you do, it's open season. Thus exorcists bind the devil to their service and force him to yield up his captives. Why not? But this was the work of magicians (another term for faith-healers), and second-generation Christians attributed Jesus' spiritual authority to his being God's Son, not to magical techniques. Thus Mark and Q, each in his own way, spin the passage. The Q version inserts a midrash, a rewritten Jesus version of Exodus 8:18-19, where Pharaoh's magicians admit defeat in their miracle contest with Moses. He has them out-gunned: "This is the finger of God." See? Mere magic wouldn't be enough to do what Jesus (like Moses) does.

Third Day or Three Days? (12:40)

Matthew seems to have added to the traditional "Sign of Jonah" saying a typological explanation, implying that the resurrection of Jesus will fulfill the sign of Jonah's deliverance from the fish's gullet. Matthew gives the duration of Jesus' being dead as a full three days and three nights. This is odd since elsewhere we read of Jesus coming back to life "on the third day" (Matt. 17:23; 20:19; Mark 9:31; 10:34; 16:2; Luke 9:22; 18:33; 24:7, 21, 46) or "after three days" (Matt. 27:63; Mark 8:31). Of course, Matthew derived the variant figure from Jonah, from whence he quotes it. But it does not match the chronology elsewhere, even in his own gospel. But Matthew does have something special in mind here. By having Jesus explain how the enigmatic sign of Jonah anticipates his own coming burial and resurrection, Matthew creates a scene in which Jesus publicly predicts, *in the presence of his enemies*, that he will rise from the dead. Matthew will need this once he gets to chapter 27, where he has the Sanhedrinists warn Pilate of a possible resurrection hoax: "Sir, we remember how that impostor said, while he was still alive, 'After three days, I will rise again.'" (verse 63). When did he say that? Right here in Matthew 12:40.

Royal Family (12:46-50)

Mark 3:20-21, 31-35 had Jesus' relatives arrive to take custody of him for his own good. He had, they thought, gone off the deep end. And Jesus, realizing this, refused to meet with them, preferring the company of his devoted hearers. Matthew 12:46-50 preserves enough of the scene to keep it awkward, but he has omitted the occasion for the visit. No more do we hear that his relatives thought him insane. Why this change? Simply because, unlike Mark, Matthew had included a Nativity story. Once having experienced such events, it seemed impossible that Mary and the others could ever think anything Jesus did was crazy.[259] So why did they come? Maybe to bring him some manna sandwiches?

Parable Marathon (chapter 13)

Mark had devoted a whole chapter, 4, to a collection of Jesus' parables. Matthew greatly expanded it. In Mark, Jesus says his parables are designed to veil the truth from the unworthy, but in Matthew he says that misunderstanding is an unfortunate by-product of the method. Mark had Jesus say he used parables "*in order* [Greek: *hoti*] that they may indeed see but not perceive," etc. Matthew changes that crucial conjunction from *hoti* to *hina* ("so that"). Mark had Jesus trying to make sure the wrong people did not understand him, while Matthew has Jesus use parables with the unfortunate result that the thick-headed will not get it.

Born Too Soon! (13:16-17)

Despite what I said about Matthew's use of the ancient *pesher* method of interpreting scripture in his "formula quotations," verses 16-17 ("But blessed are your eyes, for they see; and your ears, for they hear. For truly I say unto you, that many prophets and righteous men

---

[259] Strauss, *Life of Jesus*, p. 394.

desired to see the things you see, and did not see them, and to hear the things you hear, and did not hear them") seem to introduce the traditional Christian "proof from prophecy," assuming that there were many clearly messianic prophecies that anyone should have recognized as coming true in the events of Jesus' ministry. It does not say the ancient prophets and saints were ignorant of God's plans for the future. No, just the reverse. It was precisely because they *did* know what to expect that they were sorry they would not live to see it happening in the flesh. This is why Simeon, local Jerusalem prophet, rejoiced that, an old man, he had just managed to live long enough to see the Messiah Jesus, whom he knew was coming (Luke 2:25-32). To the degree that Matthew did view prophecy in this sense of clairvoyant predictions by Old Testament seers, he fully invites the scathing scorn of Joseph Wheless (see above at 1:22-23).

Day of the Triffids (13:24-30, 36-43)

Farmer Smith seems to have snuck into Farmer Jones's newly-planted wheat field and sprinkled seeds of the darnel plant in the same rows.[260] When the plants begin to push up through the soil, the farmhands notice something odd and report back to their boss, who concludes, "An enemy has done this." Very likely, this refers to Paul, sometimes called "the Enemy" by Jewish Christians.[261] The tares are his converts, fake Christians, imagined as antinomian radicals. In view is the mixed character of the Antiochene church, which contained Paulinist, Petrinist, and Jamesian factions.[262] Should the Torah-Christians try to "purify" the congregation of the Pauline heretics? No, the parable wisely says: the resulting schism would do more harm than good. The stirred-up strife would probably destroy the church. Best leave it to God (cf., 1 Cor. 4:1-5).

Let Goods and Kindling Go,

---

[260] Dale Gribble did pretty much the same thing to his neighbor Hank Hill's front lawn in an episode of *King of the Hill*.

[261] Barth, "Matthew's Understanding," p. 160; Hans-Joachim Schoeps, *Jewish Christianity: Factional Disputes in the Early Church*. Trans. Douglas R.A. Hare (Philadelphia: Fortress Press, 1969), pp. 50-51.

[262] Price, "Antioch's Aftershocks," p. 238.

This Mortal Life Also (13:49-50)

Matthew seems to have added his own interpretation (Matt. 13:49-50) to the parable of the Dragnet (Matt. 13:47-48). Note how poorly the hell-fire business fits the fate of the rejected fish in the parable: while the fish are set free, the reprobate are consigned to a fiery hell. Verses 42 and 50 are two instances of Matthew taking the phrase "weeping and gnashing of teeth" from the Q saying also underlying Luke 13:28 and using it to describe in glowing colors a hell of torment.

Collection, Not a Colloquium

Like the Sermon on the Mount (chapters 5-7) and the Missionary Discourse (chapter 10), this parable chapter (13:1-52) was not, as Matthew says, a transcription of what Jesus said on a single occasion. Nor does it matter to Matthew. It is merely part of the narrative frame for the teaching. The fact of the fivefold discourse arrangement makes it clear what he was really getting at. But strict inerrantism cannot afford to recognize so simple a thing because, "If Matthew *said* Jesus wrapped up his speech and left, then, by God, that's the way it happened!"

Just for That—No Healing for You! (13:53-58)

Note the cosmetic changes from Mark's original (Mark 6:1-6): Mark had Jesus astonished at the stubborn unbelief of his former townsmen. Matthew gives no hint of this. Safeguarding a higher Christology than Mark's, Matthew thinks it untoward to imagine Jesus not having anticipated the outcome, so he omits Mark's comment. And, whereas for Mark Jesus' ability to heal appears *limited by* their lack of faith ("he *could do* no miracles there"), for Matthew the lack of miracle healings was a *punishment for* their lack of faith: "he *did* no mighty works there." Matthew's Jesus, unlike Mark's, is sovereign. He could heal the devil himself if he so desired, but he does not deign to heal unbelievers.

The Headless Ghost (14:1-12)

Mark 6:14-29 depicted Herod Antipas as essentially forced to arrest John the Baptizer since, as Machiavelli would have assured him, he could not afford to have a champion of the people continue to condemn him publicly. But he knew John was right: he should never have sent his wife packing so he could marry his brother's wife instead. And he was afraid to lay hands further on the man of God. In fact, he often sought his counsel in the depths of his fortress. Seeing this, his new wife, Herodias, knew the only path to settling her score with the prophet who had so publicly shamed her was to trap Herod into doing her will by attacking him at his weakest point, his lust. So she has her daughter dance before Antipas and his drunken guests. Pleased with the spectacle, the tetrarch swears to grant any request she may make. Herodias tells her to demand the execution of John. Cheated out of her choice of a prize, the girl Salome acquiesces, and Herod finds himself outmaneuvered. But to hear Matthew tell it, Herod himself wanted the Baptist dead but feared public outcry, perhaps revolt. This is why Herodias has to intervene and choreographs the death. Matthew thus makes Herodias into even more of a New Testament Jezebel, supplying the evil backbone her royal husband lacked.

Forgotten Flashback (14:13-21)

Matthew has lost track of his own story, having forgotten that the episode of John's death was a flashback told retrospectively to explain why Herod, hearing of Jesus, feared him to be the risen John the Baptist, perhaps returning for revenge. Matthew goes back and tells the story of John's martyrdom, then picks up his narrative from that point, John's disciples telling Jesus about it, and Jesus departing for less dangerous climes, as if it were all happening in the narrative present.

Bear but a Touch of my Hand There
And You Shall Be Upheld in More than This (14:28-33)

166

Mark 6:45-53 and John 6:16-21 tell the story of Jesus walking on the water. But, as Heinz Joachim Held[263] again points out, Matthew 14:22-33 elaborates the story to make it into a lesson in answered prayer. This time he adds considerably to the original story, and the effect is splendid. Peter, still afraid that Jesus is a bodiless ghost despite Jesus' reassurances otherwise, asks for proof. He knows that he himself is no insubstantial phantom, so if Jesus can cause *him* to defy gravity, too, that will show Jesus need not be a ghost either. It works. But then Peter comes to his senses, realizes where he is and just what he is doing, and gravity reclaims him. Here he stands for every Christian, in danger of sinking into the stormy waters of temptation, but immune so long as he keeps focused on his Lord (Hebrews 12:1c-2a: "Let us run with perseverance the race that is set before us, looking to Jesus, the pioneer and perfecter of our faith."). But should our eyes wander and come to rest on the trials that plague us, we will sink. Nonetheless, it is not too late, for Jesus condescends to rescue even the faltering and the faithless. The closing acclamation of the disciples in the boat is no longer "utter astonishment" as in Mark 6:51, but rather worshipful Christological confession (Matt. 14:33), a cue to Matthew's readers.

And all this means that Matthew created this portion of the story. Or very possibly he borrowed it from a Buddhist original in which a disciple of the Buddha, afraid he will miss his Lord's discourse, walks cross-country, including an intervening lake. As long as he meditates upon the Buddha, he speeds along on the surface, but if his thoughts wander just for a second, he begins to sink.[264] If the one version is not historical fact, why should the other be? And if Peter's stroll on the waves had happened, is there any chance not one but both of the other evangelists who tell of Jesus' walking on the waves would have omitted it?

This is one of the places where we can see Peter's[265] character going up and down like a yo-yo. If you look closely, you notice that 14:28-29 say that Peter did successfully make it across the water to join Jesus. That must have been the extent of the original expansion of the Markan original. It glorifies Peter by having him repeat Jesus'

---

[263] Held, "Matthew as Interpreter," pp. 204-205.
[264] Michael Lockwood, ed., *Buddhism's Relation to Christianity: A Miscellaneous Anthology with Occasional Comment* (Tambaram, Chennai: Tambaram Research Associates, 2010), p. 41.
[265] Nau, *Peter in Matthew*, pp. 100-104.

own feat. This version must be the contribution of the pro-Peter redactor who wanted to rehabilitate the impression left by Mark that Peter was a thick-headed bumbler unworthy of respect. But a subsequent redactor from the James party (I should think the evangelist "Matthew" himself) has taken Peter back down a peg by having him sink, like Wile E. Coyote, beneath the waves as soon as he realizes nothing is holding him up.

From Foundation Stone to Stumbling Block in Ten Seconds (16:17-23)

Whereas Mark 8:27 has Jesus ask, "Who do men say that I am?" Matthew 16:13 alters it to "Who do men say that *the son of man is?*" The meaning is the same, but the inerrantist must account for the difference: which did Jesus say? Not both. The rest of us can recognize editorial license when we see it.

Most important, though, is the way the confession of Peter has grown in the telling. In fact, it is different in every gospel, implying that each evangelist wanted to use Peter as the apostolic mouthpiece for his own Christology. For Mark (8:29), Jesus is the Christ. For Luke (9:20) he is the Christ of God, for John (6:69) the Holy One of God. But for Matthew, a messianic mouthful: "Thou art the Christ, the Son of the living God." Thomas (saying 13) admits he cannot put the truth about Jesus into words. Which did Peter say? Matthew's version, which the other evangelists then trimmed down? That seems a bit unlikely. On the other hand, we have seen Matthew improving on Mark's Christology at various points. No doubt he has done so again here.

Beyond this, we must ask, if Jesus really handed Peter pontifical authority as he does here, how the other evangelists just happened to miss it. As the Gospel of Matthew seems to be based on Mark, it becomes clear that a Matthean scribe/redactor has augmented Mark's account so as to beef up the clout of the Antiochene church which boasts Peter as its founder. So Peter's stock goes back up from its Markan low. My guess is that this elevation replaced Mark's Jesus denouncing Peter as Satan. The redactor would have omitted it. Peter looked good at this stage.

But then poor Peter is called Satan, the Adversary, after all! A subsequent redactor who favored James over Peter shot Peter back down by restoring Mark's Satan insult.[266] And Jesus' delegation to Peter of unique stewardship and authority, granted in Matthew 16:19, gets distributed among the twelve generally (or to congregations generally) only two chapters later in Matthew 18:18.[267] Ouch!

A Fish Story (17:24-27)

Peter is approached by men collecting the two-drachma tax for the upkeep of the Temple. Does Peter's rabbi Jesus pay it? (It was every Jewish male's duty though not actually required by law.) It looks as if the original story stopped with verse 26. Peter assumed Jesus planned to donate, but Jesus catches him up short with an analogy suggesting that God is like a king who taxes his subjects but not his family, who are exempt. Jews worshipping King God in his palace, the Temple, are his subjects and thus owe the tax. But Jesus and his disciples are God's children and, by rights, need not pay it. Nonetheless, why make unnecessary trouble? Jesus tells Peter to pay it for both of them anyway. The issue here for the Torah-keeping Jewish Christians of Antioch is that of relations with the Yavneh rabbis.[268] The Matthean leaders, including our evangelist, regard themselves as the true heirs to Jewish leadership (Matt.21:43; Mark 12:9) but want to maintain their standing as loyal Jews (Matt. 23:1-3).

    The predicted miracle of finding four drachmas to pay the tax is impossible, not simply because Jesus seems to know the future in an effortless, magical manner, but because no fish, once hooked, could retain a coin in its mouth. Besides, the money-mouthed carp loans Peter only enough money to cover Jesus and Peter; what about the other eleven disciples? The story focuses on Jesus and Peter in the manner of medieval tales of the pair as a kind of first-century Hope-and-Crosby team.[269]

---

[266] Nau, *Peter in Matthew*, pp. 108-114.

[267] Nau, *Peter in Matthew*, pp. 112.

[268] J. Andrew Overman, *Matthew's Gospel and Formative Judaism: The Social World of the Matthean Community* (Minneapolis: Fortress Press, 1990), pp. 145-146.

[269] A.S. Rappoport, *Medieval Legends of Christ* (London: Ivor Nicholson and Watson, 1934), Chapter VII, "The Wanderings of Christ on Earth," pp. 142-174.

We Are Poor Little Lambs Who Have Lost our Way (18:12-14)

The parable of the Lost Sheep, shared with Luke 15:3-7, comes from Q, where it had no narrative context. Luke applies it to Jesus' outreach to sinners for whom most religious folks had given up hope. But Matthew applies it to matters of congregational life.[270] If any of the brethren should go astray or backslide, let the church leaders seek him out, show concern, and try to win him back. The next verses (15-20) further apply the parable to congregational discipline, how to mediate disputes between members of the brotherhood (rather than taking a fellow Christian to small claims court before unbelievers; cf., 1 Cor. 6:1-6). The shepherd looking for the straying sheep here stands for the offended person trying to settle with, and so reconcile with, the offender. The three-step process stipulated in these verses is reminiscent of the procedure prescribed in the Dead Sea Scrolls and seems to presuppose the same sort of monastic living situation:

> When anyone has a charge against his neighbour, he is to prosecute it truthfully, humbly and humanely. He is not to speak to him angrily or querulously or arrogantly or in any wicked mood. He is not to bear hatred [towards him in the inner recesses] of his heart. When he has a charge against him, he is to proffer it then and there [on the selfsame day] and not render himself liable to penalty by nursing a grudge... Furthermore, no man is to bring a charge publicly against his neighbour except he prove it by witness. (*Manual of Discipline*)

If the alleged offender refuses to come clean and make restitution, he must be excommunicated: "let him be to you as a Gentile and a tax-collector." This sounds odd given Jesus' own policy of freely associating with sinners and toll-collectors in order to win them to repentance, but I suppose the three steps before excommunication correspond to Jesus' efforts among the sinners. Anyway, the ejection

---

[270] Joachim Jeremias, *The Parables of Jesus*. Trans. S.H. Hooke (New York: Scribners, 1972), pp. 38-40.

from the fellowship is effected by the mysterious presence of the risen Jesus:

> Truly, I say to you, whatever you bind on earth shall be bound in heaven, and whatever you loose on earth shall be loosed in heaven. Again I say to you, if two of you agree on earth about anything they ask, it will be done for them by my Father in heaven. For where two or three are gathered in my name, there am I in the midst of them. (Matt. 18:18-20)

First Corinthians 5:3-5 mandates the very same procedure, only Paul's hovering presence is to be invoked alongside Jesus'.

> For though absent in body I am present in spirit, and as if present, I have already pronounced judgment in the name of the Lord Jesus on the man who has done such a thing. When you are assembled, and my spirit is present, with the power of our Lord Jesus, you are to deliver this man to Satan for the destruction of the flesh, that his spirit may be saved in the day of the Lord Jesus.

The conceptuality is present also in Judaism, where we read that "If two sit together, and words of Torah [are spoken] between them, the Shekinah rests between them." (Rabbi Hananiah ben Teradion, d. 135, in *Pirke Aboth* 3, 2)

It must be noted that, for what it may be worth, the premise of the parable is absurd; no shepherd would risk the ninety-nine's safety to recover a single stray. This implies the creator of the parable was not a rural dweller and knew nothing of shepherding.

Grace under the Gun (18-21-35)

The parable of the Unforgiving Slave makes a point similar to that in 1 John 4:20-21,

> If any one says, "I love God," and hates his brother, he is a liar; for he who does not love his brother whom he has seen, cannot love God whom he has not seen. And this

commandment we have from him, that he who loves God should love his brother also.

God, a mighty Being of infinite majesty, has condescended to cancel your crushing debt of sin and guilt; and *you* are going to be more high and mighty than *him?* Come *off* it!

It does not seem to occur to Matthew that it might be difficult to forgive (or to do anything else) freely, genuinely, "from the heart"—under the Damoclean Sword of damnation threats! One may be pathetically cowed into pretending one has let go all feelings of bitterness, but the duress under which one tries it will forever torment him: does he really mean it? *Can* he? Because if he doesn't forgive "from his heart," the torturers have a rack waiting for him! The parable poisons the motives it seeks clumsily to inculcate.[271]

Well, on Second Thought... (19:9)

Matthew has amended what he took to be the Markan divorce prohibition[272] (Mark 10:11-12), in effect placing Jesus on the side of

---

[271] Paul Watzlawick, *How Real Is Real? Confusion, Disinformation, Communication: An Anecdotal Introduction to Communications Theory* (New York: Random House/Vintage Books, 1976), p. 19, calls this "the 'Be Spontaneous' Paradox." "It occurs whenever somebody demands of another person behavior that by its very nature must be spontaneous but now cannot be because it has been demanded."

[272] Martin Dibelius, *The Sermon on the Mount* (New York: Scribner's, 1940), relates how the sayings of Jesus, originally offered as radical insights on the human condition, become, in the Christian community, a reified scripture of "new Law": "all commandments of Jesus handed down to the communities assume the character of a testament. The Christians feel that Christ has instructed them to live in accordance with these sayings. They are not any longer proclamations of the will of God in all its radicalism; they become rules of conduct for the life within the communities and are adapted to the conditions of this life. They are no longer single sayings spoken at different occasions and to different people. They are brought together and codified to form systems of ordinances like the new law of the Sermon on the Mount" (p. 88).

the strict Rabbi Shammai in the ancient debate. Matthew adds the phrase *mē epi porneia*, i.e., divorce is without valid pretext *except for prostitution* (or immorality, or consanguineous marriage, or whatever "*porneia*" meant to him). The inerrantist must admit that Matthew has "erred" by saying that Jesus said something he actually did not say. But anyone else will recognize that Matthew did not so view it. For him, it was just that the sacred text of the community required amendment in light of tragic experience, so he amended it. It was a question of law, not of history.

Only in Matthew does Jesus go on to command celibacy for those who can stand it (19:10-12).

The Rich Young Ruler (19:16-22)

Just as Matthew took pains to banish any suspicion that Jesus had gotten in line to be baptized for the same reason most people did, to confess his sins and repent (3:13-15), so he rewrites the account of the Rich Young Ruler from Mark 10:17-22 in order to erase Jesus' declining the flattery of the inquirer. In Mark, the man had addressed Jesus as "Good teacher," then asked, "What good deed must I do to inherit eternal life?" Jesus caught him up short: "Why do you call me 'good'? No one is good but God only." For Matthew such humility is heretical, since Jesus certainly *was* good and in some way he might even be God ("God with us," 1:23). So for Matthew Jesus must say, "Why *do you ask me concerning* the Good," meaning by "the Good" the Torah whose commands he then begins to enumerate. And Matthew's point is that one cannot isolate any single commandment as the requirement for salvation. The Law is indivisible, as in James 2:10-11.[273] And the result is that Matthew's Jesus denies neither being good nor being God.

But did the historical Jesus say this? Of course not. He cannot have said both versions on the same occasion, and Mark, followed by Luke 18:18-25, has preserved the original. Was Matthew, then, trying to perpetrate a hoax, like the forger of the Hitler Diaries?

---

[273] O. Lamar Cope, *Matthew: A Scribe Trained for the Kingdom of Heaven.* Catholic Biblical Quarterly Monograph Series 5 (Washington, D.C.: Catholic Biblical Association of America, 1976), pp. 111-119.

Obviously not. He did not see it as correcting or distorting history, only as improving a sacred story. And, by the way, he noticed that, though Mark depicted Jesus as beginning to list the Ten Commandments, he had included one not on the official list, "Do not defraud." Matthew omits it from his version.

Matthew plugs in a Q saying at this point that Luke inserted into a very different context, 22:28-30. In Matthew it is a fitting reward for the disciples having abandoned everything to follow him. "Truly, I say to you, in the regeneration, when the Son of man shall sit on his glorious throne, you who have followed me will also sit on twelve thrones, judging the twelve tribes of Israel" (Matt. 19:28). Matthew's version is more specific than Luke's. Matthew counts twelve thrones for twelve disciples to govern twelve tribes; Luke does not specify the number of thrones, though he has Jesus speaking to the same disciples. Luke may have omitted the number twelve so as to deny one to the traitor Judas. Or Matthew may have *added* "twelve" to restrict to the disciples a statement originally addressed to Christians in general (cf., 1 Cor. 6:2-3; 2 Tim. 2:11; Rev. 2:26-27). Want to have a séance and ask him?

.

What Would Caesar Chavez Do? (20:1-16)

The parable of the Laborers in the Vineyard is usually understood as defending, against Pharisaic disapproval, Jesus' promising repentant sinners the same reward as the long-time righteous.[274] That makes sense except that it seems odd to picture Pharisees complaining about sinners repenting (though Jonah sure did!). Another possibility is that the parable means to defend the extension of salvation to the late-comer Gentile converts from paganism. Yes, Jews have been faithful to God for many centuries, but that is no reason to begrudge the late-in-the-day inclusion of Gentile believers. All are equal in God's eyes, so why not in ours?

This parable bears a striking resemblance to a rabbinic parable and may be a new version of it. This would hardly be surprising given Matthew's Jewish context. The rabbinic version takes the form of a eulogy for a brilliant Torah scholar who died very young.

---

[274] Jeremias, *Parables*, p. 38.

whom shall I liken Rabbi Bon, son of Chaija? To a king that hath hired laborers, among whom was one of great power. This man did the king summon to himself, and held speech with him. And when the night fell, the hired labourours came to receive their hire. But the king gave to the favoured labourer the same hire which he had given unto others. Then they murmured and said, "We have laboured the whole day, and this man hath labored but two hours, yet there is given unto him the same wages that we have received." And the king sent them away, saying: "This man hath done more in two hours than ye have done in the whole of the day." Even so hath the Rabbi Bon done more in the study of the Law in the twenty-eight years of his life than another would have done who had lived in a hundred years. (*Beracoth* 5.3c)

Stage Mother (20:20-21)

Matthew tries to improve the image of James and John, sons of Zebedee, from Mark 10:35-37, where they are depicted as trying to secure first dibs on the catbird seats on Jesus' dais. Matthew has the lads' *mother* make the request, leaving us to imagine the brothers embarrassed in the background: "Mom!"

Two More Blind Mice (20:29-34)

Why re-tell Matthew? 9:27-31?

Double Dumb Ass on (or under) You (21:1-11)

Hebrew poetry, while it could rhyme, more often employed parallelism: saying a thing, then paraphrasing it or contrasting it with its opposite. The effect is quite beautiful, as any glance at the Psalms will reveal. While later rabbis understood this and even wrote new verse of their own in the old style, they treated *biblical* poetry in a

175

literalistic and prosaic manner, as a technique for multiplying information from the text.[275] Matthew's doubling of the donkeys in 21:17 is a perfect example. He no longer allows this quote from Zechariah 9:9 to use parallelism but insists on taking it literally—with ludicrous results. John 12:15, too, quotes the passage, but without the doubling. John further says (12:16) that no one at the time realized they were witnessing the messianic Parousia in Jerusalem. Yet, like Luke 19:38 and Matthew 21:9, John phrases the acclamation of the crowd as if they are welcoming the anointed king (John 12:13). Only Mark 11:9-11 has them welcome Jesus among the pilgrim throng and hail the impending Messianic kingdom—with no hint that Jesus is the king. Nor do Matthew, Luke, and John agree in their wording, implying all were dissatisfied with Mark's non-messianic original and could not resist messianizing the scene, though each in his own way. It is literature, not history.

The Accursed Tree (21:18-22)

Mark 11:12-14, 20-21 has Jesus curse the bare tree, but it does not immediately wither up. Instead, the next day the disciples notice it is dead. Matthew 21:18-19 has the tree shrivel up on the spot. Why? The answer is no doubt a matter of literary preference: Matthew favored the power of a direct, one-shot miracle, leaving no doubt. By contrast, Mark, by leaving the actual withering off stage and at some undetermined time, creates the suspense and ambiguity that are basic to mystified awe.[276] In Mark's version, there remains the possibility that Jesus' words were not the cause of the tree withering,

---

[275] James Kugel, *The Idea of Biblical Poetry: Parallelism and Its History* (Baltimore: Johns Hopkins University Press, 1998), Chapter 3, "Rabbinic Exegesis and the 'Forgetting' of Parallelism," pp. 96-134.

[276] Tzvetan Todorov, *The Fantastic: A Structuralist Approach to a Literary Genre.* Trans. Richard Howard (Ithaca: Cornell University Press, 1975), pp. 24-40. "The fantastic occupies the duration of this uncertainty. Once we choose one answer or the other, we leave the fantastic for a neighboring genre, the uncanny or the marvelous. The fantastic is that hesitation experienced by a person who knows only the laws of nature, confronting an apparently supernatural event" (p. 25).

since no one saw it happen. And yet it is too close for coincidence. The result is all the more eerie. Both versions are effective in different ways. But if it ever happened either way, it did not happen both ways.

Pipe Down, for Christ's Sake! (21:15-16)

Matthew describes the irritation of the Jerusalem scribes hearing young children acclaiming Jesus for his healings: "Hosanna to the Son of David!" They snap at him, "Do you hear what these are saying?" as if they expect Jesus will think it excessive. He doesn't. He replies with an out-of-context quote from Psalm 8:2. Luke, a moment earlier, during the Triumphal Entry, has something oddly similar despite its difference: "And some of the Pharisees in the multitude said to him, 'Teacher, rebuke your disciples.' He answered, "I tell you, if these were silent, the very stones would cry out" (Luke 19:39-40). I have to think there is some sort of ambiguous Q original lurking somewhere here, because of an underlying Hebrew pun on "sons" (*banim*) and "stones" (*abanim*),[277] the same pun occurring in Matthew3:9/Luke 3:8 ("God is able from these *stones* to raise up *children* to Abraham").

Prodigal Parallel? (21:28-32)

A parable about second-thought repentance defends Jesus' outreach to sinners, telling them it is by no means too late to return to God. One son says he will do the chore his father assigns him but goes to the movies or the race track instead. His brother openly defies their father at first but winds up thinking better of it and does his chores after all. It is the latter who does his father's will, not the former. The one who winds up obeying stands for repentant sinners rescued by Jesus, while the ultimately disobedient son must stand for ostensibly pious Jews who refuse to follow Jesus.[278] On the other hand, possibly it is pagan Gentiles who are in view in the first case, Jews who

---

[277] Schonfield, *Authentic New Testament*, p. 91.
[278] Jeremias, *Parables*, p. 80.

begrudge them in the second. In the latter case, the parable must have originated during the Gentile Mission.

Though the wording of this passage displays a clear Matthean signature mark, the favorite phrase "the will of [my] Father in heaven" (cf., Matt. 7:21 in contrast with the Q parallel at Luke 13:25-27), I suspect it was originally a Q parable that Luke has heavily rewritten as the parable of the Prodigal Son (Luke 15:11-32).

Dress for Success (22:1-14)

Matthew here appears to combine two independent parables, the longer being that of the Great Supper, a Q parable found in something closer to its original form over in Luke 14:26-34. I will defer discussion of it to my chapter on Luke, except to note the invited guests not only, to a man, decline but *kill* those who delivered the engraved invitations, whereupon the host of the supper becomes so furious that "he sent his armies, and destroyed those murderers, and burned their city"! Of course, in Matthew's version the banquet was the Marriage Supper of the Lamb, and the murderers are Jews who stood aloof to Jesus. The military assault on them is the destruction of Jerusalem in 70 C.E. All this is absent from Luke. Matthew did not think his rewrite through very carefully because, when he again takes up the Q original, the food is still hot on the table after an intervening military campaign!

The shorter parable is found in Matthew 22:2, 11-13a.[279] There is a wedding feast given by a king for his son. The guests *do* show up at this "fish and goose soiree,"[280] but attention focuses on one man (implicitly a party crasher) not appropriately dressed for the occasion.[281] He is accorded the bum's rush. This appears to be another version of a parable told by the great first-century Rabbi Johanan ben Zakkai.

---

[279] Jeremias, *Parables*, p. 65.

[280] Jack Torrance to Delbert Grady in *The Shining*.

[281] This reminds me of the time my pal Chuck Hoffman decided to show his disapproval of a friend's marriage by showing up to the wedding wearing a *Star Wars* T-shirt and an orange leisure suit!

It is like a king who invited his servants to a feast and did not specify a time for them. The astute ones among them adorned themselves and sat at the gate of the palace. They said, "There is no lack in the palace" [to delay the feast]. The foolish ones among them went to their work. They said, "There is no feast without preparation." Suddenly the king asked for his servants. The astute ones among them came into his presence as they were, adorned; and the foolish ones among them came into his presence as they were, dirty. The king was pleased with the astute ones and angry with the foolish ones. He said, "Let those who adorned themselves for the feast sit down and eat and drink. Let them who did not adorn themselves for the feast stand and look on." (*Shabb.* 153a).

The point is to "wear the garments" of repentance at every moment so as to be ready whenever either death or the Final Judgment arrives. When the Angel of Death or the Messiah suddenly appears, you don't want to be caught wearing your "Sex Olympics" T-shirt, like a student of mine wore to class one day. On the same theme, see also Matthew's parables of the Talents (25:14-30), the Bridesmaids (25:1-13), and the Sheep and Goats (25:3146).

To this, as to other parables (Matt. 13:41-42, 49-50; 24:51), Matthew has added the prospect of hell-fire or the equivalent.

Tirade against the Pharisees (chapter 23)

Matthew appears to have been written in the heat of sectarian competition between Matthew's Jewish Christian community and the post 70 C.E. Yavneh Judaism of Johanon ben Zakkai. Thus the lampooning we read in chapter 23 of Jewish honorific titles "Rabbi" (= Teacher, Master) and "Abba" (Father). Thus also the wrangling over the niceties of vows, tithing, etc. In the midst of this bitterness, it is sad but not surprising to discover this wholesale vilification of the Pharisees *en masse*. In fact, they were the most pious of Jews and showed real imagination in humanizing the application of the Law. Much of their supposed casuistry was a means of making the Torah less confining. Their own traditions contain savage satires of certain types of Pharisees, especially hypocrites and fanatics.

An ancient baraita enumerates seven classes of Pharisees, of which five consist of either eccentric fools or hypocrites: (1) "the shoulder Pharisee," who wears, as it were, his good actions ostentatiously upon his shoulder; (2) "the wait-a-little Pharisee," who ever says, "Wait a little, until I have performed the good act awaiting me"; (3) "the bruised Pharisee," who in order to avoid looking at a woman runs against the wall so as to bruise himself and bleed; (4) "the pestle Pharisee," who walks with head down like the pestle in the mortar; (5) "the ever-reckoning Pharisee," who says, "Let me know what good I may do to counteract my neglect"; (6) "the God-fearing Pharisee," after the manner of Job; (7) "the God-loving Pharisee," after the manner of Abraham (Yer. Ber. ix. 14b; Soṭah 22b; Ab. R. N., text A, xxxvii.; text B, xlv.) [282]

Though the denunciations listed here in Matthew 23 are still edifying in the sense of pointing out religious abuses we need to avoid, the gospels have distorted the real historical situation.

Verse 37 mentions a martyr named Zechariah son of Barachiah, murdered in the Temple. Josephus (*Jewish Wars* IV.5.4) calls him Zachariah son of Baruch (the same name minus the theophoric suffix) and says the Zealots killed him in the Temple during the Roman siege, accusing him of conspiring to open the city to Vespasian. There is some confusion here in Matthew between the Old Testament prophet Zachariah son of Barachiah (not murdered as far as we know) and Zachariah son of Jehoiada back in 2 Chronicles 24:20-21, whose murder in the Temple supposedly prompted God to abandon Jerusalem to the Babylonian conqueror Nebuchadnezzar. Matthew has Jesus calling down the wrath of God to avenge all the martyrdoms, murders of prophets from the beginning of history to the end, such vengeance to coincide with the fall of Jerusalem in 70 C.E. Thus Matthew must be thinking of Josephus' Zachariah son of Baruch, not a biblical character from centuries before. But this would be anachronistic for Jesus to speak about in ca. 30. It is all related from Matthew's later standpoint.

[282]   Kaufmann   Kohler,   "Pharisees,"   *Jewish   Encyclopedia* http://jewishencyclopedia.com/articles/12087-pharisees.

There are other anachronisms as well. Matthew 23:2 mentions "Moses' seat," a special chair reserved for synagogue elders (like the Bishop's Chair in Episcopalian churches today). These thrones date from no earlier than the second century C.E.[283] Matthew 23:6 says the Pharisees love to display themselves on the chief seats in the synagogues, but there appear to have been no synagogue buildings in Galilee, except in a couple of Herodian strongholds, till after 70 C.E. Even the title "Rabbi" only came to be used at the end of the first century C.E.[284]

The denunciation of the Pharisees is really aimed, not at the contemporaries of Jesus, but at Matthew's rivals, the rabbis of Yavneh. Matthew's Jesus tells Matthew's Christians that, granted, the "scribes and the Pharisees sit on Moses' seat: so practice and observe whatever they tell you" (verses 2-3a). Thus Christians are obliged to keep the Torah, including halakhic stipulations, like their fellow Jews. Matthean Christians have their own leaders (the gospel author himself was obviously one of them), but, like most sectarian movements, they see themselves as democratic and egalitarian (Matt. 23:11-12), resenting the authority of leaders of the institution from which they have withdrawn. Thus "But you are not to be called rabbi, for you have one teacher, and you are all brethren. And call no man your father on earth, for you have one Father, who is in heaven. Neither be called masters, for you have one master, the Christ" (23:8-10). "Rabbi," "Abba," and "master" were all honorific forms of address in late first-century Judaism.

In verse 15 we appear to have a Paulinist addition,[285] condemning the "circumcision party" (Acts 15:1, 5; Gal. 5:1-12; Phil. 3:2-3) that told Paul's converts they needed to undergo the rite if they were to be counted as true Christians. Paul viewed theirs as "another gospel" (Gal. 1:6-7) and a false one. Hence converts to it were not children of God but rather newly hatched spawn of Satan. "Woe to you, scribes and Pharisees, hypocrites! for you traverse sea and land to make a single proselyte, and when he becomes a proselyte, you make him twice as much a child of hell as yourselves" (Matt. 23:15).

---

[283] Overman, *Matthew's Gospel*, pp. 47, 145.
[284] Overman, *Matthew's Gospel*, pp. 44.
[285] Price, "Antioch's Aftershocks," pp. 248-249.

The Olivet Discourse (chapters 24-25)

For chapter 24, Matthew has reproduced Mark 13, possibly also consulting the original Little Apocalypse Mark himself had previously used and slightly edited.[286] I will here restrict myself to comments on a few of Matthew's additions to Mark 13.

Mark 13:1-2 has Jesus shock the disciples by, out of the blue, predicting matter-of-factly the utter demolition of the Temple. Stunned, four of them wait till they can follow up in private to ask, "When will this be, and what will be the sign when these things are all to be accomplished?" (verses 3-4). But Matthew changes it to "when will this be, and what will be the sign of your coming *and of the close of the age?*" (24:3). "The close of the age" is one of Matthew's favorite phrases (see 13:40, 49; 28:20). He adds the explicit mention of the end of the age in order to anticipate the broadening of the scope of Jesus' answer. In Mark, the four disciples[287] asked only about the time of the Temple's overthrow, not knowing it would signal the End.

Mark 13:6 had Jesus warn that "many will come in my name, saying, 'I am he.'" This looks a little different in Matthew 24:5: "many shall come in my name, saying, 'I am *the Christ.*'" What is the difference? Why bother changing it? I suppose Matthew thought Mark might have meant that in the last times imposters would show up claiming to be Jesus himself returned. Matthew rewords it to suggest that these troublemakers would be claiming to be messiahs in their own right. This is confirmed when we get to Matthew 24:26: "If therefore they shall say unto you, 'Behold, he is in the wilderness, do not go forth," a reference to various messianic revolutionists leading up to the fall of Jerusalem in 70 C.E., such as Theudas the Magician

---

[286] Hermann Detering, "The Synoptic Apocalypse (Mark 13 par): a Document from the Time of Bar Kochba." Trans. Michael Conley and Darrell J. Doughty, *Journal of Higher Criticism.* Fall 2000 (7/2), pp. 161-210.

[287] Why only these four disciples? It is a device common in Gnostic revelation texts, where Jesus is depicted confiding some juicy secrets only to a select inner circle. The point of this gimmick was to explain why this revelation had not been generally known till this particular Gnostic text blabbed it. It had been known only to the illuminati till now. The Olivet Discourse was unknown till its revelation (composition) and publication on the eve of the fall of Jerusalem.

and the unnamed Egyptian (Josephus, *Jewish War* 2:13.5; *Jewish Antiquities* 20:8:6; Acts 21:38).[288]

To Mark 13:18 ("Pray that it may not happen in winter") Matthew 24:20 adds "or on a Sabbath," implying that Matthew's readers are strict sabbatarians who would hate to have to violate the Sabbath rest merely for the sake of escaping a Roman invasion!

Matthew 24:37-41 comes not from Mark but from Q. Luke used the same text in Luke 17:26-27, 34-36.

There are a number of Matthean additions to the Olivet Discourse intended to soften the blow of the failure of the Parousia. Mark 13:36-37 depicts a lazy, negligent servant put in charge by his master, away on business, and unpleasantly surprised upon his boss's untimely return. But Matthew 24:48 changes it so that the servant grows lax when his master is *delayed*. Likewise, the parable of the Wise and Foolish Virgins (bridesmaids), unique to Matthew, is entirely predicated upon the Second Coming being delayed. That is why there is such a danger of letting things slide and growing lax.

Even the wonderful parable of the Talents (Matt. 25:14-30) concerning one's responsibility at least to try to make something of one's life before God calls in the loan of it, contains this element of retrofitting Parousia expectation, adjusting it to the discouraging delay. We read that the businessman is away for "a long time" (verse 19). As we will see, Luke rewrites this Q parable as heavily as Matthew rewrote that of the Great Supper, and Luke makes the delay absolutely central to his version (19:11-27).

.

Catch 22 (25:31-46)

Here is the famous parable (unique to this gospel) of the Sheep and the Goats, which envisions the Final Judgment when the Danielic Son of Man[289] separates the righteous ("sheep") from the sinners

---

[288] Lena Einhorn, *A Shift in Time: How Historical Documents Reveal the Surprising Truth about Jesus* (New York: Yucca Publishing, 2016).

[289] John A.T. Robinson, *Twelve New Testament Studies*. Studies in Biblical Theology No. 34 (London: SCM Press, 1962), Chapter VI, "The 'Parable' of the Sheep and the Goats," pp. 76-93, argues that Matthew has adapted an earlier text featuring God as the Judge and King, adding the figure of the Son of Man from gospel sayings which he uses elsewhere (Matt. 16:27;

("goats"). It is worth noting that the standard "social gospel" reading of the story fits Matthew's wider agenda less well than another interpretation. Who are "my brethren" whom some of "the nations" (verse 32) are going to pay hell for neglecting? Probably not the poor and destitute, the foreigner and the downtrodden in general, but rather the itinerant missionaries and prophets sent by Jesus to preach his gospel (Matt. 8:19-20; 10). The sheep gave the missionaries the aid and comfort Jesus told the itinerants to expect from their hearers (6:25-33; 10:9-11, 40-42), which means they accepted the gospel. But for those towns (collectives, not individuals) who spurned them *because they spurned their preaching*, terrible judgment awaits (10:14-15; 11:24), like that which devastated Sodom and Gomorrah, Tyre and Sidon. That's what will happen to the *nations* of the goats. Acceptance or rejection of the gospel, not conscience-salving social service, is the criterion for salvation of nations and peoples.[290]

Here is an irony: the parable urges its readers to be like the sheep, who unwittingly lent aid to Christ himself when they spontaneously helped the brethren of the Son of Man. One is to avoid emulating the goats, who had no compassion on them—but *would* have helped them had they realized what was at stake. The trouble is, Matthew has, by this very parable, rendered it impossible to do this! Now the reader knows all too well what is at stake, and he will be happy to help the sufferers in order to save his own skin. But this, of course, is to encourage just the attitude that got the goats damned to everlasting fire. Thanks, Matthew.[291]

Throwing Money Away (27:3-10)

Matthew adds a few interesting tid-bits to Mark's story of Judas Iscariot. For the most part, he derives them, not from his own or the
19:28).

[290] George Eldon Ladd, "The Parable of the Sheep and the Goats in Recent Interpretation." In Richard N. Longenecker and Merrill C. Tenney, eds., *New Dimensions in New Testament Study* (Grand Rapids: Zondervan, 1974), pp. 197-198.

[291] Watzlawick, *How Real*, ibid., "If a significant other gives injunctions that both demand and prohibit certain actions, a paradoxical situation arises in which the individual... can obey only by disobeying."

Christian community's memory of the ostensible events, but from the Old Testament prophet Zechariah. Judas is one of the clearest cases of a gospel writer embellishing, even creating, the Jesus narrative "according to the scriptures" (1 Cor. 15:3-4).[292] Sometimes, it seems, early Christians began with a story about Jesus, whatever its origin (history? Borrowings from the tales of Pythagoras or Apollonius of Tyana? Who knows?), and scoured the Old Testament for phrases that, context be damned, could be read as "hidden" predictions of that story's events.[293] But sometimes they seem to have spotted phrases from scripture with certain "theological triggers" like "my son," "that day," etc., and built up stories to "fulfill" them.[294] Judas has been the recipient of such treatment, especially in Matthew.

First, one subtle Matthean change to Mark. In Mark 14:10-11 no particular motive is ascribed to Judas for betraying Jesus to the Sanhedrin, but Matthew makes him a bounty hunter who needed a few extra bucks: "Then one of the twelve, who was called Judas Iscariot, went to the chief priests, and said, '*What will you give me*, if I will deliver him to you?' And they paid him thirty pieces of silver" (Matt. 26:14).[295] Ever wonder how Matthew "knew" the extent of the filthy lucre Judas received? None of the other gospels gives a figure. How could anyone but Judas himself and his paymasters have known? As it happens, Matthew appropriated the number from Zechariah 11:12, "Then I said to them, 'If it seems right to you, give me my wages; but if not, keep them.' And they weighed out as my wages thirty shekels of silver."[296]

Where on earth did Matthew get his "information" about Judas returning the blood money? The very next verse of Zechariah: "Then

---

[292] Earl Doherty, *The Jesus Puzzle: Did Christianity Begin with a Mythical Christ?* (Ottawa: Canadian Humanist Press, 1999), pp. 44-45.

[293] Robert J. Miller, *Helping Jesus Fulfill Prophecy* (Eugene, OR: Cascade Books, 2016).

[294] Robert M. Price, "New Testament Narrative as Old Testament Midrash." In Jacob Neusner and Alan J. Avery-Peck, eds., *Encyclopedia of Midrash: Biblical Interpretation in Formative Judaism*. Volume II, (Leiden: Brill, 2005), pp. 534-573.

[295] C.H. Dodd, *Historical Tradition in the Fourth Gospel* (New York: Cambridge University Press, 1963), p. 27.

[296]Many a frustrated pastor has wanted to say these words to his or her employers.

[Yahweh] said to me, 'Cast it into the treasury'—the lordly price at which I was paid off by them. So I took the thirty shekels of silver and cast them into the treasury in the house of [Yahweh]" (11:13). Here's an odd thing: the Hebrew text of this verse reads as I have just quoted it, "cast it into the treasury," but the ancient Syriac version has "cast it to the *potter*." What do you know? In Matthew 27:3-10 we read.

> When Judas, his betrayer, saw that he was condemned, he repented and brought back the thirty pieces of silver to the chief priests and the elders, [uh, while they were having their audience with Pilate?] saying, "I have sinned in betraying innocent blood." But they said, "What is that to us? See to it yourself." And *throwing down the pieces of silver in the temple*, he departed; and he went and hanged himself. But the chief priests, taking the pieces of silver, said, "It is not lawful to put them into the treasury, since they are blood money." So they took counsel, and *bought with them the potter's* field, to bury strangers in.

Remember those etymological legends from Genesis and Exodus? Stories spun out to account for (or to redefine) puzzling names of people or places? The etymological imagination has been at work with Judas as well. And not just in the case of modern New Testament scholars trying to figure out what the heck "Iscariot" means,[297] but with ancient Christians trying to determine the meaning of "Akeldama," the Field of Blood. Matthew 27:8 derives it from the Sanhedrin's purchase of the indigents' burial ground with Judas' blood money, while Judas is stringing himself up at some undisclosed location elsewhere. But in Acts 1:18-19 Judas himself purchases the land and dies there (no method is mentioned) in spectacular fashion, pretty much swelling up and exploding! And for this reason the place got the descriptive name "Field of Blood."

My guess is that the original sense of the name was to denote that blood-soaked battlefield on which Baal was slain by Mot, the death monster of Canaanite myth. It was there that Anath

---

[297] Bertil Gärtner, *Iscariot*. Trans. Victor I. Gruhn. Facet Books. Biblical Series-29 (Philadelphia: Fortress Press, 1971).

discovered her consort's fate and departed to avenge him, after which Baal rose from the dead.

Matthew 27:9 considers these events leading to Judas' death as the fulfillment of prophecy, no surprise, since he created them for that purpose. But, er, *which* prophet? "Then was fulfilled what had been spoken by the prophet *Jeremiah*, saying, 'And they took the thirty pieces of silver, the price of him on whom a price had been set by some of the sons of Israel, and they gave them for the potter's field, as the Lord directed me." Actually, though, as we have seen, the quoted text comes from *Zechariah* 11:12-13. What was Matthew thinking? No doubt he simply confused this text with a couple in Jeremiah in which that prophet buys a field from his cousin for seventeen silver shekels (Jer. 32:9) plus another in which God tells him, "Go buy a potter's flask," etc. (Jer. 19:1).[298] It's an easy mistake to make, especially when you have no computer searches or even chapter and verse divisions to facilitate looking up Bible verses.

Finally, Matthew "knows" Judas hanged himself because that was the fate of David's traitorous counselor Ahithophel (2 Sam. 17:23), whom scribal tradition took to be the subject of Psalm 41:9, which the gospels apply to Judas (John 13:18).

God Is my Co-Pilate (27:11-26)

Matthew's embellishments to Mark's story of Pontius Pilate's involvement are quite interesting. First, according to some Old Latin[299] manuscripts, Matthew 27:17 reads, "When therefore they were gathered together, Pilate said unto them, 'Whom do you want me to release for you? Jesus Barabbas, or Jesus who is called Christ?'" Of course, plenty of people were named "Jesus" for the Old Testament hero Joshua (for which *Iesous* is the Greek equivalent, "Jesus" being the Latin), and "bar-Abbas" is a patronymic, specifying which Jesus you are talking about by identifying him as So-and-so's son. So it is

---

[298] Miller, *Helping Jesus*, pp. 131-132.
[299] The predecessor to Jerome's Vulgate translation.

entirely plausible for the two men up for release both to be named Jesus. No big deal. And this may well be the way the text of Matthew originally read. We can easily imagine some early Christian scribes, who had come to regard the name "Jesus" as especially sacrosanct, being affronted that this profane murderer should bear it and snipping it from the text.

But when we also realize that "bar Abbas" means "son of the father," we can't help wondering if something strange is going on here. Is it possible this passage was originally intended as a piece of *docetism* in which the real Jesus ("Jesus, Son of the Father") escaped crucifixion while "another Jesus" (2 Cor. 11:4) went to Golgotha in his place? Muslims still believe this today. We'll never know, as with so many other biblical enigmas.

Second, Matthew adds the episode of Procula's[300] ominous dream. Matthew, as he taught Mark's gospel in his congregation, must have often been asked, "Rabbi, why on earth would a man like Pilate be so urgent to set Jesus free?" Matthew thus supplies narrative motivation: "while he was sitting on the judgment-seat, his wife sent word to him, 'Have nothing to do with that righteous man; for I have suffered much over him today in a dream'" (27:19). This, we may suppose, sent a chill of superstitious fear through Pilate, hence his urgency in trying to let Jesus off the hook. But what did his wife mean? Maybe no more than that she had tossed and turned in a nightmare somehow involving Jesus. But some early interpreters of Matthew thought Procula had a precognitive dream in which she would someday convert to Christian faith and *suffer* martyrdom. As we do read of this kind of thing in evolving Christian legend,[301] this verse may be cut from the same cloth.

Third, once Pilate sees he is getting nowhere with the menacing crowd of Jesus-haters and Barabbas fans (whose permission to release Jesus he seems to think he needs), he still seeks to avert responsibility for executing "that righteous man" by shifting the blame to the crowd. "So when Pilate saw that he was gaining nothing, but rather that a riot was beginning, he took water and washed his hands before the crowd, saying, 'I am innocent of this man's blood; see to it

---

[300] So early Christian tradition names Mrs. Pilate.
[301] Robert M. Price, *The Widow Traditions in Luke-Acts: A Feminist-Critical Scrutiny.* SBL Dissertation Series 155 (Atlanta: Scholars Press, 1997), Chapter 6, "Chaste Passion: The Chastity Story of Joanna," pp. 127-151.

yourselves'" (27:24). This detail Matthew borrowed from Susanna 46 (Dan. 13:46 LXX): "I am innocent of the blood of this woman."

Fourth, we come to the most notorious verse in the Gospel of Matthew. "And all the people answered, 'His blood be on us, and on our children!'" Traditionally, Matthew 27:25 has been taken as depicting Jews inviting divine retribution upon themselves and their progeny, in the form of Christian persecution, for their role in hounding Jesus to death. (Such persecution was, of course, far more heinous than the crucifixion of Jesus.) But can we be sure this was Matthew's intent? The evangelist may well have created this exclamation on the basis of the Q saying in Matthew 23:35 ("that upon you may come all the righteous blood shed on the earth."), in which case the point *is* to show Jews condemning themselves out of their own mouths. Their children would then be mentioned in order to allow for the occurrence of the 70 C.E. destruction as the fulfillment of this prediction. But one might also read the text in a very different way, as an ironic (in the sense that they didn't understand what they were really saying, a la John 11:48-51) invocation of that "blood of the new covenant which is poured out for many for the forgiveness of sins" (Matt. 26:28).

> And Moses took half of the blood, and put it in basins; and half of the blood he sprinkled on the altar. And he took the book of the covenant, and read in the audience of the people: and they said, "All that [Yahweh] has spoken will we do, and be obedient." And Moses took the blood, and sprinkled it on the people, and said, "Behold the blood of the covenant, which [Yahweh] has made with you concerning all these words. (Exod. 24:6-8)

I should say the parallel is quite striking, especially in view of how hard Matthew tries to portray Jesus as a new Moses bringing a new Pentateuch.

At the Cross (27:33-56)

Mark 15:34-35 tells us that the crucified Jesus let loose an anguished cry of "*Eloi, Eloi, lama sabachthani*," Aramaic for "My God, my God, why have you forsaken me?" Sadistic idlers loitering around the cross thought he was summoning the prophet Elijah, whom legend depicted as occasionally descending from heaven to rescue the righteous in their distress.[302] Matthew (27:46) changed the Aramaic to Hebrew ("*Eli, Eli, lama sabachthani*"), realizing that bystanders would not easily mistake "*Eloi*" for "Elijah," whereas "*Eli*" would sound similar enough.

And as if Mark's rending of the Temple veil and darkness at noon were not spectacular enough markers of Jesus' death, Matthew adds an earthquake so violent that it shattered boulders nearby and cracked opened mausoleums in the immediate vicinity (27:51-52a). "And many bodies of the saints who had fallen asleep were raised; and coming out of the tombs after his resurrection they went into the holy city and appeared to many" (27:52b-53). The astonishing reference to a resurrection of the recently dead (not the ancients, since they have to be recently deceased persons recognizable to the people of Jerusalem, or their appearance to them is moot) is without parallel in any other gospel. It appears to be a clumsy narrative cameo illustrating the idea of Jesus as the first fruits of the End-Time resurrection. Thus someone has added "after his resurrection" so as to preserve the priority of Jesus' own rising (1 Cor. 15:20; Col. 1:18).

Jehovah's Witnesses, I am told, attempt to salvage some credibility for this story by suggesting that it means only that dead bodies were exposed to public view by the turbulence of the quake ruining the graves, as one sometimes sees in the aftermath of floods. Their relatives would naturally be horrified at the sight when they came to see what had happened. But of course, that is not exactly what the text describes, is it? But I am willing to take the proposal seriously. Instead of positing that Matthew concocted such a piece of apocryphal silliness, we might suggest that some very early copyist changed just a few words to have the "walking dead" hike into town rather than having the living trek to the cemetery to see if their dead

---

[302] Louis Ginzberg, *Legends of the Jews, Volume IV: Bible Times and Characters from Joshua to Esther*. Trans. Henrietta Szold and Paul Radin (Philadelphia: Jewish Publication Society of America, 1909-1938; rpt. Portland, OR: Dragon Key Press, n.d.), pp. 100-104.

loved ones required reburial. It's just speculation, obviously, but an attractive one nonetheless.

Guarding an Empty Tomb (27:57-28:15)

The Sanhedrinists know Jesus had predicted his resurrection because *only in this gospel* (12:40) Jesus has told them to expect it. How convenient: Matthew was preparing for this scene (27:62-66). The whole notion of the tomb of Jesus being garrisoned with Roman guards is a Matthean invention; otherwise, how is it that no other gospel mentions it? If it were known, how could any evangelist *fail* to mention it?[303] Roman guards could not keep him in the tomb! The ensuing narrative suggests Matthew is trying to counter the Jewish charge that the tomb was found empty only after the disciples absconded with their master's corpse. They could not have done it, protests Matthew, because there were Roman soldiers there to forestall such mischief. But it is Matthew who has posted them. And the sealing of the tomb has been borrowed from Daniel 6:17: "And a stone was brought, and laid upon the mouth of the den; and the king sealed it with his own signet, and with the signet of his lords; that nothing might be changed concerning Daniel."

As in his source, Mark, Matthew sends Jesus' ladies auxiliary to discover the open tomb of Jesus. But where in Mark they found the tomb open when they got there, Matthew has brought the supernatural action onstage in full view: they get there in time to see an angel drop down out of the sky and shoulder the millstone away from the opening, then sit on top of it (Matt. 28:2). There is another earthquake, but this time it doesn't cause the tomb to open, so what's the point? The angel's "appearance was like lightning and his clothing white as snow" because he is on loan from the Book of Daniel: "His body was like beryl, *his face like the appearance of lightning*, his eyes like flaming torches, his arms and legs like the gleam of burnished bronze, and the sound of his words like the noise of a multitude" (Dan. 10:6) and "his raiment was white as snow" (Dan. 7:9). The soldiers guarding Jesus' tomb were understandably

---

[303] Hermann Samuel Reimarus, *Reimarus: Fragments.* Trans. Ralph S. Fraser. Ed., Charles H. Talbert. Lives of Jesus Series. Fortress Press, 1970), p. 155.

disoriented: "and for fear of him the guards trembled and became like dead men" (Matt. 28:4). This, too, comes straight out of Daniel: "Because the king's order was strict and the furnace very hot, the flame of the fire *slew those men that took up Shadrach, Meshach, and Abed-nego*" (Dan. 3:22).

Matthew has decided the youth Mark had posted was an angel. On the other hand, it occurs to Matthew that the young man in Mark's empty tomb might have been intended as the risen Jesus himself, so Matthew introduces an explicit appearance of Jesus to the women after the appearance of the angel. That the two appearances were originally the same is evident from the fact that the risen Jesus merely reiterates the message of the angel, a gross anticlimax. The derivative character of it shows the appearance of Jesus here cannot be based on a separate piece of tradition.

The guards eventually snap out of it and decide they'd better give an accounting of the fiasco to the Sanhedrin who got Pilate to post the guards. There is no hint that the Jewish elders disbelieved them; they are portrayed like corrupt politicians caught in the act and paying to make it all go away. In other words, they know Jesus really did rise as he said he would, but they are in no way daunted by that inconvenient little fact and want only to cover their villainous butts. So they bribe the guards to tell people, "His disciples came by night, and stole him away while we slept—yeah, *that's* the ticket!"

Verse 15 implies that the Jews of Matthew's day rebutted the resurrection preaching with the alternate supposition that the disciples stole the body, period. Matthew added the guards to the story in order to refute that rejoinder. After all, the other gospel writers knew nothing of a guarded tomb; if they had, it would have sounded too good to be left out. And pray tell, how did the guards know what had or had not happened while they were *unconscious?* And how would such an excuse convince anybody? It is a Christian parody.

Class Reunion (28:16-20)

Mark ends on a mysterious note: the women are commanded by the young man to go and tell Peter and his colleagues to return to

Galilee to rejoin a now risen Jesus, but the women disobey. *The End.* Matthew, Luke, and John all follow Mark's Empty Tomb story but carry it further, each in his own direction. (So did early copyists of Mark who added two or three new endings to Mark 16). The importance of this fact, usually seemingly unnoticed, must not be minimized. Continuations of the Empty Tomb story into scenes in which the women *do* carry out their orders, and in which the disciples *do* meet with Jesus are entirely predicated on *changing Mark's ending.* Matthew, Luke, and John did not merely add new material; they rejected the original ending in Mark and substituted one they liked better. This by itself is enough to disqualify the resurrection appearance stories as being historical.

Matthew, dependent upon Zechariah for his version of Judas, is even more derivative of Daniel in his resurrection narrative (though it hardly even qualifies *as* a narrative, it is so short). Verses 18-19a are based on a conflation of two Greek versions of Daniel 7:14. In the Septuagint, it says, "to him [the one like a son of man was] ... given the rule... the authority of him [the Ancient of Days]." In Theodotion's version, he receives "authority to hold all in the heaven and upon the earth." The charge to make all nations his disciples comes from Daniel 7:14, too: "that all people, nations, and languages should serve him."

As for the Great Commission, it is issued by Matthew to his church's missionaries, not by Jesus to his disciples. The turmoil in the early church over the question of preaching to Gentiles (Acts chapters 10-11) shows they originally had no such guidance from Jesus but had to find the way forward themselves. Can you imagine the scene otherwise? "Yeah, I know the parting words of the resurrected Son of God commanded us to evangelize the Gentiles, but I'm still not convinced." *Riiight.*

Again, it is plain that Matthew possessed no information, no independent traditions, about resurrection appearances since he had to create the two he has entirely on the basis of reinterpreting Mark and cribbing from Daniel.

12

The Gospel According to Luke, The Acts of the Apostles
The Middle of Time

Authorship and Sources

Gone are the days when one could blithely take for granted the Sunday School party line about Luke and Acts, that they were the work of "Luke the beloved physician" (Col. 4:14), one of Paul's entourage who wrote down the gospel as his favorite apostle preached it and followed it up with a history of the early church in which he himself figured as a player, writing up his notes while Paul was under house arrest in Rome, awaiting trial. And all this literary activity was supposedly finished before 62 C.E., the traditional date of Paul's beheading. No, all of this originated as apologetical propaganda, serving the agenda of emerging Catholicism. And it is all bogus. And the fierceness with which conservative Christian scholars still defend it only confirms the suspicion that it is a question of faith rather than of scholarship.

Why nominate Luke as the author (assuming for the moment that a single author was responsible for both the gospel and Acts)? Irenaeus, Bishop of Lyon in ancient Gaul, writing about 180 C.E., claimed that Luke wrote the gospel based on Paul's preaching. It looks like he was simply duplicating what an earlier bishop, Papias of Hierapolis, had written about the Gospel of Mark having been written by John Mark, a character in the Book of Acts, on the basis of the memoirs of Jesus shared by Simon Peter. These bishops were trying desperately to connect the traditional names of these two gospel writers ("evangelists") with major apostles, an attempt, basically, to make Peter the real author of the Gospel of Mark and Paul the real author of the Gospel of Luke. What was at issue here?

We have to take a step backward to ask how the names Mark and Luke (names absent from all gospel lists of Jesus' disciples) became attached to these works in the first place. The texts of all four gospels are technically anonymous; no name appears in the body of the text, unlike, say, the epistles ascribed to Paul. Whether Paul actually wrote them or not, whoever did write them included the name "Paul" in the letter. Even if, e.g., the Epistle to the Ephesians is pseudonymous, it does give a name. No gospel does. Nor was there any need to come up with a hypothetical name until churches had more than one gospel to read from on Sundays. Until then, the worship leader would say, "And now a reading from the Gospel." But once you got copies of other gospels and started using them in church, you had to find a way to differentiate them. The names must have been added at that time.

Matthew was the most popular of the gospels in the ancient churches. In virtually all ancient gospel books collecting all four, Matthew comes first. No doubt this was because of the handy organization of the work. I think the name is a pun on the Greek word *mathētēs*, "disciple." But of course, whoever picked the name was thinking of the disciple Matthew and was trying to secure the authority of the book as the deposit of eye-witness testimony. The gospels we call Mark and Luke were judged secondary because of differences in the order of events from the "normative" version of Matthew. Hence the names of second-string New Testament characters were chosen. This was no real criticism of their teaching; otherwise they'd have shared the fate of the Gospel of Thomas and the Gospel of Truth: the dumpster instead of the canon. Schleiermacher in the nineteenth century was still approaching it the same way: why did Luke think there was only a single Gerasene demoniac while Matthew thought there were two? Luke's informant must not have had as clear a vantage point as Matthew's! It was a kind of harmonization gimmick.

John's gospel was hugely different from the other three (the so-called Synoptics). How on earth did *it* manage to get christened with an apostolic name? Initially it didn't. In fact there was a whole school of opinion called the Alogoi (= those against the gospel that opened with "In the beginning was the Logos") who (rightly) considered the fourth gospel a tissue of Gnostic heresies. Specifically, some believed it to be the work of the Gnostic Cerinthus. So how did it get to be "the Gospel of John"? As Bultmann demonstrated, an "ecclesiastical redactor" had to sanitize the gospel for Catholic use, and part of the rehabilitation program was to ascribe the approved version to no less a personage than an eyewitness apostle, in fact the closest confidant of Jesus, the unnamed "Beloved Disciple" mentioned a few times in the story. He had to be one of the Twelve, and early Christian guesswork had narrowed down his identity to John son of Zebedee.

The same sort of thing happened at about the same time in the case of the Song of Solomon. There's really nothing expressly religious about it. It's a love song, and a pretty spicy one. In fact, the rabbis tried to get Jews to stop singing it as a bawdy drinking song in taverns! So some sages thought it did not belong in the canon of scripture. The parallel with the fourth gospel was even stronger because, just as the original version of "John" was Gnostic, the Song of Songs had originally been a collection of liturgical texts for the worship of Ishtar and Tammuz. Their names had to be cut out of the text, shorn of their original meaning, if the text was to be retained in monotheistic Jewish synagogue worship. To rebut the disapproval of devout Jews who wanted to dump the Song of Songs, its partisans countered that it was the holiest of all scripture scrolls! To touch it "defiled the hands" (i.e., rendered them temporarily exempt from secular use). From the negative extreme to the positive! Even so: Cerinthus? *Hell* no! John the Beloved Disciple! You know the rule: "For every action there is an equal and opposite reaction."

As we will see, an ecclesiastical redactor had to rehabilitate Luke before it could be considered legitimate, too.

A second apologetical[304] goal in attaching the name Luke to the gospel and Acts was to hide the fact that the Pauline Epistles make virtually no reference to anything in the gospels despite the pathetic attempts of apologetically inclined scholars even today. If Paul knew the gospels (*any* of them), or even any of the sayings ascribed to Jesus, why does he never cite such material when to do so must have won any argument? He says nothing of a teaching or healing ministry of an earthly Jesus, nothing about any miracles wrought by him, nothing about the circumstances of his crucifixion and even suggests it was the work of evil angels!

The reason (excuse?) for making Luke the author of this gospel and of Acts is a plausible (though hardly necessary) inference from the several "we" passages in Acts. Wouldn't that make sense as the signature of one of Paul's companions on the journeys where the first-person plural narration occurs? Indeed it would, but then you'd have to ask why its use is restricted to sea-voyage passages (or directly adjacent to them). I prefer the theory of Vernon K. Robbins[305] that the "we" narration is a vividness device commonly used in ancient sea-voyage sections set in larger narratives otherwise using the normal third-person form. (It is equivalent in effect to the sporadic use, especially in Mark, of present-tense verbs to make the action more immediate to the reader when the rest of the verbs are past-tense.) "All is as it was then, only *you are there!*"

This is important, not just interesting, because the notion that the author of Acts was Paul's traveling companion allows or even requires a very early date for both Luke and Acts. If he ended the

---

[304] Why do I persist in using the older form of the word, "apologetical" rather than the shorter "apologetic"? Simply because I don't want to give anyone the impression that I'm talking about "apologizing." By contrast, "apologetical" has to denote "apologetics," the defense of the faith. I'm still using the phrase "argue that so-and so is true" to mean "argue for" a position. Today the term is more and more used to mean "to dispute a position." But there's still a window of opportunity to use the phrase in its traditional, more useful, sense.

[305] Vernon K. Robbins, "By Land and by Sea: The We-Passages and Ancient Sea Voyages," in Charles H. Talbert, ed., *Perspectives on Luke-Acts.* Perspectives in Religious Studies Series No. 5 (Edinburgh: T&T Clark, 1978), pp. 215-242.

Acts narrative where he did, with Paul awaiting the trial before Nero (Good luck on *that* one!), doesn't that imply it hadn't happened at the time of writing? If the author of Acts knew of Paul's heroic martyrdom, why the heck didn't he even *mention* it?[306]

Oh, but he *did*. The whole narrative structure of Acts parallels Paul's career with that of Jesus: both undertake an itinerant preaching mission, performing healings and exorcisms, only to wind up at the Jerusalem Temple, sparking a disturbance there, which leads to arrest by the Romans and trials before the Jewish Sanhedrin, Herodian kings, and Roman procurators. You mean this writer didn't know Paul wound up being put to death by Rome? If that weren't enough, Paul even makes Passion predictions (Acts 20:22-25; 21:10-14). Do you seriously believe the author did not only know that Paul was dead as a doornail but that his readers already knew it, too?[307]

And do we even *know* when Paul died? The only indications are found in the anonymous and undateable 1 Clement and the grossly legendary Acts of Paul. In other words, we *don't* know.

A number of factors serve to locate Luke-Acts (as we call the linked pair) in the second century, not long before the first known reference to either work, by the afore-mentioned Irenaeus of Lyon, about 180 C.E. Luke-Acts shares genre conventions with both the Apocryphal Infancy Gospels and the Apocryphal Acts of the Apostles, all products of the second (and/or third) century. The Apocryphal Acts are, in turn, heavily influenced by the Hellenistic novels.[308] They also manifest the apologetical and theological agendas[309] of the emerging "nascent Catholicism"[310] that is on full

---

[306] Adolf Harnack, *The Date of Acts and of the Synoptic Gospels*. Trans. J.R. Wilkinson. Crown Theological Library. New Testament Studies IV (New York: Putnam's, 1911), pp. 93-99.

[307] Ernst Haenchen, *The Acts of the Apostles: A Commentary*. Trans. Bernard Noble, Gerald Shinn, Hugh Anderson, and R. McL. Wilson (Philadelphia: Westminster Press, 1971), pp. 592, 593, n. 2.

[308] Richard I. Pervo, *Profit with Delight: The Literary Genre of the Acts of the Apostles* (Philadelphia: Fortress Press, 1987); Pervo, *Dating Acts: Between the Evangelists and the Apologists* (Santa Rosa: Polebridge Press, 2006).

[309] Charles H. Talbert, *Luke and the Gnostics: An Examination of the Lucan

display in the Pastoral Epistles. With the late second-century Apologists and heresiologists Irenaeus and Tertullian, Luke-Acts asserts possession of a definitive way of interpreting scripture allegedly received from the original apostles. Paul, for instance, tells the elders of the Ephesian church that God has appointed them bishops (*episcopoi*, "overseers, supervisors") of the flock of Christ (Acts 20:28). Here is the "apostolic succession of bishops," the cornerstone of the church governance policy of Orthodoxy and Catholicism even today. Acts 21:29-30 has Paul warn "in advance" that the heretics of Asia Minor will, after his death, appeal to him as the source of their Gnostic, Marcionite, and Encratite heresies. This represents our author's attempt to wrest the apostolic figurehead away from these sects, and it plainly presupposes a standpoint long after Paul.[311]

Luke-Acts is the prime example of what F.C. Baur identified as the Catholicizing tendency of the second-century church. Baur saw how earlier strata of the New Testament writings tended to fall in line with either of two broad factions (each with various subdivisions). One was committed to what we would call a Judaic Christianity or a Christian Judaism, championing Jesus as the Messiah of Israel and devoted to strict Torah observance. Some of these opposed any preaching of their gospel to non-Jews, believing that God would one day bring them into the fold via miraculous conversion (a la Isaiah 2:2-4).[312] Others believed the preaching of

---

Purpose (New York: Abingdon Press, 1966). Ever notice how British New Testament scholars use "Lucan" while Germans use "Lukan"? I gather that Americans choose to follow one tradition or the other. I'm with the Deutschers.

[310] Ernst Käsemann, *New Testament Questions of Today* (Philadelphia: Fortress Press, 1969), Chapter XII, "Paul and Early Catholicism," trans. Wilfred F. Bunge, pp. 236-251.

[311] Walter Bauer, *Orthodoxy and Heresy in Earliest Christianity.* Robert Kraft and Gerhard Kroedel, eds., Trans. by a team from the Philadelphia Seminar on Christian Origins (Philadelphia: Fortress Press, 1977), p. 84; Haenchen, *Acts of the Apostles,* pp. 596-597.

[312] Joachim Jeremias, *Jesus' Promise to the Nations.* Trans. S.H. Hooke. Franz Delitzsch Lectures for 1953. Studies in Biblical Theology. No. 24 (London:

Jesus should be shared with the Gentiles (at least the Gentile "God-fearers" who were already attracted to Diaspora Judaism), but that these Gentiles must be required to become full Jewish proselytes, getting circumcised and signing on for all the ceremonial aspects of the Torah. They venerated either of at least two distinct leadership groups, the Twelve and the Heirs of Jesus (= the "Pillars" of the Jerusalem Church). Sometimes these two groups were at odds, sometimes not. The Jewish Christians strongly rejected Paul as a false prophet and even as an (or the) Antichrist. To this wing of Christianity belonged the Gospel of Matthew, the Letter of James, and the Book of Revelation.

The opposing faction (or family of factions) was Hellenistic Christianity, already underway before Paul, primarily Diaspora Jews in, or from, the Hellenistic world who had come to embrace Greek customs and identity. They were willing or even eager to slough off the ethnic markers intended to preserve Jewish identity and safeguard it from assimilation and the ultimate dilution/dissolution of Judaism per se. After all, during the Hasmonean struggle with the Seleucid Empire, many Jews were willing to turn from Yahweh to Dionysus, or to equate the two, or even to identify Yahweh with Zeus. Hellenistic Christianity understood the Messiah not as the champion of the Jewish Law but rather as the stultifier of it, the initiator of a new Torah-free dispensation. Such a Christianity was tailor-made (whether by intent or effect) for assimilating Diaspora Jews and for the Gentile God-fearers who loved Judaism but balked at full conversion. Obviously, the heroes of this wing of the faith included Paul, Barnabas, Apollos, Andronicus and Junia, Priscilla and Aquila. The Gnostics and Marcionites were parts of this movement and even claimed Paul as their founder. New Testament writings stemming from Hellenistic Christianity include the Pauline Epistles, the Gospels of Mark and John, Hebrews, and the "Johannine" Epistles.

Baur believed that the two factions attained a rapprochement some years or decades later, Hellenistic Christians tenaciously

---

SCM Press, 1967).

clinging to the Jewish scriptures even while excusing themselves from ceremonial obedience. Jewish Christians came to acknowledge the right of Gentiles not to be circumcised, etc., as long as no one told Jewish Christians to give up their inherited Torah-piety. Baptism replaced circumcision. One might say that strict Paulinists sat out this reconciliation and continued to exist at the margins. These were Gnostics and Marcionites, rejecting the Old Testament and the Jewish Jehovah lock, stock, and barrel. On the other end of the spectrum sat the Ebionites and Elchasites who continued to evolve theologically along their own consistent trajectories. These marginalized sects produced their own gospels, epistles, acts, and revelations, several of which still survive, but they do not appear in the present Christian canon because the canon was itself the creation and expression of emerging Catholicism. Not surprisingly, we find specifically Catholicizing New Testament writings: 1 and 2 Peter, 1 and 2 Timothy, Titus, and Luke-Acts. All of them, in one way or another, try to reconcile Peter and Paul, i.e., the factions whose figureheads they were.

A good case can be made for Bultmann's ecclesiastical redactor being also the compiler of the familiar twenty-seven book New Testament canon,[313] and that it was he who penned the three Pastorals, padded out Luke, composed Acts, tamped down the Gnosticism of John, and perhaps edited down Secret Mark. It was likely he who chose the letters of James and Jude on the chance that they were written by characters mentioned in the gospels and Acts. It would have been he who decided the letters of "the Elder" were written by John. Polycarp, Bishop of Smyrna in the mid-second-century, has long been nominated as the author of the Pastorals.[314] It

---

[313] Of course this list was officially endorsed by Saint Athanasius in his Easter Encyclical of 367 C.E., but that did not mean this particular list of writings was being newly unveiled. Rather, it was an attempt to restrict usage to Polycarp's edition, already about two centuries old. Nor did adoption of this edition become universal for some centuries thereafter, as surviving manuscripts from after Athanasius' time still include various other books not on the official list.

[314] Hans von Campenhausen, *The Formation of the Christian Bible* (Philadelphia: Fortress Press, 1972), p. 181, note 172; Von Campenhausen,

is the natural next step to identify the ecclesiastical redactor[315] as Polycarp.

Once we see that Luke-Acts belongs in the mid-to-late second century and is, in its present state, the creation of Polycarp, two other old questions receive new answers. First, who was "most excellent Theophilus," to whom both Luke and Acts are dedicated? There are several traditional guesses. One is that this Theophilus was some otherwise unknown Roman official, a Christian convert, who acted as Luke's literary patron. Or he might have been a non-Christian Roman official to whom Luke-Acts was addressed as an apologia, a defense of Christianity, such as Aristides, Justin, Tertullian, and others addressed to fair-minded Romans to allay their suspicions.[316] Finally, "Theophilus" ("Lover of God") might be meant to stand for all Christian readers. None of these guesses is implausible, but if the author was Polycarp, we ought to take very seriously Joseph Wheless's proposal that Luke's dedicatee was none other than Bishop Theophilus of Antioch.[317]

> It is very significant, for the date of the authorship of "Luke," to note the fact that the only Theophilus known to early Church history is a certain ex-Pagan by that name, who, after becoming Christian, and very probably before being instructed in the certainty of the faith by "Luke," himself turned Christian instructor and Father, and wrote the Tract, in three Books, under the title Epistle to Autolychus, preserved in the Collection of Ante-Nicene Fathers, vol. ii, pp. 89-121. This Theophilus became Bishop of Antioch

Polykarp von Smyrna und die Pastoralbriefe. Sitzungberichte der Heidelberger Akademie, Philosophisch-Historischen Klasse, Jahrg. 1951, Bericht 2 (Heidelberg: C. Winter, 1951).

[315] From here on in, I'm going to capitalize "Ecclesiastical Redactor" as a kind of title.

[316] Hans Conzelmann, *The Theology of St. Luke.* Trans. Geoffrey Buswell (New York: Harper & Row, 1961). p. 85.

[317] Joseph Wheless, *Forgery in Christianity: A Documented Record of the Foundations of the Christian Religion* (Moscow, ID: Psychiana, 1930), p. 166.

about 169-177 A.D. (CE. xiv, 625); and thus illuminates the date of "Luke."

Where was Luke-Acts written? Suggestions include Syria, Caesarea, Asia Minor, and Rome. But if it was the work of Polycarp, we can narrow it down to Smyrna, one of the seven churches of Revelation. But that doesn't mean all of the underlying source material originated there. And that brings us to the matter of Source Criticism.

The second-century Carthaginian theologian Tertullian ridiculed Marcion as "the Pontic mouse," because he thought Marcion of Pontus in Asia Minor had excised ("nibbled away") from our Gospel of Luke passages that contradicted his radical Paulinist theology. The great Tübingen critics of the nineteenth century, however, thought Tertullian was turning the tables on Marcion. It was, they contended, Marcion who had the original, shorter version and that his Catholic opponents had padded out that text to make it amenable to Catholic Christianity. I find myself convinced by the recent revival of the Tübingen position by John Knox,[318] Joseph B. Tyson[319] and others.[320]

This document contained material (stories and sayings) drawn from the itinerant charismatics who made the rounds of Christian communities teaching, healing, exorcizing, and prophesying in the name of the Son of Man. There were also materials generated by the main sympathizers in those churches, the itinerants' fellow ascetics, the celibate consecrated women, who were also prophetesses. It is no wonder that Marcionites, themselves radical ascetics, would appreciate and preserve such sayings and tales. Everyone else preferred to ignore them. We still do. The Lukan (Polycarpian) redaction of such material is quite revealing, especially in view of the

---

[318] John Knox, *Marcion and the New Testament: A Chapter in the History of the Canon* (Chicago: University of Chicago Press, 1942).

[319] Joseph B. Tyson, *Marcion and Luke-Acts: A Defining Struggle* (Columbia: University of South Carolina Press, 2006).

[320] Jason D. BeDuhn, *The First New Testament: Marcion's Scriptural Canon* (Salem, OR: Polebridge Press, 2013).

"early Catholic" silencing of these holy women and the attempted suppression of their ministry (exactly as in the Pastorals, which come from the same source and represent the same stage of church history).

What about Acts? C.C. Torrey[321] maintained that the first fifteen chapters of Acts are a Greek translation of an Aramaic original. It reads, he said, much like the Septuagint, a Greek translation of the Hebrew-Aramaic Old Testament. (This section of Acts, this originally separate book, Torrey dubbed "1 Acts.") But as of chapters 16-28, the Greek changes, no longer sounding like a translation. This extension of 1 Acts was composed by whomever translated 1 Acts. (Of course, Torrey called this section "2 Acts," though not implying it had ever circulated as a separate document.) The redactor who combined 1 and 2 Acts will have inserted similar-sounding summaries at 6:7; 9:31; 12:24; 16:5; 19:20; and 28:31 to punctuate the progress of the narrative,[322] precisely parallel to the five summary statements marking the five sections of Matthew (7:28-29; 11:1; 13:53; 19:1; 26:1-2). Nor should we be surprised (indeed we should expect) to find redactions serving the complier's Catholicizing project.

Given the anti-Marcionite tendency evident in 2 Acts, we would naturally have to nominate Polycarp as the translator of 1 Acts and the author of 2 Acts[323] (along with the additions to the originally shorter Luke, as well as the Pastoral Epistles and the Catholicizing additions to the Pauline Epistles). Polycarp thus becomes recognized as a major New Testament author! As Polycarp appears to have been the architect/compiler/editor of the canonical New Testament as we now know it,[324] we can see that canonization was actually part of the

---

[321] Charles Cutler Torrey, *The Composition and Date of Acts.* Harvard Theological Studies I (Cambridge: Harvard University Press, 1916).

[322] C.H. Turner first noticed these dividers and their function. See Haenchen, *Acts,* p. 105, note 1.

[323] We will see how this division into 1 and 2 Acts sheds new light on Baur's understanding of the Peter-Paul balancing act so crucial to the Catholicizing theme.

[324] David Trobisch, *The First Edition of the New Testament* (New York: Oxford University Press, 2000); Trobisch, "Who Published the New Testament?"

process of *writing* the New Testament, not just hammering out the table of contents.

The Nativities of Jesus and John (1:1-2:52)

The first two chapters of Luke's gospel serve as a kind of Old Testament in miniature put there to preface the adult ministry of Jesus. Why bother? There are two reasons, and they are not alternatives. First, this prologue has been added by our Ecclesiastical Redactor in order to counter the Marcionite claim that Jesus and his new religion had nothing to do with Judaism or the Old Testament. Jesus' Father, Marcion held, was not the Creator God of Israel who issued the Torah. "Luke"[325] (i.e., Polycarp) thus repudiates the very popular Marcionite understanding of Jesus right from the start, just as he did by starting Matthew's Sermon on the Mount with the warning that one should not believe those (i.e., Marcionites) who teach that the mission of Jesus was to abolish the scriptures ("the Law and the Prophets," Matthew 5:17).

Second, these chapters, by providing an Old Testament cameo, clarify Luke's organization of the material into a kind of dispensational time-line of salvation history ("*Heilsgeschichte*"), partitioning it into three periods. The first is the time of Old Testament Israel, leading up to and including John the Baptist, whose real goal was to pave the way for Jesus to inaugurate the second, very brief, central period.[326] This is the time of Jesus preaching the gospel, driving Satan and his minions from the field,

---

Free Inquiry 28/1 (December 2007/January 2008), pp. 30-33.

[325] I will refer to the Catholicizing author of canonical Luke and Acts as "Luke" to avoid confusion, even though I identify him with Polycarp.

[326] Hans Conzelmann, who worked all this out, called it "the middle of time," which was the original title, in German, of his great book *The Theology of St. Luke*. Though Conzelmann sees no real connection between the first two chapters of Luke, i.e., the Infancy Narratives, and the rest of the gospel, I would suggest that his understanding of the Baptizer's "hinge" position, opening the door to the new era but himself belonging to the old, is strengthened by comparing it with that of old Simeon in Like 2:25-35. Simeon rejoices at the sight of the promised Christ, who will bring a salvation *that the aged prophet will not actually live to see.*

and arranging the furniture for the third period, that of the Church, God's institution of salvation, sovereignly administering the saving grace of God through the Twelve Apostles and their delegates (including Paul, who is not to be granted true apostolic standing, contrary to what his epistles say) and their successors, the bishops (Acts 20:28; 1 Tim. 3:1-7; 2 Tim. 2:1-2). This third period would not be a short one. Luke knew that because too much time had already passed before he entered the game (Luke 1:2, cf., Heb. 2:3b[327]) and who knew how long it would continue? Here the Delay of the Parousia has become foundational to a whole new paradigm.[328] Delays of Jesus' return were uncomfortable hiccups for Mark, to be dealt with (explained away) as they occurred, but still expected around the *next* corner. But for Luke, Christians might as well unpack their suitcases and settle down for the long haul, "redeeming the time" by preaching the gospel (Acts 1:6-8) and providing a living example of the commendable Christian lifestyle (1 Tim. 2:1-4; cf. Matt. 5:16).

Luke's double Nativity story is clearly based on that of the prophet Samuel. The old priest Eli is the prototype for both Simeon and Zachariah. The barren Hannah "gives birth" to old Elizabeth (as well as Mary, provided we follow the majority of manuscripts in ascribing the Magnificat, Luke 1:46-55, to Mary, though I think it makes more sense if we go with the few manuscripts crediting the hymn to Elizabeth (or just "she," which would have to refer back to Elizabeth). The Magnificat is obviously just a paraphrase of Hannah's song in 1 Samuel 1-10. And the refrain about Jesus continuing to

---

[327] Some think Luke-Acts and Hebrews are the work of the same author. See C.P.M. Jones, "The Epistle to the Hebrews and the Lucan Writings," in D.E. Nineham, ed., *Studies in the Gospels: Essays in Memory of R.H. Lightfoot* (Oxford: Basil Blackwell, 1967), pp. 113-143; F.J. Badcock, *The Pauline Epistles and the Epistle to the Hebrews in their Historical Setting* (London: SPCK, 1937), pp. 190-198. This is hard to accept, however, given the centrality of the blood atonement in Hebrews and its absence from Luke-Acts.

[328] Martin Werner, *The Formation of Christian Dogma: An Historical Study of its Problem.* Trans. S.G.F. Brandon (Boston: Beacon Press, 1965), shows how the delay of the Parousia fundamentally shaped the whole evolution of the Christian belief system throughout its history.

grow in wisdom and favor with God and men (2:40, 52, cf., 1:80) is right out of 1 Samuel 2:26, "Now the boy Samuel continued to grow both in stature and in favor with [Yahweh] and with men."

When Gabriel announces to Mary her coming pregnancy, the story is cut from the same midrashic cloth as the annunciation to Sarah of Isaac's birth (Gen. 17:19, "Sarah your wife shall bear you a son, and you shall call his name..."; cf., 18:9-15) and that of Samson (Judg. 13:2-5, "you shall conceive and bear a son... and he shall begin to deliver Israel..."). The story also borrows the commissioning formulae of Moses (Exod. 3:10-12) and Jeremiah (Jer. 1:4-8), where God's reluctant draftee tries to wiggle out of it, only to have his objection overruled (see Luke 1:18, 34).[329]

Some of the Nativity sources are what we might call quasi-biblical texts. One is the account of Moses' birth in Pseudo-Philo's *Biblical Antiquities*. In the course of Pharaoh's *Endlösung* attempt to eradicate any and all future generations of resident alien Hebrews by killing their babies, Amram resolves to defy Pharaoh by having a son. God sends an angel to the virgin Miriam.

> And the Spirit of God came upon Miriam one night, and she saw a dream and told it to her parents in the morning, saying, "I have seen this night, and behold a man in a linen garment stood and said to me, 'Go, and say to your parents, "Behold, he who will be born from you will be cast forth into the water; likewise through him the water will be dried up. And I will work signs through him and save my people, and he will exercise leadership always."'" (9:10)[330]

In Luke 1:32-33, 35, the angel Gabriel's predictions look like

---

[329] Raymond E. Brown, *The Birth of the Messiah: A Commentary on the Infancy Narratives in Matthew and Luke* (Garden City: Doubleday, 1977), pp. 156-157; Gerhard Lohfink, *The Bible: Now I Get It! A Form-Criticism Handbook.* Trans. Daniel Coogan (Garden City: Doubleday, 1979), Chapter 8, "The Annunciation of the Birth of Jesus," pp. 114-126.

[330] Trans. D.J. Harrington. James H. Charlesworth, ed., *The Old Testament Pseudepigrapha.* Vol. 2. Anchor Yale Bible Reference Library (New Haven: Yale University Press, 1985), p. 316.

they're borrowed from an Aramaic version of Daniel discovered among the Dead Sea Scrolls:

> [And when the Spirit] came to rest up[on] him, he fell before the throne. [Then Daniel rose and said,] 'O king, why are you angry; why do you [grind] your teeth? [The G]reat [God] has revealed to you [that which is to come.] ... [Peoples will make war,] and battles shall multiply among the nations, until [the king of the people of God arises... [All the peoples will serve him,] and he shall become gre[at] upon the earth... He will be called [son of the Gr]eat [God;] by his Name shall he be designated. He will be called the son of God. They will call him son of the Most High... His kingdom will be an eternal kingdom, and he will be righteous in all his ways. (4Q246, *The Son of God*).[331]

Luke has Mary visit her older cousin Elizabeth, and she gets quite a greeting! The fetal John the Baptizer leaps in Elizabeth's womb in excitement at the approach of his embryonic superior, Jesus.[332] It seems he just cannot wait thirty years to start testifying about Jesus— even though, in Luke's gospel, he never does! Here Luke is working from Genesis 25:22, where Rebecca groans in agony when her two sons strive within her, anticipating their future rivalry.[333] Luke is thinking of the Greek Septuagint (LXX), which reads, "And the babes *leaped* within her." Luke wants to reverse the original prediction of rivalry. Jacob and Esau may have been bitterly opposed, but John and Jesus (standing for their respective sects in Luke's day) will get along just fine (or so Luke desires). More than that, however,

---

[331] Michael Wise and Robert H. Eisenman, eds. and trans., *The Dead Sea Scrolls Uncovered: The First Complete Translation and Interpretation of 50 Key Documents Withheld for over 35 Years* (Rockport, MA: Element Books, 1992), p. 70.

[332] Did the zygote John clairvoyantly behold the Holy Fetus of Prague in all his creepy glory?

[333] David Friedrich Strauss, *The Life of Jesus Critically Examined*. Trans. George Eliot (Mary Ann Evans). Lives of Jesus Series (Philadelphia: Fortress Press, 1972), p. 151; Brown, *Birth of the Messiah*, p. 345.

John defers to Jesus, the attitude Luke wants the Baptist sectarians of his time to take toward Jesus.

He wants them to come join the Christian fold. Here is another Lukan concern and technique. When he wants to reconcile rival sects or factions, he tells parallel stories about their figureheads. Here it is John and Jesus. Later, in Acts, we will see him depict the Hellenist leader and martyr Stephen in terms borrowed from the Passion narrative of Jesus, his goal being to make Stephen and the Hellenists look good to Jewish Torah-Christians who blamed them for a persecution. And he will, famously, construct an elaborate series of striking parallels between Peter and Paul as well, to rehabilitate each man in the eyes of the other's partisans.

It has been plausibly proposed[334] that Luke did not freely compose the Nativities of John and Jesus, but rather combined and interlaced pre-existent infancy traditions derived from each of the two rival sects. "You Christians don't like John? You Baptists don't like Jesus? Look at their Nativities! How can you think God was active in one and not in the other?" The underlying tensions are attested in the Pseudo-Clementines, where Christians seem to consider John the fountainhead of heresies, and Baptists argue that John was the Messiah, Jesus his subordinate,[335] and in the Mandaean Book of John, where Jesus is denounced as a false Messiah. Luke 7:31-33/Matt. 11:16-19, a Q saying, seems to reflect the standpoint of an outsider disgusted at this dispute. By placing in tandem their respective Nativity traditions, both based on Old Testament texts, our author seeks to bury the hatchet (i.e., to co-opt the Baptizer's

---

[334] Alfred Loisy, *The Origins of the New Testament.* Trans. L.P. Jacks (London: George Allen & Unwin, 1950), p. 149; Jack T. Sanders, *The Jews in Luke-Acts* (Philadelphia: Fortress Press, 1987), p. 160.

[335] "And, behold, one of the disciples of John asserted that John was the Christ, and not Jesus, inasmuch as Jesus Himself declared that John was greater than all men and all prophets. 'If , then,' said he, 'he be greater than all, he must be held to be greater than Moses and than Jesus himself. But if he be the greatest of all, must he be the Christ'" (Pseudo-Clementine *Recognitions*, Book I, 60:1-3). Trans. Thomas Smith. Quoted in J. Louis Martyn, *The Gospel of John in Christian History: Essays for Interpreters* (Eugene: Wipf & Stock, 2004), p. 139.

sect).

It is not absolutely clear that Luke meant to say that Jesus was miraculously conceived. There is an anomaly in the annunciation canticle of Gabriel: unlike the canticles of Simeon, Zechariah, and the Magnificat, this one gets interrupted. Not just that, but the interruption makes no sense. Mary is puzzled at the news that she will bear a son because "I know not a man," i.e., she is a virgin. But Luke has already told us (1:27) that Mary is betrothed to Joseph. Had Mary stopped Gabriel with this objection, one can imagine the archangel's reaction: "Uh, you *are* engaged to be *married*, right? Have I got the wrong house?" It seems to me that Mary's interjection makes sense, not within the flow of the narrative, but rather as a clumsy attempt by a scribe, who believed in a miraculous conception, to insert a reference to it in a narrative that lacked one. In fact, a couple of manuscripts lack Mary's protest. That's enough for me.

The four canticles appear to be (or to be based upon) hymns composed for the use of pious sectarian groups somewhere between the Dead Sea Scrolls sect and the *haberim*, these latter being dining clubs of devout Jews, somewhat akin to the Pharisees, who met together to encourage one another and to reinforce their members' practices of piety.

Whiz Kid Avoids a Whippin' (Luke 2:41-51)

The tale of the adolescent Jesus accompanying his parents to the Temple is the tip of an apocryphal iceberg. Many more of these amusing stories were collected in books like the Infancy Gospel of Thomas, the Infancy Gospel of Matthew, and the Arabic Infancy Gospel. In all of them Jesus is portrayed as mentally an adult and essentially a god. He barely tolerates the buffoonish mortals among whom he finds himself perforce marooned. Joseph, a carpenter, cannot seem to get the legs of a chair the same length until, that is, young Jesus intervenes. He exposes the ignorance of tutors who do not suspect he knows more than they do. He is annoyed to have to prove, by a miracle, that he did not strike a playmate dead. Here in

211

Luke, he is taken aback at the dull-wittedness of his parents: why did they bother searching all the Jerusalem video arcades and comic book shops? Why didn't they make a beeline for the Temple? Where else would he be? But he apologizes to his scholarly colleagues for suspending their *halakhic* dialectic and condescends to return home with his idiot parents to have some milk and cookies.[336]

Baptismal Begetting (Luke 3:1-23a)

John the Baptizer gets his fifteen minutes of fame in this passage, which has a few interesting points of variance from the baptism accounts of both Mark and Matthew. The chapter begins with what is called a *synchronism*, the coordination of the events to be recounted with known historical facts, in this case the reigns of various figures over various territories, assuming the reader will be familiar with them. Some of the Old Testament Prophets begin this way (Jer. 1:1-3; Ezek. 1:1-3; Hosea 1:1; Amos 1:1; Micah 1:1; Zeph. 1:1; Hag. 1:1; Zech. 1:1; cf., Isa. 6:1). Some have theorized that verses 1-3 were the original beginning of the Gospel of Luke before the addition of the infancy narratives.

Verses 3-9, 16-17 reproduce the John the Baptist material from Mark and Q. But verses 10-14 are new. John has exhorted the crowds to repent and to prove the reality of their decision by improving their behavior. This is pretty general, but Luke adds some specifics, defining the fruits of repentance for specific groups within his following. Anyone with anything extra should share with anyone in need. Tax-collectors must stop charging more than is actually required (even though that's how these guys made their living). Soldiers about to ship out (for that is the nuance of the Greek word here[337]) must not extort money from the citizens they are supposed

---

[336] You catch a whiff of the same thing in Mark 3:19b-21, 31-35, where Jesus' relatives see nothing more important than that he not miss lunch, and Jesus says these poor fools do not understand the duties of being his real kinfolk.

[337] Robert Eisler, *The Messiah Jesus and John the Baptist According to Flavius*

to protect. Conzelmann's[338] keen eye notices a significant shift of emphasis from the earlier hysterical demands to repent while mere moments remain before the End. What we are reading here are rules for conduct in an ongoing world in which little has changed except the character of the repentant. Do we not detect here the same spirit that permeate the household codes (*Haustafeln*)[339] that form part of the Pastoral Stratum[340] added to the Marcionite Pauline canon (1 Cor. 14:33b-35; Eph. 5:21-6:1-9; Col. 3:18-4:1; 1 Pet. 2:13-20)?

Luke has ingeniously augmented the Q passage used in Luke 3:16-17 and Matthew 3:11-12 by making it the answer to a question, albeit an unspoken one: "As the people were in expectation, and all men questioned in their hearts concerning John, whether perhaps he were the Christ, John answered them all..." (3:15-16a). Again, this is aimed at John the Baptist sectarians in Luke's own day (cf., Acts 19:1-7). It is exactly like the saying of Jesus in the Koran where he is made to repudiate Christian belief about him: "And when Allah saith: 'O Jesus, son of Mary! Didst thou say unto mankind: "Take me and my mother for two gods beside Allah?"' he saith: 'Be glorified! It was not mine to utter that to which I had no right'" (5:116a).[341]

Verses 19-20 seem to want to round off the John the Baptist episode by inserting a notice of the Baptizer's public rebukes of the corrupt tetrarch Herod Antipas, and his subsequent imprisonment. And only then, in a flashback, and in a subordinate clause—Jesus gets baptized! Uh, by *whom*? John is gone, isn't he? Luke seems to want to

---

Josephus' Recently Rediscovered 'Capture of Jerusalem' and the other Jewish and Christian Sources. Trans. Alexander Haggerty Krappe (New York: Dial Press, 1931), p. 265.

[338] Conzelmann, *Theology of St. Luke*, p. 102.

[339] John Howard Yoder, *The Politics of Jesus* (Grand Rapids: Eerdmans, 1972), Chapter 9, "Revolutionary Subordination," pp. 163-192.

[340] Winsome Munro, *Authority in Paul and Peter: The Identification of a Pastoral Stratum in the Pauline Corpus and I Peter*. Society for New Testament Studies Monograph Series 45 (New York: Cambridge University Press, 1983).

[341] Mohammed Marmaduke Pickthall, *The Meaning of the Glorious Koran: An Explanatory Translation* (New York: Mentor Books / New American Library, n.d.), p. 107.

obscure the issue, to leave it open whether Jesus was baptized by John. Why? Simply because Jesus' baptism by John, once seen as a valued endorsement, has become a point of vulnerability in the struggle against the Baptist sect. Does not the greater baptize the lesser? Is it not the lesser who appeals to the greater? (For the same reason, as we will see, the Gospel of John omits the baptism altogether!)

And when the Spirit descends upon Jesus, the heavenly Voice utters, "You are my beloved Son; with you I am well pleased" (verse 22). Or does he? According to other ancient manuscripts the Voice says, "You are my beloved Son; today I have begotten you," which of course makes God quote Psalm 2:7, the climax of the old Judean enthronement rite. This would mean that Luke retained the adoptionism of Mark, though he did tone it down a bit by changing Mark's "descended *into* him" to "descended *upon* him" (as Matthew also did). Matthew also changed the Voice's address, "You are" to "This is." For Matthew, God is talking to the crowd, revealing Jesus' messianic identity to *them*, since Matthew thinks Jesus *already knows* because he *already is*. Luke, of course, has shown Jesus manifesting divine maturity and prodigious knowledge, but here he has simply retained Mark's version, where Jesus seems first to learn his identity as he steps out of the Jordan. Likewise, Luke retains Mark's lack of any recognition between Jesus and John, despite Luke having made them previously acquainted as cousins. He just didn't harmonize every patch he sewed into the quilt.

The genealogy (Luke 3:23-38) is completely different from Matthew's. The often-heard attempt to solve this problem, suggesting that Luke is offering the genealogy of Mary, is nonsense born of desperation. Again, there no ancient Jewish custom of supplying the mother's family tree, not under her own name, but under her husband's. And it fairly swarms with Levitical names, pretty odd if Jesus is supposed to descend from David.

The original gospel, which is sometimes called the Ur-Lukas, lacked the first three chapters. There was no baptism and no desert Temptation scene.[342] Canonical Luke therefore did not derive his

Temptation narrative from Q (which didn't have one), but from Matthew, who based the whole sequence on Deuteronomy 34:1-4, where Yahweh takes Moses to the top of a high mountain to show him the various kingdoms his people will conquer.

Nastiness in Nazareth (4:16-30)

The Ur-Lukas contained the core of this passage, but it began with verse 16 and continued immediately with verse 23, then 28-30. What is missing here?[343] Or, better, what has Luke added? The scripture quotes and allusions, that's what. Jesus does not read from Isaiah. He does not taunt the congregation with examples from Elijah and Elisha. He just baits the crowd: they're only interested in him because of the rumored healings he performed in the last village he visited. (The point is the same as in John 6:26, "Jesus answered them, 'Truly, truly, I say to you, you seek me, not because you saw signs, but because you ate your fill of the loaves.'" Or Mark 8:11-12, "The Pharisees came and began to argue with him, seeking from him a sign from heaven, to test him. And he sighed deeply in his spirit, and said, 'Why does this generation seek a sign? Truly, I say to you, no sign shall be given to this generation.'") This riles up the audience to the point that they try to lynch him, a climax missing from other Synoptic versions. Luke must have taken Jesus' escape from the mob from the Ur-Lukas, since it does not occur in Mark. Marcion was some kind of docetist and Marcionites no doubt read the ending as implying that Jesus slipped through the hands of the mob like a ghost, and indeed that may have been the point. If the idea was to show Jesus standing up to them and the mob chickening out, that

---

[342] All comparisons between canonical Luke and the Ur-Lukas are based on numerous comments by church fathers who actually had access to copies of the latter, used by Marcionites.

[343] By the way, Luke is the only evangelist to specify the location of this story as Nazareth. Mark 6:1 and Matthew 13:54 have only "his own country."

would have been easy to say, but it doesn't say that.

Note, too, that neither Luke nor the Ur-Lukas contains the list of Jesus' brethren. Luke has added a mention of Joseph as Jesus' well-known father, unlike Mark who has the audience identify Jesus as Mary's son. If the Ur-Lukas was not only *used* by Marcionites but actually *written* by them, it is no surprise either that the episode would feature no Old Testament texts or that there would be no mention of family members, since Marcion taught that Jesus descended from heaven as an adult.

But canonical Luke does, of course, add a section from Isaiah and Jesus' application of it to himself, pretty much blabbing the Messianic Secret. Luke no longer quite understands the secrecy motif.[344] Despite what one usually hears, it is not Jesus' claim that Isaiah 61:1-2 has been fulfilled that very hour that turns the crowd against him, for Luke, in verse 22, says the congregation greeted these words with enthusiasm. No, like a stand-up comic insulting his audience, Jesus says, "Look, I know you're just buttering me up for some of those miracles you've heard about, but you can just forget it!"

The Ur-Lukas went that far, but Luke actually has Jesus back up his harsh words with scripture. "You think that's unfair? You think charity ought to begin at home? Well, let me tell you how both Elijah and Elisha skipped their own countrymen to do miracles for foreigners!" Talk about rubbing it in! Luke had Mark on hand as well, and he must have felt that Mark was right in trying to justify the proverb, "A prophet is not without honor, except in his own country," etc. But Luke saw how arbitrary Mark's abrupt change in the mood of the crowd was, so he decided to provide some motivation for it. And what better than to have Jesus anticipate Paul's parting shot to Diaspora synagogue Jews that God had washed his hands of them and was sending the gospel to Gentiles instead (Acts 14:46-48; 18:6-7; 28:25-29). Likewise, Jesus announces that he will follow the example of Elijah and Elisha in spurning Jews for

---

[344] William Wrede, *The Messianic Secret*. Trans. J.C.G. Greig. Library of Theological Translations (Cambridge: James Clarke, 1971), pp. 178-179.

Gentiles. "Tough luck!"

Find the Fish! (Luke 5:1-11)

And that's not the only gap in narrative motivation Luke noticed in Mark and decided to supply. Doesn't it seem a bit strange for Peter, Andrew, James, and John to drop everything to follow some Svengali appearing out of nowhere? I think the Markan version is very powerful simply as is, but it is easy to see how one might find it puzzling, and Luke figures it must have taken a pretty good miracle to elicit this reaction from the four anglers. The miraculous catch of fish seems ultimately to be derived from a tale of Pythagoras. A vegetarian, the sage was dismayed at the sight of a huge pile of fish flopping on the shore, fresh from the nets. He hated to think of them winding up as refrigerated fish sticks and approached the fishermen with a proposal: if he could tell them the exact number of the ichthyic hostages, would the fishermen dump them back into the water? He ventured his "guess," and, after counting them (none having died in the meantime), the astonished fishermen freed the fish. And don't worry, Pythagoras paid them the market price and went on his way.

John's gospel uses the story as well, even retaining the exact count of fish. It seems, then, that, as so many did, this story circulated independently, coming to rest in two gospels. But upon closer examination, something interesting pops out. In Luke, the story introduces the call of Peter, especially, to his apostolic ministry, "fishing for men." The version found in the Johannine Appendix (John 21) also has a brief exchange between Jesus and Peter, issuing in Jesus' calling Peter to his apostolic ministry, shepherding men (and women, obviously). And in John, the story is a resurrection appearance. In Luke the disciples-to-be suddenly see Jesus on the shore while they are busy fishing. They do not recognize him, never having seen him before. In John 21 they see him on shore while they are fishing and do not initially recognize him because, last they heard, *he was dead.* Maybe it *was* originally a resurrection appearance story (albeit fictive, derived from Pythagorean lore), and Luke's placement of the fish story at the commencement of Jesus' ministry is a holdover from a time when readers understood the circular narrative logic of Mark: that the Galilean reunion of the risen Jesus with the disciples occurs in Mark 1:16-20.

Why does Peter react to the sudden draught of fish with penitential sorrow? "Depart from me, O Lord, for I am a sinful man!" Traditionally, we have taken Peter's abashment to denote his sudden awareness of being in the presence of the Numinous.[345] His reaction, then, would be much the same as Isaiah's: "Woe is me! For I am lost; for I am a man of unclean lips, and I dwell in the midst of a people of unclean lips; for my eyes have seen the King, [Yahweh Sabaoth]!" (Isa. 6:5). And that makes good sense.

But I think another possibility makes even more. It has been suggested that Peter's words are a vestige of a longer exchange between the risen Jesus and a disciple who had grievously denied him (Luke 22:54-62). We might have another piece of it over in Luke 7:40-43:[346]

> And Jesus answering said to him, "Simon, I have something to say to you." And he answered, "What is it, Teacher?" "A certain creditor had two debtors; one owed five hundred denarii, and the other fifty. When they could not pay, he forgave them both. Now which of them will love him more?" Simon answered, "The one, I suppose, to whom he forgave more." And he said to him, "You have judged rightly."

Perhaps this Simon was originally Simon *Peter*, and this passage is the other shoe dropping after the first, namely Jesus' Last Supper

---

[345] Rudolf Otto, *The Idea of the Holy: An Inquiry into the Non-Rational Factor in the Idea of the Divine and its Relation to the Rational*. Trans. John W. Harvey (New York: Oxford University Press, 1924), p. 52.

[346] Adolf Harnack, *Luke the Physician: The Author of the Third Gospel and the Acts of the Apostles*. Trans. J.R. Wilkinson. Crown Theological Library XX (London: Williams & Norgate, 1911), p. 227; A.H. Dammers, "Studies in Texts: A Note on Luke vii., 36-50," *Theology* 49 (1946), p. 80.

prediction of both Peter's denial *and restoration* (Luke 22:31-34). Interestingly, Jesus does not call the Pharisee character in chapter 7 "Simon" until verse 44, implying that Luke got the idea of calling him Simon once he had interpolated verses 40-43 into their present context.

Luke 5:12-6:16 closely parallels Mark 3:19. But one especially interesting note demands comment. The Markan pericope about fasting (Mark 2:18-22) features an analogy involving wine and wineskins: no one puts new, still fermenting wine into old wineskins, because these have stretched as much as they can from the fermenting of their previous contents. So new wine would stretch the leather skins past the breaking point, spilling the wine all over the place. Elementary. And, Mark's Jesus said, it ought to be equally clear that you can't confine a new spiritual reality in the forms of old-time religion. To this, Luke adds an unexpected modification: that's only if you're interested in new wine in the first place! Real connoisseurs are not: they know the old wine is always better. This has to be a dig at Marcionites who jettisoned the Old Testament (fine wine) in favor of the New (Grape Nehi).

Plain Speech (Luke 6:17-49)

Where Matthew has the Sermon on the Mount, Luke has the Sermon on the Plain. Both are based on a collection of sayings from the Q source. Luke's is much shorter, probably about the same length as the Q Sermon. As for the extra sermon materials in Matthew, Luke does have much of it but places it in different contexts. The rest of the so-called M material (shared with neither Mark nor Luke) is very likely Matthew's own creation. The location on a mountain must also be Matthew's idea, since it fits with Matthew's depiction of Jesus as a new Moses promulgating a new Torah from a new Sinai.

The remaining notable difference between Matthew and Luke is the two sets of Beatitudes (benedictions, blessings). Matthew has nine of them, Luke only four, and Luke counterbalances these with four corresponding Woes. Matthew's "extras" bless the meek (5:5), the merciful (5:7), the pure in heart (5:8), the peacemakers (5:9), and the persecuted (5:10). The first eight of Matthew's are in the third person ("those," "the meek," etc.), with the ninth in the second person, whereas all four of Luke's are in the second person ("you"). Were Luke's four the only ones in Q, with Matthew adding five more? Or does Matthew have the original, five of which Luke cut? Did Q contain Luke's four Woes, which Matthew cut, or did Luke add them? Alfred Loisy[347] thought that Luke's four beatitudes were original to Q, Matthew adding the other five, but that Luke fabricated the four matching Woes.

And look at the wording of two of them. Did Q have Matthew's "poor *in spirit*" (which would seem to amount to what Schleiermacher called "the feeling of absolute dependence" upon God)? Or was the original reading simply "the/you poor," as Luke has it? Did Q have Matthew's "hunger and thirst *for righteousness*" or Luke's simpler "hunger now"? Many think Matthew has spiritualized a more down-to-earth original. Others argue that Luke has politicized a more strictly religious original which Matthew preserves. Since the general tendency in the New Testament seems to be to de-politicize in order to avert Roman suspicions, I suspect Matthew has spiritualized a more political original. But who knows?

The Centurion's Child and the Son of the Widow of Nain (7:1-17)

First Kings 17 serves as the basis for a pair of miracles.[348] The Elijah original stipulates (1 Kings 17:1) that the famine shall be relieved only by the prophet's permission, just as the word of Jesus by itself is sufficient to heal the centurion's servant (or child, same Greek word) from a distance (Luke 7:7b). And Elijah goes to the Transjordan

---

[347] Loisy, *Origins of the New Testament*, pp. 153-154.

[348] Thomas L. Brodie, "Luke the Literary Interpreter: Luke-Acts as a Systematic Rewriting and Updating of the Elijah-Elisha Narrative in 1 and 2 Kings." Ph.D. dissertation presented to Pontifical University of St. Thomas Aquinas, Rome. 1988, pp. 136-137.

region and encounters a Gentile, the widow of Zarephath (1 Kings 17:5, 10a), exactly as Jesus arrives in Capernaum and meets a Roman officer. In both, the Gentiles are in great need: the widow and her son are on the verge of starvation (17:12), while the centurion is desperate to prevent his son's/servant's looming death (7:2-3). Each parent briefs each miracle worker, and these latter issue a series of commands (1 Kings 17:10c-13; Luke 7:8), and the desired boon is granted, the multiplication of food in the one case (17:6), the return of health in the other (7:10).

The story of the centurion's son came to Luke (by way of the Ur-Lukas) from the wider gospel tradition, attested in both Matthew 8:513 (hence in Q) and in John 4:46-54. Christian scribes had already modeled it upon the Elijah story. Luke didn't have to do the work. But he has added a new Jesus tale, unique to his gospel, basing it on the 1 Kings sequel to the story of Elijah and the widow. Elijah later resurrects the widow's son; likewise, Jesus next happens upon a funeral procession, stops the mourners in their tracks, and raises the man who was about to be buried, another widow's son, this one from Nain. Luke has held back one feature from the first Elijah episode in order to use it in his second Jesus episode: Elijah met the widow at the city gate of Zarephath, which Luke transforms into the gate of Nain (even though archaeology reveals that historical Nain, now called "Ain," had no gate).

But back up a step: Luke (or Ur-Lukas) started his second episode with the same opening from 1 Kings 17:17a: "And it happened afterward." It reappears in Luke as "after this...." The widow's son is dead in both 1 Kings 17:17b and Luke 7:12b. Elijah cries out in anguish (1 Kings 17:19-20); Jesus does not (probably because Luke deemed such a reaction unbecoming for the unflappable Son of God). But he does tell the widow not to cry (Luke 7:13). In both stories a gesture raises the dead: Elijah prays for the boy's spirit to return, v. 21, while Jesus orders the boy to rise (7:14). Both lads prove the reality of their recovery by crying out (1 Kings 17:22; Luke 7:15). Then, in both anecdotes, the wonder-worker "gave him to his mother" (1 Kings 17:24; Luke 7:15b, verbatim identical between Luke and the Septuagint). And the bystanders burst into acclamation (1 Kings 17:24; Luke 7:16-17).

If Luke himself (as Brodie thinks)[349] composed the first episode directly from the first Elijah episode, instead of taking it from Q, he also transformed the widow's lament that Elijah has come to punish her sins into the centurion's confession that he is unworthy to have Jesus come under his roof.

Luke 7:18-35 comes from Q and does not differ materially from Matthew's version.

Risqué Repentance (7:36-50)

According to Brodie,[350] Luke has constructed the cumbersome story of the sinful woman using a couple of Elisha's miracles, the bottomless cruse of oil (2 Kings 4:1-7) and the resurrection of the Shunammite woman's boy (2 Kings 4:8-37). Some disciple of Elisha's has died, bequeathing his widow a pile of debts, and her creditors, not satisfied with harassing collection calls, threaten to take her two children in payment (2 Kings 4:1). In effect, the children would be held hostage till she could post "bail" for them with the sum she owes. Luke has changed her monetary debts into a debt of sin (Luke 7:37, 40-42). Elisha miraculously multiplies the widow's oil so she can use it to pay what she owes. Jesus cancels the woman's debt of sin (Luke 7:44-50). The widow's oil has become the myrrh which the woman uses to anoint Jesus' feet (Luke 7:38). Simon the Pharisee has invited the itinerant Jesus to dinner (Luke 7:36), echoing the Shunammite woman's invitation of Elisha to stay and eat with her whenever he's in the neighborhood (2 Kings 4:8-11). Elisha rewards her by miraculously enabling her (*ahem!*) to conceive a son. Some years later, the lad succumbs to sunstroke, and his mother makes the trek to Elisha's office for help, like a complaining customer. She falls at his feet (2 Kings 4:27), just as the suppliant woman anoints Jesus' feet (Luke 7:38). Luke need not have created the anointing story out of whole cloth; he must have gotten the core of it from Mark 14:3-9,

---

[349] Brodie, "Luke the Literary Interpreter," pp.136-152.
[350] Brodie, "Luke the Literary Interpreter," pp. 174-184.

but he has largely rewritten it in light of 2 Kings.

As it stands, the story is incoherent. Why would the Pharisee invite Jesus as a dinner guest, then neglect the basic social amenities? It is only subsequently that the host is said to infer that Jesus is a false prophet, so why had he disrespected him earlier? And how on earth did the unnamed woman, already notorious as a local streetwalker, manage to gain entry to the dinner? And if somehow she had, why was she not immediately ejected? Instead, she is allowed to carry through her fairly elaborate procedure of copiously sobbing onto Jesus' feet, drying them with her long hair, and then anointing them with oil. If this was such a scandalous scene, how did the host allow it to continue? (Okay, maybe to give Jesus enough rope to hang himself.) But the problems do not stop: when were the woman's sins forgiven? The parable of the two debtors implies that her show of devotion means she has already been forgiven by Jesus, since it is he to whom she is grateful, yet Jesus actually pronounces forgiveness at the end of the story. *What a mess.* I believe that the first version of the story, once adapted from 2 Kings and Mark, came from the consecrated widows' community. It casts Christian bishops as the Pharisee. The bishops were no fans of these women's ministries and refused to welcome the itinerant charismatics, rivals of institutional authorities but natural allies of their fellow ascetics, the widows. The bishops leave such menial chores to the widows (1 Tim. 5:9-10). But Lukan redaction (favoring institutional authority) vilifies "the younger widows" who are liable to "become wanton" (1 Tim. 5:11) by casting a prostitute as their representative.

The Joanna Romance

A number of odd bits scattered throughout Luke's gospel would make sense as vestiges of a distinct pre-existent source, one of the Chastity Narratives that abound in the second-century Apocryphal Acts of the Apostles.[351] These novelistic documents are Christianized versions of the many Hellenistic Romance novels in which star-crossed lovers are separated and overcome great odds in their attempts to reunite. In the Christian version, the love of the heroine for her lover/fiancé/husband becomes the devotion of a new female convert to the apostle (Paul, John, Thomas, Peter, Andrew, Matthias) whose preaching of the Encratite celibacy gospel has alienated her entirely from her pagan spouse or lover. The spurned husband, etc., a highly placed noble, reports on his misfortune and prevails on the king to have the apostle arrested and executed (martyred). The woman disciple visits the apostle in prison and carries on his work after he is gone (to heaven). I feel sure that such a tale was once told of Joanna, a follower of Jesus not mentioned in any gospel but Luke's. Some have suggested that Luke had a special source of Herod material from which he drew the following:

> and also some women who had been healed of evil spirits and infirmities: Mary, called Magdalene, from whom seven demons had gone out, and Joanna, the wife of Chuza, Herod's steward, and Susanna, and many others, who provided for them out of their means. (Luke 8:2-4)

> Herod said, "John I beheaded; but who is this about whom I hear such things?" And he sought to see him. (Luke 9:9)

> At that very hour some Pharisees came, and said to him, "Get away from here, for Herod wants to kill you." (Luke 13:31)

> When Herod saw Jesus, he was very glad, for he had long desired to see him, because he had heard about him, and he was hoping to see some sign done by him. (Luke 23:8)

> He leads our women and children [i.e., virgin daughters] astray. (Marcionite text of Luke 23:2)

---

[351] Robert M. Price, The Widow Traditions, in Luke-Acts: A Feminist-Critical Scrutiny. SBL Dissertation Series 155 (Atlanta: Scholars Press, 1997). Chapter 6, "Chaste Passion: The Chastity Story of Joanna," pp. 127-151.

> And Herod with his soldiers treated him with contempt and
> mocked him; then, arraying him in gorgeous apparel, he sent
> him back to Pilate. (Luke 23:11)

The "Herod source"[352] was the Chastity story of Joanna. These
snippets would find a natural home in such a context. Joanna, now a
follower of Jesus, seems to have deserted her husband, a childhood
friend (so the Greek implies) and trusted servant of Herod Antipas.
Chuza, affronted by his wife's alienation, tells Herod what happened,
how his wife was led astray by this charlatan magician (hence Herod's
curiosity about Jesus' reported miracles). And why should Herod
want Jesus' dead? As a favor to Chuza, of course. All this is standard
issue for the Chastity Story genre. And in this version, it was Herod
who not only tried Jesus and allowed his soldiers to make sport of
him, but who put him to death. In Mark, the soldiers' mockery was a
preliminary to crucifixion, and originally it served the same purpose
here. But Luke did not want to reject Mark's Passion narrative, so he
clumsily tried to harmonize the two. It didn't work: Pilate tries to
pass the Jesus buck to Herod, leaving the verdict up to him. But
Herod does not condemn him, so why doesn't he set Jesus free? Why
the heck send him back to Pilate? Just so the narrative can rejoin
Mark's.

These Chastity Stories were the stock-in-trade of the consecrated
women,[353] the so-called (not necessarily) widows and virgins, several
of whose traditions appeared in the Ur-Lukas and were then
modified by canonical Luke.[354]

Luke's Re-marks on Mark

---

[352] Loisy, *Origins of the New Testament*, p. 167.

[353] Ross S. Kraemer, "The Conversion of Women to Ascetic Forms of
Christianity." *Signs: Journal of Women in Culture and Society* 6 (Winter 1980),
pp. 298-307; Virginia Burrus, *Chastity as Autonomy: Women in the Stories of
Apocryphal Acts*. Studies in Women in Religion, Vol. 23 (Lewiston and
Queenston, New York: Edwin Mellen Press, 1987).

[354] Price, *Widow Traditions*.

Luke 8:4-18 adheres closely to Mark chapter 4, though Luke goes easy on the disciples who do not invite Jesus' rebuke for their stupidity, omitting Mark 4:13 (though he doesn't go as far as Matthew 13:51-52, where Jesus actually commends the disciples for their acuity).

In Luke 8:19-21 the evangelist similarly rehabilitates the family of Jesus. Not only does he omit the occasion for Jesus' relatives' visit (thinking him mad and intending to take custody of him, Mark 3:20-21), but he also tactfully skips Jesus' repudiation of them in favor of his followers as his true kin (Mark 3:33-35). In Luke the door is left open to read the saying of Jesus as praise for his wonderful family who are those who hear the word of God and put it into practice, just as Mary did back in Luke 1:38. Thus it is no surprise to see Jesus' mother and brothers gathered with the apostles in the Upper Room for Pentecost (Acts 1:14).

Luke 8:22-9:50 is, again, based on Mark, with just a couple of interesting changes. When Jesus raises up Jairus' daughter, Luke has him say, "Child, arise!" Luke's Jesus pointedly does *not* first use the Aramaic words *Talitha cumi*, as in Mark 5:41. Luke has an aversion to Hebrew and Aramaic, apparently fearing Greco-Roman readers would think it barbarous speech (cf., 1 Cor. 14:10-11). No cries of *Hosanna* at the Triumphal Entry either. Luke does, however, make use of the magic words from Mark 5:41 over in Acts 9:40, in a widow story parallel to the story of Jairus' daughter. The woman is, not accidentally, named Tabitha, enabling Peter to raise her up with the words, "Tabitha, rise!" The similarity to Mark's *Talitha cumi* is not coincidental.

Then there's the "Great Omission." Between Luke 9:17 and 18 we would expect to find a Lukan version of Mark 6:45-8:27, but we don't. In the chapter on Mark's gospel, I mentioned how Mark included side-by-side two sets of miracle stories so closely parallel to one another that they appear to be variant versions of a pre-Markan mini-collection.[355] What Luke is missing, then, turns out to be the

---

[355] Paul J. Achtemeier, *Jesus and the Miracle Tradition* (Eugene, OR: Cascade Books, 2008), Chapter 4, "Toward the Isolation of Pre-Markan Miracle

second of these miracle-chains. What happened to this material? Some scholars believe that Luke would have included the set of stories had they been available to him, but that they were not. Perhaps Luke's copy of Mark was defective, missing the material,[356] or maybe he was using an earlier version of Mark which contained only one of the miracle-sets. Matthew, then, which features both miracle-chains, was using a version of Mark which either had not suffered the omission of one group or to which the second group had since been added.

Others believe that Luke intentionally omitted the second group,[357] perhaps on account of its redundancy and because he needed to make room for non-Markan material he wanted to add. It also seems possible that Luke made the common scribal error of *homeoteleuton* ("same ending"), but on a large scale. This is when copyists write down a line, then look back to the manuscript from which they are copying and spot a different line, further down, that happens to end with the same word as the line they just finished writing. Thinking they have returned to their stopping point, they start copying from the end point of that line they think was their last, skipping all the lines of text in between. It is conceivable that, given the similarity between the two miracle sequences in Mark, Luke got to the end of the first but then his eye returned to the end of the second and went on from there.

In Luke's version of Peter's confession (Luke 9:18-22), the main difference from Mark is that Luke slightly beefs up Peter's affirmation of Jesus' status from "You are the Christ" to "You are the Christ of God" (Luke 9:20). The only thing to note here is the malleability of the sayings ascribed to Jesus, especially the theological ones. The evangelists do not seem disinclined to let well enough

---

Catenae," pp. 55-86; Chapter 5, "The Origin and Function of the Pre-Markan Catenae," pp. 87-116.

[356] Burnett Hillman Streeter, *The Four Gospels: A Study of Origins Treating of the Manuscript Tradition, Sources, Authorship, & Dates* (London: Macmillan, 1951), pp. 175-176.

[357] Vincent Taylor, *Behind the Third Gospel: A Study of the Proto-Luke Hypothesis* (Oxford at the Clarendon Press, 1926), pp. 139-140.

alone. Luke's change may seem insignificant, but it is, so to speak, a transitional form on the way to more evolved versions, like Matthew's "You are the Christ, the Son of the living God" (16:16), John's "You are the Holy One of God" (6:69), and Thomas' "Master, my mouth is not able to say what you are like" (saying 13).

As in Mark, the messianic confession is followed up with sayings on discipleship. Mark 8:34 had "If any man would come after me, let him deny himself and take up his cross and follow me." But Luke has added the word "daily" after "take up his cross." This is to change an encouragement to martyrdom for Christ in the turbulent context of the End Times into a timeless preachment about Christian devotion in day-to-day life under normal circumstances (cf., Phil. 2:5). As Conzelmann[358] showed, the shift is part of Luke's "de-eschatologizing" agenda, a readjustment to life in an ongoing world *not* about to be cut short by the Parousia at any moment. The same goes for Luke 9:27: "I tell you truly, there are some standing here who will not taste death before they see the kingdom of God." By itself, this saying would sound as apocalyptic as the old Jehovah's Witnesses bumper sticker, "Millions now living will never die." But if you take a look at the Markan original, there has been an important change. In Mark 9:1 we read, "Truly I say to you, there are some standing here who will not taste death before they see the kingdom of God come *with power*." Why would Luke have shortened the text? The qualifier "with power" is elsewhere used in conjunction with the miraculous resurrection of the dead (Mark 6:14; Rom. 1:4; 1 Cor. 15:43). For Luke to cut that particular phrase implies that, in the readers' time, the Church Age, "to see the coming of the kingdom of God" means something spiritual,[359] i.e., metaphorical (cf., Luke 17:20-21). This is just what all embarrassed end-of-the-world sects do: "Oh, er, ah, you see, the End, uh, *did* come, *in a sense*, visible only to the eye of faith! Yeah, *that's* the ticket!"

These may seem to be over-subtle inferences, but they do form a pattern,[360] as we will see. Also, I think it is the same logic as

---

[358] Conzelmann, *Theology of St. Luke*, pp. 96-97.
[359] Conzelmann, *Theology of St. Luke*, p. 104.

with Freudian slips:[361] if it's only random, you *could* have said *any*thing; why'd you say *this*?

Appointment in Samaria (9:51-56)

It does not require any great Higher-Critical acumen to spot the connection between Luke 9:51-56 and 2 Kings 1:1-2:1. After all, the one makes explicit reference to the other (Luke 9:54). But Brodie[362] demonstrates how Luke's story is simply cloned from its prototype. In 2 Kings the anticipation of the hero's being taken up into heaven occurs at the end of the section on Elijah's clash with the Samaritan troops (2 Kings 2:1). Luke switches the anticipation to the beginning of his story of Jesus and the Samaritan village (Luke 9:51a). Back to Elijah: the king of Samaria has sent messengers to inquire of the oracle of Baal-zebub in the Philistine city of Ekron, but Elijah intercepts them before they have gone far and tells them to save themselves a trip; he can tell them what the king wants to know (2 Kings 1:2-5). In Luke this has become the rebuff accorded Jesus' messengers whom he sent ahead to arrange accommodations in Samaria. For Luke, the Samaritans are no longer those turned back but those who turn others back in their travels. The prophet is now the one who sends the messengers, not the one who turns them back. But there's more: once the king of Samaria dispatches troops to arrest Elijah, the prophet conjures fire from the sky to incinerate them (2 Kings 1:9-10). The same thing happens in verses 11-12. Third time's the charm: Elijah agrees to come along quietly (1 Kings 1:13-15; cf., John 18:3-8). In Luke James and John want to repeat Elijah's miraculous firestorm attack on the Samaritans (now villagers, not troops), but Jesus will have none of it. Instead he takes the role of the angel of Yahweh who persuaded Elijah to show mercy.

The disciples' angry reaction provides one of the clearest

---

[360] Conzelmann, *Theology of St. Luke*, p. 125.
[361] Sigmund Freud, *A General Introduction to Psychoanalysis*. Trans. Joan Riviere (New York: Pocket Books, 1953), p. 36.
[362] Brodie, "Luke the Literary Interpreter," pp. 207-214.

examples of the completely fictive nature of these stories. Can you imagine a sane adult seriously proposing that they summon fire from the sky to roast a hostile city? Maybe if he was the Human Torch or Firestorm... oh, but they're comic book characters, aren't they?

Goodbye to All That (9:59-62)

Mark's stories of Jesus recruiting Peter, Andrew, James, and John (Mark 1:16-20) and Levi (Mark 2:14) are all rewritten from the 1 Kings 19:19-21 episode of Elijah calling Elisha to abandon his plowing chores to become his disciple and successor. Luke has created another discipleship paradigm which implicitly critiques the prototype.[363] Elisha requested, and received, from his new master permission to go to his startled (but no doubt proud) parents and bid them farewell. But in Luke 9:59-62 Jesus expressly forbids what Elijah allowed. He refuses to permit a would-be recruit to delay long enough to pay filial respects. Elijah, it seems, was too much of a pushover! Luke retains the element of plowing, obviously, but, while plowing was the worldly pursuit Elisha had to forsake for a prophetic ministry, Luke uses plowing as the very metaphor for apostolic ministry. Second Timothy 2:15 uses the same metaphor for ministry, "plowing a straight furrow with the word of truth." This would be easily explained (as would much else) if canonical Luke had the same author as the Pastoral Epistles.

Deutero-Deuteronomy: Luke's Central Section (10:1-18:14)

The Transfiguration scene in Mark implicitly portrays Jesus as a new Moses on the peak of a new Mount Sinai. Both Matthew (17:1-8) and Luke (9:28-36) were quick to take the hint and to present Jesus as the Prophet like unto Moses (Deut. 18:15) issuing a new Torah. Matthew's version is a whole new Pentateuch. This is what he was doing when he organized the sayings of Jesus into five major sections:

---

[363] Brodie, "Luke the Literary Interpreter," pp. 216-227.

the Sermon on the Mount (chapters 5-7), the Mission Charge (chapter 10), the Parables chapter (13), the Manual of Discipline (chapters 18-19), and the denunciation of the Pharisees plus the Olivet Discourse (chapters 23-26). The fact that he jammed together two very different subjects in the fifth section only shows how important it was to him to squeeze all his material into five "books." Luke, on the other hand, decided to have Jesus delivering a Deutero-Deuteronomy, a "second law" like the one Moses promulgates in the Book of Deuteronomy. C.F. Evans[364] first pointed this out. Like Matthew, Luke not only organized some traditional materials but also created some of his own, riffing on the scripture texts he was emulating (or replacing).

Sending out Emissaries (Deut. 1; Luke 10:1-3, 17-30)

Moses chose twelve men to survey the land which stretched "*before your face*," sending them through the *cities* of Canaan. Luke, following Mark, has Jesus send the Twelve on a preaching mission, then a second group, this time of seventy, symbolizing the seventy (as then counted) nations of the earth who are to be "conquered" with the gospel in the Book of Acts. Jesus sends them out "*before his face*" to every *city* he plans to visit (in Canaan, too, obviously).

Luke wants to match the return of the spies with samples of the fruit of the land (Deut. 1:25), so he plugs in the Q saying (Luke 10:2; Matt. 9:37-38), "The harvest is plentiful, but the workers are few; therefore beg the Lord of the harvest to send out more workers into his harvest." And Jesus' emissaries return with a glowing report, just as Moses' did.

Judgment for Rejection (Deut. 2-3:22; Luke 10:4-16)

[364] C.F. Evans, "The Central Section of St. Luke's Gospel," in D.E. Nineham, ed., *Studies in the Gospels: Essays in Memory of R.H. Lightfoot* (Oxford: Basil Blackwell, 1967), pp. 37-53.

Moses sent messengers to Og, King of Bashan, and Sihon, King of Heshbon, with peace terms; Jesus sends his seventy out with the offer of blessing: "Peace be to this house." The Israelite messengers are rebuffed, and God punishes their un-welcoming committee by sending the Israelite armies to destroy them. Likewise, Jesus warns that in case the targeted cities reject his agents, they will face terrible future judgment. This missionary material is from Q (cf. Matt. 10). Luke may have decided to use it here because it features the image of the missionaries "shaking the dust" (i.e., the contagion) of an unresponsive village "from the soles of their feet" (Luke 10:1), recalling "the sole of the foot" in Deuteronomy 2:5.

Praying to the Lord of Heaven and Earth (Deut. 3:23-4:40; Luke 10:21-24)

"At that time" Moses prayed to God, who has no rival "in heaven or on earth" (Deut. 2:23-24). The Q saying Luke 10:21-24 and Matthew 11:25-27 may have been suggested originally by that Deuteronomy passage. Jesus "at that time" praised his Father, "Lord of heaven and earth" (Luke 10:21). He thanks God for revealing his wonders to "children," not to the supposedly "wise" (cf., Gal. 2:6). Even this reflects the wording of Deuteronomy 4:6, where Moses reminds his people to cherish the commandments as their *wisdom* and 4:9, where he urges them to tell what they have seen to their *children*. Moses' recital of all the wonders their eyes have seen (Deut. 4:3, 9, 34, 36) may have inspired the Q benediction on the disciples for having seen with their own eyes the great deeds the ancient prophets and kings were not privileged to witness (Luke 10:23-24). But for Q it is the ancients who failed to see what their remote heirs did see.

The Commandments and the Shema (Deut. 5-6; Luke 10:25-27)

Chapters 5 and 6 of Deuteronomy give us both the Decalogue and the Shema. Luke alludes to this section when Jesus asks a scribe to summarize the gist of the Torah, and he suggests the Shema's assertion of monotheism (adding Leviticus 19:18), but none of the Ten Commandments. This is Luke's rewrite of Mark 12:28-34, which did list a few specific commandments from the Decalogue. Luke's concluding comment, "Do this and you will live," comes straight from Leviticus 18:5, "You shall therefore keep my statutes and my ordinances, by doing which a man shall live."

(No) Mercy to the Foreigner (Deut. 7; Luke 10:29-37)

Moses strictly charges the Israelites to destroy the heathen Canaanites, showing no mercy (Deut. 7:2). To counter this, Luke has Jesus tell the parable of the Good Samaritan, which depicts a despised foreigner/heretic showing mercy (Luke 10:33) for a Jew beaten to a pulp by bloodthirsty highwaymen. Like all the uniquely Lukan parables, this one is Luke's own work. Matthew certainly did not imagine Jesus sympathizing with Samaritans (Matt. 10:5). Luke's pro-Samaritan viewpoint (also evident in the uniquely Lukan narrative of the Samaritan leper, 17:1-19) no doubt stems from his advocacy of the Samaritan mission (Acts 8:5-17 ff.; cf., John 4:1-42). Luke's contrast of Jesus' compassion with Moses' mercilessness reminds us of Luke's Elijah/Jesus contrast in Luke 9:54, where Jesus refuses to call down fire from heaven upon cold-shouldered Samaritans, unlike his counterpart Elijah who was happy to barbeque them (2 Kings 1:10, 12).

The parable of the Good Samaritan, like most of Luke's, is a genuine story, not merely an extended simile. They typically compare two type-characters, in this case the indifferent priest and Levite versus the compassionate Samaritan, just as Luke elsewhere contrasts the Prodigal with his straight-arrow brother, the destitute Lazarus with the uncaring Rich Man, the self-righteous Pharisee with the self-loathing Publican, the persistent Widow with the Unjust Judge, contemplative Mary with fussbudget Martha, and the Importunate Friend with the Irritated Householder.

The Truth Shall Make You Gluten Free (Deut. 8:1-3; Luke 10:38-42)

The Mary and Martha episode is Luke's commentary on Deuteronomy 8:3, "Man does not live by bread alone, but... man lives by every word that proceeds from the mouth of the LORD [i.e., Yahweh]." Luke champions the placid Mary who hungers for Jesus' ("the Lord's") "words." He is less pleased with the harried Martha (whose name means "Lady of the House," thus an ideal, fictive character). Her preoccupation with domestic chores, especially cooking and serving, threatens to crowd out spiritual nourishment (cf. Deut. 8:11-14). The story must originally have been part of a "recruitment paradigm" told by the consecrated women ("widows" or "virgins") in the Christian communities of Luke's day (cf. 1 Tim. 5:3-16).

Heavenly Father Knows Best (Deut. 8:4-20; Luke 11:1-13)

In Deuteronomy Moses says that God's disciplinary blows to disobedient Israel are like the chastisement accorded a son by a dutiful father (though that usually doesn't include plagues and poisonous snakes), then promises the new generation security, prosperity, and sufficient food in their new land. For this Luke substitutes his version of the Lord's Prayer (from Q), which shares the same basic themes of fatherly provision and of asking God to spare his children "the test," recalling the "tests" sent upon the people by God in the wilderness. On top of that, Luke adds the Q material about God giving good gifts to his children (Luke 11:9-13; Matt. 7:7-11), which is the point of the corresponding Deuteronomy text, together with his own parable of the Importunate Friend, which (like the parable of the Unjust Judge, 18:1-8, is also unique to Luke) urges the seeker not to give up praying "How long, O Lord?"

In Matthew's version of the Lord's Prayer (Matt. 6:9-13) it is implicit that the prayer is understood as a liturgical text intended for regular verbatim use, though Protestants with an anti-formalist bias would like to think of it as only a sample prayer: "keep it simple; don't pray God's ear off!" Form criticism compels us to recognize it as a piece of liturgy, since otherwise we would not be reading it. It must have been constantly repeated as it still is today. And this feature, so clear in this case, should help us see the formulaic, even liturgical, character of all other gospel forms: healing stories were repeated as incantations. Likewise exorcism stories, Eucharistic sayings, pronouncement stories, etc. Well, what was implicit in Matthew is explicit in Luke when Jesus says, simply, "When you pray, say this" (Luke 11:2).

But even repeated texts tend to get modified over time, as a comparison of, say, earlier and later versions of the Book of Common Prayer makes clear. Or a comparison between Matthew and Luke. Luke's Lord's Prayer is shorter, Matthew's more poetic, adding Hebrew poetic parallels here and there. It comes out sounding quite a bit like ancient Jewish synagogue prayers. You can trace the process by which ancient copyists tended more and more to assimilate Luke's version to Matthew's, probably without realizing it. More familiar with the Matthean version from using it in their worship, they simply added the extra material reflexively. Finally, the late manuscripts on which the Textus Receptus (which underlies the King James Version) was based, wound up with the Luke 11 version differing from the Matthew 6 version only in that Luke's still reads "debts," while Matthew's has "trespasses."

But this process of reshaping Luke's version began even earlier than that; the original Lukan version is preserved in the Marcionite text of the Ur-Lukas, where, instead of "Thy kingdom come," we read, "Thy Spirit come upon us and sanctify us,"[365] quite a change!

The Harder They Fall (Deut. 9:1-10:11; Luke 11:14-26)

On the verge of Israel entering the land of Canaan, Moses rehearses the wilderness generation's rap sheet of rebellion, yet he promises

---

[365] Loisy, *Origins of the New Testament*, p. 158.

victory over the formidable nations awaiting them, including the half-mythical Anakim, descended from a race of titans. Later imagination accounted for these "mighty men of old" as the product of cross-breeding between the Sons of God (now understood as fallen angels) and the daughters of men (Gen. 6:1-6). This background "information" made it possible for Luke to see a parallel between this text and the Q/Mark account of the Beelzebul controversy, where Jesus evicts demons (fallen angels?), depriving Satan, the strong man, of his "possessions." On this analogy, the hapless demoniacs correspond to the Promised Land, while the demons controlling the poor wretches match the Anakim holding the land until God boots them out because of their wickedness, even though, like their master Satan, they are much stronger than any human.

In the Beelzebul controversy, the Q comparison of Jesus with the "sons" of the Pharisees and his own use of "the finger of God" to cast out demons is a midrash on the Exodus contest between Moses and the priestly magicians of Pharaoh. Matthew uses it in a different context, but Luke places it where he does because of Deuteronomy's reference to "the finger of God" engraving the commandments on the stone tables. The "strong man" business common to both Mark's and Q's versions of the Beelzebul episode originated in Isaiah 49:24, but it seemed to fit the Deuteronomic reference to stronger nations here.

Impartiality and Clear Vision (Deut. 10:12-11:32; Luke 11:27-36)

To the Deuteronomic praise of God as impartial to all, not a deity to play favorites, Luke matches an anecdote, which he probably created on the basis of Mark 3:31-35, showing that not even the mother of Jesus is more "precious in his sight" than the least of his brethren.

Moses warns Israel not to copy the sins of the doomed Canaanites, since the same fate would await them if they did. Luke matches to this the Q saying on how even ancient non-Israelites appreciated the divine witness of their day more than Jesus' contemporaries did (Luke 11:29-32//Matt. 12:39-42).

Lastly, Luke places the Q material about the eye being the lamp of the body (Luke 11:34-36; Matt. 6:22-23) in the same slot as Deuteronomy 11:18's charge to treasure the commandments in one's heart and to place them as frontlets on one's forehead. The implicit middle term between the one image and the other was Psalm 19:8 ("the precepts of [Yahweh] are right, rejoicing the heart; the commandment of [Yahweh] is pure, enlightening the eyes") or maybe Psalm 119:105 ("Your word is a lamp for my feet and a light for my path").

Clean and Unclean (Deut. 12:1-16; Luke 11:37-12:12)

Deuteronomy 12:1-14 prohibits sacrifice on the hilltop shrines ("high places"), restricting worship to the (Jerusalem) Temple. This finds no real echo in Luke; he waits to apply roughly parallel material to Deuteronomy 12:15-16, a text allowing the preparation and eating of meat at home, i.e., just as a meal, no longer as a sacrifice. Thus one needn't be in a state of ritual purity to have a steak. Luke takes the opportunity to introduce the Q material on the Pharisees' inability to tell the real difference between clean and unclean (Luke 11:39-52; Matt. 23:4-7, 23-36, also shared between Mark 7:1-5 and Luke 11:37-38), as well as the Q material Matthew 10:26-35; Luke 12:2-9. The connection is merely that of catchwords, also the case with the Q phrase "the blood of all the prophets shed" (Luke 11:50; cf., Matt. 23:35, "all the righteous blood shed on earth"), which just barely recalls Deuteronomy 12:16, "you shall not eat the blood; you shall pour it out upon the earth."

Inheritance (Deut. 12:15-32; Luke 12:13-34)

Someone in the crowd asks Jesus, an inspired and impartial prophet, to adjudicate an inheritance dispute, but Jesus will not cooperate: "Man, who made me a judge or divider over you?" (Luke 12:14). The episode is surely derived from Exodus 2:14a, "Who made you a prince and a judge over us?" Moses had tried to mediate a dispute between two Hebrew laborers in Egypt, but the men told him to get lost. Jesus' intervention is requested, but he rebuffs the request. Here is another Moses-Jesus side-by-side comparison, at the expense of Moses, since one greater than Moses is ostensibly here. Luke 12:30 tells disciples not to worry about life's necessities as "the nations" do, corresponding to Deuteronomy 12:29 which warns Israel not to emulate "the nations" in their religious observance.

The parable which follows, Luke 12:16-21, must be based on Ecclesiastes 6:-2, "a man to whom God gives wealth, possessions, and honor, so that he lacks nothing of all he desires, yet God does not give him the opportunity to enjoy them, but a stranger enjoys them." See also Ecclesiastes 2:18-21. The connections with the corresponding Deuteronomy passage are slight, but Luke must have thought them sufficient: both texts treat of inheritance, and both envision "sitting pretty" with accumulated possessions. Finally, both speak of the *psuche* (soul, life, or self). Luke's Rich Fool says, "I will say to my soul, 'Soul, you have ample goods,'" etc., while Moses, in the Greek Septuagint, says, "You may eat after the desire of your soul" (Deut. 12:20).

Chock Full o' Gods (Deut. 13:1-11; Luke 12:35-53)

Deuteronomy has no love for what it considers false prophets, spokesmen for rival deities. Moses direly warns Israel to turn a deaf ear to their seductions. But, surprisingly, it is Yahweh himself who has sent them, as a test for his people, like a sting operation. To parallel this theme, Luke uses parable material based on the Mark 13 apocalypse (verses 34-37). Luke expands Mark 13::37, "What I say to you I say to all: watch," into an exchange between Jesus and Peter: "Peter said, 'Lord, are you telling this parable for us, or for all?'" (Luke 12:41 ff.). The Markan original had the departing master assign tasks to his servants, tests to prove their mettle. By connecting this parable with the Deuteronomy passage, Luke characterizes the church's job while their Lord is away in heaven as remaining steadfast against the blandishments of other saviors and prophets (Luke 21:8).

Since Deuteronomy does not exempt from punishment even family members who convert to the service of forbidden gods (13:6-11), Luke adds the Q saying Luke 51-53; Matthew 10:34-36, which is based on an unacknowledged quotation of Micah 7:6, "for the son treats the father with contempt, the daughter rises up against her mother, the daughter-in-law against her mother-in-law; a man's enemies are men of his own household."

Lowering the Boom (Deut. 13:12-18; Luke 12:54-13:5)

The Deuteronomic Moses, like some modern-day Jihadi caliph, orders that entire cities that lapse into heathen apostasy are to be wiped off the map, never to be rebuilt. So seriously does Yahweh take spiritual infidelity. No less gravely does the Lukan Jesus take the lack of repentance by Galileans and Jews. The tragedies and atrocities of the past will come to be seen as foreshadowings of the judgments to fall upon an unrepentant people. Of course, Luke's Jesus "prophesies" long after the fact, referring to the triumph of Rome in Galilee and Judea culminating in 73 C.E.

The Third Year (Deut. 14:28; Luke 13:6-9)

Luke decided just to skip Deuteronomy 14:1-21, a list of clean and unclean animals, as well as 14:22-27, which just repeats 12:17-31. Deuteronomy 14:28 commands every Israelite to offer a tithe of one's produce every three years. Luke employs this law as a springboard to launch a retrospective parable accounting for the Roman defeat of Judea and Galilee, continuing his discussion begun in the preceding verses. He likens the Jewish nation to a barren fig tree which has produced nothing (no fruit of repentance) three years straight. The vinedresser begs his employer to allow one more year before getting rid of the tree. I have to think this is a Lukan explanation for the delay of the Parousia, exactly as in 2 Peter 3:8-9.

Release of the Bond-slave (Deut. 15:1-18; Luke 13:10-21)

Deuteronomy commands that all debts be cancelled every seventh year (an utterly impractical measure that makes one suspect Deuteronomy was never really a binding legal code, but rather a utopian manifesto). This amounted to a release from indentured servitude and from incarceration in debtors' prison. The last case in the list is that of the bondwoman (Deut. 15:17). From this Luke develops his story of Jesus liberating an old woman, a bondservant of Satan for eighteen years by virtue of a bent spine (cf., Acts 10:38). Does the bondservant metaphor imply the woman was working off a debt of sin by suffering in this way?

Luke and Matthew have inherited both the Markan story of the man with the withered hand (Mark 3:1-6), a controversy about healing on the Sabbath, and the Q saying "Which of you, having one sheep [Luke: "a son/ass or ox"] that falls into a pit [Luke: "well"] on the sabbath, will not lay hold of it and pull it out?" (Matt. 12:11; Luke 1414:5). Matthew inserted the Q saying into the Markan story, while Luke rewrote Mark's story of the man with the withered hand as the healing of the man with dropsy (Luke 14:1-6), inserting the Q saying into it at the equivalent spot. But he also created the story of the woman with the bent spine, basing it on the same Q saying, adapted to the case suggested by Deuteronomy, the release from a bond; thus the parallel cited becomes *releasing* a farm animal from its *tether* on the Sabbath.

All Roads Lead to Jerusalem (Deut. 16:1-17:7; Luke 13:22-35)

Deuteronomy commands Israelites to undertake a pilgrimage to the Jerusalem Temple three times a year. In this Deuteronomic slot Luke has Jesus announce that nothing will deter him from meeting his destiny in Jerusalem. The wording of his declaration presupposes the Lukan redactional agenda of the Central Section itself, as well as the distinctive Lukan "prophet" Christology[366] (Luke 4:24; 7:16, 39; 9:19; 13:33; 24:19; Acts 3:22; 7:37), so we can be sure the saying is itself a redactional creation.

Guess Who's Coming to Dinner? (Deut. 16:18-20; 17:8-18; Luke 14:1-14)

The fit here is pretty loose, but the strained Deuteronomy-Luke correspondence itself demonstrates how dead-set Luke was to have something correspond to the next section of Deuteronomy. The Deuteronomy passage is concerned with people submitting to the oracular verdict of priests and judges, and with limiting the easily-abused prerogatives of the king. It was enough for Luke to set his scene in the house of a "ruler" and to tell the story of the dropsical man in order to exalt Jesus' judgment over that of the scribes.

The rest of the Lukan passage refers back to the preceding Deuteronomic verse, 16:14, where various guests are ranked. Inspired by this, Luke appends a piece of table etiquette lifted from Proverbs 25:6-7 ("Do not put yourself forward in the king's presence or stand in the place of the great; for it is better to be told, 'Come up here,' than to be put lower in the presence of the prince."). Deuteronomy 16:14's specific inclusion of the widow and the sojourner has resulted in Luke's command to skip one's friends and relatives and to invite the poor, the maimed, the blind, and the lame to dinner. While Luke's admonition at first sounds more radical

---

[366] Johannes Weiss, *Jesus' Proclamation of the Kingdom of God.* Trans. Richard Hyde Hiers and David Larimore Holland. Lives of Jesus Series (Philadelphia: Fortress Press,1971), p. 120; Weiss, *Earliest Christianity: A History of the Period A.D. 30-150* , Volume I. Trans. Frederick C. Grant. Harper Torchbooks (New York: Harper & Brothers, 1959), p. 120; Weiss, *Christ: The Beginning of Dogma.* Trans. V.D. Davis (Boston: American Unitarian Association, 1911), p. 16.

than Deuteronomy's inclusion of the poor *alongside* one's family, it actually mitigates the awkwardness of the situation: one can bask in playing the benefactor to one's poor clients without having to embarrass one's fellow sophisticates with the crude manners of the poor at the same table. Luke 14:12 points out that the reciprocation by your friends and kin would be an insignificant reward compared to the eternal reward due the benefactor of the poor, whereas in fact such largesse would win greater honor in the eyes of one's peers.[367] One would still be doing one's pious acts "to be seen of men" (Matt. 6:1), thereby forfeiting any reward from God.[368]

[Luke has omitted Deuteronomy 19's discussions of cities of refuge and of false witnesses.]

Draft Dodgers (Deut. 20; Luke 14:15-35)

All commentators recognize the similarity between the excuses offered by those invited to the great supper in Q (Matt. 22:1-10; Luke 14:16-24), implicitly sneered at by the narrator, on the one hand, and, on the other, the circumstances exempting an Israelite from serving in holy war in Deuteronomy 20: building a new house, planting a new vineyard, getting married. The Q parable represents a tightening up of what were considered by an enthusiastic sect to be lax standards, just as early Christians stiffened divorce rules. Think also of the stricter demands of itinerant discipleship as compared with Elijah's leniency on Elisha in Luke 9:61-62. But are not holy war and accepting God's grace very different propositions? Maybe not: "Onward Christian soldiers, marching as to war!"

---

[367] Bruce J. Malina, *The New Testament World: Insights from Cultural Anthropology* (Atlanta: John Knox Press, 1981), p. 142: "What patrons want of their clients is recognition of honor, submission, a following."

[368] In 1 Corinthians 11:18-22 we learn that some "solved" the problem by segregating the two groups at the same event! Gerd Theissen, *The Social Setting of Pauline Christianity: Essays on Corinth.* Trans. John H. Schütz (Edinburgh: T&T Clark, 1999), p. 151.

The Great Supper parable appears already in Q (Luke 14:16-24; Matt. 22:1-10 ff.) and in the Gospel of Thomas, saying 64. It seems to be an adaptation of the rabbinic story of the tax-collector Bar-Majan.[369] He chafed at his social outcast status[370] and hit upon a scheme to improve his reputation by inviting the respectable rich to a great feast. But every one of them, no fools, refused to cooperate. So the tax-collector decided he'd share the food with the poor in order not to waste it. Shortly thereafter, Bar-Majan died. The good karma accrued by his act of charity did win him a stately funeral, but it was not enough to keep him out of hell (Jerusalem Talmud, *Hagigah*, II, 77d).

The rest of Luke 14:25-33 owes its place here to the discussion of warfare in the parallel section of Deuteronomy, though the connection is really only that of catchwords, as is often the case in the Central Section.

[Luke skips Deuteronomy 21:1-14, the treatment of corpses and female captives. It is hard to imagine what he could have come up with as a parallel section.]

Prodigality (Deut. 21:15-22:4; Luke 15:11-32)

The poignant parable of the Prodigal Son is Luke's own work, as witness not only the juxtaposition of two representative characters, but also the uniquely Lukan device of character introspection in a tight spot: "What shall I do? I shall..." The Prodigal, having painted himself into a corner, reflects, "I will arise and go to my father, and I will say to him..." (15:18). The Unjust Judge, exasperated, "said to himself, 'I will vindicate her...'" (Luke 18:4-5). The Dishonest Steward "said to himself, 'What shall I do? ... I have decided what to

---

[369] Joachim Jeremias, *The Parables of Jesus*. Trans. S.H. Hooke (New York: Scribners, 1972), pp. 178-179.

[370] Luisa Schottroff and Wolfgang Stegemann, *Jesus and the Hope of the Poor*. Trans. Matthew J. O'Connell (Maryknoll: Orbis Books, 1986), pp. 7-13; Malina, *New Testament World*, pp. 83-84.

do...'" (16:3-4). And the Rich Fool "thought to himself, 'What shall I do...? I will do this...'" (12:17-18). Don't tell me this is not a signature mark of a distinctive author, all the more since we never see the like in Matthew, Mark, or John.

He likely got the idea for the parable from the Deuteronomic treatment of sons and their inheritance in 21:15-21. Luke combined the elements of division of property between a pair of sons, the possibility of favoring the wrong one, and the problem of a rebellious son who shames his family. But, as he does elsewhere, Luke mitigates the harshness of the original legal provision (no doubt because he writes for a Diaspora audience for whom some of these laws can no longer apply) with an example of mercy. Here the rebellious son is accepted and embraced, not executed.

Though the basic inspiration (or at least its placement here) comes from Deuteronomy, Luke borrowed his building materials from another source, the *Odyssey*.[371] The Prodigal is Luke's version of both the long-absent Odysseus and his son Telemachus who returns from his own long quest to find his father. Both the elements of wandering far from home and of the father-son reunion stem from this source. The cavorting of the Prodigal with loose women in distant lands is based on Odysseus' dalliance with Calypso. But the motif of the Prodigal's having "devoured [his father's] estate with loose living" comes from the similar judgment passed more than once by Telemachus and Eumaeus on the "gang of profligates" mooching off Odysseus' estate during his absence, the suitors for Penelope's hand.

The Prodigal's employment as a swine herder, a galling "transformation" for a Jew, reflects Circe's literal, magical transformation of Odysseus' men into swine, especially since the hungry Prodigal wants to stuff himself with the pods the pigs eat, i.e., act like a pig. Then again, his swineherd job may stem from

---

[371] Robert M. Price, "Rhoda and Penelope: Two More Cases of Luke's Suppression of Women," in Amy-Jill Levine with Marianne Blickenstaff, eds., *A Feminist Companion to the Acts of the Apostles.* Feminist Companion to the New Testament and Early Christian Writings, 9 (Edinburgh: T&T Clark, 2004), pp. 98-104.

Eumaeus' having been one. The latter's frequent characterization as a "righteous swineherd" may have suggested the depiction of the Prodigal as a repentant swineherd. The return of the Prodigal mirrors the return of Odysseus, as well as the homecoming of Telemachus. The Prodigal hopes to enter his father's household as a mere slave, whereas the returning Odysseus actually disguises himself as a slave on his own estate. The happy welcome given the Prodigal by his father recalls the reunion of Odysseus and Telemachus, also father and son, but even more the reunion of Telemachus and Eumaeus, his father's faithful servant.

> The last words were not out of his mouth when his [Odysseus'] own son appeared in the gateway. Eumaeus jumped up in amazement, and the bowls in which he had been busy mixing the sparkling wine tumbled out of his grasp. He ran forward to meet his young master. He kissed his lovely eyes and then kissed his right hand and his left, while the tears streamed down his cheeks. Like a fond father welcoming his son after nine years abroad, his only son, the apple of his eye and the centre of all his anxious cares, the admirable swineherd threw his arms around Prince Telemachus and showered kisses on him as though he had just escaped from death.[372]

Next Luke splits Odysseus into two characters, the two brothers. The elder brother, too, returns from being away, albeit only out in the field (the scene of conflict between another famous pair of brothers, Cain and Abel). Returning, he is dismayed, like Odysseus, to discover a feast in progress. (Luke may also be thinking of Exodus 32:18, "It is not the sound of shouting for victory, or the sound of the cry of defeat, but the sound of... *singing* that I hear!") It is a feast in honor of a profligate, as the elder brother is quick to point out, just like that of Penelope's suitors. And, just as their feast is

---

[372] Homer, *The Odyssey*. Trans. E.V. Rieu. Penguin Classics (Baltimore: Penguin Books, 1961), p. 245.

predicated upon the assumption of Odysseus' death, the Prodigal's father explains to the elder son that they must feast since the Prodigal was dead and has now returned alive, as Odysseus is about to do.

Deuteronomy 22:1-4 lists all kinds of lost objects which must be returned if found, just as the sequence Luke 15:3-7, 8-10 concerns lost things zealously sought and found. The first of these parables comes from Q, the parable of the Lost Sheep (also in Matthew 18:10-14), while the second, the parable of the Lost Coin, is presumably Luke's own creation, a doublet of the uniquely Lukan parable of the Leaven (13:20-21) plus his story of Martha (10:38-42), both featuring a busy housekeeper.

Masters, Slaves, Money, and Divorce (Deut. 23:15-24:4; Luke 16:1-18)

Luke skips Deuteronomy 22:5-23:14, a miscellaneous grab bag. But he has borrowed the Deuteronomy 23 provision for the welcoming of an escaped slave to live in one's midst to use as the basis for his parable of the Dishonest Steward. Given his pink slip, the too-clever Steward manipulates his master's accounts to guarantee himself a new position with his master's clients.

Luke lacks anything special about cult prostitutes and vows, discussed in Deuteronomy, but the Deuteronomic treatment of debts and usury inspires him to accuse the Pharisees of being "lovers of money." Greed like theirs is an "abomination" (bdelugma) before God, a word he has borrowed from the Septuagint version of the same Deuteronomic passage's condemnation of a man remarrying his divorced wife after a second husband has also kicked her out. On the matter of divorce, Luke opposes to the Deuteronomic provision the diametrically opposite Markan rejection of divorce (Mark 10:9), even while insisting that the Torah is forever unalterable!

Publican Enemy Number One (Deut. 24:6-25:3; Luke 16:19-18:8)

To take the place of Deuteronomy's instructions about fair treatment of the poor, Luke has created the parable of the Rich Man and Lazarus, probably basing it upon the ending of the same rabbinic story of the tax-collector Bar-Majan (*Hagigah*, II, 77d) which formed the basis also of the Great Supper parable. Bar-Majan, rapacious tax-collector, wound up in the frying pan. At least it wasn't simply his wealth that damned him in that version. But perhaps we are to infer that Dives (as tradition names him) was damned for his callous indifference to Lazarus' misery, though Luke doesn't actually say so.

Luke inserts the Q saying about the millstone (Luke 17:1-2; Matt. 18:6-7) to match the Deuteronomic mention of a millstone as the irreplaceable tool of one's trade (24:6), a mere catchword connection.

The instructions for a leper's cure and certification (Deut. 24:8-9) plus Deuteronomy 24:14's counsel to treat the sojourning foreigner fairly inspire a new Lukan pro-Samaritan story, that of the nine Jewish lepers whom Jesus cures without thanks versus the single Samaritan who returns to thank him. The motif of praising God for a miracle, which Luke frequently adds to older miracle stories, forms the whole premise of this one, branding it as completely Lukan.

Deuteronomy 24:17-18, 25:1-3 commands fair judgments on behalf of the poor and fair treatment of widows. Luke's counterpart is his parable of the Unjust Judge. This scoundrel rebuffs a widow too poor to bribe him till she finally drives him to distraction. This Luke uses to urge patience in prayer: if even a corrupt judge will at length give in to a just petition, won't a righteous God answer prayers in his own time?

I'm Humble and Proud of it![373] (Deut. 26; Luke 18:9-14)

---

[373] This was a tongue-in-cheek slogan circulated by the Chaplain's Committee at Wheaton College back in 1975. I wish I had one of those lapel buttons!

Luke skips another piece of Deuteronomy, namely 25:4-19 which deals with Levirate marriage, false weights, etc. He picks back up with Deuteronomy 26:12-15 which says that, as one offers the first-fruits of his crops, he may confess his own perfect obedience to the commandments (provided it's true!), and so may rightly claim God's blessing on his farmland. This seems to have struck Luke as pretentious and pompous, so he spoofs the section with his parable of the Pharisee (whose self-praise in the guise of prayer sounds a lot like that in Deuteronomy) and the Publican (counted righteous by virtue of his humble self-condemnation).

Zach and Jesus Sittin' in a Tree (Luke 19:1-10)

Zacchaeus wants to get a glimpse of the famous Jesus, so he shinnies up a tree "because he was short." Who was vertically challenged, Zacchaeus or Jesus? It might be Jesus, with a Zacchaeus of average height unable to see the diminutive sage over the heads of the crowd. But I think generations of Sunday Schoolmarms are probably correct that Zacchaeus is supposed to be the short one.

The fictive character of the tale is evident from the fact that, though Jesus and Zacchaeus have obviously never met, Zacchaeus is already on Jesus' divinely ordained appointment schedule. Jesus is made to sound like the Grim Reaper or the Angel Moroni.

Are we to understand that Zacchaeus is so blown away by Jesus' unexpected attention that, like Peter seeing the miraculous catch of fish and recognizing the presence of the divine, is reflexively cut to the quick and repents of his sins on the spot? That would indeed make good sense. But I wonder if Zacchaeus, hearing the crowd hissing at him for being a no-good tax-collector, rises to his own defense, declaring his innocence. Does he mean to protest that he makes it a policy to donate half his income to the poor and that, if he finds he has overcharged anyone, he always reimburses the person four-fold?

Pounding the Parable (Luke 19:11-27)

Luke has drawn from Q what we know from its appearance in Matthew 25:14-30 as the parable of the Talents. The original point seems to have been that, as your life is on loan from God, you'd better have something to show for it when time comes for God to collect. Matthew preserves this message, but Luke confuses things, making the parable an ellipse drawn around two foci, or a planet orbiting a double star. Luke has a habit of pre-interpreting his parables for the reader. In this case, he says Jesus told this story to dampen the apocalyptic fervor of his followers who believed the End Times were around the next corner. To this end, Luke makes Q's lord of the manor into a king, implicitly Herod the Great's son Archelaus.[374] Luke supplies the occasion for the man's trip away: he is journeying to Rome to confirm his inheritance of his father's client kingship. But Archelaus is no sweetie (cf., Matt. 2:22), and the folks back home send an embassy to the emperor, pleading with him not to make Archelaus king over them. But the effort fails, and when the new king gets back, he rounds up those who sought to undermine him and liquidates them. Now what does this have to do with the date of the Parousia? Simply that the parable has the king-elect undertake a journey *far away*, i.e., heaven, where he will become king (Jesus a la Psalm 110:1) and only subsequently make the exceedingly *long* trip back.[375]

The Non-Olivet Discourse (Luke 21)

For some reason, Luke omits Mark's location of this speech atop the Mount of Olives, as he previously omitted the location of the Confession of Peter, which Mark placed at Caesarea Philippi. The content is largely the same as in Mark 13, but that only makes the alterations all the more significant. For instance, Mark had Jesus warn, "Many will come in my name, saying, 'I am he!' and they will

---

[374] Jeremias, *Parables of Jesus*, p. 59.
[375] Conzelmann, *Theology of St. Luke*, p. 113.

lead many astray" (13:6), but Luke has, "Take heed that you are not led astray; for many will come in my name, saying, 'I am he!' *and,* '*The time is at hand!*'" (21:8). Aha! Expecting the imminent Parousia is now false prophecy, precisely as in 2 Thessalonians 2:1-3.

Verses 20-24 replace Mark 13:14-19. Instead of the apocalyptic mystery of Daniel's Abomination of Desolation, Luke historicizes it into the Roman siege of 70 C.E. and the leveling of the Temple, followed by "the times of the Gentiles," a period of definite but unspecified duration. The immediate implication of the phrase is the wholesale displacement of Jews by the Romans (21:24) which, again, makes more sense if it refers to the aftermath of the Bar Kochba rebellion of 132-135. But Luke would also seem to be thinking of the period of evangelism among the nations (cf., Rom. 11:25) during the (potentially very long) Church age.

All this confirms Conzelmann's reading of Luke as implicitly acknowledging the failure of the expected Parousia and its deferral to the unknown future.[376] But then why does Luke retain, in 21:32, Mark's promise that the End must come within the generation of Jesus' contemporaries? It was too well established in the tradition. So in classical scribal style, Luke had to be content with inserting surrounding material to mitigate the thrust of this passage, so that the reader might conclude (as modern readers still do!) "I guess that 'this generation' business must not mean what it seems to mean! Otherwise, what do you make of these other verses?"

From Passover to Passion (Luke 22)

One of the numerous oddities Luke shares with John (and no one else) is the idea that Judas Iscariot was influenced or even possessed by Satan to betray Jesus. Mark offered no clear motivation for Judas' perfidy. Matthew says Judas was a little short of cash and decided, so to speak, to "pawn" Jesus to get a few extra bucks. John depicts Judas as a sneak thief but also as devil-inspired.

---

[376] Conzelmann, *Theology of St. Luke*, p. 123.

In 22:15 Luke has Jesus refer to the Last Supper as "this Passover," which is interesting, as Mark (followed by Matthew) does not, within the Last Supper pericope itself, call the meal a Passover seder. It is only the context which makes it one, and remember, the narrative is composed of individual, rounded units, subsequently strung together. And nothing in the actual description of the Last Supper implies it is a seder. No lamb, no spices, not even a reference to the Exodus story![377] And in John, the meal is explicitly *not* a Passover but takes place the night before.

Where we expect the traditional Words of Institution of the Eucharist (Holy Communion), we find something amiss:

> And he took a cup, and when he had given thanks he said, "Take this, and divide it among yourselves; for I tell you that from now on I shall not drink of the fruit of the vine until the kingdom of God comes." And he took bread, and when he had given thanks he broke it and gave it to them, saying, "This is my body."

In Mark 14:22-25 we read this.

> And as they were eating, he took bread, and blessed, and broke it, and gave it to them, and said, "Take; this is my body." And he took a cup, and when he had given thanks he gave it to them, and they all drank of it. And he said to them, "This is my blood of the covenant, which is poured out for many. Truly, I say to you, I shall not drink again of the fruit of the vine until that day when I drink it new in the kingdom of God."

The differences are immediately apparent. The shared cup comes

---

[377] The Eucharist was undoubtedly borrowed from neighboring dying-and-rising god cults with which Israel had been familiar (and even practiced!) for centuries (Ezek. 8:7-17; Zech. 12:11). The devotees of Dionysus and of Osiris drank wine and/or beer as the gods' blood and ate bread as their flesh.

second in Mark but first in Luke. Luke has nothing to say of any sacramental or symbolic meaning of the cup. Instead, as if it explained the sharing of the cup, he has Jesus, after offering the cup, take his vow of abstinence: no more wine for him till the kingdom of God comes (which implies it will be but hours or days away). The temperance vow in Mark's version was last, after the whole bread-and-cup complex. In Luke, the bread is mentioned last, and only very minimal explanation follows: it is somehow to be identified with Jesus' body, though nothing is said of any sacramental purpose for eating it.

The abruptness of the ending, "This is my body," has caused many ancient scribes and modern scholars to try to fill the gap they perceive because they insist that Luke be like Matthew and Mark. So in later manuscripts we find a clumsy and artificial continuation, to harmonize Luke's Last Supper with Mark's and Matthew's: "'which is given for you. Do this in remembrance of me.' And likewise the cup after supper, saying, 'This cup which is poured out for you is the new covenant in my blood.'" Okay, now that's more *like* it! But it's not authentic; it produces a three-stage sequence of cup, bread, cup. It couldn't be more obvious that someone wanted Luke to read more like Mark but didn't dare to erase the Lukan original and rewrite the whole thing to make it just like Mark. It was sacred text already. So all he could do was to add on text that would produce a bread-cup sequence after the original "false start" cup (as he viewed it).

The situation here is precisely parallel to that of the brakes-slamming conclusion of Mark 16. Scribes added Mark 16:9-20 to replace what they felt *must* be missing. Matthew and Luke did the same. And a few modern scholars follow them in declaring the longer ending authentic, though it patently is not. Same here: some scholars[378] want the longer version of the Last Supper text to be original because they don't know what to make of the shorter version.

Just to be clear ("Fat chance," you say?), I admit that there was a

---

[378] Joachim Jeremias, *The Eucharistic Words of Jesus*. Trans. Arnold Ehrhardt (Oxford: Basil Blackwell, 1955), pp. 87-91.

longer version that got truncated, but that longer version was in Luke's source, and it was he who truncated it. The "This is my body," *period*, certainly implies that. So why, pray tell, did Luke cut the text? Apparently he was well aware of the widespread Christian belief in Jesus' death as an atoning sacrifice—and *rejected* it. Notice another Lukan alteration of Mark to the same end. Mark 10:45 had "For the Son of man also came not to be served but to serve, and to give his life as a ransom for many." Luke 22:27 substitutes for this a rather different version: "For which is the greater, one who sits at table, or one who serves? Is it not the one who sits at table? But I am among you as one who serves." Two differences: "the Son of man" becomes Jesus, as if to clear up any doubt that Daniel's Son of Man *is* Jesus and not someone else. And there is nothing in Luke about Jesus giving his life as a ransom for many. Luke seems to have wanted to suppress this notion of Jesus' saving death,[379] so important to Paul and John.

Accordingly, in Luke-Acts' summaries of the gospel message (Luke 24:19-27; 46-47; Acts 2:22-38; 3:18-26; 4:10-12; 5:30-32; 7:51-53; 10:36-43; 13:26-39; 17:2-3; 22:16; 26:22-23) a definite pattern emerges: it was prophesied that the Messiah must first suffer and die and only then enter into his triumph. Once he had done so, he should become the source of salvation. All who believed in his name and called upon it in baptism should receive forgiveness of sins. And what was the role of Jesus' death in all this? It was simply a credential: had he not suffered and died, he could not qualify as the real Messiah, but he did. And he is. There is nothing about his shed blood washing away sins.

Acts 20:28 ("Take heed to yourselves and to all the flock, in which the Holy Spirit has made you overseers, to care for the church of God which he obtained with the blood of his own Son") may seem an exception, but there is some textual uncertainty here. Some

---

[379] Conzelmann, *Theology of St. Luke*, p.201; C.H. Dodd, *The Apostolic Preaching and its Developments: Three Lectures* (New York: Harper & Row, 1964), p. 25; Henry J. Cadbury, *The Making of Luke-Acts* (London: SPCK, 1961), pp. 280-281.

manuscripts read "with his own blood." And this, in turn, could as easily be rendered "with the blood of his own." So what did it originally say? We don't know, so any polemical citation of this verse gets hamstrung by the crippling asterisk that must be placed beside it.

Luke 22:28-30 is a Q passage shared with Matthew 19:28. It promises to the Twelve pretty much what sounded so delusional when James and John requested it: privileged seats on the messianic dais with Jesus. The main difference between Matthew and Luke is that Matthew has "twelve thrones judging the twelve tribes of Israel," while Luke has no specific number of thrones for the judges, hence no restricted number of judges. Who has changed it? And why? If Luke has the original, it might imply that this promise, uttered by some Christ-prophet, was directed to Christians in general, as in 1 Cor. 6:2-3; 2 Tim. 2:12a; Rev. 2:26-27; 3:21. That would mean Matthew has restricted the promise to the Twelve. On the other hand, you could argue that Matthew's was the Q original and that Luke has omitted the number of thrones because, had Jesus promised thrones to the Twelve, this would have included Judas Iscariot. This seems a bit far-fetched to me in light of Acts 1:21-26, where Luke makes clear that the college of the Twelve Apostles is stable in number though open to replenishment. So I think Luke lacks the number of thrones because the promise was not intended only for Peter and his colleagues.

So jealous is he for the reputation of Peter as Prince of the Apostles, Luke (22:31) actually has Jesus predict Peter's restoration before he predicts what it is from which Peter is restored! Notice that Satan has *demanded* to test the disciples, as he tested Jesus in the wilderness, to see if they will prove worthy of the trust Jesus has placed in them. As in the Book of Job, it is his right and proper function.

Jesus already knows his men will fail! Of course, nothing like this was ever spoken by Jesus to Peter. It is all aimed at the reader. The story of the disciples running like scared rabbits and, worse yet, Peter's denials of Jesus, was too widely believed (at least by Pauline Christians)[380] that the best Luke can do is to picture Jesus giving poor Pete a vote of confidence despite the inevitability of his great failure! He's hoping his readers will be as willing to forgive Peter.

Conzelmann[381] took verses 35-36 as another turning point in Luke's dispensational progression, marking the end of "the middle of time" and turning the corner to the Church age. Jesus contrasts it with the halcyon period of unmolested and successful gospel preaching in which his missionaries operated under a shield of divine protection. From here on in, Satan's vicious mischief can be expected to return with fury. Indeed, it has already begun with Satan's manipulation of Judas to betray Jesus.

What does it mean when Jesus tells them to prepare for the worst, advising them to sell the shirt off their back and buy a sword with the money? S.G.F. Brandon[382] took this to be an historical detail that Mark never would have divulged (and didn't), while Luke is not particularly on his guard, since the time when Rome suspected Christians of sedition was long past. But this seems unlikely to me in view of Luke's numerous apologetical attempts to whitewash Christianity as politically harmless. Brandon believed, quite reasonably, that Jerusalem Christians fought alongside fellow Jews in the war against Rome. And in doing so they were the heirs of a revolutionary Jesus who had been crucified forty years earlier for being what he actually *was*, a rebel against Caesar.

But Luke could scarcely have wanted to depict Jesus this way. No, he has reinterpreted the saying as if, a la Hugh J. Schonfield,[383] Jesus had no revolutionary plans that day (or any day) but was merely setting the stage for acting out a scheduled prophetic fulfillment: "he was counted as one of the transgressors" (Isa. 53:12). This meant Jesus had to appear to be a violent revolutionary for the authorities

---

[380] Alfred Loisy, *The Birth of the Christian Religion*. Trans. L.P. Jacks (London: George Allen & Unwin, 1948), p. 102.

[381] Conzelmann, *Theology of St. Luke*, pp. 13, 16, 36, 50, 81-82, 91-92,103, 170, 187, 199, 201, 232, 234..

[382] S.G.F. Brandon, *The Fall of Jerusalem and the Christian Church: A Study of the Effects of the Jewish Overthrow of A.D. 70 on Christianity* (London: SPCK, 1951), pp. 103, 207.

[383] Hugh J. Schonfield, *The Passover Plot: New Light on the History of Jesus* (New York: Bantam Books, 1967), pp. 125, 134.

to arrest him. Thus the swords were mere stage props. As ludicrous as this sounds as a description of anyone's behavior outside of a sitcom, it makes good sense as part of Luke's fictionalizing program of sucking up to Rome. And we will very shortly be seeing more of the same.[384]

The scene in Gethsemane (though Luke doesn't call it that) has been condensed from Mark in order to make room for new material. Now Jesus prays to escape the cross a single time, not three, and he receives a remarkable reply. "And there appeared to him an angel from heaven, strengthening him" (Luke 22:43), a detail borrowed from 1 Kings 19:7-8, where angels come to strengthen the prophet Elijah. But in some manuscripts it gets even more interesting: "And being in agony he prayed more earnestly; and his sweat became like great drops of blood falling down upon the ground" (22:44). Is the idea that Jesus was sweating actual drops of blood? Or just that he was perspiring so profusely that it was like blood pouring out? And is this scene a Lukan counterpart to John 19:34?

The most fanciful miracle in the New Testament is found in Luke 22:50-51: the disciples unlimber their swords and start to defend Jesus from those who've arrived to arrest him, and Jesus puts a stop to it. But before he can, one of his men has taken a swing at one of the goon squad and, failing to split the man's skull, only manages to slice off an ear. Jesus to the rescue! He picks up the severed ear, dusts if off, and sticks it back on (using divine spittle as his glue?)! In case you haven't noticed, there is no other healing story in which Jesus restores a severed limb. This ought to give us pause. Why does no other gospel document this feat? Okay, it's just an ear, but it's still a pretty big deal. Surely, what happened was this: some earlier version had Jesus halt the fray, saying, "Let it be restored to its place!" Matthew made the correct inference and had Jesus say, "Put your sword back into its place" (Matt. 26:52). Likewise John 18:11, "Put your sword into its sheath." But Luke figured the "it" was the ear, not the sword![385] And so a miracle was born.

---

[384] Conzelmann, *Theology of St. Luke*, pp. 137-142.

[385] G.A. Wells, *The Jesus of the Early Christians: A Study in Christian Origins*

Luke adds a novelistic touch of poignancy[386] in verse 61, where Jesus, hearing Peter's cowardly denials, turns to give him that "Toldja so!" look, and poor Pete breaks down crying. Unless Luke has lost control of his narrative, he must intend that Jesus is out in the courtyard though removed just a bit from Peter, surrounded as he is by guards. Otherwise, how could Jesus hear Peter denying him and turn to look at him? Readers tend to harmonize Luke with Matthew and Mark and so create a needless difficulty, imagining Jesus and Peter able to see and hear one another while Jesus is on trial inside the house. Mark and Matthew place the denials during the Sanhedrin hearing, inside the priestly mansion, but Luke places the denials before the hearing begins, while Jesus is in the courtyard awaiting trial.

Once the elders convene, Luke has some differences from Mark. He has transferred the business about Jesus supposedly threatening to destroy the Temple (Mark 14:57-58) to the trial of Stephen (Acts 6:14). And when Jesus is asked, "If you are the Christ, tell us," Jesus gives an even more equivocal response than he does in Matthew 26:64 and a few manuscripts of Mark 14:62: "You have said so" (i.e., "If you say so!"). Luke's Jesus replies, "If I tell you [i.e., that I am?], you will not believe, and if I ask you [a question of my own?] you will not answer." Huh? I think of Jesus answering a question with a question in Luke 20:3. Is he saying he would like to use the same strategy here but knows it would be futile because they would only stonewall him again? Maybe, but what would be the point of saying that? Why would Jesus say it? Why would Luke? Well, I'm not planning to lose any sleep over it.

Luke does have Jesus asked if he is God's son and give the familiar evasion a few verses later (verse 70). So what was the point of the confusing exchange up in verse 67? It looks like Luke is trying to splice together two slightly different versions of the story. Or maybe scribes interpolated the Matthew/Mark version of his reply in order to harmonize the Synoptics. At any rate, Luke makes a crucial change

---

(London: Pemberton Books, 1971), p. 197.

[386] Loisy, *Origins of the New Testament*, p. 166.

to part of Jesus' reply. Mark and Matthew have Jesus predict that "you will see the Son of man sitting at the right hand of Power, and coming with the clouds of heaven." Not Luke. He has Jesus say, "from now on, the Son of man shall be seated at the right hand of the power of God." No longer does he predict that they will live to see the Parousia of the enthroned Danielic Son of man. History betrayed that promise. All these men died while things went on, business as usual. So Luke merely says that the Son of man will be enthroned alongside God, whether any mortal eye beholds it or not. Tradition assigns the sharp-eyed eagle as the symbol for John the evangelist, but maybe we should award it to Conzelmann![387]

An Innocent Man (Luke 23)

Luke generally follows Mark's Passion Narrative but does add interesting bits of his own. Mark said the chief priests "accused [Jesus] of many things" (Mark 15:3) without specifying what they were, "many charges" (Mark 15:4). Luke fills in that blank: "We found this man perverting our nation, and forbidding us to give tribute to Caesar, and saying that he himself is Christ a king." Of course, that's about what you'd expect, since the Sanhedrin would know issues of blasphemy would be of no particular interest to the Roman procurator (cf., Acts 18:14-16). Uh, can we be sure these are false accusations as the gospel writers would have us believe? Suppose they were true. After all, if the Jewish Sanhedrin did not possess the authority to carry out executions (John 18:31), they could have simply explained the case to Pilate (as they do in John 19:7) and ask his approval for them to put Jesus to death. It's not as if Rome forbade Jews from stoning blasphemers; they just had to have it approved by Rome first. Instead they charge him with sedition. This implies Jesus *was* a rebel. It is impossible to know, but it is very clear that, throughout Luke and Acts, Luke is engaging in an apologetical

---

[387] And don't think I'm saying this just because I got my doctorate under Darrell J. Doughty, who got his under Conzelmann!

"charm offensive," as when in this very chapter he has Pilate declare Jesus innocent no less than three times (verses 4, 14, 22)!

We have already seen that Luke could not bring himself to choose between the Joanna Chastity story and the Markan Passion narrative but, like ancient "scissors-and-paste historians,"[388] he feels obliged to harmonize them rather than leaving anything on the cutting room floor. Thus he tries to combine one version, in which it was Herod who sentenced Jesus to death, with another that held Pilate responsible. But the result is not entirely successful. If Pilate was happy to let Herod Antipas pass judgment, and Herod found him innocent (as Pilate expressly says he did in 23:15a), why did Pilate continue his involvement in the case?

Verses 27-31 offer us a new moment during the *Via Dolorosa*, a new station of the cross. Here we see the beginning of the trend of embellishment that would before too long give us Veronica with her veil and the Wandering Jew. What Jesus says to his female devotees functions here as an anticipation of the doom to befall Jerusalem (cf., Luke 13:1-9; 19:41-44; 21:20-24), but I suspect Luke has placed it in this context as a way of robbing it of its originally intended force, a blessing on women who embrace consecrated celibacy and reject maternal duties.

In any event, the resulting scene is of a type known elsewhere in the same milieu. Midrash Genesis Rabbah 65:22 tells a tale of Rabbi Yosi b. Yoezer of Zeredah, who served as Nasi (chief rabbi) around 191 B.C.E. The Seleucid general Bacchides had him seated on a horse on his way to the place he was to be hanged, i.e., crucified. His nephew was a stooge of the persecutors, having renounced Judaism. He came riding up to his uncle, mocking the old man: "See the horse upon which my master lets me ride and see the horse upon which *your* Master [God] lets *you* ride." Yosi retorted, "If it is thus with those who do His will, all the more so with those who anger Him." The apostate smartass was brought up short in a fit of self-loathing and soon killed himself, hoping in this manner to

---

[388] R.G. Collingwood, *The Idea of History*. A Galaxy Book (New York: Oxford University Press, 1956), pp. 33, 235, etc.

atone for his terrible sins.

Bultmann[389] passes on another couple of examples with obvious similarities to Luke's scene.

> It was customary to weep for those who were led to their crucifixion. When R. Chanina b. Teradjon was led to execution his daughter wept for him, and he responded: "If you weep for me and beat yourself it were better that an (earthly) fire that is kindled should consume me than the fire (of Hell) which is not kindled."

> [A] Rabbi who is taken out to his cross (and there is clearly mockery going on) says, "If this (crucifixion) is what happens to those who do the will [of God], what will be the lot of those who offend against it?"

The crucifixion scene itself features more Lukan innovations. First there's Jesus' cry (so we readers can "hear" it): "Father, forgive them; for they know not what they do," 23:34a, which some manuscripts quite surprisingly lack. One wonders if possibly the texts that include the famous saying were made from a first draft, before Luke composed Acts, his second volume. In Acts 7:60 Luke gives the dying Stephen pretty much the same line. When Luke transfers something from Mark into Acts, he usually skips it in his retelling of Mark. Perhaps, having decided to use the prayer for forgiveness in Acts, he went back and removed it from the Jesus' crucifixion scene, and the manuscripts lacking the prayer are based on that revised version?

Then there's the Good Thief who chides his big-mouth colleague for giving Jesus grief. "*You're* criticizing *him*? Look, you and I are scum. We deserve what we get, but this guy's done nothing! Luke vouches for him, and that's good enough for me!" And hopefully for any Roman readers, too! See? In case Pilate's three declarations weren't enough to convince you, take it from an expert

---

[389] Rudolf Bultmann, *The History of the Synoptic Tradition.* Trans. John Marsh (New York: Harper & Row, 1972), p. 37, n. 3.

who ought to know (cf. Titus 1:12)!

Wait a sec! Don't Mark 15:32 and Matthew 27:44 have *both* men (*lestai*, thieves or revolutionaries) ridicule Jesus? Common Bible readers have been taught to read this scene according to an old apologist trick: at first both joined in the fun, but then one thought better of it and told the other to shut up. But no gospel says this. It is just a lame attempt to split the difference, hoping no one will notice. And yet this "theory" is unwittingly close to the truth. Originally, I am willing to bet, Luke (or the underlying Ur-Lukas) had both of the men crucified with Jesus mocking him, neither one repenting. The one man's words, "Jesus, remember me when you come to your throne!" was not a desperate statement of last-minute faith, as we now read it, but rather one of the sarcastic barbs hurled by one of Jesus' mockers. As it happens, Luke's fellow second-century author, Diodorus Siculus, wrote a scene in which a nobleman mocks a household slave who harbors dreams of nobility: "Remember me when you come into your kingdom!" Lukan redaction has made this cruel jest into a deathbed confession of faith. So, in a sense, one crucified mocker *did* change his tune, just not within Luke's narrative, rather between one draft and another!

The story encourages those who, like Luke's Prodigal Son, fear it is too late to return to God. This is all the more evident from the fact that the salvation Jesus promises the man makes sense only as envisioning the beatific bliss of the Christian upon death. By contrast, if we consistently read it as a prediction made by Jesus on that particular occasion, it clashes rudely with Jesus' predictions of his death and resurrection sprinkled throughout this gospel. "Today you will be with me in Paradise"? Really? I thought Jesus was to languish in the grave till the third day and then ascend bodily into the highest heaven where God's throne is. But no? He's just going to heaven to play his harp next to pious old Aunt Matilda?

Hey, *wait* a minute! Where's Jesus' notorious cry of despair, "My God, my God, why did you forsake me" (Mark 15:34; Matt. 27:46)? If they were frank, all Christian readers wish Jesus hadn't said it. Ditto Luke, who chops it and replaces the quote from Psalm 22:1 with a more positive one from Psalm 31:5, "Father, into thy hands I commit my spirit." Okay, Jesus didn't die in disappointed despair after all! *Whew!*

In the next verse, the centurion on duty, beholding the events attendant upon Jesus' death, exclaims, "Truly, this man was the Son of God!" Right? No, that's what he says in Mark 15:39 and Matthew 27:54. By contrast, Luke's centurion quips, "Certainly, this man was [wait for it...] innocent!" What an anti-climax! Or was it? Here Luke's apologetical agenda is very clearly on display. Luke is again telling his story for Roman eyes; it is most important for him that a Roman officer reiterates Pilate's declaration that Jesus was not guilty.

It's about time for Joseph of Arimathea to come on stage, and he does not disappoint. But Luke is uncomfortable with Mark's perhaps unwitting implication that, despite Joseph's generosity in seeing to Jesus' burial, he had cast his vote in the Sanhedrin against Jesus. He *couldn't* have! So, for Luke (23:51), he *didn't!*[390]

Higher and Higher, Baby; It's a Livin' Thing[391] *(Luke 24)*

Mark has some of Jesus' female followers visit Joseph's tomb in order to prepare the body properly for burial. They are startled to find the tomb already standing wide open with a young man sitting there, dressed in white, apparently waiting for them. Who, or what, was he? Many scholars plausibly suggest that Mark expected the reader to recognize the "young man" as an angel, since angels are often obliquely described this way in ancient sources. Luke makes that explicit, and adds a second one for good measure; he says the two "men" are clad in phosphorescent garb, not just white. Like Jesus atop the Mount of Transfiguration. Once again, they tell the women to go and report the news of Jesus' resurrection. In Mark, you'll recall, they are too freaked out, and they keep their mouths shut. The End. But Luke did not like that ending, so he changed it. Now,

[390] Sanders, *Jews in Luke-Acts*, p. 229.
[391] Of course, this is a line from a song by Yasser Kilowatt and the Electric Liberation Organization.

in Luke, they obey orders and do bring the news to the disciples. This is not to say Luke simply tacked on more material. No, in order to do that he had to *discard* Mark's ending. This means that Mark's ending does not allow any continuation. Either the women told the disciples or they didn't, and if they didn't, there can be no continuation.

When the women make their report, the men laugh it off as some crazy tall tale. But in some manuscripts, Peter is curious enough to go and check the tomb for himself, though he finds nothing, the angels having packed up and left. One suspects this verse (12) is an interpolation since it seems incompatible with the disciples' utter incredulity, just reported. Does this leave room for Peter to think there may in fact be something to the women's report after all?

But let's not leave the empty tomb as quickly as the angels did. There is another strategic rewrite to be noticed. Mark had his young man say, "But go, tell his disciples and Peter that he is going before you to Galilee; there you will see him, as he told you" (16:7). Luke has rearranged the furniture a bit: "Remember how he told you, *while he was still in Galilee,* that the Son of man must be delivered into the hands of sinful men, and be crucified, and on the third day rise." Hmmm... sounds like Luke doesn't want the disciples going to Galilee. And indeed they do not.[392] There are no Galilean resurrection appearances in Luke's gospel, contrary to Matthew and John. In Luke Jesus appears in and around Jerusalem.[393] This is because Luke wants Christianity to expand like the Big Bang from the Holy City. In Acts we will see how Peter and his Jerusalem colleagues pioneer new mission initiatives from Jerusalem and keep a close eye on the missions of their subordinates like Philip, Paul, Barnabas, and Silas.

The real substance of Luke's Easter chapter is, of course, the story of the two disciples on the road to Emmaus. It looks like a pre-Lukan story to which Luke has added a big chunk of dialogue.

---

[392] Conzelmann, *Theology of St. Luke,* p. 202.
[393] Conzelmann, *Theology of St. Luke,* p. 93.

Bracket verses 17-27, 32-35 and see what you've got. It is a coherent story, swiftly proceeding to the climax, the shocking revelation of the identity of their incognito companion. It is a variant of the classic myth of "entertaining angels unaware" (Heb.13:2) placed in the service of Eucharistic liturgy. No one can miss the symbolism of the climax: in the course of the breaking of bread the risen Jesus is invisibly present. In fact, the symbolism is so dominant, one must wonder if the story is even intended as a real event.

But what about the dialogue? Luke has Jesus talk, ostensibly, to the two disciples, but really to the reader. What the disappointed disciples tell Jesus summarizes events from the previous chapter. Jesus replies with the distinctive Lukan understanding of Jesus' death: it is the sign of the true Messiah because the Messiah's death was predicted all over the place in scripture. (Too bad Luke doesn't happen to *quote* any of these ubiquitous texts!) Had Jesus escaped death he could not qualify. So, far from debunking Jesus' messiahship, the cross confirms it. The fulfilled prophecy motif tends to eclipse the original Eucharistic theme.

We find an astonishing parallel to the Emmaus episode in an old testimonial inscription (fourth century B.C.E.) from the Epidaurus shrine of the healing god Asclepius.

> Sostrata, a woman of Pherae, was pregnant with worms. Being in a very bad way, she was carried into the Temple and slept there. But when she saw no distinct dream she let herself be carried back home. Then, however, near a place called Kornoi, a man of fine appearance seemed to come upon her and her companions. When he had learned from them about their bad luck, he asked them to set down on the ground the litter in which they were carrying Sostrata. Then he cut open her abdomen and took out a great quantity of worms--two wash basins full. After having stitched her belly up again and made the woman well, Asclepius revealed to her his presence and enjoined her to send thank-offerings for her treatment to Epidaurus. (Stele 2.25)[394]

---

[394] Emma J. Edelstein and Ludwig Edelstein (ed. and trans.), *Asclepius: Collection and Interpretation of the Testimonies* (Baltimore: Johns Hopkins

Now you might be tempted to disbelieve this story, but that would leave you open to the charge of harboring naturalistic presuppositions.

When Jesus appears out of thin air to the huddled disciples back in Jerusalem (verse 36) he sends mixed signals.[395] Despite his Jacob Marley-like entrance, Jesus insists that he is no ghost and tries to prove it by showing them his hands and feet (presumably for them to touch) and asks for something to eat, since the common belief was that angels and spirits, lacking physical bodies, could not eat. But what exactly is he trying to prove? Does he mean to show he has risen from the dead in a physical form? Or is he trying to convince them that he is *still* alive, that he has survived the cross? Consider the parallel with Apollonius of Tyana's reunion with his disciples, who had mistakenly given him up for dead.

> Damis groaned out loud, and said something like, "Gods above, will we ever see our good, noble comrade?"
>
> Apollonius, who was now standing at the entrance of the grotto, heard this and said, "You will, in fact you already have."
>
> "Alive?" asked Demetrius, "But if dead, we have never stopped weeping for you."
>
> Apollonius stretched out his hand, and said, "Take hold of me. If I elude you, I am a ghost come back from Persephone's domain, like the ghosts which the gods below reveal to men when mourning makes them too despondent. But if I stay when you grasp me, persuade Damis, too, that I am alive and have not lost my body." (Philostratus, *Life of Apollonius of Tyana* 8:12)[396]

The two stories are quite similar. Are they trying to make the same

---

University Press, 1998), p. 234; also available in Mary R. Lefkowitz and Maureen B. Fant, eds., *Women's Life in Greece and Rome: A Source Book in Translation* (Baltimore: Johns Hopkins University Press, 1982), p. 122.

[395] A.J.M. Wedderburn, *Beyond Resurrection* (Peabody: Hendrickson Publishers, 1999), p. 31.

[396] Philostratus, *The Life of Apollonius of Tyana*. Trans. C.P. Jones (Baltimore: Penguin Books, 1970), p. 232.

point? Or were they before Luke got ahold of one of them? You tell me.

Luke's ascension narrative (the only one in the gospels) is based closely on the story of Elijah's ascension in 2 Kings 2,[397] though he has added elements of Josephus' story of Moses' ascension as well.

> And as soon as they were come to the mountain called Abarim..., he was going to embrace Eleazar and Joshua, and was still discoursing with them, [when] a cloud stood over him on the sudden, and he disappeared in a certain valley. (*Antiquities* V. 1. 48)[398]

In 2 Kings 2:9, Elijah grants Elisha's request that he shall inherit a double share of Elijah's mighty spirit, i.e., his power. Likewise, just before Jesus ascends, he announces to his disciples his own bequest: "the promise of my father" (Luke 24:49). The disciples will be "clothed" with power, recalling Elijah's miracle of parting the Jordan with his own rolled-up mantle (2 Kings 2:8) and Elisha's successful repetition of it (2 Kings 2:13). Elijah and Jesus are then assumed into heaven (1 Kings 2:11; Luke 24:50-53: Acts 1:1-1), Elijah aboard Apollo's sun-chariot. Both, we read, are separated from their disciples (2 Kings 2:11; Luke 24:51). After this, the promised spirit comes, empowering the disciples (2 Kings 2:15; Acts 2:4). And just as Elijah's ascent is witnessed by his disciples, whose search failed to turn up his body (2 Kings 2:16-18), so is Jesus' ascension witnessed after his disciples find only an empty tomb (Luke 24:3; Acts 1:9-11).

The Acts of All the Apostles

Is that a typo? No, this version of the title is used in the second- (or possibly fourth-) century list called the Muratorian Canon.[399]

---

[397] Brodie, "Luke the Literary Interpreter," p. 254-264.

[398] *The Works of Flavius Josephus.* Trans. William Whiston (London: Ward, Lock & Co.), p. 123.

Whether original or not, that title perfectly sums up the point of the book, namely to counterbalance the Marcionites' exclusive focus on Paul as the only real apostle of Jesus. Marcionites believed, quite plausibly, that the Twelve failed to grasp the meaning of Jesus' teachings. How can you read Mark's gospel and get any other impression? Mark's unremitting drubbing of the disciples[400] can't be ignored. Ever noticed that Acts does not quite call Paul an apostle (we'll discuss Acts chapter 14 later)? Paul defers to the Jerusalem apostles and appears to be no more than one of their delegates, like Barnabas or Silas. Why? Luke (Polycarp) exactly reverses the Marcionite picture of Paul as the *only* legitimate apostle. And it seems to be Luke who created the whole idea of "the Twelve Apostles." No other New Testament writer ever refers to them this way. We read of "the Twelve," "the disciples," and "the apostles," but only Luke has "the Twelve Apostles."[401] So Luke transforms the Twelve into a "college of apostles" which must not be depleted, which is why he alone speaks of the replacement of the fallen Judas Iscariot with the cipher "Matthias," a kind of screen echo of Matthew. It is no surprise that many subsequent writers found it difficult to distinguish them.

It is significant that, despite the seeming importance of the Twelve Apostles, Acts tells us almost nothing about any of them but Peter. This ought to make us suspect they were not as important as the anti-Marcionite theology implies they should have been. John sometimes is a silent sidekick for Peter, and James bar Zebedee's big accomplishment is getting executed.

But Acts does not share the antipathy for Paul felt by the hostile Ebionites who considered him the veritable Antichrist.[402] No,

---

[399] Geoffrey Mark Hahneman, *The Muratorian Fragment and the Development of the Canon.* Oxford Theological Monographs (Oxford: Clarendon Press, 1992).

[400] Theodore J. Weeden, *Mark: Traditions in Conflict* (Philadelphia: Fortress Press, 1971).

[401] Günter Klein, *Die Zwölf Apostel: Ursprung und Gehalt einer Idee.* Forschungen zur Religion und Literatur des Alten und Neuen Testaments (Göttingen: Vandenhoeck und Ruprecht, 1961).

Acts is a compromise document, offering a sanitized version of the origin of the Church. It is an attempt to recruit and co-opt Paulinists in precisely the same way the Gospel of Luke redefines the relationship between the two great sect figureheads Jesus and John the Baptist. In the gospel, Luke wanted to show Christians could make room for Baptists by according John a place of honor, albeit second banana to Jesus. In Acts he wants to attract Paulinists to leave the ranks of Marcionites, Gnostics, and Encratites and come under the wing of Mother Church. To do so, Paulinists would have to be satisfied with Paul as a "top aide" to the real apostles, the Twelve, but in practical terms Peter's equal. This is the reason for paralleling every major achievement of Peter with those uncannily similar feats of Paul. After all, Paulinists were not the only ones who would need some convincing. Not long after Acts was written, Tertullian would call Paul "the apostle of the heretics and of Marcion." Gnostics and Marcionites claimed him as their founder, so Catholics cursed his name. Acts had to rehabilitate his image so Petrine (Catholic) Christians could stand thinking of him as "Saint Paul."

At the same time, it was equally important to define the boundaries of allowable Paulinist doctrines. Like a baggage check at the airport, the Church would tell inquiring Paulinists what they might and might not bring aboard with them. This is why Simon Magus, a Gnostic version of Paul,[403] is condemned. This is why Encratism is attacked in Paul's name in the Pastorals.[404] And this is why the Holy Spirit prevents Paul and his party (Acts 16:6-7) from evangelizing Asia Minor—the home of Marcion![405]

The Long Goodbye (1:1-11)

---

[402] Just like many theologically liberal Christians today, at least those who do not turn Paul into an eco-feminist, anti-American, interfaith ventriloquist dummy.

[403] Or was it the other way around? See below.

[404] Dennis Ronald MacDonald, The Legend and the Apostle: The Battle for Paul in Story and Canon (Philadelphia: Westminster Press, 1983).

[405] Tyson, Marcion and Luke-Acts, p. 77.

Acts opens with another aside to Theophilus but launches right into the action. Verses 1-2 say that the Gospel of Luke dealt with "all that Jesus *began* to do and teach until the day when he was taken up." Some have said that "began" refers to all Jesus' deeds and words in the first volume, implying that now volume two will recount the *further* deeds and teachings of Jesus working through the apostles. But I think it more likely that the "began" sets up one end of his ministry, with the ascension on the other end ("until he was taken up"). Another minor puzzle occurs in verse 2. What does it mean that the risen Jesus gave the apostles a "command through the Holy Spirit"? This would make more sense if the reference were to John 20:21-23, where Jesus commissions the disciples to go forth, remitting or retaining people's sins as they see fit. To empower them for the job, Jesus breathes the Holy Spirit into their mouths like Yahweh Elohim's mouth-to-nose resuscitation in Genesis 2:7. And Acts might actually *be* referring to that scene in John, given the puzzling apparent cross-influence between various editions of John and Luke-Acts. So this might not be the worst place to set forth the series of parallels between the two works, unparalleled in Mark and Matthew.

Some thought John the Baptist might be the Christ (Luke 3:15; John 1:20), but the Baptist denies it (Acts 13:35; John 1:20; 3:38).

John had an extensive itinerant ministry (Luke 3:3; John 1:28; 3:23; 10:40).

Luke implicitly denies John is Elijah by omitting Mark's reference to his hair shirt, while John's gospel has the Baptist pointedly deny he is Elijah (John 1:21).

John avoids having Jesus get baptized by John, while Luke carefully avoids saying it was John who baptized Jesus.

Jesus' ministry begins in the hill country near Nazareth (Luke 4:14-16; John 2:1-11) instead of around the Sea of Galilee.

Possible three-year duration of Jesus' ministry (Luke 13:7; John's references to three Passover celebrations in 2:13, 23; 6:4; 13:1).

Miraculous catch of fish (Luke 5:1-11; John 21:1-14).

Jesus or others teach in Solomon's Portico (John 10:22; Acts 3:11; 5:12).

Special interest in the mother of Jesus (Luke 1:26-56; 2:1-20; 2:48-51; 11:27; John 2:1-5; 19:25-27).

A single miraculous feeding (Luke 9:10-17; John 6:1-14). Luke locates it at Bethsaida, while John has Jesus ask Philip, a native of Bethsaida (as John has told us), where one might buy a great quantity of bread in the vicinity.

Jesus is favorable to Samaritans (Luke 9:51ff; 17:11-19; Acts 8:4-25; John 4:4-43).

Mary and Martha host Jesus in their home (Luke 10:38-42; John 12:1-2).

Even should Lazarus return from the dead, sinners would not repent (Luke 16:19-31; John 11:45-48, etc.).

A woman anoints Jesus' feet, not his head (Luke 7:38; John 12:3).

The Jerusalem crowd hails Jesus as king (Luke 19:38; John 12:13).

Jesus is encouraged by an angel before the Passion, or at least some think so (Luke 22:43; John 12:27-29)

Judas betrayed Jesus because Satan invaded him (Luke 22:3; John 13:27).

Jesus' retreat outside Jerusalem, where he is arrested, is not called Gethsemane.

At the Last Supper Jesus neglects to say the Words of Institution (Luke 22:15-19a; John 13).

Jesus is as one who serves (Luke 12:37; 22:27; John 13:1-15).

Jesus predicts Peter's denials at the Supper table (Luke 22:31-34; John 13:36-38), not on the way to the Mount of Olives.

Only Luke and John mention "Siloam" (John 9:7, 11; Luke 13:4).

Jesus is Deuteronomy's "prophet like Moses" (John 5:46; 6:14; Acts 3:22; 7:37; 26:22-23).

Jesus refers to "my kingdom" only in John and Luke (John 18:36; Luke. 22:30).

Jesus prays for his disciples not to lose their courage during the upcoming ordeal (John 17:15; Luke 22:31-32).

It was the right ear of the priest's servant that Jesus' disciple hacked off (Luke 22:50; John 18:10).

At the trial Jesus is asked a double question about his messiahship and sonship (Luke 22:67, 70; John 10:24, 36).
At the trial, Jesus/Paul talks back to the high priest and gets slapped for it (John 18:19-23; Acts 23:1-5).
Jesus answers Pilate's questions instead of remaining silent (Luke 23:3; John 18:33-38).
Pilate asserts Jesus' innocence three times, and the crowd responds, "Crucify him! Crucify him!" (Luke 23:20-23; John 19:4-6).
Jesus is mocked and scourged (or threatened with scourging) before Pilate pronounces sentence (Luke 23:10-16; John 19:1-3).
Jesus was buried in a tomb never before used (Luke 23:53; John 19:41).
Two men/angels were posted at the empty tomb (Luke 24:4; John 20:12).
We are told what Mary and her sisters told the disciples about what they saw at the tomb (Luke 24:9-11; John 20:20:1-12, 18).
Peter goes to the empty tomb but leaves not knowing what to make of it (Luke 24:12; John 20:9ff).
The risen Jesus appears in and around Jerusalem, not Galilee (Luke 24:13ff; John 20:11-31).
Jesus suddenly appears in the midst of the disciples in a locked room and shows his hands and feet/side (Luke 24:36-40; John 20:19-20).
Jesus seeks to prove the reality of his resurrection in the flesh by asking for something to eat (Luke 24:41; John 21:5).
Peter is restored to grace (Luke 22:31-32; John 21:15-17).
Jesus imparts the Holy Spirit after the resurrection (Acts 2:1-4; John 20:22).
Jesus will/does ascend to heaven (Luke 24:51; Acts 1:9; John 6:62; 20:17).
Both have a purpose statement aiming at securing the reader's belief. Each insists on his accuracy, based on eye-witness sources (Luke 1:1-4; John 21:24), and mentions other books (actual or hypothetical) on the same subject (Luke 1:1; John 21:25). Each speaks of "we/us," then "I."

(Acts' "We-passages;" John 21:24-25).[406] [Here and above, the spacing between items is inconsistent.]

Pierson Parker[407] explains the parallels as the result of Luke and John (whom he identifies with the "John Mark" of Acts 12:25) working together in evangelistic ministry. John Amedee Bailey[408] chalks it all up to fortuitous use of common oral traditions. F. Lamar Cribbs[409] argues for Luke's use of John or of the pre-Johannine Signs Gospel.[410] Mark A. Matson[411] argues that Luke used John's gospel, at least in the Passion narrative. Note that wherever Luke has a parallel to Matthew/Mark, he follows it, but where there is a Johannine version as well as a Matthean/Markan version, Luke skips Matthew/Mark and uses the material parallel to John instead (or opts for a version like none of the other evangelists).

Luke 24:51 had Jesus launch into heaven on the same day the empty tomb was discovered, but Acts 1:3 and 9 have the lift-off occur a full forty days later! This is one of those situations where even the critic must search for a harmonization since, as it reads, the contradiction is so blatant, so outrageous, that you have to suspect there's something else going on behind the text. And this may be it. Some manuscripts of Luke are missing the words "and was carried up into heaven" from 24:51. If they have preserved the original reading, we could take it to mean Jesus simply left for the moment, though he would rejoin the disciples from time to time during the forty days to impart new teachings, as in Acts 1. But where would he be going? A sleeping bag on the Mount of Olives? Lazarus' house in

---

[406] Bartosz Adamczewski, *The Gospel of the Narrative 'We'* (Frankfurt-am-Main: Peter Lang, 2010).

[407] Pierson Parker, "Luke and the Fourth Evangelist" *New Testament Studies*, vol. 9, July 1963, pp. 331-336.

[408] John Amedee Bailey, *The Traditions Common to the Gospels of Luke and John* (Leiden: E.J. Brill, 1963).

[409] F. Lamar Cribbs, "A Study of the Contacts That Exist Between St. Luke and St. John." *Society of Biblical Literature: 1973 Seminar Papers* (ed. George MacRae. Vol. 2; Cambridge: Society of Biblical Literature, 1973) 1-93.

[410] Robert T. Fortna, *The Gospel of Signs: A Reconstruction of the Narrative Source Underlying the Fourth Gospel.* Society for New Testament Studies Monograph Series 11 (Cambridge at the University Press, 1970).

[411] Mark A. Matson, *In Dialogue with Another Gospel? The Influence of the Fourth Gospel on the Passion Narrative of the Gospel of Luke.* Society of Biblical Literature Dissertation Series 178 (Atlanta: Scholars Press, 2001).

Bethany? And why? He didn't mind bunking with Peter and the rest before. And it's entirely likely the words "and was carried up into heaven" *were* the original reading, and that some scribe, noticing the contradiction and looking both ways, skipped the troublesome words. After all, that's one of the most important axioms of textual criticism: the more difficult reading is probably the original, since it is easier to imagine a scribe trying to smooth out a difficulty ("Huh? That *can't* be right!") than to screw it up and have subsequent scribes continue copying the screwed-up version.

The longer pre-ascension period uses the same device various Gnostic texts employ, having the risen Jesus remain on earth for as long as eighteen months in one text and eleven years in another![412] The point is to explain why the unheard-of doctrines of the Gnostic apostles (Simon Magus, Valentinus, Basilides, et. al.) could not be found in any of the more widely-familiar gospels: "Oh, well, you see, no wonder you don't find the Fallen Sophia, the Archons, and Ialdabaoth in Matthew, Mark, and the rest! Jesus taught the *advanced* stuff, the *inside* stuff, only after he released the public material you find in those 'Jesus for Dummies' gospels!" In Acts, Luke is doing the same thing, since there was just as wide a gap between the Catholic theology of his own day and the contents of even *his* gospel.[413]

It is not quite clear whether the Acts author means that Jesus was constantly among his disciples during the forty days, as he had been before the crucifixion, or whether there was a forty-day period during which Jesus made numerous discrete resurrection appearances as if "beaming down" from heaven. He spent at least part of this time performing "proofs" of the reality of his resurrection, as in Luke 24:36-43, where he demonstrates his corporeality by eating, something, it was believed, impossible for a fleshless ghost. One wonders what else he did. Luke says there were "many proofs," just as he tells us that Jesus provided many scriptural proofs of his messiahship without, however, supplying any specifics (Luke 24:25-27, 44-45). One suspects this is more vacuous puffery.

---

[412] Gerd Lüdemann, *Early Christianity according to the Traditions in Acts: A Commentary* (Minneapolis: Fortress Press, 1989), p. 28.

[413] In precisely the same way, one finds precious little of the complex and fascinating Mormon theology in the Book of Mormon because it was only after writing it that Joseph Smith began to elaborate his new theology and had to create a new volume of scripture, *Doctrines and Covenants*, to contain the new material.

Acts 1:4 says Jesus was staying with the disciples, but the same word could just as easily be translated "eating." Are we to suppose Luke means to imply that he was resuming his habitual, uninterrupted association with them, sharing regular meals with them? Or does "eating with them" refer to Luke 24:42? Was this eating one of the "proofs," the same *one* offered in Luke 24? If this is Luke's intent, he was presumably thinking of sporadic "pop-ins" like that in Luke 24:36-49. Who knows?

In verses 4-5, 8a, Jesus tells the Twelve (actually, at this point, just the eleven) to stay put in Jerusalem (which fits with all the resurrection appearances being confined to Jerusalem and its environs in Luke 24) where they will soon receive the Holy Spirit. This command, obviously, looks forward to Pentecost in chapter 2.

Verse 3 informs us that, over this period of forty days, Jesus was teaching the newly-minted apostles about the coming kingdom of God. But then in verse 6, we read that the disciples, newly catechized as to the true nature of the kingdom of God, prove themselves fully as thick-skulled as *Mark* made them! They ask, "Lord, will you at this time restore the kingdom to Israel?" You can just see poor Jesus, eyes rolling, slapping his forehead with its thorny scars. How damn *stupid* can these guys be? But Luke is not trying to make fools of the disciples and probably didn't notice that he had. Rather, he is using the cardboard cut-outs of the disciples to set up the Christian readers' question. It is like Paul's use of the Stoic diatribe ("Ah, but someone will say..."), an anticipatory rejoinder. Luke knows his readers either still eagerly expect the apocalyptic wrap-up in their own day, or they are depressed and disappointed that it failed to happen on schedule. Luke has Jesus just shut down the question, as it does not tend unto edification: "What are you worried about *that* for? *Your* only concern is spreading my gospel! Get *to* it!"

This missionary mandate for world evangelization would seem pretty clear, right? Peter and the elders of the Jerusalem church all seem to have somehow forgotten it in Acts 10-11, where it takes visions from the Holy Spirit and the on-scene observation of a Roman centurion embracing the faith to convince these men to drop their stubborn opposition to any Gentile Mission.[414] But this is because we are reading theological fiction, not ecclesiastical history.

---

[414] Hermann Samuel Reimarus, *Reimarus: Fragments*. Trans. Ralph S. Fraser. Ed. Charles H. Talbert. Lives of Jesus Series (Philadelphia: Fortress Press, 1970), pp. 102-103.

Luke is happy to make pretty much any of his characters appear idiotic in order to anticipate and pre-refute the preconceptions of his readers.

The artificiality of the missionary commandment is glaringly apparent (as is the Matthean Great Commission) from the fact that the job of the Twelve was to oversee the congregations *in Palestine*, as implied in the Q saying (Matt. 19:28; Luke 22:29-30) about their sitting on thrones judging (governing) the twelve tribes of Israel, not to mention the fact that Paul was known as "*the* Apostle to the Gentiles." See also Galatians 2:7-8. The common picture of the Twelve fanning out across the globe is a later idea occurring in the Apocryphal Acts, motivated by various competing churches (bishops) claiming a (fictive) apostolic foundation.

So Jesus has shown to characters within the narrative many scriptural proofs of Jesus' messiahship, but none to us, the readers. Luke has told us Jesus did many wonders to prove his resurrection, but he doesn't bother recounting any of them for us (unless Luke 24:41-43 is intended). Right up front, he told us there were "many" hagiographies of Jesus but left the claim in generalities (though, by comparing Luke's gospel with Matthew and Mark, we know he did at least use *two* previous documents, i.e., Mark and Q).[415] And now he says Jesus vouchsafed deep secrets concerning the true nature of the kingdom, but he doesn't share it with us—though Conzelmann managed to sniff it out!

In verses 9-11 a pair of white-robed men appear. They are "interpreting angels" such as we find in ancient apocalypses, including the New Testament Apocalypse of John. You have to think they're the same duo who greeted the women at the empty tomb. There (Luke 24:5) they asked a question that would be stupid if it were not rhetorical: "Why do you seek the living among the dead?" Here, too, they ask a rhetorical question: "Men of Galilee! Why do you stand looking into heaven? This Jesus who was taken up from you into heaven, will come in the same way you saw him go into heaven." It is not too hard to imagine that Luke 9:30-31, the Transfiguration narrative, originally read "two men talked with him, who appeared in glory and spoke of his departure, which he was to accomplish at Jerusalem." Maybe the names "Moses and Elijah"

---

[415] He doesn't seem to think much of Mark and Q, since he says he found it necessary to supplant them with his own version—and he bases it on theirs! I guess it's another case of the "anxiety of influence."

represent a subsequent interpolation meant to harmonize Luke with Mark and Matthew. Maybe originally the two figures were the same two angels who appear at the tomb and at the ascension.[416]

Take a close look at the two stories. The two men in Acts 1, like those in Luke 9, are there to discuss the ascension, not with Jesus this time, but with the disciples. In Luke 9, a cloud obscures everyone atop the Mount of Transfiguration. Jesus remains behind while the two visitors return to heaven. In Acts 1, it is Jesus who rides the cloud into heaven, while the two men remain below to discuss Jesus' departure (literally, his "exodus") with the disciples. Is Acts 1:9-10 a reshuffling of Luke's Transfiguration narrative?

Cast of Characters (1:12-14)

After the ascension, Jesus' orphaned followers make the short trip back to Jerusalem from the Mount of Olives, "a Sabbath day's journey." I remember reading a skeptic's gleeful gloating over this "mistake": "Aha! From the Mount of Olives to Jerusalem was a short trip! It wouldn't take a whole day to make it!" Of course it wouldn't. A "Sabbath day's journey" was a technical term for a Torah loophole invented by the Pharisees, who were trying to make it a bit easier for pious Jews. The Torah commanded that one remain at home on the Sabbath, but this proved a major inconvenience. Since the Sabbath was made for man and not man for the Sabbath, the Pharisees posited that one might designate a larger radius of 960 yards as one's "home" (cf., one's "haunts") for the Sabbath, allowing brief travel on the holy day. That was a Sabbath day's journey. The whole point is to say that Jesus' followers had only a short trek.

This section is mainly there to set the stage for Pentecost. We get a list of the Twelve, minus the Iscariot, plus the mother and brothers of Jesus, plus "the women," who must be intended as Mary Magdalene, Joanna, Susanna, and the rest, though it is no surprise that Luke names none of the females. Anyway, Luke might have saved some ink here, because the only ones on this passenger manifest who we are ever going to see again in Acts are Peter; his mute shadow, John son of Zebedee; James his brother, who gets decapitated; and James the Just (assuming that Luke considered him one of Jesus' brothers). This latter James is a pretty important figure

---

[416] This is not original with me, but I can't remember where I read it.

in the book, appearing in a couple of crucial scenes. This is quite a crowd to be staying for ten days, cheek by jowl, in a single "Upper Room" (cf., Luke 11:7).

Job Opening (1:15-26)

The first order of business for the gathered micro-church is replacing Judas Iscariot, and, for the benefit of the reader, Luke has Peter tell everyone what they must already know: Judas did not return his bounty money to the Sanhedrin. No, he invested in some real estate, but whatever plans he had for it (maybe to build a Noah's Ark theme park?) were cut short when he was walking around, surveying his property, and suddenly exploded like Mr. Creosote in *Monty Python's The Meaning of Life*! There's no hint that he committed suicide a la Matthew 27:5. Luke got the nasty idea from the Greek Septuagint version of 2 Samuel 20:10, which tells us how the traitor Amasa's "bowels poured out upon the ground." Verily, *yecch*. But at any rate, he had to be replaced.

What was the apostolic job description? A viable candidate had to have belonged to Jesus' entourage from the day Jesus was baptized all the way to the ascension. Why? Because Luke views the function of the Twelve Apostles as witnesses able to attest everything Jesus did during his ministry (cf., Luke 1:2). But this is clearly fictive, not a historical recollection, since, on Luke's own account, none of the Twelve could have met the requirement! Which of them was there at the Jordan when Jesus got baptized? Granted John's gospel says a couple of Jesus' first disciples were there as fans of the Baptizer. And even if Luke was familiar with John, this is not the way Luke tells the story. Besides, most of them could not have been there from the start since Jesus only recruited them later on.

So why does Luke have Peter make this stipulation? His goal is not to legitimate either the Twelve or Matthias, but only *to exclude Paul*. For Luke, Paul, great as he is, still is no apostle.[417]

Why do the gathered disciples make the big decision by *casting lots*? Luke understands the indeterminacy of a coin toss as an open window for divine Providence to intervene.[418] The Philistine

---

[417] Conzelmann, *Theology of St. Luke*, p. 216, note 1.

[418] It is possible that at some point Jesus' whispered statement, "It is one of the twelve, one who is dipping bread in the same dish with me" (Mark

277

shamans had the same idea when they loaded the captured Ark of Yahweh into an ox-cart and let the animals take it wherever they wanted. In this way they hoped to discover whether the plagues afflicting Philistia were reprisals from the deity whose Ark they had stolen. If the oxen headed for the border with Israel, which they did, that ought to prove it was Yahweh who was afflicting them. This seems pretty silly, true, but is it really any more plausible when, after much political wrangling and a series of votes, the Vatican announces the choice of a new Pope as the will of the Holy Spirit?

Holy Ghost Jamboree (chapter 2)

As we have seen, the reference in Acts 1:2 to Jesus "giving commandment through the Holy Spirit" brings to mind the "Johannine Pentecost" (John 20:21-23). I suspect Luke knew this story and expanded it into the longer process we observe in Luke 24:36 through Acts chapter 2. In the Johannine version Jesus commissions the apostles to continue his mission, imparting the Spirit to them on the spot. Luke changed it, I imagine, so that during that scene in the room with the disciples, Jesus predicts that they will receive the Spirit, enabling them to undertake the apostolic mission, sometime in the near future, which turns out to be some ten days later. Why would Luke do this? I should think he wanted to Christianize the Jewish Feast of Weeks, or "Pentecost" (the "Fiftieth Day" after the first day of Passover). This implies an underlying tension over the question of old wine (Judaism) and new wineskins (Christianity): should Christians continue to observe traditional Jewish holy days (cf., Col. 2:16)? Christianizing Pentecost was a way of splitting the difference: if you can't retain the Jewish holy day, why not insert a new Christian holy day into the same calendar slot? This is probably why we celebrate Christmas on December 25: Gentile

---

14:20; cf., John 13:26) meant that whoever happened to be dipping his bread into the dish at the precise moment Jesus did, would be assigned the task of "betraying" Jesus to his enemies. He did not know who it would turn out to be but left it to God to make his will known through coincidence. See Robert M. Price, *Deconstructing Jesus* (Amherst: Prometheus Books, 2000), Chapter 6, "Sacred Scapegoat," p. 198. Oddly, modern Theistic Evolutionists entertain the same superstition when they say God uses the wiggle room made possible by quantum indeterminacy to prod a creature's DNA to mutate the way he wanted it!

Christians were in the habit of celebrating the Mithraic holiday of Brumalia, sending Brumalia cards, going to office Brumalia parties, etc., so the Church decided to give them something else to celebrate on that day. It worked pretty well: you don't see many "Merry Brumalia" cards any more, do you?

There is something hidden in plain sight here, namely the death blow to a very often repeated apologetics argument, namely that if Jesus' tomb were empty because the Sanhedrin had taken custody of Jesus' body, beating Jesus' disciples to Joseph's tomb, they could easily have squelched the apostles' preaching of Jesus' resurrection by simply producing the body: "Yeah? Here's your 'risen savior'!"[419] But Reimarus refuted this reasoning two hundred years before these apologists wrote.

> The *corpus delecti* was not to be found, and even if anyone should come and point out that it was somewhere to be found, more than fifty days had passed over since the death of Jesus, and decay must have done its work. Who would be able to recognize him now, and say, "This is the body of Jesus"? The lapse of time secured them from detection, and made investigation useless.[420]

The descent of the Holy Spirit upon the gathered apostles and their associates appears to be based (along with much else in Acts) on the great play of Euripides, *The Bacchae*,[421] which depicts the advent of the ecstatic cult of Dionysus among the women of Thebes. For instance, the resting of tongues of fire above the heads of the newly Spirit-baptized Christians comes straight from *The Bacchae* (lines 757-758): "Flames flickered in their curls and did not burn them."

What does our author intend by "speaking in tongues"? Is it

---

[419] Michael Green, *Man Alive!* (Downers Grove: Intervarsity Press, 1967), p. 38; John R.W. Stott, *Basic Christianity* (Grand Rapids: Eerdmans, 1958), p. 50; J.N.D. Anderson, *Christianity: The Witness of History, A Lawyer's Approach* (London: Tyndale Press, 1969), p. 93. All these writers use the same language: the authorities needed only to "produce" the body. It has become a kind of liturgy.

[420] *Reimarus: Fragments*, pp. 250-251.

[421] All my quotations from the play come from the translation by William Arrowsmith in David Grene and Richmond Lattimore, eds., *Greek Tragedies Volume 3* (Chicago: University of Chicago Press, 1960), pp. 189-260.

simply ecstatic speech, "unutterable utterances" (2 Cor. 12:4), "sighs too deep for words" (Rom. 8:26), "the tongues of angels" (1 Cor. 13:1)? Or, as Pentecostals believe, unlearned foreign languages? The story does not really clear things up. Many Diaspora Jews have come to Jerusalem for the festival, or possibly they have permanently moved there.[422] In either case, crowds of these people, thronging the streets in celebration, hear the sudden ruckus of one hundred twenty Spirit-enthusiasts, all Galileans (though it is not clear how their hearers know this), proclaiming the mighty works of God. Were they speaking in unison without a script? If not, how could anyone cut through the cacophonous babble to hear *what* they were saying? The puzzled reactions of the crowd do not help us much. "How is it that we hear, each in his own native language?" Does this mean each and every hearer is able to pick out from the general din one individual speaking in whatever language the hearer speaks back home? There is no narrative plausibility in this. It seems to make more sense if we infer that the hundred twenty were spouting inspired gibberish, and each hearer thought he heard all one hundred twenty Christians speaking in unison in the hearer's accustomed tongue. Thus, in terms of 1 Corinthians 12, Acts 2 would be recounting a miracle of glossolalia and, simultaneously, of the interpretation of tongues.

We mustn't ignore the significance of the fact that Jews had already reinterpreted this feast as the commemoration of the giving of the Torah on Mount Sinai. Luke must have known the tradition that, on that ancient occasion, God had offered all the nations the Torah covenant, to each in its own language, though all but Israel rejected it. Thus, for Luke, the descent of the Spirit at Pentecost is a kind of repeat of that first Sinai revelation: the new covenant is being offered to Jews and Gentiles, and this time God will have better luck.

Peter comes to the fore once the "Holy Ghost noise"[423] has

---

[422] Haenchen, *Acts*, p. 175.

[423] My pal Ken Blank once told me about a radio preacher he heard who had lost control of his congregation and could be heard over the microphone trying to calm everyone down so he could get on to his sermon: "Cut out the Ho-ly-Ghost noise! Cut out the Ho-ly-Ghost noise, I say!" This tide of chaos took up all of the air time, and the broadcast ended

subsided, and he preaches in Greek (or Aramaic?). But why? Didn't the crowd just hear a sermon? "We hear them in our own tongues telling the mighty works of God" (Acts 2:11). One wonders: is the glossolalic spectacle itself supposed to have been the mighty work of God to which they were referring?

Apparently only those receptive to the gospel were able to make sense of the tongues outburst. Others who happened to be loitering about heard nothing but verbal salad and thought that either the hundred twenty speakers or those in the audience who professed to understand what they said, were drunk and hallucinating. "They are filled with new wine!" (2:13). Peter addresses these hecklers first: "These are not drunk, as *you* suppose, since it is only the third hour of the day!" That's nine o'clock, and the taverns were not yet open for business. The whole scene recalls 1 Corinthians 14:23-25:

> If, therefore, the whole church assembles and all speak in tongues, and outsiders or unbelievers enter, will they not say that you are mad? But if all prophesy, and an unbeliever or outsider enters, he is convicted by all, he is called to account by all, the secrets of his heart are disclosed; and so, falling on his face, he will worship God and declare that God is really among you.

This is pretty much what we see in Acts 2, both reactions. But I'm pretty sure Luke was thinking of *The Bacchae*, lines 683-687: "There they lay in the deep sleep of exhaustion, some resting on boughs of fir, others sleeping where they fell, here and there among the oak leaves – but all modestly and soberly, not, as you think, drunk with wine." Compare Acts 2:17-18.

Peter's sermon is based on Joel 2:28-32, interpreted ventriloquistically via the *pesher* method on display in Matthew's gospel and the Dead Sea Scrolls. But I cannot help thinking Luke's choice of text was suggested by affinities to *The Bacchae*, lines 693-694. There we read a description of the Maenads (women devotees

---

abruptly just as the preacher finally began his sermon.

of Dionysus) awakening from sleep: "a lovely sight to see: all as one, the old women and the young and the unmarried girls."

Peter gives a succinct summary of Jesus' life and ministry, his crucifixion and resurrection. "God raised him up, having loosed the pangs of death, because it was not possible for him to be held by it" (2:24). This reminds me of the words of Dionysus in *The Bacchae*, lines 515-516: "I go, though not to suffer, since that cannot be."

The sermon jumps like a frog from one textual lily pad to another, appropriating first Psalm 16, then Psalm 110, again, in the context-be-damned fashion of the Dead Sea Scrolls. This is only one of the dead give-aways that this speech (like all the rest in Acts) is a literary creation of Luke, not a transcript of anything anyone said on the Day of Pentecost. The use of scripture here presupposes a tradition of early Christian scribal study. We must picture scholars squinting over scrolls and weighing possible esoteric references to their Messiah, not a preacher winging it, no matter how deeply "in the zone" he might have been at the time.[424]

Then there's the problem of Peter quoting extemporaneously from the Greek Septuagint. In 2:7, the crowd thought it impossible that the Galilean hicks would have known a variety of foreign languages, and the same problem occurs here: would Peter, hillbilly that he was, have known, much less been able to quote from memory, the Greek Old Testament?[425]

Two items in this sermon attest the early Christology of adoptionism, i.e., that Jesus was a righteous mortal rewarded by God with divine honors, like the Genesis patriarch Enoch. Acts 2:22 describes Jesus as "a man attested to you by God with mighty works and wonders and signs which God did through him," while 2:36 says, "God has *made* him Lord and Christ, this Jesus whom you crucified."

---

[424] Haenchen, *Acts*, p. 188.

[425] We see the same device in Acts 4:13; John 7:15; Exod. 4:10; the unlettered simplicity of the prophet only underlines the reality of his revelations because the prophet couldn't have been clever enough to compose them himself. The same apologetic was offered on behalf of Muhammad and Joseph Smith.

Verse 37 tells us the audience was "cut to the heart," reminding us again of 1 Corinthians 14:24-25, since this is the response expected there when outsiders hear prophecy or interpreted glossolalia.

Verse 38 makes no mention of any atonement wrought by Christ's blood in its prescription for salvation. Repentance and baptism in the saving name of Jesus Christ are enough to secure salvation, which seems to be equated with receiving the Holy Spirit. We must not read into this passage the modern theological distinctions that fuel Pentecostal-Holiness-Keswick[426] versus Evangelical[427] debates. In Acts 2:38 reception of the Spirit is coincident with baptism and salvation, and the reference is plainly to the charismatic endowment experienced by the hundred twenty. In other words, Luke knows nothing of a distinction between initially being "born again of the Spirit" (John 3:3, 8) and a subsequent "second blessing" of being "baptized in the Holy Spirit" (Acts 1:5) for sanctification and/or empowerment for Christian service.[428] Of the various modern Christian positions, I should think that of the United Pentecostal Church most closely approximates the understanding implied in Acts 2:38. They make the initially startling claim that if you don't speak in tongues, you are not saved.[429] But they don't mean to reduce glossolalia to an arbitrary shibboleth. Rather, their point is that there is a single experience of the Spirit, not a division of it into subsequent stages, and that tongues signifies that single reception of the Spirit, so, if you lack the "initial evidence" of glossolalia, you lack the Spirit of which it is the evidence. "Any one who does not have the Spirit of Christ does not

---

[426] R.A. Torrey, *The Baptism with the Holy Spirit* (Minneapolis: Dimension Books / Bethany Fellowship, 1972).

[427] John R.W. Stott, *The Baptism and Fullness of the Holy Spirit* (Downers Grove: Inter-Varsity Press, 1964).

[428] For the evolution of the various Holiness and Pentecostal doctrines of the Baptism of the Holy Spirit, see the definitive book by Donald W. Dayton, *Theological Roots of Pentecostalism* (Grand Rapids: Francis Asbury Press / Zondervan, 1987).

[429] Or, as Ken Blank quoted another radio preacher as saying, "If you ain't got *tongues*, you ain't got *nuthin!*"

belong to him" (Rom. 8:9).

Acts 2:39 hints that Luke is speaking over the heads of the Pentecost pilgrims to his much later readers: "the promise is to you *and your children and to all who are far off.*" When Peter's words continue with "every one whom the Lord our God calls to him," is he talking about predestination? That is to read too much into these few words. All they need to mean is "every one who hears the gospel preached." (Acts 13:48, on the other hand, *does* seem to presuppose predestinarianism, as I read it.)

Verses 41-47, describing the baptism of three thousand converts in a single day and the blissful, communistic paradise that ensued, as well as the (unspecified) miracles worked by the super-powered apostles, form a typical foundation legend of a golden age of power and purity.[430] As Conzelmann[431] aptly observes, the purpose of the idealized portrait is not to provide a model for the churches of the readers' day, but rather to authenticate the tradition in which they stand, in the same way Christians reading of the miracles performed by Jesus are not to reproach themselves for their inability to repeat them,[432] but rather to rejoice in knowing the

---

[430] Robert L. Wilkin, *The Myth of Christian Beginnings: History's Impact on Belief* (Garden City: Doubleday Anchor Books, 1972), pp. 20-21, 31-37; Haenchen, *Acts*, p. 189.

[431] Conzelmann, *Theology of St. Luke*, pp. 211-212, 233.

[432] Failing (quite understandably) to grasp this distinction has led to regrettable results. Oral Roberts, *The Call: Oral Roberts' Autobiography* (New York: Avon Books, 1971), pp. 39-40: "I kept comparing my ministry and my church with that of the disciples and the Early Church. They preached in the marketplace and in the arena of need. I was preaching three times a week in my little church to the same people. The disciples ministered to the sick wherever they found them and miracles happened. The sick, the crippled, the afflicted seldom darkened the door of our church and little happened when they did." Ronald A. Knox, *Enthusiasm: A Chapter in the History of Religion* (New York: Oxford University Press, 1950), describes the "enthusiast" who holds himself obliged to live up to the model of the early church: "He expects more from the grace of God than we others. He sees what effect religion can have, does sometimes have, in transforming a man's whole life and outlook; these exceptional cases (so we are content to think

foundation of their faith is/was truly divine.

Will This Do? (3:1-10)

This story of Peter (with the superfluous John in tow) surprising a lame beggar with an instantaneous healing has two significant parallels. First, the story is so close to the episode of Jesus healing the man born blind in John chapter 9, including its aftermath and the confirmation of his identity (Acts 4:22),[433] that you have to count this as another of those suspicious Luke/John overlaps, whatever you want to make of them. Some kind of influence in one direction or the other seems likely.

Second, the miracle parallels Paul's healing of the crippled man of Lystra in Acts 14:8-11. This is, by my count, the first of the striking sets of miracles, etc., designed to persuade Petrinists (Catholics) that Paul (the hero of the Marcionites) wasn't so bad and, likewise, to persuade the Paulinists (potential converts from Marcionism, Gnosticism, and Encratism) that Peter was just as good as Paul. It seems not unlikely that one of the twin items in these pairs has been rewritten from the other in the same way we have seen that Luke and his fellow evangelists (or their oral-tradition predecessors) have rewritten various stories of Elijah, Elijah, Moses,

---

them) are for him the average standard of religious achievement. He will have no 'almost-Christians', no weaker brethren who plod and stumble, ... whose ambition is to qualify, not to excel. He has before his eyes a picture of the Early Church, visibly penetrated with supernatural influences; and nothing less will serve him as a model... Quoting a hundred texts - we also use them, but with more of embarrassment - he insists that the members of his society, saved members of a perishing world, should live a life of angelic purity, of apostolic simplicity" (p. 2).

[433] What does his age have to do with it? I think it is a shorthand (or, if you prefer, garbled) allusion to the Johannine Blind Man story (John 9:18-23), "He is of age, ask him."

and David as Jesus stories.

The utility of Torrey's division of the book into an Aramaic 1 Acts (chapters 1-15) and a Greek 2 Acts (chapters 16-28), composed by the translator of 1 Acts into Greek, is shown strikingly when we observe that all the Peter episodes occur in 1 Acts, while most of the Pauline versions appear in 2 Acts: each raises someone from the dead (Peter in 9:36-40, Paul in 20:9-12); each heals a paralytic (Peter in 3:1-8, Paul in 14:8-10);[434] each heals by extraordinary, magical means (Peter in 5:15, Paul in 19:11-12); each gets the better of a pseudo-Christian prophet (Peter in 8:18-23, Paul in 16:16-18); each miraculously escapes prison (Peter in 12:6-10, Paul in 16:25-26). This is exactly what we should expect on the Tübingen hypothesis that the Catholicizing composer of Acts was trying to fabricate a Petrine Paul. How natural that the Peter-glorifying original should be an originally Aramaic document, stemming from conservative Torah-Christians! And this would settle the question of which apostle was the original and which the Xerox. The Paul parallels must have been rewritten from the Peter originals.

Waiting in the Wings (3:11-26)

Peter promptly uses the healing as an object lesson for a sermon, and in verses 13 and 17 he denounces his Jewish audience for having railroaded Pilate into crucifying Jesus. He did the same on the Day of Pentecost, lambasting the Diaspora Jews, who just happened to be present, for killing Jesus. What? *These particular guys?* Peter (actually Luke) simply lumps all Jews together as stereotypical Christ-killers. You're circumcised? You killed Jesus. All the Jews are interchangeable in Luke's eyes—until they become Christians, of course.

There are a couple of points of special theological interest in

---

[434] Both healings of the lame appeared already in 1 Acts, so the writer of 2 Acts (Polycarp) saw no need to create a second Pauline cure of a paralytic to match Peter's in 3:1-8.

verses 19-21:

> Repent therefore, and turn again, that your sins may be blotted out, that times of refreshing may come from the presence of the Lord, and that he may send the Christ appointed for you, Jesus whom heaven must receive until the time for establishing all that God spoke by the mouth of his holy prophets from of old.

Verse 19 reflects the traditional Jewish belief that the kingdom of God will not come until Jews prove themselves worthy of it by doubling down on repentance. "If you were *serious* about it, you'd *get* somewhere!" This is rather different from the usual New Testament eschatological urging, where Christians are warned to watch their step lest Jesus catch them in a compromising position. "He's coming! You just better be ready!"

Verses 20-21 seem to enshrine "the most primitive Christology of all,"[435] the notion that Jesus was not yet enthroned as Messiah upon his resurrection but rather was only the Messiah-elect, waiting to assume the messianic mantle only upon his apocalyptic coming in judgment. What was he doing up in heaven until that day? Acting as an intercessor with God on behalf of his believers down on earth.[436] The turning point at which Christians began to believe Jesus had been enthroned upon his resurrection/ascension was, as Eric Franklin[437] suggests, a general Christian disillusion at the repeated failure of the Parousia to arrive on schedule. Jesus would still appear at the End of Days, but in a real and most important sense, the messianic reign had already begun. I see this maneuver as quite similar to that of Jehovah's Witnesses when their 1914

---

[435] John A.T. Robinson, *Twelve New Testament Studies*. Studies in Biblical Theology No. 34 (London: SCM Press, 1962), Chapter X, "The Most Primitive Christology of All?" pp. 139-153.

[436] Benjamin W. Bacon, *The Story of Jesus and the Beginnings of the Church: A Valuation of the Synoptic Record for History and for Religion* (London: George Allen & Unwin, 1928), pp. 283-284.

[437] Eric Franklin, *Christ the Lord: A Study in the Purpose and Theology of Luke-Acts* (Philadelphia: Westminster Press, 1975).

deadline passed and Jesus did not descend from heaven. They then changed their tune, concluding that Jesus *did* take his throne, ahem, in *heaven* to rule the world invisibly from there.

No Good Deed Goes Unpunished (chapter 4)

The healing, but even more, the sermon, does not go unnoticed by the authorities. The Sadducees (from *sundikos*, councilman)[438] are the elders of the people.[439] They are, of course, not upset about a poor cripple getting healed. There is nothing about it happening on the Sabbath. But there is nonetheless a theological reason for their alarm: Peter takes the occasion to preach about the resurrection of Jesus, and that was a doctrine the Sadducees most definitely rejected. They held on to the older doctrine of Sheol, the ectoplasmic garage where the shades of the dead were store-housed. They dismissed the resurrection belief as a syncretistic borrowing from Persian Zoroastrianism (which it was). The Sadducees had gotten used to the Pharisees believing such stuff. The trouble here is that Peter is appealing to the supposed resurrection of Jesus as Exhibit A for the truth of the disputed doctrine. Thus, this time, it doesn't seem it is Christian preaching as such that leads to the arrest, but rather a subordinate issue. Had somebody been spreading the rumor that the beggar Lazarus had come back to life, the Sadducees would have arrested him, too, as in John 12:10. (The same thing happens over in Acts 23:6-9, when Paul gets the Pharisee faction of the Sanhedrin to side with him over the issue of resurrection against the Sadducees.)

Once the hearing is underway, the issue mysteriously changes: suddenly, the problem is no longer resurrection *per se*, but Jesus as the source of the healing. "By what power [i.e., angel] or what name did you do this?" In other words, what divine, angelic, or demonic name did you invoke to perform the miracle? (Think of the scribes charging that Jesus was able to exorcise demons by invoking the

---

[438] Hmmm... Does this mean Hans Conzelmann ("Councilman") was a Sadducee?

[439] T.W. Manson, *The Servant Messiah: A Study of the Public Ministry of Jesus* (Cambridge at the University Press, 1961), pp. 16-20.

name of Beelzebul in Mark 3:22.) Peter answers, "by the name of Jesus Christ of Nazareth" (4:10).[440]

In light of this observation, we must take a fresh look at 4:12, which is usually interpreted as a claim that only by invoking the name of Jesus (in baptism) can one gain salvation. Buddhists, Hindus, Muslims, Jews? Better put on your asbestos pajamas! But I would suggest that, in the context, the word *sothenai*, which is usually translated "saved" in this verse, should instead be translated as "*healed*" (another perfectly acceptable dictionary definition). This puts, I should think, quite a different face on the matter: is the verse really claiming no one can be saved from damnation if they do not call on the name of Christ, as we have always heard? I'm not so sure anymore. It might just as well mean that Peter is discounting any other means of healing via invocation.

Verses 14-18 present the Sanhedrin in a pretty bad light. It sounds like they wish they could discount the healing as a fraud, but Peter has them beat. The fact of the healing means nothing to them but a dratted inconvenience. It seems not to occur to them that they should perhaps reevaluate their position in light of the miracle! They don't want to be confused with the facts. There certainly are plenty of people like this, religious and non-religious, but it is still hard to believe this portrayal is not mere vilification of the Jewish authorities. Besides, how could Luke have known *what* they said in private?

The Unhappy Couple (5:1-11)

In 1 Kings 20:1-21:21, King Ahab and Queen Jezebel conspire to cheat righteous Naboth out of his vineyard. From this sad tale Luke mined the building materials for the episodes of Ananias and Sapphira and of Stephen.[441] Ahab becomes covetously obsessed with Naboth's vineyard. He must possess it! If only there were a *way...*! Sick of her spineless husband's moaning and pining, Jezebel tells him

---

[440] This particular phrase was always Oral Roberts's favorite formula when he laid hands on the sick.

[441] Brodie, "Luke the Literary Interpreter," pp. 271-275.

to remember that he is the *king*, for Pete's sake! He can *take* what he wants, by fair means or foul. So they falsely accuse Naboth, have him killed, and appropriate his vineyard (cf., 2 Sam.12:1-4; Mark 12:7-8). In Acts, Luke has made *Naboth* into the righteous Barnabas, and now it is the latter's donation, not possession, of a field that excites a wicked couple's jealousy. Ananias is Luke's Ahab, Sapphira his Jezebel. But their crime is not murder, an element Luke reserves for the martyrdom of Stephen. The transgression of Ananias and Sapphira is borrowed instead from that of Achan (Judg. 7), who helped himself to a bit of loot ear-marked for Yahweh. Ananias and Sapphira have sold a field (desiring the esteem accorded Barnabas), but they have kept back some of the money while claiming to have donated the full price. Big mistake! They lost the right to keep any of the sale price once they dedicated it as "devoted to the Lord."

Peter confronts Ananias and Sapphira, just as Joshua called out Achan (Josh. 7:25) and as Elijah confronted Ahab (1 Kings 20:17-18). Luke has taken the note about Ahab being disturbed in spirit (1 Kings 20:4) and made it into the accusation that Ananias and Sapphira have lied to the Spirit of God (Acts 5:3b-4, 9b). Both Elijah and Peter pronounce death sentences on the guilty, and Ananias and Sapphira (like Achan) get speedier justice than they'd have liked (Acts 5:5a, 10a)! Nemesis procrastinates visiting Ahab and Jezebel for some time. Fear seized everyone who heard of Ananias' and Sapphira's fate, reminiscent of the fear of God kindled in poor Ahab when he heard Elijah's doom oracle (1 Kings 20:27-29). Shortly after the Naboth travesty the "young men of Israel" overcome the greedy Syrians (21:1-21), giving Luke the idea of having the "young men" (who never pop up any place else in Acts) dispose of the bodies of the unlamented Ananias and Sapphira (Acts 5:6, 10b).

The story is, of course, a cautionary tale meant to put the fear of God into any who might be contemplating skimping on their church pledge. It cultivates superstitious fear in a disgraceful manner.[442]

---

[442] Loisy, *Origins of the New Testament*, p. 173.

Me and My Shadow (5:12-16)

Reminiscent of Jesus' involuntary healing of the hemorrhagic woman (Mark 5:28-30) who merely touches his prayer shawl, Peter now becomes a veritable dynamo of therapeutic energy: any across whom the Petrine umbra chances to fall is at once delivered of his or her affliction. Good thing it wasn't a cloudy day! This is another of those sets of matching miracles that place Peter and Paul on an ecumenical par: over in Acts 19:11-12, Paul, too, works extraordinary miracles without even trying, as his fans manage to snitch his handkerchiefs and work aprons as "pieces of him" with which to touch the sick and demoniacs, who were at once healed. Need I say, this is superstitious medievalism of the most flagrant kind? What's next? Splinters from the True Cross? Feathers from the Holy Spirit? Breast milk from the Virgin Mary? Used diapers from the Holy Infant of Prague?

Breakout Kings (5:17-32)

All this publicity riles up the Sanhedrin's Sadducees, who are envious of their competitors' success. In fact, this invidious attribution of base motives to the Jewish authorities occurs again and again throughout Acts (e.g., 13:45; 17:5), and the more we see of it, whether in Jerusalem or in Diaspora synagogues, the more anachronistic it reveals itself to be. Surely the ascriptions of "jealousy" refer to the competition between church and synagogue in Luke's day,[443] the mid-second century, when Jews and Christians were engaged in mimetic rivalry[444] over the prize of calling themselves the chosen people of God. As Christianity, which was easier to join and to practice, progressively overtook Judaism in numbers, Jewish jealousy was understandable (just as one perceives a jealousy-generated Christian antipathy to Islam).

---

[443] Cf., Sanders, *Jews in Luke-Acts*, p. 286.

[444] Rene Girard, *Violence and the Sacred*. Trans. Patrick Gregory (Baltimore: Johns Hopkins University Press, 1977), Chapter Six, "From Mimetic Desire to the Monstrous Double," pp. 143-168; Richard L. Rubenstein, *After Auschwitz: Radical Theology and Contemporary Judaism* (New York: Bobbs-Merrill, 1966), pp. 9-10, 58.

So the Sadducees have the apostles rounded up and put behind bars. However, during the night, an angel smuggles a golden file into the prison and saws through the bars, letting the apostles escape and telling them to use their new-found freedom to resume preaching the Christian gospel. When morning comes and the sleepy Sanhedrinists take their seats and call for the bailiff to bring in the prisoners, they are greeted with the news that the cell is empty! Still locked and guarded, but empty! Huh? Then someone rushes in with an update: "They're in the Temple preaching right now!" Hearing this, the elders dispatch armed guards to apprehend them~again! Maybe they'll have better luck this time! Once the apostles are once again hauled in, the Sanhedrin makes no mention at all of their escape or how they pulled it off. It is, as Edward Zeller[445] implied, quite comical.

I believe I detect here an echo of 2 Kings 1:9-15, where the king of Israel sends a party of fifty soldiers to bring in Elijah, but the prophet, in a cranky mood, calls down fire from the Empyrean heaven to roast them. A second arresting party fares no better, but the third time Elijah condescends to come along quietly, whereupon he tells off the king. Of course, the big difference is that Luke doesn't have the apostles barbecue the solders. But we know from Luke 9:51-55 not to expect that.

Another parallel is visible, this time with Matthew 27:62-28:14. Jesus, dead, has been placed in a tomb with guards posted outside. Jesus (offstage) vacates the tomb. An angel comes down to open the door of the sepulcher, even as one of his winged colleagues now descends to open the door to the apostles' jail cell. He tells them to go preach, even as Matthew's angel commanded the women to go tell the disciples. Meanwhile, the stupefied soldiers, whose efforts had proven futile, return to their superiors and report the absence of Jesus, just as their counterparts in Acts report the vanishing of the apostles. In both cases, the Jewish authorities seem to take the

---

[445] Edward Zeller, *The Contents and Origin of the Acts of the Apostles Critically Investigated* (London: Williams & Norgate, 1985; rpt. Eugene: Wipf & Stock, 2007), Volume One, p. 222.

mysterious miracle in stride and begin to work on damage control. Has Luke borrowed the story from Matthew or vice versa? Or were there two (mutated) versions of the rumor mentioned in Matthew 28:15, one concerning Jesus, the other his apostles?

The divinely aided jail break looks like still another borrowing from Euripides, this time from lines 444-451:

> As for those women you clapped in chains and sent to the dungeon, they're gone, clean away, went skipping off to the fields crying on their god Bromius [= Dionysus]. The chains on their legs snapped apart by themselves. Untouched by any human hand, the doors swung wide, opening of their own accord. Sir, this stranger who has come to Thebes is full of many miracles. I know no more than that.

Note that there is not only the motif of their bonds falling away and the prison doors opening by themselves; there is also the mystified report of it by the persecutor's servants.

Don't Know Much about History (5:33-42)

What to do about those pesky apostles? Some want the firing squad. But as tempers grow hotter, the eminent scholar Rabban Gamaliel[446] calls for silence and offers these words of caution:

> Men of Israel, take care what you do with these men. For before these days Theudas arose, giving himself out to be somebody, and a number of men, about four hundred, joined him; but he was slain and all who followed him were dispersed and came to nothing. After him Judas the Galilean arose in the days of the census and drew away some of the people after him; he also perished, and all who followed him were scattered. So in the present case I tell you, keep away

---

[446] Can't you see him played by Morgan Freeman in a movie?

from these men and let them alone; for if this plan or this undertaking is of men, it will fail; but if it is of God, you will not be able to overthrow them. You might even be found opposing God!

Of course, this is more of Luke's public relations campaign: "Hey! Listen to *this* guy! You can't go wrong leaving Christians in peace!" Gamaliel never said such things. Instead, Luke is cribbing from Josephus, who discussed various Jewish rebels against Rome. He mentioned Theudas the Magician who promised his followers he would repeat Joshua's feat of causing the Jordan to dry up. Then, *in a flashback*, he refers to the *earlier* revolt of Judas of Galilee during the Roman taxation census of 6 C.E. But Luke seems not to have noticed that the discussion of Judas *was* a flashback, so when he summarizes the Josephus passage, he writes as if Theudas was chronologically *prior* to Judas. Yikes. Worse yet, Theudas was active only in the decade of the 40s, some years *after* Gamaliel supposedly recounts his adventure![447] Hoo boy.

But there is more. Euripides has a very similar scene in which King Pentheus' counselor, the venerable Cadmus, urges him to think again about his plan to persecute the followers of Dionysus. "Even if this Dionysus is no god, as you assert, persuade yourself that he is. The fiction is a noble one" (lines 334-36). Later Dionysus himself advises Pentheus, "I warn you once again: do not take arms against a god" (line 789).

The Magnificent Seven (6:1-6)

Luke appears to portray the second-century church institution of widow relief as if it were up and running already in the early years of the Jerusalem church.[448] A difficulty has arisen over the neglect of

---

[447] Haenchen, *Acts*, pp. 256-257.

the Hellenist widows in the daily distribution of food and supplies. The widows of the Hebrews were getting theirs right on schedule. These "Hellenists" were apparently Diaspora Jews, Greek-speakers, who had resettled in the Holy Land. The Hebrews must have been born-and-bred Palestinian Jews, Aramaic-speakers. Most probably, the story presupposes that the slighting of the one faction was inadvertent, the result of a language barrier and difficulty communicating. When some bring the issue to the high-and-mighty apostles, they reply that they cannot be bothered with such trivia, and Peter suggests the Greek-speakers choose a group of their own administrators. But they need to be filled with the Spirit and wisdom, in order to mediate any future practical difficulties. The whole passage looks to be based on Exodus 18, where Jethro advises Moses not to wear himself out by hearing every minor dispute among the people from morning to evening. Moses accepts the advice and appoints seventy honest men to act as lower court judges. They receive a share of Moses' Spirit to equip them for their task (Num. 11:24-25). Likewise here: to lighten the burden on the hard-working apostles, a group of seven is appointed to handle the small stuff while the apostles are busy preaching the gospel and performing miracles. But, as things develop, the Seven, too, find time to engage in foreign evangelism and wonder-working, as we shall soon see.

Rough Crowd (6:8-8:1)

Luke is not done with Naboth, Ahab, and Jezebel yet. Now he makes the hapless Naboth into the bold proto-martyr Stephen. Remember, Naboth was framed by the witch-queen Jezebel. She managed to get the elders and *freemen* to bear false witness against a bewildered

---

[448] N. Walter, "Apostelgeschichte 6.1 und die Anfänge der Urgemeinde in Jerusalem," *New Testament Studies* 29 (1983), pp. 370-393; cf., F.C. Baur, *Paul, the Apostle of Jesus Christ: His Life and Work, His Epistles and Doctrine.* Trans. Edward Zeller (London and Edinburgh: Williams & Norgate: 1875), vol. 2, p. 103

Naboth. Stephen suffers the same treatment at the hands of the Synagogue of *Freedmen*. Both righteous men were accused of double blasphemy, Naboth supposedly defaming both God and king, Stephen reportedly badmouthing Moses and God. Both men are carried outside the city limits and stoned to death. When Ahab hears of the outcome, he tears his garments in self-reproach. This note of sartorial suicide Luke has transformed into the detail of young Saul of Tarsus checking the coats of the stoning mob.

The very name "Stephen" is a clue to the fictitious nature of the story, as it translates as "crown," and (what do you know?) Stephen wins the crown of martyrdom. He is thus an ideal figure, "Mr. Martyr." But there may nonetheless be a historical core to the martyrdom of Stephen, or at least an earlier legend lying behind it. Both Hans-Joachim Schoeps[449] and Robert Eisenman[450] have suggested that the Stephen story is a reworking of the story of the martyr death of James the Just. Indeed, there are vivid similarities. Josephus briefly notes the event in his *Antiquities of the Jews*, Book XX, chapter IX.

> But this younger Ananus, who, as we have told you already, took the high priesthood, was a bold man in his temper, and very insolent; he was also of the sect of the Sadducees, who are very rigid in judging offenders, above all the rest of the Jews, as we have already observed; when, therefore, Ananus was of this disposition, he thought he had now a proper opportunity [to exercise his authority]. Festus was now dead, and Albinus was but upon the road; so he assembled the sanhedrim of judges, and brought before them the brother of Jesus, who was called Christ, whose name was James, and

---

[449] Hans-Joachim Schoeps, *Theologie und Geschichte des Judenchristentums* (Tübingen, 1949), p. 441; Schoeps, *Jewish Christianity: Factional Disputes in the Early Church* (Philadelphia: Fortress Press), pp. 43-44.

[450] Robert Eisenman, *James the Brother of Jesus: The Key to Unlocking the Secrets of Early Christianity and the Dead Sea Scrolls* (New York: Viking, Penguin, 1997), Chapter 14, "The Stoning of James and the Stoning of Stephen," pp 411-465.

some others, [or, some of his companions]; and when he had formed an accusation against them as breakers of the law, he delivered them to be stoned.[451]

In his *Ecclesiastical History* (Book 2, Chapter 23), Eusebius (fourth century) claims to be preserving extracts from a second-century work by a Jewish-Christian church historian named Hegesippus. One of these recounts the martyrdom of James.

> James, the Lord's brother, succeeds to the government of the Church, in conjunction with the apostles. He has been universally called *the Just*, from the days of the Lord down to the present time. For many bore the name of James; but this one was holy from his mother's womb. He drank no wine or *other* intoxicating liquor, nor did he eat flesh; no razor came upon his head; he did not anoint himself with oil, nor make use of the bath. He alone was permitted to enter the holy place: for he did not wear any woollen garment, but fine *linen only*. He alone, *I say*, was wont to go into the temple: and he used to be found kneeling on his knees, begging forgiveness for the people-so that the skin of his knees became horny like that of a camel's, by reason of his constantly bending the knee in adoration to God, and begging forgiveness for the people. Therefore, in consequence of his pre-eminent justice, he was called *the Just*, and *Oblias*, which signifies in Greek *Defence of the People*, and *Justice*, in accordance with what the prophets declare concerning him.
>
> Now some persons belonging to the seven sects existing among the people, which have been before described by me in the Notes, asked him: "What is the door of Jesus?" And he replied that He was the Saviour. In consequence of this answer, some believed that Jesus is the Christ. But the sects before mentioned did not believe, either in a resurrection or in the coming of One to requite every man according to his works; but those who did believe, believed because of James. So, when many even of the ruling class believed, there was a

---

. [451] *Works of Flavius Josephus*, pp. 529-530.

commotion among the Jews, and scribes, and Pharisees, who said: "A little more, and we shall have all the people looking for Jesus as the Christ."

They came, therefore, in a body to James, and said: "We entreat thee, restrain the people: for they are gone astray in their opinions about Jesus, as if he were the Christ. We entreat thee to persuade all who have come hither for the day of the passover, concerning Jesus. For we all listen to thy persuasion; since we, as well as all the people, bear thee testimony that thou art just, and showest partiality to none. Do thou, therefore, persuade the people not to entertain erroneous opinions concerning Jesus: for all the people, and we also, listen to thy persuasion. Take thy stand, then, upon the summit of the temple, that from that elevated spot thou mayest be clearly seen, and thy words may be plainly audible to all the people. For, in order to attend the passover, all the tribes have congregated *hither*, and some of the Gentiles also."

The aforesaid scribes and Pharisees accordingly set James on the summit of the temple, and cried aloud to him, and said: "O just one, whom we are all bound to obey, forasmuch as the people is in error, and follows Jesus the crucified, do thou tell us what is the door of Jesus, the crucified." And he answered with a loud voice: "Why ask ye me concerning Jesus the Son of man? He Himself sitteth in heaven, at the right hand of the Great Power, and shall come on the clouds of heaven." [Cf., Acts 7:56]

And, when many were fully convinced *by these words*, and offered praise for the testimony of James, and said, "Hosanna to the son of David," then again the said Pharisees and scribes said to one another, "We have not done well in procuring this testimony to Jesus. But let us go up and throw him down, that they may be afraid, and not believe him." And they cried aloud, and said: "Oh! oh! the Just himself has been deceived!" Thus they fulfilled the Scripture written in Isaiah: "Let us away with the just man, because he is troublesome to us: therefore shall they eat the fruit of their doings." So they went up and threw down the just man, and said to one another: "Let us stone James the Just." And they began to stone him: for he was not killed by the fall; but he turned, and kneeled down, and said: "I beseech Thee, Lord God our Father, forgive them; for they know not what they do." [Cf., Acts 7:60]

And, while they were thus stoning him to death, one of the priests, the sons of Rechab, the son of Rechabim, to whom testimony is borne by Jeremiah the prophet, began to cry aloud, saying: "Cease, what do ye? The just man is praying for us." But one among them, one of the fullers, took the staff with which he was accustomed to wring out the garments *he dyed*, and hurled it at the head of the just man.

And so he suffered martyrdom; and they buried him on the spot, and the pillar erected to his memory still remains, close by the temple. This man was a true witness to both Jews and Greeks that Jesus is the Christ.[452]

Is the story true? Who can say? There are certainly big question marks to be placed beside it. First, there is serious doubt as to whether Josephus intends to refer to the biblical Jesus and "James the brother of the Lord" (Gal. 1:19). It seems at least as likely that Josephus is talking about James the son of Damnaeus, newly appointed high priest, being gotten out of the way by his rival Ananus, who was then removed from office, the honor passing to the slain James' surviving brother Jesus, also a priest.[453] At any rate, Christian readers took it for granted Josephus was referring to the two New Testament characters, and the Stephen version may have grown from there.[454] Hegesippus, too, may have been dependent

---

[452]Roberts-Donaldson translation,
http://www.earlychristianwritings.com/text/hegesippus.html.

[453] As high priest he had the epithet "Christ," Anointed, as in Daniel 9:26, because priests, like kings, were anointed with oil upon investiture.

[454] And Luke seems to be acquainted with Josephus at other points, so this text was presumably known to him, too. Steve Mason, *Josephus and the New Testament* (Peabody: Hendrickson Publishers, 1992), Chapter 6, "Josephus and Luke-Acts," pp. 185-225; Pervo, *Dating Acts*, Chapter. 5, "Acts among the Historians: Luke and Josephus," pp. 149-199.

upon Josephus, or a highly embellished version of that version, if he did not embellish it himself.[455]

The role of Paul (Saul) in the martyrdom of Stephen is a fairly minor one, holding the coats of the mob (so their wind-up would not be hampered). But this is only a vestige of the active role of Paul in fomenting the violence directed to James, actually shoving him down the steps to the Temple floor, where he was stoned. This is the version of the martyrdom told in the Pseudo-Clementine *Recognitions* (based on an earlier Ebionite Acts).[456]

One further, major hint that the Stephen story is based on that of James the Just can be spotted in 7:52, with the mention of "the Just, whom you have *now* betrayed and murdered," a reference originally not to Jesus but to James the Just, anticipating his own imminent execution.

Stephen's accusers make some pretty damning claims against him: "We have heard him speak blasphemous words against Moses and God" and "This man never ceases to speak words against this holy place and the law; for we have heard him say that this Jesus of Nazareth will destroy this place, and will change the customs which Moses delivered to us" (Acts 6:11-14). These are supposed to be the calumnies of false witnesses, but can it really be that simple? Doesn't the ensuing speech imply that Stephen *is* speaking against the Temple, as he makes it tantamount to an idol in 7:47-50?[457] It was a mistake from the beginning, he says, since it is absurd to think the universe-filling deity could be confined to some earthly building.

But we can't seriously ask *what* a man named Stephen said on this particular occasion, seeing that the whole thing has been composed on the basis of the Naboth story and the traditional martyrdom of James the Just. The business about the perjurers who

---

[455] I think it not unlikely that "Hegesippus" is itself a Christianized version of sections of Josephus. Another version of Josephus' works is called the "Josippon," and "He-*gesippus*" is not much different.

[456] Schoeps, *Jewish Christianity*, p. 45; Eisenman, *James*, p. 124.

[457] Marcel Simon, St. *Stephen and the Hellenists in the Primitive Church*. Haskell Lectures delivered at the Graduate School of Theology, Oberlin College, 1956 (New York: Longmans, Green, 1958), p. 89.

say Stephen claims Jesus will destroy the Temple is obviously lifted from the trial of Jesus in Mark 14:57-58. Style and vocabulary[458] make it clear that the speech in chapter 7 is a Lukan creation through and through, and not a Hellenist or Samaritan tract as some scholars once proposed.[459] So then we have to wonder how "false" Luke considered the charges against the fictive Stephen to be.

After all, doesn't Luke have Jesus predict the destruction of the Temple in Luke 21:20-24? Yes, but remember that, for Luke, the fall of Jerusalem is not a sign of the immediate Parousia as it is in Mark and Matthew. The whole period called "the times of the Gentiles" must pass before Jesus can return, so it is *not* Jesus who destroys the Temple. So here Luke is putting into the mouths of false witnesses what was the actual belief of an earlier generation of Christians, just as in Luke 21:8 he warns that it is only false prophets who will come announcing, "The time is at hand!"

Does Luke also think it is false to say that Jesus will or does "change the customs delivered by Moses"? Yes, he does. Later in Acts, we hear James the Just inform Paul that the Jewish Christians of Jerusalem think

> that you teach all the Jews who are among the Gentiles to forsake Moses, telling them not to circumcise their children or observe the customs. What then is to be done? They will certainly hear that you have come. Do therefore what we tell you. We have four men who are under a vow; take these men and purify yourself along with them and pay their expenses, so that they may shave their heads. Thus all will know that there is nothing in what they have been told about you but that you yourself live in observance of the law. (Acts 21:21-24)

---

[458] Earl Richard, *Acts 6:1-8:4: The Author's Method of Composition.* Society of Biblical Literature Dissertation Series 41 (Missoula: Scholars Press, 1978).

[459] Johannes Munck, *The Acts of the Apostles: A New Translation with Introduction and Commentary.* Anchor Bible 31. Revised by W.F. Albright and C.S. Mann (Garden City: Doubleday, 1967).

Luke does not uphold the Pauline teaching familiar from Galatians, Romans, and Colossians that the Torah is no longer in effect, at least for Gentiles. In Acts 15, Luke decrees that even Gentile Christians must keep a few basic laws. Plus, note that Luke uses the sociological term "customs" rather than the theological term "laws" for Jewish practices in Acts 6:14; 21:21; 26:3; 28:17, as if from an outsider's point of view.[460] This is not what Jerusalem zealots for the Torah, much less James the Just, would have said.

Again, what of the Temple? Was it a mistake from the beginning? Perhaps not. Keep in mind the late date of Acts. The Temple's demolition is long past, even if you count the laying waste (or at least the seizure) of Bar Kochba's Temple.[461] To minimize the loss of the Temple, saying it was never really necessary, sounds like the Jewish sour grapes theology current in the wake of its destruction, a rationalization to the effect, "Don't worry! No great loss! God couldn't really have lived in it anyway, right?"[462]

Simon Says (8:1-25)

Eisenman indentifies Simon Magus with a kind of Rasputin-like character mentioned by Josephus. This Simon conspired with Bernice to persuade her sister Drusilla to leave her husband, King Azizus of Emesa. The poor sap had agreed to be circumcised so he could marry her, but now Drusilla wanted to take up with the uncircumcised Felix instead. Josephus' Simon hails from Cyprus, while later Christian writers say Simon Magus came from Gitta (the Old Testament Gath) in Samaria, but, far from being a contradiction, this fact actually strengthens the connection, since it was natural to confuse "Gitta" with the "Kittim," or Sea Peoples of Cyprus. And, as Eisenman points out, some manuscripts of Josephus name the magician "Atomus," and Eisenman sees a connection with

---

[460] Sanders, *Jews in Luke-Acts*, pp. 248, 271.

[461] Leibel Reznick, *The Mystery of Bar Kochba: An Historical and Theological Investigation of the Last King of the Jews* (Northvale, New Jersey: Jason Aronson, 1996), Chapter 18, "The Bar Kochba Temple," pp. 65-76.

[462] J.C. O'Neill, *The Theology of Acts in its Historical Setting* (London: SPCK, 1961), pp. 85-89. My sentences in quote marks are my own summary of O'Neill's point, not a direct quotation from his book.

the Primal Adam doctrine implied in Simon's claim to have been the many times reincarnated Standing One.

And there is still a closer link: the episode of Saul/Paul squaring off against Elymas the sorcerer (Acts 13:8 ff) is a Pauline counterpart to Peter's contest with Simon Magus in Acts 8:9ff. (In fact, Elymas' patronymic "bar-Jesus" may reflect Simon's claim to have appeared lately in Judea as Jesus). So Elymas is simply Simon Magus. And, what do you know? The Western Text of Acts gives the name as "Etoimas" or "Etomas" instead of Elymas. Thus, Simon Magus = Elymas = Etomas = Atomus = Josephus' Simon = Simon Magus.

Then again, Simon has a second historical prototype: *Paul!* This identification, first detected by the eagle-eyed F.C. Baur, emerges toward the end of the fascinating episode in Acts chapter 8. Verse 1 offers a particularly interesting bit of information: the lynching of Stephen ignited a persecution, then a *hegira*, of the Jerusalem Christians—except for the apostles! What sense does *that* make? It might be an arbitrary literary fiat by Luke motivated by his agenda of making the Jerusalem apostles the home-office supervisors of the expansion of the church. In the midst of persecution? Maybe we are to imagine the apostles once again huddling behind locked doors and sending out communiqués by carrier pigeons. But it seems quite likely that "the apostles" are synecdoche for the "Hebrews," the Aramaic-speaking Christians who still attended Temple worship (Acts 3:1) and kept kosher (Acts 10:14). Such Jerusalem Torah-Christians are clearly in evidence in chapter 11, after all.

So why were the Hellenists singled out for persecution? Because they held, or were believed to hold, with Stephen's (real or imagined) heresies. This would imply that the faction led by the apostles was not especially odious to at least some of the Jewish authorities, a scenario implied in Acts 23:6-9, where the Pharisee members of the Sanhedrin are willing to give Paul a break, unlike the Sadducees who want him dead. And remember, it was specifically those mean old Sadducees who had Peter and his colleagues arrested and imprisoned.

As the remaining six "deacons" (as tradition dubs them) fan out from Jerusalem, they preach the gospel to whomever will listen, Jew or Gentile. Probably, as Paul is depicted in subsequent chapters, they are assumed to be speaking in local synagogues (as visitors were commonly invited to do, Acts 13:14b-16). The Gentiles to whom they preached would have been the so-called God-fearers, Gentiles who loved Judaism and attended synagogue, though unwilling to be circumcised and become full proselytes.

But the Jewish authorities were not content to have expelled the Hellenistic Christians from Jerusalem. They pursued them beyond Judea. Who led this witch-hunt? None other than Saul. Or so says Luke. But that cannot be. Luke tells us Saul carried warrants from the High Priest, enabling him to arrest Christians and to put the thumbscrews to them till they renounced their new faith (Acts 9:1-2; 22:4-5; 2:9-11). But the High Priest had no such authority to delegate; his reach did not extend beyond the Jewish homeland. Granted, as Pontifex Maximus of Judaism, he might have armed Paul with a letter to read to local synagogue rulers asking them to excommunicate any Jesus freaks from their congregations, but that would not give them the legal authority to conspire with Saul to arrest people and to drag them back to Jerusalem. And besides, such a measure of mass excommunication *was* taken, but that was decades later, via the addition to the synagogue liturgy of the Eighteenth Benediction, calling down divine wrath upon the *minim*, the heretics, and specifically upon the Nazarenes.

Well, Philip (one of the Seven, not the one belonging to the Twelve) wound up seeking refuge in Samaria, only to find himself surrounded by a religious revival. Simon Magus (i.e., the magician) was wowing the crowds with a great show of (unspecified) miracles, all to the end of recruiting followers, even worshippers, as he styled himself "the Great Power," i.e., the highest deity. All this is but the tip of a heretical iceberg, for other second-century sources tell of the thriving religion of Simon and of his Gnostic teaching. To hear him tell it, he descended from heaven in search of his soul-mate Helen, the Fallen Sophia of Gnosticism. She had left her proper estate and become trapped in the material world, in which, mired in forgetfulness, she had been many times reincarnated. She was thus the symbol of the Gnostic believer not yet awakened to his or her true nature. Simon was the Gnostic redeemer bringing her to remembrance and rescuing her from degradation in the brothel of the material world.

Simon is said to have taught that he had (only apparently) suffered on the cross as the Son, and he offered salvation by grace, dismissing the Torah which was only the creation of the angels anyway. When Luke has Peter chastise Simon, "Pray to the Lord that, if possible, the intent of your heart may be forgiven you" (8:22), he is winking to the second-century reader: the "intent" of Simon's heart is the Greek word *epinoia*, a technical term meaning "first thought," the epithet of the pre-incarnate Helen, more or less equivalent to the Logos or Sophia.[463] Luke is trying to caricature the origin of the Simonian sect which Justin Martyr says had become the dominant religion of Samaria in his day.

But I'm getting ahead of myself. Back to Philip. As we now read the tale, Philip comes across like a stand-up comic at a comedy club, waiting offstage while the comedian before him finishes his routine. Simon holds sway over the Samaritans by a series of impressive miracles. Then he retires from the field, and Philip comes on for his set. Those Samaritans are a fickle bunch! Philip's prestidigitation proves even more boffo than Simon's. Must have been that stunt sawing the Samaritan Woman[464] in half that convinced 'em that Jesus was the real savior. (This is why Paul, in 1 Corinthians 1:20-25, disdained the evangelistic appeal to miracles and philosophical dialectic: the next guy might have a more flashy Power Point display.)

Here is one of those places where the "trajectory" approach pioneered by Helmut Koester and James M. Robinson[465] comes in quite handy. The idea is that what first seems to be a later embellishment of an earlier story or idea may actually make more sense as a fuller account of an original version to which the earlier document was making glancing reference.[466] What is it that Acts is summarizing in its terse statements that both Simon and Philip were piling on the miracles? My guess is that the underlying story has been more fully preserved (though that doesn't rule out further legendary embellishment as well) in the Acts of Peter and related texts. In them Peter and Simon engage in a "Can You Top This?" miracle contest, which, of course, Peter wins.

---

[463] Gerd Lüdemann, "The Acts of the Apostles and the Beginnings of Simonian Gnosis," *New Testament Studies* 33 (1987), pp. 420-426.

[464] John chapter 4.

[465] James M. Robinson and Helmut Koester, *Trajectories through Early Christianity* (Philadelphia: Fortress Press, 1971).

[466] Gershom G. Scholem, *Jewish Gnosticism, Merkabah Mysticism, and Talmudic Tradition* (New York: Jewish Theological Seminary, 1965), pp. 7, 14, 40-41. "Are they later developments, written by people who had no direct contact with the old Merkabah speculations and visions, but who used them only in a fanciful way, to supplement by their own inventions traditions that were lost?" (pp. 7-8) Cf., Jesse L. Weston, *From Ritual to Romance* (Garden City: Doubleday Anchor Books, 1957), p. 109.

It may even be that Luke's version has replaced an original Peter with Philip in the first part of the story, returning to Peter for the conclusion. Why might he have done this? In order to construct the picture of the need for the Jerusalem apostles to "seal the deal" whenever new groups are won to Christianity. This is certainly why Luke reports the anomaly that, even after Philip converted the Samaritans, they were devoid of the Holy Spirit. It is the same thinking we see in the second- and third-century competition between major churches who sought clout by claiming they had been founded (and their first bishops instructed) by this or that Holy Apostle. Even so, the Samaritans are not quite genuine Christians, despite having been baptized, until one of the Twelve Apostles imparts the Spirit via the imposition of hands. What was lacking in Philip's baptizing? Simply that he was the one doing it! Not an apostle! This becomes even clearer once Peter comes into the picture and finishes the job, giving the Spirit to the neophytes;

Simon, himself now ostensibly a Christian convert, offers to pay Peter to teach him how to convey the Spirit (apparently with impressive effects, no doubt glossolalia). But, silly rabbit, provision of the Spirit is for apostles, and for apostles only! Philip had no more authority or ability to do this than did Simon Magus! Get it, readers? Luke needed to make this point by positing that a subordinate converted the Samaritans but couldn't quite finish the job, then bringing Peter onstage to do the trick, precisely as in Mark 9:17-18 and 2 Kings 4:29-31.

The Clementine *Recognitions* features a longer exchange between Peter and Simon Magus in which the latter is transparently a surrogate for Paul. I have already noted how Simon Magus is said to have taught salvation by grace apart from works of the Jewish Torah. In the *Recognitions*, Peter denounces Simon as a false apostle. Allow me to paraphrase: "Look, how can you say you're an apostle when you never even laid *eyes* on Jesus! He actually *taught* us in *person*! If, as you claim, he appeared to you in a vision, then wouldn't he have delivered the same teaching to you as he did to us? Did he change his mind in the meantime? Come *off* it!"

Baur[467] took the hint and took a second look at Acts 8. Isn't Simon really Paul there, too? That would certainly throw new light on Peter's giving Simon the brush-off. What is Simon asking him? He wants to buy something that is, as we were just shown, the

---

[467] Baur, *Paul, the Apostle of Jesus Christ*, vol. 1, pp. 88-92, 232.

exclusive prerogative of the apostles. But Peter will not consider it, telling Simon that he has no role in this ministry (literally, "this word," Acts 8:21; cf., Luke 1:2). Baur recognized here an invidious version of Paul's obtaining official apostolic recognition of his ministry on condition that he raise funds for the Jerusalem Church, a form of tribute (Gal. 2:6-10), as well as the seeming failure of the gesture when Jerusalem refused the money (implied in Acts 21:23-24; Rom. 15:25-31). Thus in Acts 8, Paul's acceptance of Jerusalem's stipulation of tribute is switched around so the whole thing becomes a gauche bribe-offer for apostolic status.

If Baur is correct, as I am convinced he is, why would Luke portray Paul in such a light, especially since everywhere else he is trying to make Paul look good to his Petrine readers? Ah, you see, that is exactly why Paul appears here under the name "Simon." Luke wanted to use the story but had to do a bit of editing so as not to torpedo his Pauline PR campaign. That's what Baur thought. But one can go farther, with Hermann Detering,[468] and suggest that "Paul" was the pseudonym, or, to put it differently, that the historical Paul and the historical Simon Magus were two names for the same man. And that is what I do think.[469]

The Ethiopian... er, ah, Eunuch (8:26-40)

This episode embodies several key features of the story of Elisha and Naaman the Syrian (2 Kings 5:1-14).[470] The Elisha narrative depicts both healing (from leprosy) and conversion (from Syrian Rimmon-worship), while Luke's version tells only of conversion (from Gentile God-fearer to baptized Christian). Why no healing this time? Maybe Luke didn't want to strain plausibility or good taste by having Philip physically restore a eunuch. (You know, the, ah, laying on of hands...) Anyway, both Naaman and the Ethiopian are foreign officials of high status, both close confidants of their monarchs (2

---

[468] Hermann Detering, *The Falsified Paul: Early Christianity in the Twilight.* Trans. Darrell J. Doughty. A special issue of the *Journal of Higher Criticism* 10/ 2 (Fall 2003).

[469] Robert M. Price, *The Amazing Colossal Apostle: The Search for the Historical Paul* (Salt Lake City: Signature Books, 2012), Chapter 7, pp. 185-233.

[470] Brodie, "Luke the Literary Interpreter," pp. 316-327.

Kings 5:5; Acts 8:27c). Naaman makes the trip to Samaria to ask the king's help in contacting Elisha. The Ethiopian had gone to Jerusalem to worship in the Temple, but somehow he came away unsatisfied. He would find fulfillment on his way home, just like the Emmaus disciples in Luke 24:13ff. The Israelite king at first does not understand the letter Naaman hands him, but a word from Elisha makes the meaning clear to him, just as the Ethiopian fails to grasp the import of the prophetic scroll he is reading until the hitchhiking Philip offers his commentary. In both cases salvation is to be sought by immersion. Naaman is initially unwilling until his servant persuades him. Luke has this hesitancy in mind when he has the Ethiopian ask rhetorically, "What prevents me from being baptized?" (Acts 8:36). Healing and/or conversion follow, but both officials must go back to their pagan courts alone in their new faith.

Luke also seems to have used Josephus as a magnet to hold these iron filings together, namely the fascinating story of Helen, Queen of Adiabene, a realm contiguous and/or overlapping with Edessa, whose king Agbar/Abgarus some sources make Helen's husband. Helen and her son Izates converted to Judaism. Initially Izates decided to skip circumcision because a Jewish teacher named Ananias assured him that the simple fact of worshiping God was far more important than the ritual of circumcision. Izates' mother also counseled against it, since his subjects might resent him embracing alien customs. Soon afterward, however, a stricter Jewish teacher arrived from Jerusalem, named Eliezer. He called upon Izates and found him studying the Genesis passage (17:9-14) on the Abrahamic covenant of circumcision. He asked Izates if he understood the implications of what he was reading. If so, why didn't he see how important it was to be circumcised? Izates then agreed to do it. Helen and Izates demonstrated the sincerity of their conversion by sending agents to Egypt and Cyrene to buy grain during the famine that struck during Claudius' reign,[471] and to distribute it to the poor in

---

[471] When the prophet Agabus predicts the famine, Luke has derived his name from that of Helen's husband Agbarus, who converted his small nation to the Christian faith..

Jerusalem.

There is no room for the Acts 11:28 famine relief visit in the Galatians 2 itinerary of Paul's visits to Jerusalem, but Eisenman places the event during Paul's time in "Arabia" (Gal. 1:17) which in the usage of that time could include Edessa/Adiabene. The Book of Acts refers to two Antiochs, in Pisidia and Syria, but there were others, including Edessa. Eisenman identifies Paul with Ananias, the initial Jewish teacher who tells Izates he need not be circumcised if he has faith in God, before Eliezer persuaded Izates to submit to circumcision after all. This episode would form the basis of the Antioch episode in Galatians 2:3-4, when certain "false brethren" showed up in Antioch to "Judaize" (the actual Greek word used in Gal. 2:14) Paul's converts, telling them they must be circumcised after all. Luke will have transferred the original name "Ananias" to the (fictive) Jewish Christian who initiates Paul in Acts 9. Eisenman also makes Paul one of Helen's agents who brought famine relief to Jerusalem, which he is said to do "from Antioch," in Acts 11.

Now back to Acts 8. Luke is again referring to the Helen/Izates famine relief visit when Philip intercepts the financial officer of a foreign queen going from Jerusalem down through Egypt by way of Gaza. This is of course the Ethiopian eunuch. His queen is really Queen Helen of Adiabene, but Luke disguises her as Candace, the Queen of Ethiopia (even though there actually weren't any queens in Ethiopia in this period). He is harking back to an Old Testament prototype, making Helen, a convert to Judaism, into a New Testament Queen of Sheba, visiting Jerusalem to hear the wisdom of Solomon. Even the location of the Acts episode is dictated by the Helen story, as the Ethiopian travels into Egypt via Gaza as Helen's agents must have done to buy the grain. Luke's substituted motivation for the trip, by contrast, is absurd: a eunuch could not have gone to Jerusalem to worship since eunuchs were barred from the Temple.

How did Philip get back to Azotus (the Old Testament Ashdod)? "And when they came up out of the water, the Spirit of the Lord caught up Philip; and the eunuch saw him no more, and went on his way rejoicing. But Philip was found at Azotus, and passing on he preached the gospel to all the towns till he came to Caesarea." I have always read this as meaning Philip was "raptured" by the Spirit, like Habakkuk in Bel and the Dragon 1:33-39, and that he miraculously appeared in Azotus like Jesus suddenly popping up in the midst of the stunned disciples in Luke 24:36. But I have to admit it might mean nothing more than that the Holy Spirit suddenly inspired Philip to make a hasty exit and that the next time anyone saw him he was in Azotus.

Paul's Conversion (9:1-19)

As the great Tübingen critics first realized, the story of Paul's apprehension by the risen Jesus never even comes in for mention in the Pauline epistles but is instead based on 2 Maccabees 3's story of the conversion of Heliodorus. In it a Benjaminite named Simon (3:4) informs Apollonius of Tarsus, governor of Coele-Syria and Phoenicia (3:5), that the Jerusalem Temple contains fantastic wealth and suggests that the Seleucid king might want to seize it for himself. Once the governor tells the king, the latter sends his agent Heliodorus to confiscate the treasure. The very prospect of such a heinous violation of the Temple provokes universal wailing and praying in the Jewish community. God intervenes, and Heliodorus is miraculously repulsed by a shining warrior angel who suddenly appears on horseback. The steed kicks the astonished Heliodorus to the ground, where two more angels flog him (verses 25-26). Blinded, he is unable to help himself but is placed on a stretcher and carried to safety. Pious Jews refrain from gloating and instead pray for his recovery, fearing reprisals should Heliodorus succumb to his injuries. In reply the angels return, appearing before Heliodorus to announce God's mercy: Heliodorus will recover and must from now on proclaim the majesty of the one true God. Heliodorus is not disobedient to the heavenly vision and hastens to offer sacrifice to his Saviour (3:35). Departing again for Syria, he reports all this to the king.

Acts transforms the threatened sacking of the Temple into the persecution of the church by Saul (also called Paulus, perhaps a short form of *Apollonius*), a *Benjaminite* from *Tarsus*. Heliodorus' trip to Jerusalem from Syria becomes Saul's journey *from* Jerusalem *to* Syria. Like Heliodorus, Saul is stopped in his tracks by a heavenly being, goes blind and must be taken into the city, where the prayers of his former enemies raise him up. And as Heliodorus offers sacrifice, Saul undergoes baptism. Then he is told henceforth to proclaim his new Lord, and he does.

But there is a second literary source for the story of Paul's conversion, Euripides' *The Bacchae*, in a sequence we will also find underlying Acts chapter 16, the story of Paul in Philippi.[472] Dionysus has appeared in Thebes disguised in mortal form as a missionary for his own sect. King Pentheus views the new faith as a licentious cult and decides to drive it out of the country. He arrests the apostle of Dionysus but soon finds him freed from prison by an earthquake. Dionysus plans vengeance upon the proud and foolish king, magically compelling Pentheus to undergo conversion to the very faith he sought to destroy. "Though hostile formerly, he now declares a truce and goes with us. You see what you could not when you were blind" (lines 922-924). He sends the dazed Pentheus, disguised in women's clothes, to spy upon the Maenads, Dionysus' female revelers. Pentheus' identity is discovered, and the frenzied women tear him limb from limb, led by his own mother. As the hapless Pentheus departs on his suicide mission, Dionysus wryly comments, "Punish this man. But first distract his wits; bewilder him with madness... After those threats with which he was so fierce, I want him made the laughingstock of Thebes" (lines 850-851, 854-855). "He shall come to know Dionysus, son of Zeus, consummate god, most terrible, and yet most gentle, to mankind" (lines 859-861).

Pentheus must be made an example, as must poor Saul,

---

[472] Lilian Portefaix, *Sisters Rejoice: Paul's Letter to the Philippians and Luke-Acts as Seen by First-Century Philippian Women*. Coniectanea biblica. New Testament series, 20 (Stockholm: Almqvist & Wicksell, 1988), p. 170.

despite himself. His conversion is a punishment, giving the persecutor a spoonful of his own medicine. There seems to be a similar hint of ironic malice in Christ's words to Ananias about Saul: "I will show him how much *he* must suffer for the sake of my name" (Acts 9:16).

This story of Paul caught up short on the Damascus Road is told three times in Acts (which I guess makes up for its complete absence from the Pauline Epistles!). Some details are inconsistent, to the dismay of inerrantists everywhere. In Acts 9:7 Paul's bewildered companions are said to have heard the voice addressing Saul but to have seen nothing out of the ordinary. But in Acts 22:9 we read the exact opposite: Saul's entourage saw the brilliant light but heard no one speaking but Saul. Acts 26's version makes no mention of these bystanders (who, by the way, were very likely based on Ezekiel's companions, alarmed at his wide-eyed trance state beside the River Chebar, Ezek. 3:15). Luke might just have forgotten what he had written earlier, but it also makes sense to suggest he was intentionally reshuffling details to provide a bit of variety for the reader.

The words of Jesus (or a blazing light who says his name is Jesus) owe a debt to our friend Euripides. Maybe Jesus had been up in heaven reading the *Bacchae* before descending to earth and felt like running a few lines, specifically lines 793-795, where Dionysus tells his persecutor Pentheus, "If I were you, I would offer him [Dionysus himself] a sacrifice, not rage and kick against necessity, a man defying god."

What exactly did Saul see? Jesus himself? That seems to be implied in Acts 9:17, when Ananias of Damascus says, "the Lord Jesus... appeared to you on the road." But of course the narrative itself implies Saul saw pretty much nothing, instantly blinded by a burst of light.

Saul being overtaken on the road reminds us of the appearance of the risen Jesus, unrecognized, to a pair of disciples on the road to Emmaus. As they had lost faith in Jesus but had it restored, Saul conspicuously lacked faith in Jesus but gained it from the encounter. And, as Jesus was at first unknown to the two disciples, Saul asks, "Who are you, Lord?"

While Jesus is appearing to Saul on the road, he is also appearing to Ananias in Damascus,[473] informing him that he will shortly have a visit from the notorious persecutor, news at which Ananias, in classic biblical fashion, recoils in fear: "Lord, I've, uh, *heard* of this man! He's, ah, *killing* us, and you're sending him *here*?" No doubt he's thinking maybe he should follow Jonah's example and scram! But it is a meek and beaten Saul who darkens his door, and Ananias baptizes him, laying hands on him to impart the Holy Spirit. Two things to note: Saul does not convert of his own free will. Like Pentheus and Heliodorus, he is simply conscripted despite himself. Christian theologians (masquerading as New Testament exegetes) attempt to trace the lightning-fast thought process that "must have" flashed through Saul's synapses in a split second while he was falling off his horse: "Hmmm... I assumed Jesus was a law-breaker and got crucified for it, so he couldn't be the Messiah. Now that I see he *is* the Messiah but was no less a scofflaw, I guess that means the Messiah came to negate the Torah! Yeah! *That's* it! Okay, sign me up and hand me a ham sandwich!"[474] Absurd. You wish.

Switching Teams (Acts 9:20-30)

Saul loses no time in aggressively "preaching the faith he once tried to destroy" (Gal.1:23). His turnabout is as radical as Ebenezer Scrooge's. It looks like what it is: a fictive miracle story. I can't help thinking that, in the real world, anyone who knew who Saul was and now saw him preaching Jesus would conclude, not that Saul's Jekyll-Hyde switcheroo proved the truth of his new creed, but that he had lost his mind. He would merely seem unstable. Who could predict

---

[473] Gerhard Lohfink, *The Conversion of St. Paul: Narrative and History in Acts.* Trans. Bruce J. Malina. Herald Scriptural Library (Chicago: Franciscan Herald Press, 1976), Chapter II, Section 4, "The Double Vision," pp. 73-77.

[474] See the comprehensive discussion in James D.G. Dunn, *Jesus, Paul and the Law: Studies in Mark and Galatians* (Louisville: Westminster John Knox Press, 1990), Chapter 4, "'A Light to the Gentiles', or 'The End of the Law'? The Significance of the Damascus Road Christophany for Paul," pp. 89-107.

what off-beat sect he might espouse next? Mithraism? The friggin' Sabazius cult?

He causes such a stir debating with Damascene Jews and recruiting new converts that the Jews conspire to eliminate him (9:23-25), but Saul's resourceful disciples get him to safety by lowering him down the city wall in a big basket. Did people lower cargo over the wall all the time? Not exactly inconspicuous. Second Corinthians 11:32-33 tells a different version: "At Damascus, the governor under King Aretas guarded the city of Damascus in order to seize me, but I was let down in a basket through a window in the wall, and escaped his hands." A contradiction? It's possible, of course, that the Jews of Damascus prevailed upon the governor to arrest Paul, but who knows? At any rate, the striking parallel on the basket escape is one of the Acts-Epistles concurrences that lead Richard I. Pervo[475] to conclude that Luke knew and used the Pauline letters. Maybe he did. Hard to know for sure.

He goes next to Jerusalem and tries to associate with the Christians there, but, like Ananias, they were afraid of him. Given his former activities, they had to suspect his new profession of faith was, as Ed Norton would say, "a clever ruse" to smoke out the Christians so he could arrest them. But the apostles take his conversion story seriously and welcome him. Here we discover two clashes with Galatians. First, Galatians says Paul pointedly did *not* go directly to Jerusalem or meet the apostles right after his conversion (Gal. 1:15-17). Second, Galatians 1:22-23 says he remained personally unknown to the Jerusalem Christians, contra Acts 9:28. Though Pervo may be correct that Luke used the Pauline Epistles, making some changes, it can also be argued pretty persuasively that Galatians 1-2 were written (very late) to *rebut* the story in Acts![476]

---

[475] Richard I. Pervo, *Dating Acts*, Chapter 4, "Acts among the Apostles: The Letters of Paul," pp. 51-147; William O. Walker, Jr., "The Letters of Paul as Sources for Acts: A Cameo Essay," in Dennis E. Smith and Joseph B. Tyson, eds., *Acts and Christian Beginnings: The Acts Seminar Report* (Salem, OR: Polebridge Press, 2013), p. 116-117.

[476] Frank R. McGuire, "Galatians as a Reply to Acts," *Journal of Higher Criticism* 10/1 (Spring 2003), pp. 1-22.

Ever wonder why Ananias is never mentioned in Paul's letters? There is a very good reason: Paul claims that he received his gospel directly from God with no human intermediary (Gal. 1:1, 11-12). If Frank McGuire is right, this bold claim is a direct repudiation of the Acts 9 version, where Ananias is most certainly the kind of intermediary mentioned in Galatians 1. But was Ananias' role in Acts 9 itself a Catholicizing attempt to relegate Paul to the subordinate status of one more Christian convert, albeit a very important one? Another oddity of the same kind is on display over in Matthew 16:17, where Peter, despite having been in the company of the earthly Jesus (the very basis of Peter's superiority to Paul in the *Recognitions*), is now said to have learned the truth about Jesus only via direct divine revelation, *not through flesh and blood*. Paul's claim is being appropriated for Peter, redundant as it might seem.

The Aeneid (9:32-35)

This brief episode, in which Peter heals a second paralytic (cf., Acts 3:1-10), is an "establishing shot" to introduce the next episode, the raising up of Tabitha. Luke seeks in the Aeneas healing to create an image of Peter as a second Jesus, an itinerate healer. Aeneas is a reprise of the paralytic whose friends lowered him before Jesus through the roof of Peter's house back in Luke 5:15, based in turn on Mark 2:1-12.[477]

From Talitha to Tabitha (9:36-42)

Luke has rewritten this miracle story from that of Jesus' raising up Jairus' daughter (Mark 5:22-24a, 35-43; Luke 8:41-42a, 49-56), itself rewritten from 2 Kings 4:32-37, where Elisha excludes the gawkers and raises up the child behind closed doors, as do both Jesus (Mark 5:40) and Peter (Acts 9:40). Both New Testament stories are based on the meaning of names. "Jairus" means "he will awaken," while

---

[477] Mark had the man's friends rip up the thatched roof (implicit in 2:4), while Luke has them take off the clay tiles (Luke 5:19), a roofing material more familiar to Luke's Hellenistic readers.

Luke has turned Mark 5:41's Aramaic incantation, *Talitha* ("little maid") into the name of the dead widow *Tabitha* (Acts 9:40). Tabitha (the Greek equivalent being "Dorcas") is a consecrated widow wealthy enough to provide for a group of consecrated widows and virgins in her home (precisely the same situation envisioned in 1 Timothy 5:16, "If any pledged woman has widows, let her assist them; let the church not be burdened, so that it may assist those who are literal widows." Why, in effect, call the widow by a name that means "little girl"? Simple: women consecrated to celibacy and Christian service were called "widows" or "virgins" interchangeably to denote their removal from sexual activity (cf., Ignatius' Epistle to the Smyrnaeans 13:1, "the virgins who are called widows"). In light of this, there is no way to know the physical age Luke envisioned for this character.

The preceding Aeneas episode was, again, intended to prepare us for the reputation of Peter as a miracle-working superhero.[478] "This is a job for Simon Peter!"

Brighten the Cornelius Where You Are (Acts 10:1-16)

Cornelius is a Roman centurion and a God-fearer, nothing all that unusual since Judaism was quite attractive to many Gentiles who appreciated the ethical monotheism of the Semitic faith yet balked at full conversion. Many became Christians, full participants in what they must have regarded as a variety of Judaism of which they could be full members without submitting to all sorts of cultural mores alien to them. He is a generous almsgiver and loves the Jewish people. He is described in the same terms with which Luke embellished the centurion back in Luke 7:1-10 (based on the Q story also used in Matthew 8:5-13). One often hears the Cornelius story told as if Cornelius was like the Rich Young Ruler, already devout yet aware of his need for greater spiritual fulfillment and praying, like young Joseph Smith, for guidance to that end. But the story says

---

[478] Zeller, *Contents and Origin*, vol. I, p. 271.

none of this. When we meet him, the centurion is simply engaged in his customary semi-Jewish devotions. He seeks nothing, but God rewards his piety by sending Peter to him to share the Christian gospel. He is so receptive that he receives the Holy Spirit before Peter can even finish his sermon! And this effusion of the Spirit serves to convince Peter that maybe God wants Christians to evangelize the heathen after all (as if the risen Jesus had not commanded him to do so just before he ascended in Luke 24:46-47!). But I'm not sure we have been reading it right. Peter starts his sermon with a reminder:

> *You know* the word which he sent to Israel, preaching good news of peace by Jesus Christ (he is Lord of all), the word which was proclaimed throughout all Judea, beginning from Galilee after the baptism which John preached: how God anointed Jesus of Nazareth with the Holy Spirit and with power; how he went about doing good and healing all that were oppressed by the devil, for God was with him. And we are witnesses to all that he did both in the country of the Jews and in Jerusalem. They put him to death by hanging him on a tree; but God raised him on the third day and made him manifest. (Acts 10:36-40).

They know it already? Then I suggest Cornelius and his household are already Christians. So what is the purpose of Peter's visit? I think we are supposed to see Cornelius and company on analogy with Philip's converts in Samaria: Christian believers but not yet having received the Spirit because they were not lucky enough to have been converted by a full-fledged apostle. Cornelius would have been recruited by one of the Hellenists who preached to Gentiles after they fled from persecution in Jerusalem (Acts 11:19-21). Yes, Cornelius and his people had not yet been baptized, unlike the Samaritans who *had* gotten *that* far, but there is no consistent pattern of initiation in Acts anyway.[479] Thus Peter plays the same role here as

---

[479] Roger Stronstad, *The Charismatic Theology of St. Luke* (Peabody: Hendrickson Publishers, 1984), pp. 70, 80.

he does in Acts 8:14-18, "sealing the deal" so as to reinforce the authority of the Twelve Apostles over the whole of the expanding Church. In fact, we have just seen Peter inaugurating the Gentile Mission. Uh, wasn't that that supposed to be *Paul's* job?

Now let's backtrack to look at the vision that convinced Peter to undertake his house call. God knows Peter's own Jewish piety will make him reluctant to set foot in the home of a pork-chewing, uncircumcised Roman, so he sends Peter a dream designed to break down Peter's xenophobic resistance. The vision has been recycled from the early chapters of Ezekiel.[480] First Peter sees the heavens open (10:11), just as Ezekiel did (1:1 LXX). Peter sees a vast sheet of sailcloth, presumably stretched out like a trampoline, containing every species of animal, both ritually clean and unclean. Then a heavenly voice commands him, "Eat!" (Acts 10:13), just as Ezekiel is shown a scroll and told to "Eat!" (2:9 LXX). Peter, a faithful Jew, recoils at such a gross transgression of kosher laws, replying with a great and amusing irony: "By no means, Lord!"[481] (Acts 10:14), echoing Ezekiel verbatim (4:14 LXX), when the latter is commanded to cook his food over a dung fire. Again, not exactly kosher! Peter protests that he has never eaten anything unclean before (10:14), nor has Ezekiel (4:14 LXX).

Beware the Eleven of the Pharisees (chapter 11)

Acts 11:1-18 is an instant replay of chapter 10, underlining the point in case it wasn't clear enough the first time. The narrative occasion is that the other apostles got wind of what transpired in the previous chapter and called Peter on the carpet: "Why did you go to uncircumcised men and eat with them?" That is, "Were you out of

---

[480] Randel Helms, *Gospel Fictions* (Buffalo: Prometheus Books, 1989), pp. 20-21.

[481] Cf., Luke 6:46, "Why do you call me 'Lord, Lord,' and not do what I tell you?" Thanks to Alan Babcock, my old pastor, for pointing out the irony. You're going to call a guy "Lord" and in your very next words refuse to do what he tells you?

your mind?" This tells us something important about the Jewish-Christian[482] opposition to Gentile evangelism: it would mean violating the carefully constructed boundaries between Jews and Gentiles that minimized the danger of assimilation. Again, how was this reluctance possible if these people had been told by Jesus, not only to go spread the gospel to all nations, but to eat whatever food they might be offered while away on mission (Luke 10:7-8)? The thing is: these instructions occur, not in the mission charge to the Twelve, i.e., the missionaries to Israel, but to the Seventy, Luke's narrative anticipation of the Gentile Mission. Shouldn't that have settled the question? If we were talking about history here, rest assured, it would have, but this is all like the gospel Passion predictions: it is intended not for the ears of the characters in the story but for the readers, who cannot be told some things often enough. Luke is trying to hammer the point home that Torah regulations like kosher rules cannot be allowed to restrict the mission. That is part of the point of Peter's vision. Sure, the formerly unclean foods stand for Gentiles (Acts 10:28), but the business about eating non-kosher food is simply a direct message to Peter (to the Jewish-Christian reader) not to worry about the menu when preaching in Gentile venues.

One surprising difference in the Acts 11 retelling is verse 14, where we hear for the first time that the angel who told Cornelius to send for Peter also told him, "he will declare to you a message by which you will be saved, you and all your household." Why didn't we hear this before? Because the point in Acts 11 is to make a general statement about the Gentile Mission, whereas that in chapter 10 was to stress the importance of apostolic sanction of evangelistic work done by others.

---

[482] Jack T. Sanders makes a good case that the legalistic Pharisees of Luke's gospel (Luke 11:46; 14:3-6; 15:1-2; 18:9-14) are meant to stand for the strict Torah-Christians of Jerusalem, who attempt to impose the yoke of Torah-observance on Gentile Christians (Acts 5:15), while the Pharisees friendly to Jesus (Luke 11:37; 13:31; 14:1) stand for the Jerusalem Pharisees of Acts who side with Paul (Acts 23:6-9). See Sanders, *Jews in Luke-Acts*, pp. 95-96.

The rest of Chapter 11 looks like a flashback to the earlier aftermath of the Stephen persecution. It seems to provide an alternate account of the beginning of Gentile evangelism. Unnamed Hellenists began recruiting Gentiles while fleeing the hounds set on their trail by Saul.[483] Again we have the motif of Jerusalem sending an agent, this time Barnabas, to approve the free-lance operation in Antioch, like the Vatican deciding to authenticate (endorse) the latest Marian apparition, and that is no mere analogy. Barnabas looks things over and confers the imprimatur. Then he thinks this might be just the place for Saul to use his gifts, so he brings him in to serve in Antioch. Soon there are enough converts in this first Gentile (though mixed) congregation to catch the attention of outsiders who need a tag for them: "Hey, Gluteus! What do you make of that crazy bunch of..., ah, what d'ya call 'em?" Christians, that's what. It looks like it was a name hung on them by observers and eventually embraced by the members themselves, like "Methodists," "Moonies," or "Queers."

There is no apparent connection between this story and that of Peter and Cornelius. The second does not seem to presuppose the first. It looks to me like our redactor/compiler felt the need to insert the Peter story where he did both to accord priority to the Prince of Apostles and to legitimate Barnabas' course of action, even though, read by itself, the Barnabas/Antioch story does not seem to need it.

Verses 27-30 may be a disguised version of Paul's presentation of his collection from the Gentile churches for the relief of (i.e., tribute to) the Jerusalem Church (Gal. 2:6-10). The pieces of the puzzle have been rearranged, but it is still recognizable. In Galatians Paul and Barnabas visit Jerusalem for approval of their version of Gentile evangelism, i.e., without requiring circumcision. In Acts Jerusalem sends Barnabas to Gentile Antioch to approve (or disapprove) of this specimen of Gentile evangelism, to whose service Barnabas then commits Saul. Acts 11 immediately turns to the famine, leading to Saul and Barnabas delivering relief funds to

---

[483] In an odd way, this implies that Saul (Paul) *was*, albeit inadvertently, the founder of the Gentile Mission!

Jerusalem. Galatians, on the other hand, has the Jerusalem leaders impose on Paul and Barnabas the obligation to raise money for the home office. What Luke is doing is to paper over the final rejection of Paul's tribute money.

Peter's Resurrection (Acts 12)

Which of the many Herods hanging from the genealogical tree is the villain who has James bar Zebedee executed (murdered)? This one was Herod Agrippa I. When he saw the high ratings this evil deed garnered, he decided to knock off Peter, too. I gather this implies he planned to kill off all twelve apostles one by one, as in Agatha Christie's murder mystery *Ten Vertically Challenged Native Americans*. But the fact that the little stunt with Peter wound up not going quite as planned may have convinced Agrippa to drop it. Of course, it might also have had something to do with Agrippa's sudden death (Acts 12:20-23).

Ever wonder why God didn't send an angel to rescue James as he did shortly thereafter with Peter? Maybe he got tired of confusing James son of Zebedee with James "of Alphaeus" and James the Just. Who could blame him?

The notion of the king stationing *four squadrons* of soldiers around Peter is sheer legend. It's as if they already knew they were likely to have an attempt by God to break Peter out and were trying to be prepared for it, as in the film *The Incredible Hulk* when General Ross brings up loads of troops and heavy artillery to capture the Hulk, though he must know none of it will have any effect.

I believe that this story is a slightly modified version of a Passion and Resurrection narrative starring Peter, cut from the same cloth as the Apocryphal Acts of John and Paul. First, Peter is arrested by a Herodian king and guarded by soldiers, just as in Matthew 27:62-66. The prison was originally Peter's tomb. An angel appeared and opened the door of Jesus' tomb in Matthew 28, just as one of his haloed colleagues visits Peter in Acts 12:715. Peter's angel causes the chains to drop from his wrists, recalling Peter's words about Jesus in

Acts 2:24, "God raised him up, having loosed the pangs of death, because it was not possible for him to be held by it." The angel leads him out to the street, past the oblivious guards, who wind up getting executed for sleeping on duty, the very fate Pilate's guards feared (Matt. 28:32-14). Peter makes his way to the house of John Mark's mother where he knows his fans are gathered in a round-the-clock prayer vigil on his behalf—which apparently worked! (I guess James did not have a large enough fan-base to merit God's attention. Peter did, so he became the squeaky wheel.) When Peter gets there, the maid won't let him in, she is so flabbergasted. She rushes in to interrupt the pious petitioning of the gathered believers, to tell them with bated breath that Peter is at the door! But it doesn't even occur to these great prayer-warriors that God even *might* have granted their request! "You are mad! It must be his angel," i.e., he must be dead already, and that's his guardian angel (his ghost) who looks just like him. Absolutely hilarious! And, I am sure, intentionally so.

The skepticism of Peter's followers mirrors that of the disciples when the women brought them the news of Jesus' resurrection in Luke 24:11. Then Peter charges them to tell James the news of his release, just as the angels at Jesus' tomb told the holy women to go tell Peter about Jesus' resurrection. And then Peter pretty much disappears from the Acts narrative (though he does make a cameo appearance in chapter 15 simply as a device to remind the reader of the Cornelius episode). Peter's retreat to "another place" (as we would say, "an undisclosed location") corresponds to Jesus' removal to heaven after his resurrection.

Why does Peter direct them to tell the news to James in particular? Peter is passing the baton, or rather the scepter, to James the Just who accordingly appears in the rest of the book as the Jerusalem patriarch. Even this is part of Luke's Catholicizing agenda, as it seeks to paper over earlier disputes among rival factions of Jewish-Christians, some of whom said, "I am of Peter!" while others rejoined, "I am of James!"

Luke seems to want us to view Agrippa's death as his due recompense for his murder of James and his attempt to kill Peter. The story is similar enough to one in Josephus to raise the strong suspicion that Luke has rewritten Josephus' version.

> Now when Agrippa had reigned three years over all Judea, he came to the city C[a]esarea [...] There he exhibited shows in honor of C[a]esar [...] On the second day..., he put on a garment made wholly of silver, and of a contexture truly wonderful, and came into the theater early in the morning; at which time the silver of his garment being illuminated by the fresh reflection of the sun's rays upon it, shone out after a surprising manner, and was so resplendent as to spread a horror over those that looked intently upon him: and presently his flatterers cried out [...] that he was a god; and they added, "Be thou merciful to us; for although we have hitherto reverenced thee only as a man, yet shall we henceforth own thee as superior to mortal nature."

Upon this the king did neither rebuke them, nor reject their impious flattery. But, as he presently afterwards looked up, he saw an owl sitting on a certain rope over his head, and immediately understood that this bird was the messenger of ill tidings, as it had once been the messenger of good tidings to him; and he fell into the deepest sorrow. A severe pain also arose in his belly, and began in a most violent manner. He therefore looked upon his friends, and said, "I, whom you call a god, am commanded presently to depart this life; while Providence thus reproves the lying words you just now said to me; and I, who was by you called immortal, am immediately to be hurried away by death. But I am bound to accept of what Providence allots, as it pleases God; for we have by no means lived ill, but in a splendid and happy manner."

When he had said this, his pain became violent. Accordingly he was carried into the palace, and the rumor went abroad everywhere that he would certainly die in a little time. But the multitude presently sat in sackcloth, with their wives and children, after the law of their country, and besought God for the king's recovery. All places were also full of mourning and lamentation. Now the king rested in a high chamber, and as he saw them below lying prostrate on the ground, he could not himself forbear weeping. And when he had been quite worn out by the pain in his belly for five days, he departed this life, being in the fifty-fourth year of his age, and in the seventh year of his reign. (*Jewish Antiquities* 19.343-350).[484]

Grima Wormtongue (13:6-12)

Luke seems to me to have rewritten a story of Paul's conversion to give us the episode of Saul and Barnabas versus a magician who tries to dissuade the Roman proconsul Sergius Paulus from heeding the gospel. Something strange is going on with characters' names in this little story. The sinister sorcerer is called "Bar Jesus" in verse 6 but "Elymas" in verse 8. Luke tells us that the latter is the meaning of the former, whatever that's supposed to mean. There are two Pauls. There is Sergius Paulus, and there is (literally) "Saul who is also Paul" in verse 9. Are two originally distinct characters, Saul and Paul, being conflated here? The text does not say that Saul changed his name from a Jewish Saul to a Christian Paul, like Jacob taking on the name Israel. I have already discussed the suggestion that "Elymas" was supposed to be the same as Simon Magus, and that Simon was really none other than Paul. In Acts 13, Saul/Paul rebukes the astrologer and false prophet in terms reminiscent of Peter's rebuke of Simon. And the result is a temporary spell of blindness, which is just what happened to Saul upon his encounter with the risen Jesus on the Damascus Road. And who gets converted in Acts 13? Paul! The *other* Paul, *Sergius* Paul. Is this a game of Musical Chairs? It looks as if Luke has deconstructed the Simon Magus story and the Paul conversion story and reshuffled the deck in exactly the same way he hybridized the Old Testament stories of Achan and Naboth to create his tales of

---

Ananias and Sapphira and Stephen.

Sermon in the Synagogue (13:13-52)

Paul preaches as a guest speaker in Pisidian Antioch. There is precious little we haven't heard before, whether from Peter, Stephen, or Paul, all of whom are mere mouthpieces for the author of Acts. One very interesting tidbit, though, is Paul's (Luke's) scriptural proof-texting for Jesus' resurrection. Where did scripture predict that Jesus would rise from the dead? "This he has fulfilled... by raising Jesus; as also it is written in the second psalm, 'Thou art my Son, today I have begotten thee'" (Acts 13:33). This connection is not all that far-fetched, since Psalm 2 was, as we have seen, a piece of Judean coronation liturgy, celebrating the enthronement of the king as the earthly avatar of Yahweh who had become king of gods through his victory over Leviathan, being slain and rising again in the process. This myth does underlie New Testament Christology, though I doubt Luke had it consciously in mind.

But just as significant is another implication for New Testament Christology: the adoption of Jesus as God's Son was simultaneous with his ascension, which is in turn simultaneous with his resurrection. The notion of the resurrection as a discrete event ensuing in appearances to various individuals, followed some time later by an ascension into heaven, must have been a later notion. And it is easy to see the motive for both expansions. The postmortem apparitions we find in the Easter narratives of Matthew, Luke, John, the Markan Appendix, and 1 Corinthians 15 must have originated as credentials for the individuals named in those episodes (cf., 1 Cor. 9:1, "Am I not an apostle? Have I not seen Jesus our Lord?"). The notion of a period between the resurrection and the ascension was, as we have seen, a device to justify the later propagation of teachings ascribed to Jesus that no one ever remembered hearing before. But the original idea was that the resurrection of Jesus *was* his ascension (whether in the body or out of the body, I know not; God knows) and enthronement. I'm not

325

saying the traditional sequence of exiting the tomb, appearing to the disciples, and subsequently rising into heaven is self-contradictory or somehow incoherent. It just looks like the story was not first told that way. If it had been, we would not be reading verses like Acts 13:33.

Gods on the Ground (chapter 14)

Once upon a time, Father Zeus announced his intention to flood out an area in Phrygia where the people were notoriously inhospitable (a very serious sin the ancient world). But gentle Hermes persuaded him to accompany him on a fact-finding tour. Disguised as mortal travelers, the two deities visited three dwellings at random. No luck with two of the households, so Zeus finally decided to go ahead with his original plan. But one old couple, Baucis and Philemon, though fully as destitute as the Widow of Zarephath, welcomed the two visitors, serving them their last stale crusts and the dregs of their wine pitcher (just as the Zarephath widow offered her last meal to Elijah). Hmmm... no matter how many toasts they made, the wine never ran out. Baucis and Philemon were still sober enough to realize they were in the presence of the gods. Zeus and Hermes blessed them with the promise that, their home occupying a high elevation, they would be safe from the flood waters and, after a long life of service as priest and priestess in Zeus' temple, they would be transformed into trees upholding the structure (cf., Rev. 3:12). The story comes to us from Ovid's *Metamorphoses* 8:611-724.

Lystra was supposed to be the site of this visit, and some third-century C.E. inscriptions commemorate the "event."[485] This is the background of the story in Acts 14, where a miracle healing performed by Paul galvanizes the people who instantly "realize" that mythology is repeating itself: Zeus and Hermes have returned! [486]

---

[485] Haenchen, *Acts*, p.427, note 1.

[486] As Haenchen, *Acts*, p. 426, notes, some commentators have objected that no one was likely to have taken Paul for the youthful, handsome Hermes. How ludicrous! The whole idea is that the gods have appeared *in*

And if another flood is in the offing, the people figure they had best hop to it and give the divine duo a royal welcome! So the high priest of Zeus and his acolytes run off to haul in a pair of bullocks to sacrifice to Paul (Hermes) and Barnabas (Zeus). The two missionaries are unaware of what's going on till they see the livestock approaching, because the worshipful acclamations of the crowds were in the native Lycaonian language, which Barnabas and Paul did not know. By contrast, the Lystrans understood Paul's preaching because they, like pretty much everybody back then, spoke Greek as a universal second language.

The scene is comical! Picture Paul and Barnabas frantically running around, hands waving, trying to halt the proceedings! And imagine the puzzlement of the poor dumb Lycaonians, like painted primitives in an old Tarzan movie! Here one thinks of the quip of A.D. Loman who said that, if the historical Paul actually wrote Galatians to the rude inhabitants of that region, it would be like Hegel lecturing to New Guinea savages.[487]

Just as we saw Luke repeat Peter's visit to Cornelius[488] in the very next chapter, now we find Luke using Paul's sermon (uh, didn't he already preach one *before* they dragged the bullocks[489] into the scene?) as a kind of rehearsal for his subsequent Areopagus speech in Acts 17. He hits the same themes. He shares the exciting news that there is "a living God" who "gave you from heaven rain and fruitful seasons, satisfying your hearts with food and gladness." One can only

---

disguise! It is not their appearance, nor was it in the Baucis and Philemon story, that enabled mortals to identify the deities. Acts 14:12 expressly says they thought Paul a god because of his ability to heal. And since their hometown legend spoke of two particular gods coming to call, one of these missionaries must be Zeus and the other Hermes. Even if Paul more closely resembled hunched Hephaestus, they pegged him as Hermes, messenger of the gods, because of his eloquence.

[487] Gustav Adolf van den Bergh van Eysinga, *Radical Views about the New Testament*. Trans. Samuel Benjamin Slack (London: Watts, 1912), p. 81.

[488] "Pete, you can call me Corny."

[489] Suppose one of the bulls got converted to Christ, like the lion Paul baptizes in the Acts of Paul; would he have been known as "Ferdinand Christian"? Sure he would have.

imagine the reaction of the Lycaonians: "Amen! Isn't Zeus great?"

Paul and Barnabas appear to be just as urgent to decline the worship of the people as they were to give it. Remember how Simon Magus and Herod Agrippa were quite happy to receive divine honors from their fans and sycophants (Acts 8:10; 12:22-23). Paul, by contrast, did not dare to be implicated but hastily repudiated such vain worship (Acts 14:15), like Jesus himself (Mark 10:18), Peter (Acts 10:25-26), and even an angel (Rev. 19:10). Maybe he was thinking of Agrippa and feared God would skewer him with a lightning bolt if he basked in their adulation for so much as a moment!

But if Paul disdained extravagant estimates of himself, Luke seems to have thought Paul still regarded himself too highly! Luke, for all his lionizing of Paul, seems to exclude him from the company of the apostles. That was the point of stipulating that any candidate for that office had to have been a follower and witness of Jesus all the way back to John's baptism. Paul wasn't there. Of course, neither were several of the Twelve, by Luke's own account, but that seems not to have occurred to our author. But in Acts 14 we seem to find an exception. Verse 4 refers to Paul and Barnabas as "the apostles." Verse 14 reads, "the apostles Barnabas and Paul." But was this the way the text originally read? I'm not so sure. There is reason to think that later scribes deemed Paul and Barnabas eminently worthy of the distinction Luke had denied them and began to insert the term into the text. One manuscript substitutes "the apostle" for "Paul" in verse 9 ("the apostle, looking intently at him," etc.). And Codex Bezae does *not* have "the apostles" in verse 14. I take this as evidence of the gradual insertion of apostolic rank into a text that lacked it. Thus I think verse 4 did not originally contain the words "the apostles" either.

Acts 14:19-20 presents a bit of Pauline docetism, so to speak. Paul, pelted with stones by an angry mob, is left for dead ("supposing that he was dead"), but it turns out he survived it. "When the disciples gathered about him, he rose up." The word is *anastas*, the same word used for Jesus rising from the dead. The possible implications for the crucifixion accounts are intriguing.[490]

328

Penis Powwow (Acts 15)

Acts 15 recounts the so-called Council of Jerusalem. The story seems to be a Catholicizing version of the meeting also described in Galatians 2. In both cases the controversy is associated with the appearance in Antioch of members of the Jewish Torah-Christian faction of (former?) Pharisees who insist that these new Gentile believers have been ill-served by Paul and Barnabas who had not informed them that circumcision (presumably with the rest of the Torah commandments) was requisite for salvation. Oddly, though, in Acts the circumcision group shows up *before* the Jerusalem Council but *afterward* according to Galatians.[491]

In Acts the Antioch congregation, unable to resolve the matter by themselves, decide to send a delegation, headed by Paul and Barnabas, to Jerusalem for a ruling by the apostles and elders. Galatians has it that the idea for the embassy came via revelation, but this is no real contradiction, since, as Luke himself describes the Antiochene congregation, they enjoyed the presence of several prophets (Acts 13:3), one of whose inspired messages commanded that Paul and Barnabas should undertake their evangelistic tour. (Conceivably, this episode might originally have been another version of the scenario described in Galatians 2:1-2.) Galatians 2 leaves us with the impression that Paul's rehearsal of his evangelistic victories was sufficient to convince the Jerusalem Pillars, James the Just, Cephas (Peter?), and John, that God must have approved Paul's non-circumcision gospel and its freedom from the Torah regulations of Judaism. It doesn't actually say the Pillars officially recognized him as an apostle, but at least they agreed to a policy of peaceful co-existence—as long, that is, as Paul raised money for the Jerusalem home office.

---

[490] J. Duncan M. Derrett, *The Anastasis: The Resurrection of Jesus as an Historical Event* (Shipston-on-Stour: P. Drinkwater, 1982).
[491] Pervo, *Dating Acts*, p. 88.

Galatians implies that the pro-circumcision representatives got nowhere. Acts 15, on the other hand, has the confab issue in a compromise: Gentile converts indeed need not be required to receive circumcision, but neither are they to be completely freed from legal obligation. An encyclical is drawn up to inform the Gentile Christians that they must steer clear of idol worship (implying previous practices of Christian henotheism, the worship of plural deities one a time, simultaneous membership in several cults).

In addition, they must swear off "unchastity" (*porneia*), which probably refers to prohibited degrees of kinship marriage (Lev. 18:1).[492] So far so good; one hardly needs the revelation of Sinai to deduce these things are improper for Christians. But then we start getting into dietary restrictions. Gentiles must eat only meat butchered in a kosher fashion. And they must drain out the blood. These laws were nothing new. Leviticus laid down the same ground rules for Gentiles who chose to live among Jews (17:7; 17:10-15; 18:6-20).[493] They must not scandalize their majority Jewish neighbors. That this is the point in the so-called Apostolic Decree is perfectly clear from verse 21: "For from early generations Moses has had in every city those who preach him, for he is read every Sabbath in the synagogues."

But none of this has anything to do with criteria for salvation, the original matter of debate. It is more like Paul's line of argument in 1 Corinthians chapter 8, that "stronger brethren" who understand that idols (rival gods) are empty figments, and that therefore eating their meat-offerings has no more religious significance than dinner at Texas Steakhouse, should nonetheless refrain from such behavior for the sake of "weaker brethren" whose inherited Jewish scruples make such practices abhorrent.

So the circumcision faction seems to have entirely lost out. But what exactly was their position in the first place? Judaism did not rule out the salvation of "righteous Gentiles," as witness their

---

[492] O'Neill, *Theology of Acts*, p.102.

[493] O'Neill, *Theology of Acts*, p. 101; Nina E. Livesey, "The So-called Noahide Laws: A Cameo Essay," in Dennis E. Smith and Joseph B. Tyson, eds., *Acts and Christian Beginnings: The Acts Seminar Report* (Salem, OR: Polebridge Press, 2013), pp. 175-177.

welcoming such people to synagogue worship. Perhaps the Christian circumcision faction held that only Jesus-believers could be saved, but that, as Jesus was the Jewish Messiah, he cannot have abolished the Torah. In that case, would-be Christians (Gentile converts) who rejected it would be committing apostasy. It would be analogous to Benjamin B. Warfield's reasoning that, in itself, biblical inerrancy might not be integral to Christian faith, but, since Jesus taught inerrancy, Christians were stuck with it. Had he taught that, say, Moses had had three nostrils, we'd be obliged to believe that, too.

Luke brings Peter back on stage to take a bow in this chapter. And his job there is to one-up Paul. Though Paul has impressed everyone (except his opponents!) with his reports, it is Peter whose (second) review of his visit to Cornelius seems to clinch the decision. Of course, Peter cannot have said such a thing as Luke has him say in verse 10: "why do you make trial of God by putting a yoke upon the neck of the disciples which neither our fathers nor we have been able to bear?" No Jew would feel this way about the Holy Torah. It was ingrained in them to view the Law as a wonderful gift of God. They were raised in a culture defined by the commandments, and they took them for granted, like a fish in water. And so it is in all cultures.

The idea of the Law as a crushing burden is certainly crucial to the debate, but Luke has placed it on the wrong shoulders. To have to adopt alien cultural mores would indeed be a huge burden for Gentiles, which is why most of them who came to love and admire Judaism were nonetheless content to remain on the margins, attending synagogue but stopping decidedly short of circumcision, kosher laws, a schedule of new holidays, etc. But Luke makes his mouthpiece, Peter, a Jew, voice the Torah-dreading sentiments as his own.

The elders and apostles do not settle the question by voting, as the bishops did at the Council of Nicea. No, James the Just listens to all opinions, and *he* decides (verse 19, "my judgment is...").

No such edict was ever promulgated by the Jerusalem authorities. As O'Neill shows, the Apostolic Decree (like the Apostles' Creed) was the product of the second century. It seeks to settle issues being debated in those days. We find these issues discussed widely only in the second century.[494] For that is what we find in Justin Martyr, the Book of Revelation, the Pseudo-Clementines, Tertullian, etc. It is the same problem presented by the risen Jesus' command to evangelize all the nations: if Jesus had actually issued such orders, how could the question still be up for debate in Acts 10 and 11? Luke is trying to settle these issues in his own time by retrojecting his compromise solution into the holy past in order to claim apostolic clout for it.

Paul as Dionysus (16:11-40)

Now we find ourselves in 2 Acts. The Philippi episode is permeated so thoroughly with the influence of *The Bacchae* that we might call it "Deutero-Euripides." You'll recall that the story of Paul's conversion owed a great debt to the play. Saul was Luke's version of the persecutor Pentheus. The risen Jesus who turned him around in his tracks corresponded to Dionysus, etc. But in chapter 16, the roles change: now *Paul* is Dionysus, the missionary of his own religion. The group of women Paul meets outside the city on the riverbank is a thinly disguised version of the Bacchae, or Maenads, the women followers of Dionysus who encamp outside of Thebes and frolic in inspired ecstasy. Pentheus exclaims, "reports reached me of some strange mischief here, stories of our women leaving home to frisk in mock ecstasies among the thickets on the mountain, dancing in honor of the latest divinity, a certain Dionysus, whoever he may be" (lines 216-220). Teiresias warns Pentheus, "Moreover, this is a god of prophecy. His worshippers, like madmen, are endowed with mantic powers" (lines 297-299).

This last detail is carried over by Luke in his story of the unnamed Pythoness (Luke uses the phrase, "python spirit" rather than the familiar "demon" or "unclean spirit," etc.), an oracle who announces Paul as the herald of salvation. In Luke's rewrite of

---

[494] O'Neill, *Theology of Acts*, pp. 107-116.

Euripides this sequence does not make much sense: the oracle dogs Paul's steps daily, crying out like John the Baptist hyping Jesus—and Luke has Paul exorcize her! This halfway makes sense in that Luke remembers the prophetesses were pagans in Euripides' original. In that context the prophetic women are proclaiming their savior Dionysus. But Luke has re-identified that savior as Jesus. If Acts had the woman following Paul, and proclaiming *Dionysus*, the exorcism would make sense. Meanwhile, Lydia, a local merchant, has become one of Paul's converts, a Christian Maenad.

Paul is imprisoned on account of the exorcism, just as Dionysus is clapped in the clink at Pentheus' order. But an earthquake devastates Pentheus' prison, freeing Dionysus who strolls into Pentheus' throne room gloating. Dionysus commands: "Let the earthquake come! Shatter the floor of the world!" (line 585). The Chorus responds, "Look there, how the palace of Pentheus totters. Look, the palace is collapsing!" (lines 586-587).

In Acts we see Paul and his new side-kick Silas freed from their bonds by an earthquake, too. And, though Dionysus mocks Pentheus, his former captor, Paul reassures the Philippian jailor that he and his fellow prisoners have not escaped. The jailor is greatly relieved since, had they fled, he would have paid for his "negligence" with his life. He agrees to convert to Christianity. Pentheus, at this point, converts to the cult of Dionysus, though it doesn't end happily for him.

In light of all this, it ought to be obvious that the Philippi episode has no discernible basis in historical fact.[495] I would guess that the author of the Greek 2 Acts had recognized the use of the *Bacchae* in the Aramaic 1 Acts and got the idea of repurposing the same original story in his continuation.

At the end of the next chapter we meet a new Christian convert

---

[495] Gerd Lüdemann (*Early Christianity*, p. 182) considers the occurrence of the name "Lydia" to be a vestige of some historical tradition underlying the legend, but I can't help thinking Luke picked up even that from *The Bacchae*, where Dionysus muses on his journey so far: "Far behind me lie those golden-rivered lands, Lydia and Phrygia, where my journeying began" (lines 14-16).

named *Dionysius* (17:34). I doubt that's a coincidence.

Where Is the Debater of this Age? (17:16-34)

Paul has a layover in Athens as he waits for his friends to join him, so he decides to occupy himself in the meantime by acting as guest speaker in the synagogues, where those who politely invited him got more than they bargained for. During the rest of the week he would engage passers-by who sought only to go about their shopping but gladly paused to debate, this being the major pastime of brainy Athens. Soon he came to the attention of the local Epicurean and Stoic philosophers who, tired of having the same old debates with each other, decided to invite him to speak to their club meeting at the Areopagus (= the Hill of Mars) forum. They are genuinely curious about his preaching of new gods, Jesus and his divine consort Anastasis ("Resurrection").[496] The general shape of the story matches those elsewhere in Acts where an apostle is apprehended for his preaching and must mount a defense before Jewish or Roman/Herodian authorities, but in this case, it is a "council" of intellectuals who simply want to hear first-hand what new doctrine he is offering. No danger this time.

The main thing to note here is that Luke portrays Paul as promoting a kind of natural theology strikingly different from the views expressed in Romans chapter one. If either represents the real opinions of Paul, the other does not. (Perhaps neither does!). In Romans we read a sad story of humanity sunk so deep in sin that, despite the evident glory of the one God in his breath-taking creation, they cannot see what is before their faces and instead persist in lowering their eyes to created things and worshipping as

---

[496] I think Luke has, perhaps unwittingly, preserved a fossil of very early Christian belief according to which "Mary Magdalene" was really Anastasis, the Christian counterpart to Anath, Ishtar, Cybele, Aphrodite, and Isis who raised their husbands (Baal, Tammuz, Attis, Adonis, and Osiris) from the dead. See Price, *Widow Traditions*, Chapter 12, "The God of the Widows: Anastasis and Artemis," pp. 235-245.

gods things lower than themselves. And from this gross distortion of perspective, moral behavior has spun out of control into various perversions. But addressing the Areopagus, Paul speaks instead of a human race earnestly but ignorantly groping for a God who never blamed them for their blindness but who has now shone a light unto the Gentiles, revealing that which they had so long sought. Not only is this view of things markedly different from what we read in Romans chapter 1;[497] it bespeaks a later, post-Pauline understanding, that of the second-century Apologists.[498] It is striking that, in addition to the general theological approach of Acts 16 resembling that of the Apologists, the narrative portrayal of Paul makes him a second Socrates, accosting people in the market place to challenge their beliefs,[499] and being accused of promoting "new" or "foreign" deities.[500] We are in the atmosphere of Justin Martyr who claimed Socrates as "a Christian before Christ."

The Sun God (18:24-28)

Luke tells us that one Apollos,[501] a learned Alexandrian Jew, appeared in Ephesus and began preaching accurately the facts concerning Jesus, though he knew nothing as yet about Easter,

---

[497] Philipp Vielhauer, "The 'Paulinism' of Acts," in Leander E. Keck and J. Louis Martyn, eds., *Studies in Luke-Acts: Essays presented in honor of Paul Schubert, Buckingham Professor of New Testament Criticism and Interpretation at Yale University* (New York: Abingdon Press, 1966), pp. 34-37; Haenchen, *Acts*, pp. 528-529.

[499] Haenchen, *Acts*, p. 517.

[500] Haenchen, *Acts*, p. 518.

[501] "Apollos" is the name of the Greek god of the sun, music, law, and medicine. If we rendered the Greek text of the myths strictly, we would call him "Apollos" when grammatically appropriate, but, lacking such niceties in English, we use the neutral form "Apollo," just as we shorten "Paulos" to "Paul." When the New Testament refers to "Apollos," we ought consistently to render it likewise as "Apollo." Guess why we don't?

Pentecost, or Christianity. In this respect Apollos, as Luke describes him, would have been in the same boat as the Emmaus disciples (though they at least knew about the death of Jesus, Luke 24:19-20), Herod Antipas (Luke 9:9; 23:8), Cornelius (Acts 10:36-38),[502] and perhaps even Theophilus (Luke 1:4), depending on who we think he was. A Jewish couple, Priscilla and Aquila, recent refugees from Rome, heard him discussing these matters, correct as far as he went, then took him aside to bring him up to speed. Luke never actually says Apollos became a Christian and was baptized, so we know as little about what instruction they gave him as we do about what Jesus was teaching the disciples for forty days after Easter. We are told only that Priscilla and Aquila taught Apollos "the way of God" (Acts 18:26) just as the Risen Christ taught the disciples concerning "the kingdom of God" (Acts 1:3). Neither is a specifically Christian term. Nor does Luke ever say that Priscilla and Aquila were Christians! He implies they were *not*, since he tells us Paul sought them out *for business reasons*: they practiced the same trade he did. Eventually, the couple sends him across the Aegean Sea to Corinth.

As Darrell J. Doughty discerned,[503] this kid-gloves yet clumsy treatment of Priscilla, Aquila, and Apollos makes the most sense as yet another attempt by Luke to rewrite history. It is apparent from Romans 16:3-5a and 1 Corinthians 16:19 that these three were indeed Christians, colleagues and perhaps rivals of Paul. Luke treats them as he does in order to make Paul the founder of the Christian communities of Ephesus (not Priscilla and Aquila) and Corinth (not Apollos). Luke allows that Apollos, Priscilla, and Aquila may indeed have preceded Paul on the scene, but, according to Luke, none were yet Christians, nor does Acts ever say they *became* Christians.

We do not easily see this because we automatically read into Acts' narrative information derived from the Pauline Epistles. (This is just what pre-critical readers of the gospels do, stitching together

---

[502] Notice that what Peter says "you know" extends only this far. In verse 39 Peter begins recounting what he and his fellow disciples witnessed, implying that Cornelius could not yet know of the crucifixion and resurrection.

[503] Darrell J. Doughty, "Luke's Story of Paul in Corinth: Fictional History in Acts 18." *Journal of Higher Criticism* 4/1 (Spring 1997), pp. 3-54.

the Synoptics and John in order, they think, to get "the full picture," never suspecting that some of the differences exist in the first place because one evangelist sought to correct the account of the other.) Priscilla and her husband send Apollos to Corinth without specifying what role he is to play there because Luke needs to give a nod to the well-known fact that Apollos did in fact minister there (1 Cor. 1:123:5-6; 3:22; 4:6), but he doesn't want to say so explicitly. So there were already Christians (Aquila, Priscilla, and Apollos, at least) in Ephesus and Corinth before Paul arrived, so that he was not the founder of the Ephesian and Corinthian churches, but Luke wants to cover this up, ascribing the honor to Paul. (This is, ironically, a cheap, credit-grabbing ploy of the kind Paul repudiates in his letters, e.g., Romans 15:18-20; 2 Corinthians 10:13-16.)

We Haven't Had That Spirit Here Since 1969 (19:1-7)

Paul is on his way to Ephesus and comes upon a group of "disciples." Disciples of *whom*? Luke is withholding that bit of information so he can make the reader share Paul's mystification till the punch line is revealed. Well, then how are we supposed to know these men were recognizable as "disciples" in the first place? Unless it is just clumsy writing, I have to assume that, by "disciples," he means "ascetics," a monastic community of some kind. After all, we still can't be sure what sect it was who wrote the Dead Sea Scrolls! Essenes? Ebionites? Zealots? Who knows?[504] So it's not too far-fetched.

The men turn out to be John the Baptist sectarians, implying that the Baptizer's movement was not like the Billy Graham Evangelistic Association, a series of revival rallies under the guidance of which people tearfully repented, then went their way. No, John's followers were a sect unto themselves. We knew this from the depiction of a John the Baptist sect in the Pseudo-Clementines,

---

[504] I think of Robert Bloch's story "The Feast in the Abbey" (*Weird Tales* January 1935). It might be a good idea to know what kind of sect you're dealing with!

337

maintaining in debate that John, not Jesus, was the Messiah. And, of course, the Mandaeans (or Nasoreans) of Iraq today quite plausibly claim to be the survival of John's sect. It is also significant that the group Paul encounters is in Ephesus, implying that the Baptist sect had spread further than one might have imagined.

One inevitably wonders whether this cell had been founded by Apollos, given the note that he "knew only the baptism of John" (Acts 18:25), just before the present passage. One might even wonder if a man who had apparently been baptized by or in the name of John, yet "taught accurately the things concerning Jesus" (Acts 18:25), was one of those who heard the reports of Jesus' miracles and inferred the miracle-worker must be a resurrected John (Luke 9:7). So he knew the facts of Jesus' activities accurately except that he thought them the deeds of the resurrected Baptist.

But such speculations would appear to be moot given the fictive character of all this material (see my previous section on Aquila, Priscilla, and Apollos). And the story of Paul's "upgrading" these Baptist disciples to full-fledged Christian status is yet more fiction. Uh, how is it that John the Baptist preached the imminent baptism of the repentant with the Holy Spirit, yet these guys say they've never even *heard* of the Holy Spirit?

These twelve disciples of "John" must be masks for the twelve disciples of Jesus. The underlying issue was the effort of some to supplant Paul as the traditional apostle of Ephesus with John son of Zebedee. There was no evidence of John having been active in Ephesus, but Paul's reputation as the patron and progenitor of the many heresies of Asia Minor as "predicted" (actually reflected) in Acts 20:29-30 led some to substitute for Paul a "clean" apostle.

But not the author of Acts. Precisely by having Paul warn that *after his death* heretical weirdoes would emerge out of the woodwork, ascribing their teachings to Paul (which they actually did), Luke is absolving Paul of any responsibility for them. Luke, who regards Paul very highly once he has rehabilitated him, knows that rejecting Paul would destroy any chance of co-opting ("winning back to the truth") the various Marcionites and Gnostics to whom Luke is appealing. But Luke has to veil, rather thinly, the identity of

"John" since he has no animus against him as one of the Holy Apostles.

Healing Hankies (19:11-12)

Brethren, who has not heard of the Holy Snot Rag of Ephesus? Yes, this relic dates back to the ministry of the Blessed Apostle Paul in Ephesus, of which we read in Acts 19:11-12. It seems that "God did extraordinary miracles by the hands of Paul so that handkerchiefs or aprons were carried away from his body to the sick, and diseases left them and the evil spirits came out of them." On one level, the story presupposes *contagious magic*. Just as the hemorrhagic woman knew that Jesus' prayer shawl must convey the healing power concentrated in him (Luke 8:43-44), so do Paul's garments (stripped from him by fans whose enthusiasm matched that of Elvis's devotees) seem to have soaked up the healing "radioactivity" emitted by the apostle and that rubbed off onto anyone with whom they came into contact. That is the logic of all relic-mongering. Certainly this must have been the favorite verse of Oral Roberts.

But there is another level of meaning. Luke has added (or composed) this little scene to match that of Peter's healing shadow in Acts 5:15, back in 1 Acts. But there is also this question of the legacy of Paul, which Luke wants to defend against those who want to replace Paul's tarnished legacy with John's irreproachable one. How? The notion of contagious apostolic power functions as a metaphor for Paul's continuing legacy of healing and salvation even in his personal absence (cf., 1 Cor. 5:3-5). He is long gone, but, like righteous Abel, he still speaks (Heb. 11:4) through his writings and the work of his disciples.

Carrying Paul's garments away to heal people at a distance is the same metaphor underlying the two healings at a distance wrought by Jesus in Matthew 8:5-13; Luke 7:2-10; John 4:46-53 and in Mark 7:25-30; Matthew 15:21-28. The people healed in this way, both of them children of non-Jews and lying abed back home, represent the far-off Gentiles of the next generation whom the still-powerful influence of Jesus, active in the Gentile Mission, will reach and save.

The Ephesian Wildman (19:13-17)

In Luke 9:49-50, the evangelist reproduced Mark's episode of the Lone Wolf Exorcist (Mark 9:38), not one of Jesus' circle, but nonetheless effective. But here in Acts 19 Luke scathingly lampoons a team of Jewish exorcists who invoke the great names of Jesus and Paul with disastrous results.[505] There is a contradiction here, but our goal must be to account for it rather than to try to explain it away. And that is easy to do. The Lone Wolf Exorcist story is a defense of Paul as legitimate even though he hadn't been in on the ground floor; he was not a disciple of Jesus like the Twelve, but so what? God was obviously working through him. The story of the Ephesian Maniac, by contrast, is a shot at the Paulinist heretics in the post-Paul era, "anticipated" and condemned in Acts 20:29-30. Like the two sons of Sceva, they will appeal to Paul's "brand," but in vain.

As for the Ephesian Wildman himself, he is plainly a recycled version of Mark's Gerasene Demoniac (Mark 5:1-20; Luke 8:26-37), who is in turn a New Testament reincarnation of Homer's Polyphemus. The Wildman story comes very close to a special type of miracle story that wants to show that no one but the hero himself can successfully accomplish the feat in question. Gehazi fails to raise up the son of the Shunammite, even using Elisha's wand: only Elisha himself can do the deed (2 Kings 4:31). None of the Twelve, but only Jesus, can exorcise the deaf-mute epileptic (Mark 9:17-18). Asclepius' attendant priests are stymied trying to reattach a patient's head after

---

[505] And how many of these ghostbusters *were* there? Verse 14 mentions seven, but verse 16 refers to "both of them." Hugh J. Schonfield blames scribal confusion over the similarity of the name *Skeva* (father of the exorcists) to the Hebrew *sheva*, seven. See *The Authentic New Testament*. Translated and introduced by Hugh J. Schonfield. A Mentor Religious Classic (New York: New American Library, 1958)., p. 228, note 142.

removing her tapeworm, but the god says, "Step aside!" and does it without breaking a sweat. Same here: you might expect that the Jewish exorcists could expel the Wildman's demons via the sacred names of Jesus and Paul, but they cannot. In a comical scene, they flee naked and bleeding from their failed mission[506] (a description borrowed, by the way, from the bare-assed, heavily scarred Gerasene Demoniac). Next, mustn't we expect Paul to come on stage to do the job? But no! When the conventions of the form are conspicuously violated, some special point is being made.[507] And in this case the point is that Paul is *not* present; we are dealing with the *legacy* of Paul, and the proper and improper use of it by those who in subsequent generations would invoke his name (cf. Matt. 7:22-23).

"Allah-ho-Akbar!" (19:23-41)

Acts has Paul spend two years and three months in Ephesus preaching (19:8, 10), which Luke reckons to be enough time for Christianity to have permeated Asia Minor. This considerably upsets Demetrius, president of the idol-mongers local. He can see his profits and those of his colleagues taking wing because of the wildfire success of Paul's gospel. It won't be long before chintzy Artemis souvenirs will be gathering dust on the shelves. But, historically, this seems about as probable as Peter converting and baptizing three thousand people on a single day (Acts 2:41). The same tall claim occurs in the spurious (Christian apologetic) letter ascribed to Pliny the Younger (Book 10, no. 96), which asks us to believe that the meat markets of Bithynia were closing up because so many pagans were converting to Christianity: nobody was purchasing meat for sacrifices anymore![508] Luke betrays his awareness that all this is

---

[506] Compare the great scene in the otherwise wretched 1995 movie *Casper* when, first, Ghostbuster Ray Stantz and then Father Guido Sarducci hightail it out of a haunted mansion after utterly failing to exorcise the Ghostly Trio.

[507] As when Mark cuts off the customary acclamation of the crowd after Jesus heals the daughter of Jairus (Mark 5:43) to reinforce the Messianic Secret.

anachronistic when he has Demetrius boast that "all Asia [Minor] and the whole inhabited earth worship" Artemis (v. 27). Hmmm... so the Pauline gospel has *not* conquered the world! So what's the problem? No, Luke is taking the long view and importing it into what purports to be a story set in Paul's own day. And if this were not already clear enough, there is the little fact that, again, *Paul does not appear on stage* to reason with a hostile crowd who are shouting, "Great is Artemis of the Ephesians!" A riot is brewing, and *his colleagues* are manhandled by the mob, after convincing Paul not to risk showing his face. His colleagues represent the Paulinists of Luke's day.

Pastors, How Many Times Has This Happened to You(tychus)? (20:7-12)

Luke the comedian shows his skillful hand again in the episode of Eutychus (which means "Good Luck"). Paul is preaching in a third-story room. The hour is late, but Paul talks on and on. It's apostolic preaching which we all would love to hear, but there can be too much of a good thing. The room is crowded, and, because of all the candles and oil lamps, the temperature is very warm and the air stuffy. And wouldn't you know it? A young fellow sitting on the windowsill conks out and falls backward out the window. Well, that's *one* way to stop a preacher in his tracks! Everyone rushes downstairs while Paul plays Elijah (1 Kings 17:21-23) and hugs the

---

[508] It's not that such a thing *could* not possibly happen, you understand. Something like it did happen in 1951, in Govindpur, India, with a mass conversion of the natives to a messianic movement led by one Raj Mohini. "The liquor dealers of Surguja... suffered a heavy loss. When the aboriginals abstained from liquor the liquor dealers lost their business" (Stephen Fuchs, *Rebellious Prophets: A Study of Messianic Movements in Indian Religions* [New York: Asia Publishing House, 1965], p. 91). But such a state of affairs seems anachronistic for mid-first-century Ephesus or in the early second-century Asia Minor of Pliny. The latter is obviously absurd: so many have become Christians that pagan idols are left wanting for sacrifices at a time when a mere accusation of one's being a Christian resulted in death?

unconscious lad. Perhaps he listens for a heartbeat, puts a wet finger to the boy's mouth or nose to catch any movement of breath, and announces, "His life is in him." Did Paul simply detect subtle signs of life? Or did he somehow rekindle life? Not clear, but that is true of many such cases: the son of the Widow of Nain, Jairus' daughter, even Lazarus who is only *assumed* to be dead and rotting for four days. After this momentary distraction, Paul goes back upstairs and eats with the brethren (or perhaps leads them in the Lord's Supper, depending on how one understands "breaking bread"). All converse with Paul till sunrise and plod off to a dragging workday with no sleep.

The story of the Acts of the Apostles does not stop here, but my comments on it do. I have already discussed a number of the more interesting episodes earlier in this chapter, and much of the rest does not really require comment.

12

The Gospel According to John
The Logos and the Paraclete

The Fourth Musketeer

The lucid simplicity of the language of the Gospel of John forms a stark contrast with the stubborn complexity of the work's history-of-religions background and theology. But with that complexity come great richness and depth. This may sound strange, but let me share an illustrative anecdote. I had been reading Bultmann's great commentary on John's gospel[509] earlier on the day of the funeral of my old friend and ministerial colleague Pat Wickham. Time came, and I drove down to the church. I sat on an aisle in the pew meditating on some of the Gnostic-Johannine texts discussed by Bultmann. Then, with a rush of organ music, the service started, and as Pat's coffin passed right by me, I felt a poignant sense of the Numinous, as if, with her death, Eternity had come near. Of course, I had read (and treasured) the Gospel of John dozens of times over the years, but I can only say that Bultmann's exposition of John in more cosmic depth served to heighten my spiritual sensitivity. Does scholarly biblical criticism stifle the spiritual life? Nonsense.

Where did the Fourth Gospel come from? What does it mean? The answer to this second question is necessary if we are to answer the first. Oh, you can read the text in a vacuum if you want, and most people do, but then you will just be taking a word association test, looking at a Rorschach blot, and whatever pops into your head will likely have more to do with what you want to hear than what the Fourth Evangelist wanted to tell you.

---

[509] Rudolf Bultmann, *The Gospel of John: A Commentary*. Trans. G.R.Beasley-Murray, R.W.N. Hoare, and J..K. Riches. (Philadelphia: Westminster Press, 1971).

344

Factions and Stages in the Johannine Community

Burton L. Mack[510]suggests that an important source of early Christianity was a Synagogue Reform Movement which is represented in the gospel conflict stories depicting Jesus fencing with the scribes over points of *halakah*. According to Jerome H. Neyrey,[511] proto-Christians of this type initially viewed Jesus as little more than a/the Prophet and "a teacher sent from God" (John 3:2) whose "signs" (miracles signifying some larger lesson) functioned to vindicate his distinctive, more liberal interpretations of Torah (or those ascribed to him, anyway). Some of these survive in the Johannine Sabbath controversy stories.

At this stage of the game, these Jesus-Jews would qualify as what anthropologists call "strong group."[512] Their reformist activities (or perhaps better, halakhic debates) imply both a strong mutual subgroup identity and a strong sense of identification with the synagogue, which after all they seek to reform, not to compete with. But they are "low grid." First, they do not regard allegiance to Jesus as determinative, i.e., non-adherents are not yet seen as reprobate; Jesus-Jews seem to regard fellow-members of synagogues as Jews in good standing. Otherwise, what's the point of debating with them? Here we might make a comparison with Jewish attitudes toward the great Rabbi Akiva, adherent of a "false" messiah. Simon bar Kochba failed to usher in the messianic era, but Akiva was not condemned as some kind of heretic for having endorsed him. A difference of opinion re the identity of the Messiah needn't make Jews excommunicate one another.

Second, their *halakah* tends to liberalize Sabbath restrictions. Had they instead been "high grid," they'd have raised up high walls, very stringent criteria for membership. It wouldn't have taken much for them to exclude others from their fellowship. Likewise, they would have doubled down on sabbatarian legalism, scorning others as backsliders and sinners.

Rabbinic evidence preserves three legal opinions attributed to Jesus that had been adduced in intra-Jewish debate (daughters are to

---

[510] Burton L. Mack, *A Myth of Innocence: Mark and Christian Origins* (Philadelphia: Fortress Press, 1988), pp. 94-96.

[511] Jerome H. Neyrey, *An Ideology of Revolt: John's Christology in Social-Science Perspective* (Philadelphia: Fortress Press, 1988), esp. Chapter 8, "Christ, Spirit, and Revolt," pp. 173-206.

[512] Mary Douglas, *Natural Symbols*, (New York: Pantheon Books, 1982), pp. 54-64.

inherit equally; the donation of a prostitute can be used to buy a toilet for the high priest; he has come neither to take away nor to add to the Torah).[513] This means that even in Jewish tradition Jesus was remembered as a (Jewish) source of *halakah*. This was possible given the kind of co-existence (perhaps albeit uneasy) of the Johannine Christians with their synagogue neighbors at this stage.

Somewhere along the line, one of these Synagogue Reform groups became a messianic sect. I would guess that, as their *halakah* was more and more assimilated (not being all that controversial in the first place, as Synoptic parallels in the Mishnah indicate),[514] focus and friction between these Christians and the synagogues began to center more and more on the only remaining point of difference: the importance of Jesus himself. That Jesus is a teacher sent from God is not hard to accept; that he is the Messiah is a different matter, and this now rises to new importance.[515] We don't know that all early Jesus groups developed along the same trajectory or to the same ends. Some may have begun as messianic sects; others may never have gone in that direction at all, like the Q Community, since the earliest stratum of the Q Document does not use messianic titles.[516] Not all Synagogue Reform groups necessarily did become messianic sects, or joined them. Some may have simply been assimilated into the synagogues with which they or their parents had earlier debated. But we will be following the (hypothetical) development of one segment of the Synagogue Reform Movement, that which turned into Johannine Christianity.

---

[513]F.F. Bruce, *Jesus and Christian Origins Outside the New Testament* (Grand Rapids: Eerdmans, 1974), pp. 59-62; cf., J. Louis Martyn, *History and Theology in the Fourth Gospel* (New York: Harper & Row, 1968), p. 11, note 27.

[514] Often the opinions ascribed to Jesus in the gospel controversy stories actually match those of the scribes and rabbis quoted in the Mishnah. Either the gospel writers had been caricaturing Jesus' opponents or, as time went by, Jewish opinion moved in a more liberal, lenient direction, and not necessarily from Christian influence.

[515]In the same way, arguments between fundamentalists and Pentecostals tend to major on minors, since they are in agreement on majors. But the more you agree on, the more major the minors seem to become!

[516] Burton L. Mack, *The Lost Gospel: The Book of Q & Christian Origins* (San Francisco: HarperSanFrancisco, 1993), p. 42.

Two sub-groups come into view at this point. First, there were what we might call "Nicodemus" types, who accept Jesus as a teacher whose *halakah* they follow, but who cannot go all the way with the Messiah business. They would resemble those groups within today's Lubavitcher Hasidim who continue in the idiom of piety taught by the late Menachem Mendel Schneerson but did not join many of their co-religionists when the latter came to believe their Rebbe was the Messiah. In fact, the very existence of an early stage in which Jesus was remembered as a sage and a source of *halakah* with no reference to messianism may imply that he was not first deemed Messiah but, like Rebbe Schneerson, was elevated to messiahship only after his death by the most ardent of his followers.[517]

Second, there would have been the "Joseph of Arimathea" types who believed Jesus to be the Messiah but feared to confess their faith lest they get expelled from the synagogue.[518] The man born blind in John chapter 9 is held up as the example to follow here: "Come out of the closet and confess your faith in Messiah Jesus! And let the chips fall where they may!"

At this point our Synagogue Reform group has moved to the "strong(er) group" category in that a parting of the ways has become necessary. Its members must sever ties with the parent group, the synagogue, and close ranks with one's fellow sectarians. And their "grid" rises in that the lines dividing what was formerly a sub-group have now become markers of primary identity.

Once the (or some) Johannines (if we may call them that) get excommunicated from the synagogue, they develop the doctrine of Jesus as the true Hanukkah light (John 8:12), the Good Shepherd (John 10:11), the water of life (John 2:6-9; 7:37), etc. He replaces the

---

[517] This is exactly what Bultmann believed happened to Jesus in the early Christian imagination: in life he had spoken of the soon coming of the Son of Man in the third person, but following his death and a few apparitions, his followers concluded that he himself had been, or had become, the Son of Man and Messiah. Bultmann, *Theology of the New Testament*. Trans. Kendrick Groebel. Scribner Studies in Contemporary Theology (New York: Scribners, 1951), vol. I, pp. 26-42.

[518] Raymond E. Brown, *The Community of the Beloved Disciple: The Life, Loves, and Hates of an Individual Church in New Testament Times* (New York: Paulist Press, 1979), pp. 71-73. Nicodemus might be a poster boy for this option, too, as Martyn suggests, *History and Theology*, p. 105. Reality tends to be messier than our categories.

institutions of Judaism, just as prayer and fasting replaced Temple sacrifice at sectarian Qumran.

In the gospel we witness this stage at which Johannines are excommunicated from the synagogue over their messianic confession of Jesus. This development prompts (as in Acts13:46; 18:6; 28:28 and Romans 11:25) a turning to Samaritans and Gentiles. The onus of the impurity of these groups (cf. the business about Jews and Samaritans not using the same dishes in chapter 4) comes to attach itself to the Johannine community who are consequently shunned, even persecuted. And the Johannine texts about God loving the world (sheep not of this flock, John 10:16) and sending his son to die for the world (i.e., not just Jews, as had been thought)[519]come from this period.

The contact with Gentiles and Samaritans results in assimilation of theological and mythological themes, such as the Dionysus motif of communion as blood-drinking and flesh-eating, and Jesus as the Samaritan Taheb (John 4:25-26). The fictive debates with Jews or Johannines who value their Abrahamic descent (John 8:31-40) reflect actual debates over the propriety of either the mission itself, the threat to Jewish priority in the movement, or the theo-mythical borrowings. We see parallels with Pauline Abraham polemics in Romans 4:1-25 and Galatians 4:21-31.[520] The disparaging of Jesus' brothers (John 7:3-7) stems from these tensions, as the Pillars of Jerusalem (one of whom was "James the brother of the Lord," Galatians 1:19; 2:9) disapproved and opposed the Johannines' evangelistic work.

At this stage we can see a group of Johannines falling away, unable to brook the mystery-religion sacrament, outrageous to Jewish sensibilities. The more this rite comes under attack, again, the more elevated it becomes, to the point of being needful for salvation (John 6:51, 53-58). This means a higher grid requirement, a further weeding out process, and a defensive fortress mentality, even while on another front theological/mythical assimilation denotes a shift in grid.

In chapter 13's feet-washing story (as well as chapter 20's "Johannine Pentecost") we are witnessing a raising of *internal* grids, since

---

[519] Sam K. Williams, *Jesus' Death as Saving Event: The Background and Origin of a Concept.* Harvard Dissertations in Religion 2 (Missoula: Scholars Press, 1975), pp. 32-33, 230-233.

[520] Robert Eisenman, *James the Brother of Jesus: The Key to Unlocking the Secrets of Early Christianity and the Dead Sea Scrolls* (New York: Viking Penguin, 1996), pp. 277.

now the washing of baptism is not quite enough anymore. Post-baptismal sin must be dealt with via a sacrament of penance.

Those who leave (for Judaism? Or only another Johannine or other Christian faction?) are bade good riddance since the Father hadn't really drawn them to the Son of Man anyway (1 John 2:19; John 6:44, 65). They were never of Jesus' flock and were thus incapable of hearing his voice (John 10:26). This leads to the next phase, where God does not love the world but has sent his Son to redeem his elect *out* of the world. At this point, perhaps by way of Samaritan influence,[521] Johannines begin referring to their opponents as "the Jews," and themselves as true children of Abraham (a la Paul's Gentiles) or true Israelites (John 1:47) i.e., not southern "Jews," Judeans, but Israelites from the north.

A new religion has come into being once the Johannine sect elevates Jesus to a status "equal to God"[522] (John 5:18), which inevitably represents a full and intentional severance from Judaism. (Here one thinks of recent Roman Catholic urgings to officially elevate Mary to Co-Redemptrix, a move that many fellow Catholics resisted for the danger of subverting ecumenism, hopelessly alienating otherwise sympathetic Protestants.) Once Jesus is thus exalted, we start reading Gnostic-style sneers at Jewish rituals (John 7:22-23), pedigrees (John 8:39), and scriptures (John 10:34). Jesus is now said to be greater than Jacob (John 4:12) and Abraham (John 8:53), which means they are being negated, Jesus substituted, and Jewish identity jettisoned. Again, there are all those references to "the Jews" we cringe at today. I wouldn't call it Anti-Semitism, but rather theological anti-Judaism (not much better, admittedly, but not exactly the same thing).

When the figurehead becomes God it means he has become the object of faith of a whole new self-contained communal and symbolic world[523] in which his adherents live. A savior-Christology implied redemption of the world ("Christ transforming culture"),[524] but a

---

[521] Patricia Crone and Michael Cook, *Hagarism: The Making of the Islamic World* (New York: Cambridge University Press, 1977), Chapter 4, "The Samaritan calques," pp. 21-28, show how very early formative Islam teetered in one direction after another, notably including an assimilation of Samaritan features. I see this as a parallel to the evolution of the Johannine movement.

[522] Wayne A. Meeks, "Equal to God," in Meeks, *In Search of the Early Christians: Selected Essays.* Ed. Allen R. Hilton and H. Gregory Snyder (New Haven: Yale University Press, 2002), pp. 91-105.

[523] Peter Berger and Thomas Luckmann, *The Social Construction of Reality: A Treatise in the Sociology of Knowledge* (Garden City: Doubleday Anchor Books, 1967), pp. 92-128.

Creator God Christology (John 1:3) means the public world has been abandoned for a sheltered sectarian sub-world. The result is radical isolation, loving neither the world nor the things in the world. The "out-of-this-world" alien Messiah theme denotes, a la Wayne A. Meeks,[525] a "stranger in a strange land" mentality among the Johannines, strikingly akin to Flying Saucer sects[526] in our day.

At this stage, rituals become less important, since they hadn't managed to guarantee true faith (i.e., they hadn't prevented these sectarians from dropping out of Judaism). Or, more generally, they were held in common between two groups who found occasion to dispute over other matters. Thus rituals are taken for granted, no longer serving as the shibboleth, and recede in importance. The new shibboleth is doctrinal. "Unless you believe that I am he..." (John 8:24).

The sayings tradition, still visible here and there in the gospel, becomes subject to charismatic reinterpretation just as the Jewish scriptures had already been. The Johannines are heading somewhere else.[527] Neyrey, a la Mary Douglas, says this is a case of a movement with high grid "norming" the spirit. The earthly Jesus is still used as a criterion (or really, a diving board) for new revelation. The past (of Jesus) is valued as a norm for the present (new revelations) and for the activity of the Spirit, which must function as the Spirit *of Jesus.*

Next we see the emergence of what I would call Gnostic Bodhisattvas. There is a rift occasioned by Johannine itinerant prophets (who speak by the Paraclete), some of whom are getting new docetic and Gnostic revelations, tending to greater asceticism and otherworldliness. This schism is the one lamented in 1 John 2:19; 4:1-3. We can consider these intra-Johannine schismatics to be "low grid/weak group." As Mary

---

[524]H. Richard Niebuhr, *Christ and Culture*. Harper Torchlight Books (New York: Harper & Brothers, 1951), Chapter 6, "Christ the Transformer of Culture," pp. 190-229.

[525] Wayne A. Meeks, "The Man from Heaven in Johannine Sectarianism," in Meeks, *In Search of the Early Christians*, pp. 55-90.

[526]Leon Festinger, Henry W. Riecken, and Stanley Schachter, *When Prophecy Fails: A Social and Psychological Study of a Modern Group that Predicted the Destruction of the World*. Harper Torchbooks Academic Library (New York: Harper & Row, 1956); Egon Larsen, *Strange Sects and Cults: A Study of their Origins and Influence* (New York: Hart Publishing, 1972), p. 229; Christopher Evans, *Cults of Unreason* (New York: A Delta Book / Dell Publishing, 1973), Chapter II, "The Saviours from the Skies," 148-173.

[527]Gershom G. Scholem, *On the Kabbalah and its Symbolism*. Trans. Ralph Manheim (New York: Schocken Books, 1969), pp. 14-15.

Douglas[528] says, the symbolic repudiation of "the flesh" correlates with anti-institutionalism and with disdain for "carnal" sacraments. Accordingly, Ignatius denounces Christian docetists who reject the ritual of the Eucharist (Smyrnaeans 7:1). Similarly, the Sufis, who were ascetical itinerants, circulated anecdotes about Jesus, modeled on their own lifestyle, in which the disciples addressed the earthly Jesus thusly: "O Spirit of God," not because they held the Christian doctrine of the Incarnation (perish the thought; after all, they were Muslims), but because they pictured Jesus as a fellow homeless ascetic.

The perfectionist teaching attested for the itinerants in 1 John should be seen as a complete transcendence of the Johannine concern for post-baptismal sin and purification (on display in John 13:6-10). Sin is simply wiped away in a single broad stroke: no sin anymore! "He cannot sin, for he was born of God" (1 John 3:9; 5:18). The "sinlessness" debated in 1 John was part of the spiritualism of the Johannine Gnostics. They were either ascetics or libertines ("all things are lawful"). And, as itinerants with minimal connection to "mission HQ," they are lone wolves, loose cannons, "weak group."

"Low grid" means fewer criteria, less reference to the past to "norm" the Spirit, which now "blows where it listeth" (John 3:8) and is "another Paraclete" (John 14:16; 15:26). New revelations make less effort to be faithful to the *earthly* Jesus, because "I am not of *this world*." We are rapidly on our way to the revelations (still, but only nominally, attributed to Jesus) of the Apocryphon of John. The opponents of Gnostic Johannines (see below) still attempt to use past-time reference ("Jesus Christ came in the flesh") to norm the Spirit (1 John 4:1-3a).

As for Gnostic revealers being low-grid, i.e., no sticklers for any creedal orthodoxy, Irenaeus[529]says of the Valentinians (big fans of John's gospel)[530] that they encourage each one to create his own doctrinal innovations. "Can you top this?" "Let a hundred flowers bloom."

[528] See Neyrey, *Ideology of Revolt*, Chapter 7, "Christology and Cosmology: Spirit Versus Flesh," pp. 151-172, discussing Mary Douglas, *Natural Symbols*, pp. 65-81, 156-167.

[529] "Since they differ from one another in teaching and tradition, and those known to be more recent try to discover and fructify what no one ever thought of, it is hard to describe the doctrines of all of them." *Against Heresies*, Book I. 21.5. Robert M. Grant, *Irenaeus of Lyons*. Early Church Fathers (New York: Routledge, 1997), p. 87.

[530]Elaine H. Pagels, *The Johannine Gospel in Gnostic Exegesis: Heracleon's Commentary on John*. Society of Biblical Literature Monograph Series 17 (Atlanta: Scholars Press, 1989).

The itinerants are rivals to local elders/bishops (charismatic vs. institutional authority[531]), vying for the support of congregations in general and of consecrated widows in particular. The former tilted toward the bishops, the latter toward the itinerants, who were their major advocates against ecclesiastical authorities who sought to marginalize and suppress these women's ministry. Itinerants had more to say to fellow ascetics, the widows, even though the widows, who lived in consecrated households, were "strong-group," than to householders, who admired the itinerants' radical discipleship but were not about to emulate it.

The realized eschatology (the kingdom of God is already fully, though invisibly, here) in John's Gospel stems from this group. The futuristic eschatology of the gospel comes from the older group, though it may well appear, as Bultmann[532] said, as a reaction, a "corrective" redaction, by the non-Gnostic element. Note that the realized eschatology appears prominently, as does the Paraclete theme, in the Farewell Discourse material, itself an anticipation or reflection of the same Gnostic Revelation Dialogue genre we see full-blown in the Apocryphon of John. And, ironically, as in the Pastoral Epistles (2 Tim. 2:18), the realized eschatology of the Gnosticizing schismatics tends to reinforce the futuristic eschatology of the traditionalists because the latter take the existence of the former as evidence of the coming end! "Children, it is the last hour; and as you have heard that antichrist is coming, so now many antichrists have come; therefore we know that it is the last hour" (1 John 2:18).

The Acts of John[533] enshrine (1) resumes of Johannine itinerants, and (2) their docetic Christology, which both (a) enhances their own apostolic/Christic persona[534] and (b) prescribes asceticism

---

[531] Hans von Campenhausen, *Ecclesiastical Authority and Spiritual Power in the Church of the First Three Centuries* (Stanford: Stanford University Press, 1969), Chapter VIII. "Prophets and Teachers in the Second Century," pp. 178-212.

[532] Bultmann, *Gospel of John*, p. 261.

[533] Stevan L. Davies, *The Revolt of the Widows: The Social World of the Apocryphal Acts* (Carbondale: Southern Illinois University Press, 1980), pp. 32, 117.

[534] Walter Schmithals, *The Office of Apostle in the Early Church* .Trans. John E. Steely (New York: Abingdon Press, 1969), pp. 172-175, 306; Gerd Theissen, *Sociology of Early Palestinian Christianity.* Trans. John Bowden (Philadelphia: Fortress Press, 1978), Chapter II, "The Role of the Wandering Charismatics," pp. 8-16; Dieter Georgi, *The Opponents of Paul in Second Corinthians.* Trans. Harold Attridge, Isabel and Thomas Best, Bernadette Brooten, Ron Cameron, Frank Fallon, Stephen Gero, Renate Rose, Herman Waetjenj, and Michael

(their own practice of which further enhances their clout). The Apocryphon of John preserves Gnostic revelations articulating their "stranger in a strange land" world-and-self view. This is in direct progression from the "equal with God/creator of the world" Christology: if that Christology symbolized the sectarian insularity of the Johannine community, Gnosticism fits the utter denial of the body/world--Jesus is now higher than the creator God and is not a world creator. The world creator is evil and inferior.

The emergence of an even higher Christology, docetism, becomes the watershed again, both sides repudiating one another, which also happened in the preceding stages of the conflict (e.g., over Jesus' messiahship).The Gnostic rift became evident when a few itinerants kept their new revelations to themselves until they arrived in various local Johannine communities, where they prophesied the docetic doctrine in name of the Elder, the patron of the original parent community. This new doctrine so outraged Diotrephes, a local bishop, that he expelled the itinerants, concluded that their prophecy represented the new Johannine party line, and severed all links with the Johannine movement, warning his people not to harbor or aid the itinerants anymore.

When the docetist brethren got back to mission central, they naturally did not report their ill-treatment lest their secret come out into the open. Apparently they feared the Elder would not favor their doctrine, and they wanted to continue to use the prestige of the Elder's movement to spread their views for as long as they could. So the next pair of non-docetist Johannine itinerants went forth and found every door of Diotrephes' community slammed in their faces, save only for that of Gaius who either was not aware of the ban or did not understand it. The itinerants, thus prevented from ministering in the church, moved on, mystified. Returning to headquarters, they told the Elder of their experience.

The Elder, inferring that Diotrephes simply wanted no outside supervision/interference, sat down and fired off the (unread) letter to Diotrephes mentioned in 3 John. With no answer forthcoming, he sent 3 John itself to Gaius, his only liaison with Diotrephes' church. Through all this, the Elder knew nothing of docetic prophecies, much less of Diotrephes' assumption that the Elder himself is the fountainhead of the docetic heresy. At length, as anticipated in 3 John, the Elder arrived in person to confront Diotrephes. They compared notes and realized

Williams (Philadelphia: Fortress Press, 1986), pp. 174, 244-245.

what had happened. The Elder then excommunicated the known docetist itinerants, but on the chance there were others who were keeping mum, he wrote 2 John to Kyria's ("the elect lady") church, having adopted Diotrephes' closed-door policy. He then followed this up with 1 John as an encyclical. He had no list of names, but he provided the doctrinal shibboleths: eject any docetists or separationists (those who taught that the human Jesus was merely the channeler for the Christ-Spirit who had temporarily possessed him)[535] who might show up, like Jehovah's Witnesses, at the door.

Textual Ping Pong

I suggest that each faction along this path of historical evolution and mitosis of the Johannine community had its own copy of the Gospel of John. As each new stage emerged, additions and redactions were made to update the Gospel. When, as presumably happened, a copy containing the distinctive themes of one faction came into the hands of the other faction (e.g., when a scribe switched sides, taking his copy with him), it would receive theological "corrections" in the margins, which would then be inserted right into the text during the next copying. Finally, once many of these debates were dead and forgotten, an eclectic text was produced, harmonizing all the texts these later scribes could find. This gave us our extant Gospel of John. The same thing happened with 1 John, which contains both perfectionist and anti-perfectionist readings.

The Revelation of John gives evidence of the same intra-Johannine anti-Gnostic struggle, Jezebel and the Nicolaitans corresponding to the docetists of the other Johannine writings. The "angels" of the churches are the Johannine itinerants. That textual tampering was anticipated is clear from the warning to abstain from it (Rev. 22:18-19). But it happened nonetheless: the revelation of the Seven Thunders has either been excised—or perhaps a false notice of its excision has been added to provide a toehold for the Nicolaitan scripture Thunder Perfect Mind.

But which faction of the Johannine movement wrote the Fourth Gospel in the first place?

---

[535] Bart D. Ehrman, *The Orthodox Corruption of Scripture: The Effect of Early Christological Controversies on the Text of the New Testament* (New York: Oxford University Press, 1993), pp. 14, 119-120.

Is John's Gospel Gnostic?

As far back as the fourth-century faction of the Alogoi who wanted to bar the Fourth Gospel from the emerging New Testament canon,[536] the Gospel of John has now and again been suspected of being Gnostic in character. The greatest modern exponent of this view has been Rudolf Bultmann.[537]

First, just what is Gnosticism? It is not a sharply defined set of doctrines, since there were so many Gnostic sects, schools, and gurus, but there are certain recurrent ideas that enable scholars to construct an ideal type.[538] Here it is in broad outline.[539] There is an anti-cosmic dualism. This world is considered as absolutely evil, irredeemable, and under the despotic control of evil powers and demons. Certain individuals may be saved from this vale of tears. They are the rare ones who harbor a true soul or spark of the divine light. To them God has sent a Redeemer or Revealer, who saves them by revealing to them the hitherto unsuspected fact of their heavenly identity. Knowing who they truly are, destined for better things, they will be able to slough off the gross body of flesh at death and ascend to heaven. This is basically the *soteriology* of Gnosticism.

Conjoined with it was usually a set of doctrines seeking to explain how things had come to such a pass. This was the Gnostic *theodicy*. According to it, the world was evil because matter is inherently evil, and the material world could not have been created by a good God. Instead, it was the work of an insane and incompetent Demiurge ("craftsman"), Ialdabaoth, the Old Testament Yahweh Sabaoth.

---

[536] F.F. Bruce, *The New Testament Documents: Are they Reliable?* (Grand Rapids: Eerdmans, 1960), p. 51, referring to the fourth-century Epiphanius, Bishop of Salamis.

[537] Bultmann, *Gospel of John*, "The Relation to Gnosticism," pp. 7-9. But I must draw a distinction here in that Bultmann (p. 251, etc.) also sees the Gospel of John demythologizing its Gnostic elements in an existentialist direction via the conversion from futuristic to realized eschatology.

[538] Some recent scholars have sought to dismantle the category of "Gnosticism" simply because not all ostensible instances of it are exactly alike. They appear to have been absent on the day their professors explained what an *ideal type* is. One might as well argue there is no such thing as Protestantism, or Buddhism.

[539] Bultmann, *Theology of the New Testament*, pp. 164-183.

Often Gnostics inferred from all this that when the Revealer appeared in the world, he must have only "seemed" to take on flesh; it was in fact an illusion (hence "docetism," which means "seem-ism"). I think the Gospel of John does contain Gnostic soteriology and Christology but lacks the attendant theodicy. This is a vital distinction. For failure to draw it, many scholars have rejected Bultmann's thesis, being unable to find enough Gnostic cosmology in the document to justify it. But, on the one hand, not all even of classic Gnostic writers employed all the items described above, so to lack one of them does not disqualify a text as Gnostic. On the other hand, we do not find even the Gnostic soteriology in the other New Testament gospels. We can also see John's distinctiveness in, e.g., his pre-existence Christology, unique to the canonical gospels.

The World According to John

The Johannine writings are apparently ambivalent about the world and whether or not it is properly an object of love by the righteous or by God. On the one hand, "God so loved the world that he gave his only son that whoever believes in him should not perish but have everlasting life" (John 3:16). On the other, 1 John 2:15 exhorts readers to "love not the world nor the things in the world, for if anyone loves the world the love of the Father is not in him," because "we know that the whole world lieth in the power of the Evil One" (1 John 5:19).

The world-God enmity, for John, is not the result of the world having been created by an evil power. Rather, his Demiurge, the Logos, is a part of the divine being, what later Gnostics would call one of the Aions (among whom, by the way, they, too, numbered the Logos). The trouble was that the world had perversely turned away from God to the Evil One, God's opposite number. He now rules the world as a usurper. The Fourth Gospel calls him "the Archon of this World" (12:21). I see this as simply a variation on the typical theme of Gnosticism. Marcion's lack of a multiplicity of Aions in the Godhead is a comparable variation. John's implied otherworldliness and bitter sectarianism[540] seem to me typically Gnostic.

---

[540] J. L. Houlden, *Ethics and the New Testament* (Baltimore: Penguin Books, 1973), pp. 35-41, 68. "It is hard to believe that a work such as this is not to be rightly considered as Gnostic in tendency" (p. 35).

Anti-Judaism

One of the most uncomfortable aspects of the Gospel of John for modern readers is its attitude toward non-Christian Jews. For John, Jesus' enemies are simply "the Jews," while the occasional Jesus-friendly Jew is called an "Israelite" (1:47; 3:10). Similarly, we notice that Jesus' attitude toward the Old Testament is not unambiguously positive. He calls it "your Law" (8:17) and seems to argue from it in an *ad hominem* fashion, appealing to it as an authority his opponents will accept, not that *he* does, so as to beat them at their own game.

All this strikingly recalls the double-edged attitude taken toward Judaism and the Jewish scriptures in the Gnostic Nag Hammadi texts. It is clear that Gnostic mythology grows out of Old Testament exegesis (A.D, Nock[541] once said that all one would need to come up with Gnosticism is the early narratives of Genesis and a wild imagination!), yet Gnostics took a hostile, jeering attitude towards Jews and Judaism. One way to read this phenomenon is the theory of C.K. Barrett[542] that Gnosticism grew out of a disappointed apocalyptic Judaism. The focus would have shifted from oft-debunked hopes for external redemption to an unfalsifiable, inward-looking mysticism.

Realized Eschatology

Historically, when a religion has made the mistake of predicting the near end of the world, it has had to find some sort of face-saving rationalization, or else disintegrate. Usually the strategy is to claim that the End *did* in fact come but in a hidden, spiritual manner, accessible only to the eye of faith (cf., John 3:3). Any subsequent visible coming of the apocalypse was deferred into the ever-receding future or simply dropped altogether. Whether because of disappointment or not, Gnosticism seems to have lacked a futuristic eschatology.[543] The only

---

[541] Oral tradition via Professor David M. Scholer, 1976 or 1977.

[542] C.K. Barrett, *The Gospel of John and Judaism*. Franz Delitzsch Lectures, 1967 (Philadelphia: Westminster Press, 1975). A similar case is set forth in Hyam Maccoby, *Paul and Hellenism* (Philadelphia: Trinity Press International, 1991), Chapter 1, "Gnostic Anti-Semitism," pp. 1-35. Maccoby posits Gnosticism as a bitter parody of Philonic-type Judaism to which some Alexandrians were temporarily attracted, but thought better of it and, ashamed of their near conversion, belittled the Jewish scripture, especially Genesis.

[543] They did, however, expect that, once all the sparks of divine light had

resurrection was the one to be experienced here and now in mystical initiation or baptism. As Bultmann[544] points out, in the New Testament Paul and John are both already beginning this process of realizing eschatology in the present. While Paul still also expected an external coming of the Christ, Bultmann reads John as dispensing with it entirely. Certain passages in John seem to imply not only that John had dropped the idea but that he meant to disabuse his readers of it. That is, he not only assumed a realized eschatology, but he sought to make it explicit. Such texts include John 5:24-25; 11:23-26; 14:22-23.

There are, as any reader knows, also various passages in the Gospel of John which seem clearly to teach a futuristic eschatology. These include 5:28-29; 6:39, 54; 21:22. What are we to make of these? Bultmann suggests they are the work of an "ecclesiastical redactor," a later editor who sought to "rehabilitate" the gospel for more congenial use by the emerging Catholic Church. Such "correction" in the interests of orthodoxy is a well-attested phenomenon in the ancient church (cf., Rufinus' redaction of Origen's On First Principles and 2 Peter's of Jude),[545] and it is not arbitrary to suggest in the case of John since on entirely distinct grounds we have signs of redaction and reshuffling.

Predestinarianism

The Gnostic Revealer came into the world, much like the Christ of Calvinism, to save only a select group. According to classical Gnosticism, the elect were those who carried within them one of the fragments of the divine nature of the Primal Man, a heavenly being captured and devoured by the evil Archons (rulers) of the material world. John shows no knowledge of such a myth (unless John 1:9 is a vestige of it), but, again, this simply means that he lacked or rejected this particular set of inferences from the Gnostic soteriology. All he says is that the Revealer has appeared in the world on behalf of his own, not *why* they are his own and others are not. At any rate we do indeed find a

---

escaped reincarnation in this world, the material world would collapse. See Walter Schmithals, *The Apocalyptic Movement: Introduction and Interpretation* Trans. John E. Steely (New York: Abingdon Press, 1975), p. 110; Schmithals, *Office of Apostle*, pp. 167, 218.

[544]Rudolf Bultmann, *Jesus Christ and Mythology*. Scribner Library: Religion (New York: Scribners, 1958), pp. 32-34.

[545] See also Ehrman, *Orthodox Corruption of Scripture*.

textual basis for the idea of a predestined elect in John. Primarily we find this in the Good Shepherd discourse, where Jesus taunts the Jews thusly: "you do not believe because you do not belong to my sheep. My sheep hear my voice and I know them and they follow me, and I give them eternal life" (John 10:26-27f). Note that he does not say they are not among his flock *because* they do not believe, but just the opposite. They lack the option to believe in the first place. And in view of all this, it comes as no surprise to learn that the Good Shepherd lays down his life for his sheep and for them only (10:11).

Bultmann himself seeks to distance Johannine predestinarianism from the Gnostic variety by characterizing the former as a "dualism of decision"[546] rather than as an unalterable metaphysical decree. For John, as Bultmann reads him, it is one's decision for or against the Son of God that renders him destined to receive the truth or not. One is tempted to ask whether that is not rather just the *opposite* of predestinarian doctrine, whether John's, Gnostic, Calvin's, or any other kind. But the contrast is illusory: the truth is that *all* ostensible predestinarian language is a rhetorical strategy designed to affright the hearer and to urge him to get on the right side *now!* In the Markan parable of the Soils/Sower (Mark 4:2-9, 13-20) the point is obviously not to gloat over the destined salvation of the minority and the inescapable doom of the rest; no, the point is to make the hearers get busy becoming receptive soil! Ebenezer Scrooge got the point exactly right when he looked up from the gravestone, emblazoned with his name, to the Spirit of Christmas Yet to Come, saying, "Why show me these things if I am past all hope?"

Docetism

I have already observed that many Gnostics drew the inference from their dualistic cosmology that the Revealer could not have become truly incarnate, since the flesh was altogether corrupt, totally depraved. Some have ruled out any Gnostic character for John in view of John 1:14, "The Logos was made flesh and dwelt among us."

In the first place, we must note that not all Gnostic texts are thus docetic. The Gospel of Truth says that, at the conclusion of his earthly mission, the Risen Christ gladly "divested himself of these perishing rags" (20:30-31). Similarly, the Hymn of the Pearl has the reascending Christ declare, "I stripped off the filthy garment and left it

---

[546]Bultmann, *Gospel of John*, pp. 158-159, 316-317.

in their land" (line 63). These statements do evidence an ascetic contempt for the flesh, but the sentiments are not so different from those of the Apostle Paul in 2 Corinthians 5:1-4. (In fact the disparaging reference to the fleshly body as a mere "tent"~cf. also 2 Peter 1:13-14~ recalls the word used for the temporary incarnation of the Logos in John 1:14, "and he tabernacled [i.e., pitched his tent], among us." Is the idea, then, that the fleshly covering of the Logos was a mere veil?[547] At any rate, the references in the Gnostic texts make it sufficiently clear that they need not expound docetism in order to count as Gnostic. And conversely we could show that docetism could occur in otherwise orthodox, non-Gnostic texts.

Finally, we should note that the picture of John's gospel as non-docetic is not entirely unambiguous. Ernst Käsemann[548] has argued that John is in fact guilty of a "naive docetism" in that the evangelist doesn't seem to take the implications of a real incarnation very seriously. For example, those[549] who deny a Gnostic coloring to John are quick to appeal to the scene in John 4:7-8 where Jesus is thirsty and sends the disciples into town to buy food. Ah! There is a truly human Jesus, we are told, with a growling stomach! Yet when we come to the end of the story, the disciples urge Jesus to eat, and he will not! "I have food to eat that you know not of. My food and drink is to do the will of him who sent me and to accomplish his work" (John 4:32, 34). Again, the crucified Jesus says, "I thirst," but he is only mouthing the lines prophecy has scripted for him (John 19:28). Thomas insists on touching Jesus' wounds and is invited to do so (John 20:25, 27), but apparently he *doesn't*. And in ancient ghost stories, the spectral visitant often shows his mortal wounds to convince the witnesses that it is truly their loved one,[550] which makes sense given that, as with Peter in Acts 12:15, one's ghost was expected to look like the body of the departed, though insubstantial.

---

[547] Cf., the implicitly docetic lyrics of Charles Wesley's great hymn, "Hark! The Herald Angels Sing:" "Veiled in flesh the Godhead see."

[548] Ernst Käsemann, *The Testament of Jesus: A Study of the Gospel of John in the Light of Chapter 17.* Trans. Gerhard Krodel (Philadelphia: Fortress Press, 1978), p. 26.

[549] Udo Schnelle, *Anti-Docetic Christology in the Gospel of John.* Trans. Linda M. Maloney (Minneapolis: Fortress Press. 1992).

[550] Gregory J. Riley, *Resurrection Reconsidered: Thomas and John in Controversy* (Minneapolis: Fortress Press, 1995), pp. 50-51.

The Revelation Discourses

By far the most striking evidence for some kind of Johannine dependence on Gnostic sources is the parallels between the "I am" discourses (found only in John of the New Testament gospels) and similar discourses attributed to other revealers in the scriptures of Mandaean Gnosticism. These texts must be used with some caution, as we have only medieval copies to work with,[551] but it seems to many scholars to be quite strong evidence just the same. Note the "Johannine" flavor of this self-revelation: "I am the Messenger of Light, whom the Great One sent into this world. The true messenger am I, in whom there is no falsehood... I am the Messenger of Light: whoever smells at his scent is quickened to life. Whoever receives his word, his eyes are filled with light." It is hard to miss the characteristic Johannine structure of an introductory "I am" followed by a declaration of the benefits accruing to the one who will accept and follow the Revealer. Note also the familiar phrases "sent into the world" (cf. John 3:16) and "in whom there is no falsehood" (1:47).

Even more startling are the parallels between the Mandaean writings and particular Johannine discourses. Compare John's True Vine discourse (15:1-11) with these words of the Mandaean Revealer:

> A vine am I, a vine of life, a tree in which there is no falsehood. The tree of praise, from which everyone who smells of it becomes alive. Whoever hears his word, his eyes are filled with light... The vine which bears fruit ascends, the vine which bears nothing is cut off here from the light. Whoever is enlightened and instructed by me rises and beholds the place of light. Whoever is not enlightened and instructed by me is cut off from the light and falls into the great ocean of Suf.

With the Johannine discourse of the Good Shepherd (10:1-18) compare,

---

[551]Edwin M. Yamauchi, *Pre-Christian Gnosticism: A Survey of the Proposed Evidences* (Grand Rapids: Eerdmans, 1973), goes so far as to disqualify any and all Johannine use of the Mandaean materials on this basis. On the same basis should we refuse to date the canonical New Testament gospels before the earliest manuscripts of them we have?

I am a shepherd who loves his sheep, I protect the sheep and the lambs. The sheep are upon my neck, and the sheep do not go away from the villages. I refresh them not on the sea shore, so that they do not see the whirlpool... I carry them and give them water to drink from the hollow of my hand, until they have drunk their fill.

(All these texts come from the Mandaean Book of John,[552] i.e., of John the Baptist, though he is not the speaker).[553]

The Johannine "I am" discourses are so unlike anything to be found in the Synoptic Gospels, and so much like what we find in the Mandaean texts, that Bultmann felt the author of this gospel must have used as source material a collection of revelation discourses derived from a rival Gnostic sect. Specifically, Bultmann[554] guessed that the Fourth Evangelist had been an adherent of a group which viewed John the Baptist as the Revealer. (The Mandaeans, still around today, revere John the Baptist as their founder.) Converting to Christianity, the evangelist took over some of the sacred traditions of the sect of John, reapplying them to Jesus Christ. I do not believe we need to go the whole way with Bultmann (though, personally, I do) in order to recognize the Gnostic sources and features of John.

Sources, Date, and Authorship

Bultmann[555] posited the fourth evangelist's dependence on a list of seven miracle stories, a "Signs Source."[556] These miraculous signs may have been numbered, two of the numbered introductions surviving into the resultant text of John: "This, the first of his signs, Jesus did at Cana in Galilee" (John 2:11) and "This was now the second sign that Jesus did" (John 4:54). John 20:30-31 may at first have served as the conclusion of the Signs Source: "Now Jesus did many other signs in the

---

[552] Quoted in Bultmann, *Gospel of John*, p. 368.

[553] This text is included in my *The Pre-Nicene New Testament: Fifty-Four Formative Texts* (Salt Lake City: Signature Books, 2006). See especially 2:1-8.

[554] Bultmann, *Gospel of John*, pp. 17-18.

[555] Bultmann, *Gospel of John*, pp. 6-7.

[556] Robert T. Fortna, *The Gospel of Signs: A Reconstruction of the Narrative Source Underlying the Fourth Gospel*. Society for New Testament Studies Monograph Series 11 (Cambridge at the University Press, 1970).

presence of the disciples, which are not written in this book; but these are written that you may believe that Jesus is the Christ, the Son of God, and that believing you may have life in his name." Before someone added the Johannine Appendix (chapter 21), John 20:30-31 was retained to conclude the whole gospel as well.[557] In a sense, this implies that the Signs Source served as a basic skeleton for the whole book, as the evangelist packed the meat of the Revelation Discourses and the Passion Narrative onto its bones.

Is there any evidence outside the Gospel of John for this Signs Source having circulated independently? Actually, there is. Remember the parallel chains of miracle stories incorporated into Mark? They appear to be two oral-traditional variants of the same original. By the time Mark got hold of them, they were different enough that he decided simply to include both. (This explains how, after the multiplication of loaves and fish for five thousand people, the disciples could be baffled when Jesus suggested they feed a "second" group of four thousand in the same circumstances.) Well, Paul J. Achtemaier,[558] who pointed all this out, also spotted the Signs Source as yet a third version.

It is immediately evident that John shares a sea-miracle and a miraculous feeding story with Mark. He has the five thousand version, matching Mark's first miracle-sequence (John 6:10), but in John the sea-miracle is Jesus walking on the water (John 6:19), matching the sea-walking miracle in Mark's second sequence rather than stilling the storm as in Mark's first. John has no exorcisms to correspond with those of the Syro-Phoenician woman's daughter and the Gerasene demoniac, but on the other hand, the story of the Syro-Phoenician woman's daughter appears to be a tradition-variant of Q's story of Jesus' healing at a distance of the Roman centurion's son (Matt. 8:5-13; Luke 7:1-10). And John's story of Jesus' distance healing of the royal official's son (4:46-54) seems to be, as Bultmann[559] pointed out, still another variant version of the healing of the centurion's son, of which the Syro-Phoenician woman story (in Mark's second sequence) is yet another variant! John's story of Lazarus' resurrection (chapter 11) parallels Mark's story of Jairus' daughter from Mark's first sequence, while John's episode of the man

---

[557]Bultmann, *Gospel of John*, pp. 6-7.

[558] Paul J. Achtemeier, *Jesus and the Miracle Tradition* (Eugene, OR: Cascade Books, 2008), Chapter 4, "Toward the Isolation of Pre-Markan Miracle Catenae," pp. 55-86; Chapter 5, "The Origin and Function of the Pre-Markan Catenae," pp. 87-116.

[559]Bultmann, *The History of the Synoptic Tradition*. Trans. John Marsh (New York: Harper & Row, 1963), pp. 38, 227.

born blind parallels Mark's blind man of Bethsaida, from Mark's second sequence.

As anticipated just above, another major aspect of the question of John's sources is that of his possible use of the Synoptics. It seems obvious that Matthew and Luke both incorporated much material from both Mark and the Q Source, and their general, almost verbatim, similarity only makes their frequent editorial revisions stand out more clearly. If John made use of Matthew, Mark, and/or Luke, it is harder to trace, since he would seem to have rewritten them much more freely. In John's case, it is the parallels with the Synoptics that tend to stand out. Thus there is plenty of room to argue, as C.H. Dodd[560] did, that John is based, not on other finished gospels, but on variant versions of the same basic stories and sayings, or even sentence fragments. Both approaches are strong and make good sense, but what tips the scale for me is the fact that, at certain points of the story, John appears not merely to differ from the Synoptics but actually to *correct* them, as we will see.

Bultmann, despite his belief that John used the Synoptics,[561] believed he did not rely on (or rewrite) their Passion narratives but used instead a different Passion Source,[562] and here we find the same problem in miniature, for it is also possible to understand the Johannine Passion as a wholesale rewrite of Mark's.

Reshuffling the Deck

As it stands, the Gospel of John is something of a mess. It sometimes seems events are in the wrong order, that Jesus goes to one place but suddenly finds himself in another. Or Jesus seems to pick up the thread of the same discourse we thought he had finished a chapter earlier. What happened? The Synoptics abound in disconnected anecdotes and episodes, and we have learned to see in this a combination of originally distinct, contextless mini-narratives, like pearls strung together. But with John it reads differently, suggesting a once-continuous narrative that has been disrupted, as though the wind had scattered a pile of pages and someone had not quite been able to get them all back in proper order.[563]

---

[560] C.H. Dodd, *Historical Tradition in the Fourth Gospel* (Cambridge at the University Press, 1963).

[561] Bultmann, *Gospel of John*, p. 6.
[562] Bultmann, *Gospel of John*, p. 6.

There have been several hypothetical rearrangements[564] of the gospel which do seem to improve the continuity. But, though I have utilized one of these in presenting the Gospel of John in my collection, *The Pre-Nicene New Testament*,[565] I will discuss the text here in the traditional order, for ease of reference.

There is a major alternative approach to the problem, posited by Raymond E. Brown:[566] Perhaps the discontinuities stem from a process of successive expansions of an original text. When new sections were added, on this theory, the evangelist was more interested in certain themes than dotting all the narrative "i's," leaving loose ends.[567]

When and Who?

Conservatives have painted themselves into a pretty corner on the matter of this gospel's date of composition. They would love to assign it a very early date because they want the historical Jesus to have said all the things he is made to say in John's gospel, and this for two reasons. First, they want a *revealed* Christology drawn directly from Jesus' own words about himself. They feel distinctly uncomfortable admitting that what we are reading there is someone's theological *interpretation of* Jesus. Of course, they could just reassure themselves that Jesus *must* have said these words because they are contained in Holy Scripture, inspired and inerrant. But they know this is not historical methodology. They themselves wouldn't care about the difference, but they have entered the field of New Testament scholarship, not with simple scholarly interest, but in order to defend Orthodoxy from the "destructive" character of biblical criticism, and they know that their "colleagues" (opponents) would never take appeals to inspiration seriously. So as early as possible

---

[563]Bultmann, *Gospel of John*, pp. 10-11, 220.

[564] E.g., Thomas Cottam, *The Fourth Gospel Rearranged* (London: Epworth Press, 1952); F.R. Hoare, *The Original Order and Chapters of St. John's Gospel* (London: Burns Oates & Washbourne, 1944).

[565] I adopted Cottam's arrangement in my *Pre-Nicene New Testament*.

[566] Raymond E. Brown, *The Gospel According to John I-XII: A New Translation with Introduction and Commentary* Anchor Bible vol. 29 (Garden City: Doubleday, 1966).

[567] Kim Mark Lewis, *How John Wrote the Book of Revelation: From Concept to Publication* (Lorton, VA: Kim Mark Lewis, 2015), delineates exactly such an expansion process in the composition of John's Apocalypse, using certain discontinuities as levers to pry the layers apart, restoring original patterns.

a date for John would narrow the gap between a historical Jesus and this "record" of his words. The longer the interval, the more room for distortion and embellishment (if you want to call it that).

Second, an earlier date, pushing the Fourth Gospel closer to Jesus, would come in mighty handy for pious devotions and for evangelism. It would be great if they could tell people that, in John, they are encountering directly the promises and challenges of Jesus, as if he is speaking right off the page to their conscience. That way, reading this gospel is to initiate a "personal relationship with Christ," the supposed be-all and end-all of Christianity and the Bible.

But the statements of "early" Christian writers like Irenaeus and Eusebius tell them not only that John the evangelist was one and the same with the narrative character John son of Zebedee, but also that this John must have been a mere youngster when he traveled with Jesus and his fellow disciples and that he waited many decades to record his memoirs of Jesus, about 100 C.E. That's too long an interval for comfort! But they can't discount it because they have committed themselves to accepting as historically accurate various statements of Papias, Irenaeus, Clement of Alexandria, etc., about the apostolic authorship, hence accuracy, of the Synoptics. They can't very well discard the Patristic statement about John's late date while upholding the statements about Synoptic authorship. That sword, it turns out, cuts both ways.

With that bridge washed out, apologists seek an alternate route back to authentic Jesus reporting. Using (and possibly abusing) the work of C.H. Dodd,[568]scholars like A.M. Hunter[569] and John A.T. Robinson[570] promoted a "new look on the Fourth Gospel," turning the form-critical method against its inventors and arguing that, while, okay, the discourses in John might not be actual transcripts of Jesus' words (though they might be!), and though they might not really be the memories of an eye-witness disciple, it is possible that they represent a separate chain of traditions as "old" as those collected in Matthew,

---

[568]Dodd, *Historical Tradition*, passim.

[569] Archibald M. Hunter, *According to John: The New Look at the Fourth Gospel* (Philadelphia: Westminster Press, 1976).

[570] John A.T. Robinson, *Redating the New Testament* (Philadelphia: Westminster Press, 1976); Robinson, *The Priority of John* (London: SCM/Canterbury Press, 1987). For a pitiless take-down of Robinson, see Maurice Casey, *Is John's Gospel True?* (New York and London: Routledge, 1996), Chapter 10, "The 'Priority' of John," pp. 199-217. To be honest, Casey didn't think much of *my* work, either!

Mark, and Luke, and just as likely as the Synoptic tradition to put us in touch with the historical Jesus.[571] This is really an outrageous harmonization tactic, as if the approach could account for the glaring differences between John and the Synoptics. Why does Jesus preach the kingdom of God in the Synoptics, but scarcely even mention it in John? Why does the Synoptic Jesus speak in parables, while his Johannine counterpart instead indulges in long, circuitous and repetitive monologues and dialogues? Why does the Synoptic Jesus teach many things, while the Johannine Jesus reveals *only that he is the Revealer?*[572] Why does John's "Jesus" sound scarcely like the Synoptic version, but exactly like the (equally anonymous) author of the "Johannine" Epistles—*and* the narrator of John (we often can't tell when he is speaking for himself or for Jesus)—*and* all the other characters in the gospel? It's like reading Kahlil Gibran's *Jesus the Son of Man*[573] or watching a Woody Allen movie. Everyone sounds alike. Guess why? You're hearing one ventriloquist speaking through different dummies.

The "new look" approach tries to make the Johannine Jesus potentially as historically accurate as the Synoptic Jesus and succeeds only in implying that the Synoptic Jesus may be no less a theo-literary cipher than the Johannine.

The Tübingen critics of the nineteenth century argued for a mid-second century date for John's Gospel, and naturally conservatives cannot have *that*. For decades now, the trump card played by apologists[574] has been the John Rylands Papyrus, an ancient scrap of paper containing part of a passage from John. Paleographers, who arrive at dates for ancient documents from an analysis of their handwriting, certain styles waxing and waning through the centuries, had placed this fragment at around 125-150 C.E. Allowing sufficient time for an original to have given rise to circulated copies, this would place John

---

[571] I. Abrahams, certainly no Christian apologist, in his *Studies in Pharisaism and the Gospels*, vol. I (1917), p. 181 (quoted in Bruce, *New Testament Documents*, p. 50), remarks, "My own general impression, without asserting an early date for the Fourth Gospel, is that the Gospel enshrines a genuine tradition of an aspect of Jesus' teaching which has not found a place in the Synoptics." The trouble with this judgment is that it seems to assume that Jesus was the only one possessing "knowledge of Jewish customs, beliefs, and methods of argument" (Bruce's summary).

[572] Bultmann, *Gospel of John*, pp. 160-161, 252, note 2.

[573] Kahlil Gibran, *Jesus the Son of Man: His Words and his Deeds as Told and Recorded by those who Knew him* (New York: Alfred A. Knopf, 1928).

[574] Bruce, *New Testament Documents*. pp. 17-18.

easily within the traditional dating range. Thus the Tübingen scholars could be dismissed as purveyors of unfounded speculation (exactly, one might add, as Irenaeus had dismissed the visions and inventions of contemporary Gnostics).

But, alas, in recent years, scholars have raised serious questions about this dating of the papyrus. For one thing, paleography presupposes there are enough samples of the handwriting from a particular period with which to compare the manuscript in question and to decide where (when) it belongs. But there turn out to be too few from the period in which they had placed the John Rylands Papyrus. The date was a guess. Perhaps too convenient a guess. After a thorough review of the evidence and the history of the scholarly discussion, Brent Nongbri concludes:

> What emerges from this survey is nothing surprising to papyrologists: paleography is not the most effective method for dating texts, particularly those written in a literary hand. Roberts himself noted this point in his edition of P[52]. The real problem is the way scholars of the New Testament have used and abused papyrological evidence. I have not radically revised Roberts's work. I have not provided any third-century documentary papyri that are absolute "dead ringers" for the handwriting of P[52], and even had I done so, that would not force us to date P[52] at some exact point in the third century. Paleographic evidence does not work that way. What I have done is to show that any serious consideration of the window of possible dates for P[52] must include dates in the later second and early third centuries. Thus, P[52]*cannot be used as evidence to silence other debates about the existence (or non-existence) of the Gospel of John in the first half of the second century.* Only a papyrus containing an explicit date or one found in a clear archaeological stratigraphic context could do the work scholars want P[52] to do. As it stands now, the papyrological evidence should take a second place to other forms of evidence in addressing debates about the dating of the Fourth Gospel.[575]

---

[575]Brent Nongbri, "The Use and Abuse of P[52]: Papyrological Pitfalls in the

To retrace our steps somewhat, we have to address the objection that the evangelist claims to be an eyewitness even if he does not identify himself as John son of Zebedee. What about it? The basis of this argument is a pair of brief passages, John 19:35 and 21:24. When we get to those chapters I will argue that the first is an interpolation and the second occurs in an appendix subsequently tacked onto the gospel. But for the sake of argument, let's assume both were present in the original text. Please note that both speak of the supposed witness in the third person. This means that this eyewitness claim is no different from that made on behalf of Matthew by Papias. Some *else* is claiming the narrated events go back to someone on the scene.

But suppose the author is being cagey, and he is really referring to himself (cf., 2 Cor. 12:2-7). Why must we believe him? There are many such eyewitness claims in ancient writings that are clearly spurious, merely a literary device ("These are the secret sayings which the living Jesus spoke and Didymus Judas Thomas wrote."). We still do this: "My name is Ishmael." It is the crudest error to equate the narrator, who is himself a kind of character in the narrative, with the actual author who stands behind the narrative. Do I have to believe that Captain John Carter really had adventures on Mars because author Edgar Rice Burroughs posed, within the narrative, as Carter's friend and secretary? I hope for your sanity's sake you don't.

Why do apologists make this obvious mistake? Simply because they cannot for long put their ingrained belief in biblical inerrancy on the shelf. They thought they had donned their scholar's cap, but they were still wearing their believer's jester hood. "God said it, I believe it, that settles it!"

But who *was* the author? I can't offer a name (though I will continue to refer to the evangelist as "John" for convenience's sake), but that's sort of beside the point. What we can surmise is that the author was the mysterious figure called "the Paraclete." It is he whom Jesus is made to predict at the Last Supper.

> I will pray the Father, and he will give you another Counselor [Paraclete], to be with you for ever, even the Spirit of truth, whom the world cannot receive, because it neither sees him nor knows him; you know him, for he dwells with you, and will be in you. (John 14:16-17)

Dating of the Fourth Gospel," *Harvard Theological Review* 98.1 (2005), pp. 23-48.

These things I have spoken to you, while I am still with you. But the Counselor, the Holy Spirit, whom the Father will send in my name, he will teach you all things, and bring to your remembrance all that I have said to you. (14:25-26)

I tell you the truth: it is to your advantage that I go away, for if I do not go away, the Counselor will not come to you; but if I go, I will send him to you. And when he comes, he will convince the world concerning sin and righteousness and judgment: concerning sin, because they do not believe in me; concerning righteousness, because I go to the Father, and you will see me no more; concerning judgment, because the ruler of this world is judged.

I have yet many things to say to you, but you cannot bear them now. When the Spirit of truth comes, he will guide you into all the truth; for he will not speak on his own authority, but whatever he hears he will speak, and he will declare to you the things that are to come. He will glorify me, for he will take what is mine and declare it to you. All that the Father has is mine; therefore I said that he will take what is mine and declare it to you. (16:7-15)

Bultmann[576] notes that the Paraclete was very likely originally understood to be a second (human) revealer to appear in Jesus' wake, to clarify and amplify his teachings. This would fit exactly with a centuries-long tradition in Middle Eastern esotericism on display among, e.g., the Ismail'is[577] and the Druze, who believe that, again and again throughout history, God has sent pairs of revealers, first, the Proclaimer, and then shortly afterwards, the Foundation. The Proclaimer would announce the public (exoteric) version of a new revelation, the Foundation providing the "inside stuff," the esoteric meaning of it, for the elite who were able to understand it. First Adam, then Seth; first Noah, then Shem; first Moses, then Aaron; first Jesus, then Peter (or Paul or John); first Muhammad, then Ali, and so on. The eleventh-century Druze faith,[578]

---

[576]Bultmann, Gospel of John, p. 567.

[577] Sami Nasib Makarem, The Doctrine of the Ismail'is. Islamic Series (Beirut: Arab Institute for Research and Publishing, 1972), pp, 29-34; Farhad Daftary, The Ismail'is: Their History and Doctrines (New York: Cambridge University Press, 1990), pp. 89, 139.

which taught that the Fatimid caliph of Egypt, al-Hakim, was Allah incarnate, was proclaimed initially by one al-Hamzah, then given its esoteric elaboration by a "heretical" missionary named ad-Darazi (from whom the name "Druze" derives).

Such was, I think, the character and status of the author of the Gospel of John. Nor would he prove to be the only Christian (or post-Christian) prophet to claim the title. There were also Montanus of Phrygia, his lieutenants Priscilla and Maximilla, the Apostle Mani (who claimed to be the latest manifestation of the Spirit who had previously spoken through Zoroaster, the Buddha, and Jesus),[579] and the Prophet Muhammad himself.[580] This continued use of the title (and the entailed doctrine) provides the natural context for understanding the Johannine Paraclete. Within the narrative, he appears to be represented as the so-called Beloved Disciple, an ideal figure, left unnamed because the historical individual known as the Paraclete had not been one of Jesus' original followers[581] any more than Paul, Mark, or Luke. This is why, *in the very same verse*, he can be predicted to appear only once Jesus leaves the scene (John 14:16) *and* said to be "with you" (John 14:17). The former refers to the actual subsequent appearance of the Paraclete among the Johannine Christians, while the latter refers to the literary retrojection of the Paraclete into the narrative as the Beloved Disciple.

Note that, at the Last Supper, Peter must inquire of the Beloved Disciple who reclines "in the bosom of Jesus" (John 13:23-25) if he wants to know something from Jesus, precisely as in John 1:18 no one knew the Father until he was made known by the Son "who is in the bosom of the Father." And we hear that the role of the Paraclete will be to bring to the disciples' memory what Jesus taught but that they must have forgotten! That's what we call False Memory Syndrome, but it is also clearly a device to smuggle later Gnostic doctrine into the mouth of Jesus.

And then there's the business about the Paraclete transmitting new teaching to the disciples which they just wouldn't have been able to

---

[578] Sami Nasib Makarem, *The Druze Faith* (Delmar, New York: Caravan Books, 1974), pp. 71-72.

[579] Geo Widengren, *Mani and Manichaeism.* Trans. Charles Kessler. History of Religion Series (New York: Holt, Rinehart and Winston, 1965), p. 27.

[580] Tor Andrae, *Mohammed: The Man and his Faith.* Trans. Theophil Menzel. Harper Torchbooks, Cloister Library (New York: Harper & Row, 1960), Chapter IV, "Mohammed's Doctrine of Revelation," pp. 94-113.

[581] Bultmann, *Gospel of John,* p. 484.

process back in the old days. Surely it must be obvious this is just saying somebody, namely the Paraclete, is claiming to channel the Ascended Master Jesus.[582] Why is the teaching of Jesus in John so different from that presented in the Synoptics? This is why! And John 16:12-15 is poking the reader in the ribs. "Wink wink, nudge nudge, say no more!"

In the Beginning Was the Word "Prologue"

The opening verses of the gospel are lines of poetry, and poetry of a particular type, sometimes called "staircase parallelism." Generally speaking, the structure begins each successive line with the last word of the previous line. The gimmick is not carried through here with complete consistency, but the pattern is nonetheless clearly discernible. I have slightly readjusted the Revised Standard Version translation, reflecting the Greek word order and/or grammar in order to make this a bit clearer.

> In the beginning was the Word,
> and the Word was with God,
> and God the Word was.
> He was in the beginning with God;
> all things were made through him,
> and without him was not anything made.
> What was made in him was life,
> and the life was the light of men.
> The light shines in the darkness,
> and the darkness has not overcome it.

[There was a man sent from God, whose name was John. He came for testimony, to bear witness to the light, that all might believe through him. He was not the light, but came to bear witness to the light.]

---

[582] Modern examples of this genre, channeled revelations from Jesus, include Helen Schucman, *A Course in Miracles: Original Edition* (Omaha, NE: Course in Miracles Society, 2009); William Dudley Pelley, *The Golden Scripts* (Noblesville, IN: Fellowship Press, 1941) ; Levi Dowling, *The Aquarian Gospel of Jesus the Christ: The Philosophic and Practical Basis of the Religion for the Aquarian Age of the World and of the Church Universal: Transcribed from the Book of God's Remembrances, Known as the Akashic Records* (London: L.N. Fowler, 1908).

The true *light* that *enlightens* every man
was coming into *the world*.
The world is where he was,
and *the world* was made through *him*,
yet *him* the *world* knew not.
He came to *his own* home,
and *his own* people *received him* not.
But to all who *received him*,
who believed in his name,
he authorized to *become children* of God;
who were *born*, not of blood
nor of the *will* of the *flesh*
nor of the *will* of man, but of God.
And the Word became *flesh* and dwelt among us,
full of *grace and truth*; we have beheld his *glory*,
glory as of the only Son from the Father.

[John bore witness to him, and cried, "This was he of whom I said, 'He who comes after me ranks before me, for he was before me.'"]

And from his *fulness* have we all received,
grace upon *grace*.
For the law was given through Moses;
Grace and truth came through Jesus Christ.
No one has ever seen *God*;
the only begotten Son [or "only begotten *God*"],
who is in the bosom of the Father,
he has made him known.

The business about John the Baptist is a subsequent addition (actually, two of them)[583]aimed at correcting someone's "misapprehension" that the Baptizer was the divine light. Now where would anyone have gotten *that* crazy idea? Simply from the original and traditional use of the poem, the lyrics of a hymn, by the sect of John the Baptist (ancestors of today's Mandaean sect in Iraq). Originally, then, John *was* the light as well as the Word. As Bultmann suggested, a member of the John the

---

[583] Verse 15 quotes a saying ascribed to the Baptizer only *subsequently*, in 1:30, which also refers *back* to this one!

Baptist sect must have converted to Christianity and adapted the hymn for Christian worship, in order to make it about Jesus instead. Consider a few parallels between the Logos Hymn (John 1:1-18) and some Mandaean scripture texts:

> The worlds do not know thy name [Manda d'Haiye],[584] do not understand thy light. (Mandaean Liturgy 131) Cf., John 1:5, 10.

> They noticed me not, recognized me not and concerned themselves not about me... The man who saw and recognized me receives his way to the place of life. (Mandaean Liturgy 203)[585] Cf., John 1:12.

> Manda d'Haiye revealed himself in Judah,
> a vine appeared in Jerusalem,
> before which no wickedness stands.
> No kingly pride adorns his head,
> nor does he have the form of an idol creature.
> He is the Life, which was from time immemorial,
> Kusta [Truth Incarnate], which existed away back in the beginning.[586] (Cf., John 1:4)

There is a famous ambiguity in verse 1: "And the Word was God." As I say, I have changed the word order above to reflect the wording in Greek. "God" is the predicate of the sentence of which "the Word" is the subject. "God" is what is being said about "the Word." Here's where it starts getting tricky. All nouns, including proper names, in Greek are preceded by an article if you are referring to a particular thing. When "God" is the subject of a sentence, it would be *ho theos*, "[the] God." But if you meant to say "a god," a member of a pantheon, there would be no definite article. And Greek did not have an *indefinite* article, so you would just write "*theos*." John 1:1 says, "the Word was God," with no article before "God," so does that mean the evangelist meant that the Word was *a* god? Maybe so. But we'll never know for sure because in this verse *theos* is a predicate nominative, and in Greek, for who knows

---

[584]"Knowledge of Life," one of the Gnostic revealers in the Mandaean myths.

[585]Quoted in Bultmann, *Gospel of John*, p. 57, note 4.

[586] Werner Foerster, ed., *Gnosis: A Selection of Gnostic Texts. 2. Coptic and Mandaic Sources.* Trans. R. McL. Wilson, Peter W. Coxon, and K.H. Kuhn (Oxford at the Clarendon Press, 1974), pp. 300-301.

what reason, you can skip the definite article before a predicate nominative even if, in this case, you *did* intend "the God." You don't have to, and context usually tells the tale, but in this case it doesn't.

Another nuisance in the text. Tertullian quotes verse 13 as "who *was* born not of blood nor of the will of the flesh nor of the will of a man, but of God," referring all this back, not to "all who believed," but to "him," which would of course mean John was referring to the virgin birth of Jesus. No surviving manuscripts read this way. Did Tertullian have one that did? If so, it would be earlier than any that we have. Or did he fudge the wording in order to *create* a Johannine reference to the virginal conception, because there sure isn't one otherwise. It's another frustrating toss-up.[587]

Yet another snag: two fourth-century manuscripts, Codex Sinaiticus and Codex Vaticanus, have "God" instead of "Son" in verse 18. Those are darn good manuscripts, and "God" would fit the pattern of one line echoing the one before it. But, yet again, we cannot be sure.

Finally, there is a strange remark in the same verse: "no one has ever seen God." Really? How about Moses, Aaron, Nadab and Abihu (Exod. 24:9-11; Num. 12:8; Deut. 34:10)? Not even Isaiah (6:1)? What's going on here? Marcionism, that's what. Marcionites believed that the God of Israel/Judaism was not the Father of Jesus. Moses, Isaiah, and the rest had indeed laid eyes on old Jehovah, but no one had even suspected the existence of "God the Father of our Lord Jesus Christ" (2 Cor. 1:3; Eph. 1:3; Col. 1:3) until Jesus revealed him to mankind (Matt. 11:27). In light of this, we might take a second look at the contrast in verse 17: "For the law was given through Moses; grace and truth came through Jesus Christ." Perhaps the thought is not of "progressive revelation," but rather of a contrast between two opposite revelations from two different sources.

Do You Think You're What They Say You Are? (1:19-28)

---

[587] Bart D. Ehrman, *Orthodox Corruption of Scripture*, pp.26-27, dismisses Tertullian's version as a sneaky bit of theologically motivated tampering, while Charles Cutler Torrey, *Our Translated Gospels: Some of the Evidence* (New York: Harper & Brothers, 1936), p. 153, thought the present form of the text of John 1:13 is the original reading of the Greek, but that it represents a mistranslation of an underlying Aramaic original which did have "was."

A delegation of clergy from the Temple arrives at the Jordon to interrogate John the Baptist (presumably while he is taking a quick locust break). He has made such a splash that the authorities feel they must check him out. I see this scene as based on the Markan scene (8:27-30) at Caesarea Philippi. There Jesus questions the disciples as to what the crowds make of him. There are three wrong answers leading to one right one. Might Jesus be John the Baptist? Maybe Elijah? How about one of the prophets? No, he is the Christ. John has changed it. The group (priests and Levites this time, not the disciples) asks the hero (John the Baptist, not Jesus this time) about his identity, not the other way around. The same four options are given: the Christ, Elijah, the prophet, John the Baptist. Again, Elijah and the/a prophet are ruled out. But this time the Christ is the wrong answer, while John the Baptist is the correct one. Interestingly, John sides with Luke in denying that John is the returned Elijah, (or Luke is siding with John) as against Mark 9:13 (implicitly) and Matthew 17:12-13 (explicitly), which say he *is*. (Luke 1:17 implies the Baptizer was the returned Elijah, yet Luke omits the Matthew 3:4 / Mark 1:6 description of John's Elijah-like costume,[588] so he gives mixed signals.)

The follow-up question from the Inquisitors seems like a non sequitor: "Then why are you baptizing?" Uh, why are they *asking*? Was it assumed that the Messiah, the Prophet like Moses, or Elijah would be conducting a baptismal ministry? No; that is not the point. The question is a literary artifice, giving the evangelist the opportunity to have John explain why he *is* baptizing: just to gain a bully pulpit for announcing Jesus. In this gospel, that's the whole purpose: "For this I came baptizing with water, that he might be revealed to Israel" (John 1:31). So much for repentance in the advancing shadow of the Final Judgment. So much for any saving mission of John in his own right. The evangelist wants to appeal to his former Baptist co-religionists to jump ship and join up with the Jesus sect, like a victorious presidential nominee inviting one of his former rivals to run alongside him as his vice-presidential candidate, hoping to siphon off his former rival's disappointed supporters.

---

[588] On Conzelmann's theory of the Baptist's role in Luke, he is no longer, as in Mark, the harbinger of the imminent dawning of the kingdom of God, and thus not the predicted Elijah, but "merely" the "seal of the prophets" of the pre-Christian epoch. "This modification takes the form of a conscious editorial process of omissions, additions, and alterations in the wording of the sources" (Hans Conzelmann, *The Theology of St. Luke.* Trans. Geoffrey Buswell [New York: Harper & Row, 1961], p. 27).

Hydrophobia? (1:29-34)

The Johannine Jesus apparently just did not want to get wet! Not only does he walk on water (John 6:19), but he doesn't even let the Baptizer immerse him! Look at the text: where does it say Jesus got baptized? Nowhere, *that's* where! No, John simply spots Jesus approaching and points him out to the crowd: "Behold! The Lamb of God!" And how does he know? Because God (or maybe an angel) told him he'd recognize the Son of God when he beheld the Spirit descend upon a man and stay there (John 1:33). Was Jesus approaching John in order to be baptized? That would make sense, but then you'd expect the scene to issue in the baptism. But it doesn't, and John says he had already seen the Spirit descending on Jesus, or perhaps he saw it immediately as he saw Jesus walking toward him, but in any case, it doesn't happen as Jesus is coming back onto the riverbank, dripping, as in the Synoptics.

Volunteers and Draftees (1:35-51)

When did Jesus begin acquiring his disciples? According to Mark, the process began when he appeared out of nowhere on the shore of the Sea of Galilee and summoned Peter and Andrew, then James and John. Sensing Destiny calling their names, the two pairs of brothers left their nets and signed up. But this isn't the way it happens in John. There we read that Andrew was already a follower of John the Baptist down in Judea. Simon was there, too, presumably for the same reason, though he wasn't on the scene the day Andrew (and some other Baptist disciple) met Jesus. But Andrew quickly rejoined his brother and introduced him to Jesus, too. As soon as Jesus meets him, he confers on him a new name (cf., Rev. 2:17), "Cephas," the Aramaic equivalent to the Greek "Peter." Only afterward does Jesus, presumably with two or three new disciples in tow, return to Galilee, where he accosts Philip, a neighbor of Simon Peter and Andrew. It doesn't seem to take much convincing to get him to join the team, too. But Philip's friend Nathaniel is immediately skeptical: "You mean this guy's from *Nazareth*? Since when has anything good come out of *there*?" Whence this bad reputation? It has to be an anachronism reflecting the disapproval of later Jews who held a grudge against Nazareth on account of Jesus, the false prophet, as they viewed him.

So Mark has Jesus recruit disciples beginning in Galilee, but John has it happen in Judea. The closest thing in John to the lakeshore calling scene is in the Appendix (added by the Ecclesiastical Redactor), and there it happens at the other end of the story. Nor is that the only difference. When does Jesus rename Simon? Not this early in the other gospels. Mark seems to imply Jesus christens him "Peter" when he appoints him as one of the Twelve (Mark 3:16). Matthew has Jesus bestow the new name when he appoints him the Prince of Apostles (Matt. 16:18). Sounds like nobody knew and everybody guessed.

And who is this "Nathaniel" guy? He never appears in the Synoptics at all, much less as one of the disciples. Of course, harmonizers always speculate that Nathaniel was another name for someone who *does* appear in the lists of Jesus' disciples, but that is an expedient of desperation. This episode is obviously based on Jacob's dream of the ladder/stairway between heaven and earth, with angels going up and down (Gen. 28:11-17ff), running divine errands and returning to report on them (like Clarence in *It's a Wonderful Life*). Nathaniel is a New Testament Jacob, lacking the shrewd worldliness of his prototype (cf., Luke 16:8). Compare the imagery and language here with that of a Mandaean text:

> I am the true messenger
> In whom there is no lie,
> The true one in whom there is no lie,
> In him there is no failing or fault.
> (Ginza 59:1 ff.)[589]

Water into Wine (2:1-11)

The central feature of this miracle story, transforming one liquid into another, likely comes from the lore of Dionysus.

> There is an old theatre and shrine of Dionysos between the marketplace and the Menius. The statue of the god is the work of Praxiteles. Of the gods, the Eleans worship especially

---

[589]Quoted in Bultmann, *Gospel of John*, p. 323, note 5.

Dionysos, indeed they say their god invades the Thyra [temple to Dionysos] during the annual feast... The priests carry three kettles into the building and set them down empty, when the town citizens and strangers who happen to be there, are present. The priests, and any others who wish, put a seal on the doors of the building.... In the morning they come to read the signs and when they go into the building they find the kettles filled with wine. These things the most trustworthy men of Elis, and strangers with them, swear to have happened. This is by word of mouth; I myself did not arrive at festival time. (Pausanias, *Description of Greece* 6.26.1 ff.)[590]

But the outline of the story in which Jesus' wine miracle is set owes much to the story of Elijah in 1 Kings 17:8-24 LXX.[591] The widow of Zarephath, whose son has just died, upbraids the prophet: "What have I to do with you, O man of God?" (*Tiemoi kai soi*, 17:18). John has transferred this brusque address to Jesus, rebuking his mother (2:4, *Tiemoi kai soi, gunai*). Jesus and Elijah both tell people in need of provisions to take empty pitchers (*udria* in 1 Kings 17:12, *udriai* in John 2:6-7), from which, like the Horn of Plenty, sustenance miraculously emerges. And just as this feat causes the woman to declare her faith in Elijah ("I know that you are a man of God," verse 24), so does Jesus' wine miracle cause his disciples to put their faith in him (verse 11).

What kind of miracle *is* this, anyway?[592] Admittedly, it's quite spectacular, but it's also kind of silly. Contrast it with the miraculous feeding stories where Jesus multiplies the bread and fish in order to prevent the isolated crowd from fainting dead away from hunger. Here the "problem" is trivial: the guests at the wedding reception, already

---

[590]Trans. Cartlidge. David L. Dungan and David R. Cartlidge, eds., *Sourcebook of Texts for the Comparative Study of the Gospels*. Sources for Biblical Study 1 (Missoula: Scholars Press, 1974), p. 79.

[591]Randel Helms, *Gospel Fictions* (Buffalo: Prometheus Books, 1982), p. 86.

[592] It is "not a coincidence that John 3 introduces Nicodemus on the heels of John 2's story of Jesus' instruction to fill six large stone jars with water which he then miraculously transforms into wine. We read in *bTa'anit* 19b-20a of Naqdimon (Buni) ben Gurion in Jerusalem during the time of pilgrimage (cf. John 2:13-25), at whose prayers twelve large wells were miraculously filled with water." Samuel Zinner e-mail to the author, July 21, 2016.

pretty loaded, are clamoring for even more booze. Jesus' mother nags him into miraculously producing more! Raymond E. Brown[593] was surely correct: our evangelist has repurposed a story from the fund of tall tales of Jesus' demigod childhood, the sort of stuff that coalesced into the Infancy Gospels of Matthew and Thomas and the Arabic Infancy Gospel, where Jesus must come to the rescue of stupid adults (i.e., mortals). Joseph, a carpenter, is apparently so inept that he cannot seem to get the four legs of a chair the same length; then Jesus pops in and fixes it. Same here: the idiot adults have failed to buy enough wine, and Jesus' mom wants to help them out of this faux pas. And, like Mary and Joseph in the Infancy Gospels, she knows her son can apply his powers to fix such a "crisis." She is like Ma Kent asking her son, Superboy, to whip up a bunch of cherry pies at super-speed for the church social. And then there's the petulance of Jesus toward his mother, "Look, mom, don't drag me into this, okay?" Pious readers are disturbed by this, and, to smooth their feathers, commentators hasten to assure them that "Woman, what have you to do with me?" was actually an ancient token of respect—*right*. The real answer is simply that we are hearing the voice of the bratty Jesus of these apocryphal tales. John has just added Jesus' disciples to the mix and pretended it was an account of the adult Jesus. Why did he do this?[594] He wanted to allegorize the transformation of water into wine, making it a lesson about Christianity's superiority over Judaism (cf., Col. 2:16-17).

Supermarket Sweep (2:13-22)

Here is one of the whopping chronological contradictions between John and the Synoptics, where the Cleansing of the Temple happens at the end of Jesus' ministry. One way to solve the problem is, again, to posit that the gospel's pages had gotten mixed up and clueless copyists

---

[593] Raymond E. Brown, *The Birth of the Messiah: A Commentary on the Infancy Narratives in Matthew and Luke* (Garden City: Doubleday, 1977), pp. 487-488.

[594] "In part to anticipate chapter 3's Nicodemus story and to trump Nicodemus as portrayed in the Talmud" (Samuel Zinner, e-mail to this author, July 21, 2016).]

couldn't put Humpty together again, and that originally John had placed the Cleansing of the Temple where the other gospels had it. But this strategic retreat to the unavailable "original autographs" seems a bit too redolent of B.B. Warfield, an *ad hoc* hypothesis.

But there is a more plausible explanation for the contradiction. As Hans Windisch[595] noted, John seems to extend the trial and interrogation of Jesus by the Jewish authorities backward throughout the gospel. He is on trial the whole time, appealing to the "testimony" of "witnesses," etc. (John 5:31-39; 8:13-18, 46; 10:24-25).[596] What led to the arrest of Jesus? It must have been the Cleansing of the Temple. So if the trial is to occupy the whole gospel, it only makes sense that John would transfer the event to the beginning of the story. In this gospel, it would appear that chronology is a function of theology.

And there are two other, rather remarkable issues of chronology which, however, are not so easily dealt with. First: how old is Jesus supposed to be? Luke told us that Jesus was "about thirty" when he was baptized, but Irenaeus believed Jesus died at the ripe old age of fifty! Why would he think that? Probably because of John 2:19-21. The "temple" of Jesus' body will be destroyed and raised three days later. Jesus' opponents, thinking that he refers to the Jerusalem Temple, reply sarcastically, "It took forty-six years to build this structure, and *you're* going to rebuild it in three lousy *days?*" But presumably John means for us to detect an ironic double entendre: the Jews are *still* talking about the "temple" of Jesus' body. And this would mean Jesus' physical age at the time was at least forty-six. And then how long does Jesus' ministry last from that point on? In this gospel, at least three years. This is apparent from the presence of Jesus at three Passovers (John 2:13, 23; 6:4; 11:55; 12:1; 13:1; 18:28, 39; 19:14), and this would bring him up to the verge of age fifty at the time of his crucifixion. The capper is John 8:57: "You are not yet fifty years old." Mustn't this mean he was just under fifty? If he was, say, thirty-five, wouldn't they have said, "You are not yet forty?"[597] I can't say this is implausible.

---

[595]In Bultmann, *Gospel of John*, p. 644.

[596] Note the parallel between 10:24-25 and the question asked Jesus at his trial in Mark 14:61, Matthew 26:63, and especially Luke 22:67.

Verse 22 is quite important as a frank admission that the theological significance of the events in Jesus' life, which is baked right into the Synoptic cake, actually became evident *only in retrospect* (just as in John 12:16). The case is exactly parallel to the Christian "double take" on scripture, the retrospective "recognition" that various Old Testament passages were hitherto-unknown predictions of Jesus as the Messiah (John 20:9).

Nic at Night (3:1-21)

Here is one of the best known passages in the Bible. Indeed, for many, the whole Bible is contained (or might as well be) in John 3:16.

Nicodemus is called "a ruler of the Jews," i.e., a member of the Sanhedrin. And what does his name mean? Why, it comes out to "ruler of the people." This Greek name was used by Jews, though it was uncommon. But we have to suspect that it marks John's Nicodemus as an ideal character, standing for all persons of a certain type, the poster boy for Jews who believe in Jesus but are afraid to admit it since Jesus-Jews have been threatened with excommunication (John 16:2). But didn't that happen some fifty or sixty years after the ostensible time of Jesus' death? Yes: that was when synagogue leaders added the curse on Nazarenes to the synagogue liturgy. If you are one of those Nazarene (Jewish-Christian) heretics, you're going to think twice before calling down God's judgment on your head. Your only choice is to stop attending. If you don't leave and keep on reciting that curse, why, you're denying Jesus before men (Matt. 10:33), and you know what's going to happen! This is one of those anachronisms John uses to make his Jesus character directly address the issues of a later day. Another is the statement in John 9:22 that the excommunication ban had already been decreed. But John 16:2 still remembers that this was a measure imposed long after Jesus.

I believe the nocturnal conversation between Nicodemus and Jesus

---

[597] Alfred Loisy, *The Gospel and the Church*. Trans. Christopher Home (London: Isbister, 1903), pp. 33-34.

is a reworking of the story of the Rich Young Ruler in Mark 10:17-22. A righteous, Torah-abiding man approaches Jesus and addresses him as "teacher" (Mark 10:17; John 3:2). Both discuss with Jesus the requirements for salvation, though John does not have the inquirer explicitly raise the question. Jesus abruptly warns him that, without spiritual rebirth in the baptismal waters (3:5), salvation is impossible. It makes more sense if John had in mind the Rich Young Ruler's question, "What must I do to inherit eternal life?" In both Mark and John, the response of the inquirer to the answer Jesus gives him is left up in the air, no doubt because both Nicodemus and the Rich Young Ruler are surrogates for the reader, to confront him with the challenge. And what is the challenge presented to Nicodemus and those he represents? They cannot expect to be saved as long as they are willing to say no more about Jesus than that he is a true teacher (3:2). Salvation requires coming out of the closet and publicly confessing (in baptism)[598]one's belief in Jesus as the Son of God and Messiah. It is a question of whether one will confess or else deny Jesus before men (Mark 8:38; Matt. 10:32-33; Rom. 10:9-10).

Since there were no quotation marks in antiquity, it is impossible to tell whether it is supposed to be Jesus or the narrator speaking in verses 16-21, not that it matters much, since the whole thing is really John, a theological puppeteer. We have the same uncertainty in John 3:31-36 and Galatians 2:15-21. Speaking of narrative puppetry, note how Nicodemus is depicted here as oblivious of the obviously metaphorical language of Jesus. He asks for gratuitous clarification for the same reason Dr. Watson was always asking Sherlock Holmes for an explanation: it is not for his sake but for the readers' benefit.

John 3:14-15 compares the crucified Jesus with the bronze serpent Moses held up to cure Israelites who were suffering from snakebite in Numbers 21:9. Just as every victim who looked up at Moses' caduceus (for that's what it was, just like the one Apollo traded to Hermes for his lyre) was instantly cured, all who look to the crucified Jesus will be saved. I think there is an unnoticed Gnostic significance here, not

---

[598] The mention of sacraments is always a mark of the Ecclesiastical Redactor. Wait till we get to the Bread of Life discourse!

hidden, just not recognized. As we saw earlier in the previous volume, the Moses story referred to here was supplied as a secondary legitimization for an idol of the Hebrew serpent deity Nehushtan (= Leviathan), contained in its own chapel in the Jerusalem Temple (2 Kings 18:4).[599] Nehushtan (not Satan) appears in the Eden story to bring divine knowledge to humanity, the knowledge the Creator did not want them to have. Gnostics correctly understood that, on any literal reading, Genesis 2-3 depicts Yahweh as the villain, just like Father Zeus, with the Serpent, like Prometheus, as the benefactor of mankind by imparting knowledge. Christian Gnostics, especially the Ophites/Naassenes (both meaning "serpent-ites") and the related, if not identical, Peretai, identified the Serpent of Eden as an early manifestation of Christ the Revealer. I say John is still recognizable as a Gnostic gospel, even with the Bowdlerization of the Ecclesiastical Redactor. And so I am proposing that John's Jesus is presenting himself as the ophidian Revealer of *gnosis* to everyone who looks to him. Even in the Moses version, rewritten as it is, this is apparent: the coiling of the bronze serpent about the pole depicts the Serpent of Eden, Nehushtan, wrapped around the trunk/limb of the Tree of Knowledge from whence he offers *his* fruit, the fruit of enlightenment, to those who hunger and thirst for it.

Best Man (3:22-36)[600]

Here is yet another case of theologically and polemically motivated anachronism. Did Jesus conduct his own baptismal ministry down the street from John's? There is no room for this in the Synoptics, where Jesus is said to have undertaken his own ministry only after John's arrest and imprisonment. Is the Johannine scenario a piece of some alternative tradition? No, it is obviously a retrojection into the time of Jesus and the Baptist of the situation in the evangelist's time, when the rival messianic

---

[599] Uh, didn't I argue that there *was* no Solomonic Temple, no Jerusalem Temple until the Zerubbabel Temple, then the Herodian Temple? Right-o! The thing is, Jewish monotheism was by no means so ancient as we have traditionally believed. I would surmise that Nehushtan was worshipped even in the Temple of Herod the Great.

[600] Who could resist the pun with Matthew 11:11a? I know: if you have to explain 'em...

sects of Jesus and of John competed for followers and Christians hoped to persuade Baptists to jump ship and swim on over (as our evangelist himself had done).[601] The narrator virtually admits the fictive character of the scene when, in John 4:2, he remarks that "Jesus himself did not baptize, but only his disciples." Superficially he seems to envision Jesus like Billy Graham at a Crusade: Billy preaches to the crowd, then leaves it to trained counselors to "close the deal" with those who came forward at Billy's evangelistic invitation. But the real point is not to describe a division of labor between Jesus and his staff, but rather to admit, with a wink, that Christian baptism was a post-Jesus development.

John the Baptist's disciple is jealous for his master because Jesus is surpassing him in popularity, but the Baptizer is taking it philosophically: he had a particular job to do, and now he is coming to the end of it. That is, the reader should take the hint that John's movement is now a superannuated museum relic and should dissolve, sending its members over to the Jesus religion. Now, thanks to the Fourth Evangelist, they've even got their founder's blessing (the same point as in John 1:36-37; cf., Acts 19:4-5).

The Baptizer waves away his disciple's concerns with an analogy of the Best Man who is happy to have a remotely secondary role in a wedding and is eager for his friend the groom to receive all the attention. "He who has the bride is the bridegroom; the friend of the bridegroom, who stands and hears him, rejoices greatly at the bridegroom's voice; therefore this joy of mine is now full. He must increase, but I must decrease" (John 3:29-30). Consider the parallel in language with this from Mandaean Liturgy 205: "Then the disciples heard the voice of Enosh, of the great Uthra; they honored and praised the great life [Manda d'Haiye] beyond measure."

The scene is based either on Mark 2:18-22 or on an oral variant of the same story.[602] Note the similarities: an observer is concerned over differences in ritual practice between the sect of Jesus and that of John the Baptist. In Mark it is fasting, while in John it is baptism, both penitential rites. Jesus answers the question in Mark; the Baptizer does in John. In both cases the answer draws a comparison with a

---

[601]Bultmann, *Gospel of John*, p. 186. It is the same sort of thing as the story of the Strange Exorcist in Mark 9:38-40, where what is presented as a scene from Jesus' lifetime is really referring to the tension between the Twelve and Paul (or rather between their latter-day factions).

[602] Dodd, *Historical Tradition*, p. 284.

bridegroom and the rejoicing of his friend(s). When the bridegroom has the spotlight, the appropriate thing to do is to rejoice with him.

Samaritan Woman, Listen What I Say (4:1-44)

Robert Alter[603] identifies this scene as a variant of the "type scene" which frequently recurs in the Bible: a young man leaves home, arrives at a well and encounters young women, one of whom he marries. Other tales of the same type include Genesis 24 (Abraham's servant meets Rebecca, Isaac's bride to be), Genesis 29 (Jacob meets Rachel); Exodus 2 (Moses meets Zipporah); Ruth 2 (Ruth meets Boaz); and 1 Samuel 9 (Saul meets the maidens at Zuph). But Helms[604] adds 1 Kings 17, where, again, Elijah encounters the widow of Zarephath, and this story is the one which must have provided the immediate model for John 4. Elijah and Jesus alike leave home turf for foreign territory. Each prophet is thirsty and meets a woman from whom he requests a drink of water.

In both stories the woman departs from the pattern of the type scene. As usual, she lacks a husband, but for different reasons. The woman of Zarephath is a widow, while the Samaritan has sworn off matrimony, having had five previous husbands, now dead or divorced. Now she doesn't even bother with the ceremony and just cohabits with some guy in a trailer. In both of these stories the woman stands in need more than the prophet who has asked her help. The prophet offers her a miraculous, self-renewing source of nourishment, Elijah that of physical food, Jesus that of the water of everlasting life. And, just as the widow exclaims that Elijah must have come to disclose her past sins ("You have come to me to bring my sin to remembrance," 1 Kings 17:18), the Samaritan admits Jesus has the goods on her as well ("He told me all that I ever did," John 4:39).

I believe that behind the character of the Samaritan Woman stands Helen, the paramour of Simon Magus, the Samaritan Messiah. He had supposedly rescued her from a series of sordid reincarnations as a prostitute, the origin of the "five husbands" business. Then again, I

---

[603] Robert Alter, *The Art of Biblical Narrative* (New York: Basic Books, 1981), p. 48.
[604] Helms, *Gospel Fictions*, p. 89-90.

wonder if this story has borrowed a previous Dosithean rewrite of the Elijah tale. A vestige of it survives in what are now Jesus' words to her, "If you knew the gift of God and who it is who asks you for a drink, etc." Dositheus was a rival Samaritan Messiah (the Pseudo-Clementines make both Simon and Dositheus, like Jesus, disciples of John the Baptist), and his name means "Gift of God." Thus, the original meaning of the words would be, "If you recognized Dositheus and who it is who asks you for a drink," etc. There is another Gnostic (at least docetic) touch when we read that, when the disciples return from the local deli and urge Jesus to eat, he refuses: "I have food to eat of which you do not know [...] My food is to do the will of him who sent me" (John 4:31-34). This is to say, "Man shall not live by bread *at all*, but by every word that emerges from the mouth of God," like those nuns who subsisted on nothing but communion wafers.[605]

But John has apparently used still another source, this time a Buddhist one:

> Ananda, the attendant to the Buddha, having been sent by the Lord on a mission, passed by a well near a village, and seeing Pakati, a young outcast woman, asked her for water to drink.
>
> Pakati said, "O monk, I am too humbly born to give you water to drink. Do not ask any service of me lest your holiness be contaminated, for I am of low caste."
>
> And Ananda replied, "I ask not for caste but for water;" and the woman's heart leaped joyfully and she gave Ananda water to drink. Ananda thanked her and went away; but she followed him at a distance.
>
> Having heard that Ananda was a disciple of the Buddha, the woman went to the Blessed One and said, "O Lord, help me and let me live in the place where your disciple Ananda dwells, so that I may see him and minister unto him, for I love Ananda."
>
> And the Blessed One understood the lessons of her heart and he said, "Pakati, your heart is full of love, but you do

---

[605] Did they at least dip them in Salsa?

not understand your own sentiments. It is not Ananda that you love, but his kindness. Accept, then, the kindness you have seen him practice toward you and practice it toward others.

"Pakati, though you are born low caste, you will be a model for noblemen and noblewomen. Swerve not from the path of justice and righteousness and you will outshine the royal glory of queens and kings."[606]

The Queue Source (5:1-18)

The healing of the crippled man at the healing shrine of Bethsaida (or Bethesda or Bethzatha, depending on your favorite manuscript) is a miracle story of a particular type, comparing one's favorite source of healing with another, an old and venerable one, rendering the latter "Brand X." You have seen a thousand TV commercials of the same kind. The healing of the hemorrhagic woman in Mark 5:25-34 is another such miracle, contrasting conventional medicine, bankrupting the old lady and improving her health not one whit, with Jesus who heals her without even trying! In the same way, John's lame man had practically moved into the Bethsaida shrine despite the fact he had quickly realized it was one big Catch-22: first one into the water gets healed! But what if your ailment prevents you from competing? Hence Jesus asking him, "Uh, do you even *want* to be healed?"[607] Here is another such story, this one showing the superiority of Apollonius of Tyana to the renowned healing shrine of Asclepius.

> As I am describing the life of a man whom even the gods thought highly of, it would not be right to pass over his actions in the shrine. A youth had come from Assyria to visit Asclepius, but indulged himself even on his sickbed; drinking was his whole life, or rather his death, for in fact he had dropsy and

---

[606] "The Woman at the Well," adapted from the *Agamas*, trans. E. Burneuf and P. Carus. In Jack Kornfield, ed., *Teachings of the Buddha, Revised and Expanded Edition* (New York: Barnes & Noble Books, 1996), pp. 105-106. Many scholars automatically scoff at the very notion of Buddhist influences in the gospels, but this is sheer theological distaste. Buddhist missionaries had been active, e.g., in Egypt and Syria for at least two centuries before the gospels were written.
[607] Dodd, *Historical Tradition*, pp. 176-177.

because of his love of wine was failing to dry up his condition. For this reason Asclepius did not help him or even visit him in his dreams. But when the youth reproached him for this he appeared to him and said, "If you talk with Apollonius, you will be cured." So he approached Apollonius and said, "Asclepius has told me to converse with you: what can your wisdom do for me?"

"Something very valuable in your present condition," was the reply, "for I suppose you want a cure?"

"Indeed I do," he said; "a cure is what Asclepius has promised but not given me."

"Don't blaspheme," Apollonius said; "he gives a cure to those who want it [cf., John 5:6], but in your self-indulgence you are doing the opposite of what your disease requires. You are burdening your intestines with rich food when they are soft and bloated, and pouring water on mud." [And] Apollonius restored the youth to health by expressing himself wisely and simply. (Philostratus, *Life of Apollonius* I:9)[608]

You see, this kind of contrast between effective healing in Jesus' name with futile efforts in some other name is the issue underlying Acts 4:12.

But of course, in John's gospel the miracle has little importance in itself, being mainly the springboard for a revelation discourse. The story quickly introduces the issue of sabbatarianism: has Jesus violated the commandment? The Jewish authorities say yes. But it is really Jesus' rebuttal that gets him into serious trouble. God works on the Sabbath all the time! If he didn't exercise his providential power for twenty-four hours, the world must fall to ruin. (This was an object of rabbinic debate: *had* God, *did* God, truly rest on the seventh day?) And if it's okay for God to do it, it's okay for Jesus to do it. After all, like any son, he is only following his father's example. Yikes! So Jesus is not only a no-good Sabbath-breaker, but a blaspheming megalomaniac as well! John says these Jews had already decided to have Jesus killed and that this remark only steeled their determination. Compared to the Synoptics, this is pretty early in the day for the Jewish elders to be gunning for Jesus.

Often in this gospel, Jesus' opponents are depicted as misunderstanding Jesus' metaphors in a crudely literal way, but this time it looks, from Jesus' own elaboration of his words, that they are on the

---

[608]Philostratus, *Life of Apollonius*. Trans. C.P. Jones. Penguin Classics (Baltimore: Penguin Books, 1970), p. 34.

same wavelength; they just don't like what they hear. And then he rubs it in, upping the ante re his divine prerogatives. God has given him the authority to raise the dead for judgment.[609] Of course, Jesus never said anything of the kind. This is the Paraclete channeling revelations from the ascended Christ (cf., the reading of some manuscripts of John 3:13, "No one has ascended into heaven but he who descended from heaven, the Son of man, *who is in heaven*"). And from here we move into realized eschatology: "Truly, truly, I say to you, he who hears my word and believes him who sent me, *has* eternal life; he does not come into judgment, but *has passed from death to life*." Here we find ourselves deep into Mandaean/Baptist Gnostic territory, as witness:

> The true and faithful Nazoreans
> will ascend and see the place of light...
> They will not be kept back (in the world)
> and in the great judgment they will not be called to account.
> On them the judgment will not be pronounced
> which will be pronounced on all beings.
> (Ginza 323:13 ff.)[610]

> Thou shalt not come before the court of judgment,
> On thee no judgment shall be passed...
> For thou hast done the works of an upright man.
> (Ginza 512:22 ff.) [611]

But it gets better in verse 25: "Truly, truly, I say to you, the hour is coming, *and now is*, when the dead will hear the voice of the Son of God, and those who hear will live." Forget the future: the resurrection is right now! Exactly as in John 11:24-25: "Martha said to him, 'I know that he will rise again in the resurrection at the last day.' Jesus said to her, '*I am the resurrection!*'" But the Ecclesiastical Redactor, who agrees with Martha on this one, feels compelled to walk this back in verses 28-29: "Do not marvel at this; for the hour is coming when all *who are in the*

---

[609]The great (life) has created and commissioned thee,
has arrayed, commissioned and sent thee,
and given thee authority over every thing.
(Ginza 70:3 ff.) Quoted in Bultmann, *Gospel of John*, p. 165, note 4.

[610]Quoted in Bultmann, *Gospel of John*, p. 155, note 2.
[611]Quoted in Bultmann, *Gospel of John*, p. 155, note 2.

tombs will hear his voice and come forth, those who have done good, to the resurrection of life, *and those who have done evil, to the resurrection of judgment.*" Whew! I was afraid for a second there that Jesus was saying some kind of Gnostic bunk about the only resurrection being now! I hate to tell you, but he *was*. The dead who rise in response to his voice are the same as the sheep of his flock who hear his voice and follow. Just like the Mandaeans:

> Thereupon there called a voice of life;
> A watchful ear hears.
> Many heard and revived;
> many wrapped themselves round
> and laid themselves down (to sleep).
> (Ginza 596:9 ff.) [612]

> He who hears the speech of life, finds room in the Skina [=dwelling] of life. (Ginza 275:19 f.)[613]

The notion that Jews, even Jewish scripture scholars, poring over the texts, should have recognized their prophecies being fulfilled in Jesus is yet another evidence that this gospel is far distant, not only from any historical Jesus but even from the earliest Christianity, since it has been forgotten that ostensible predictions of Jesus could be discerned only with the eye of (an already Christian) faith, like the pesher exegesis of the Dead Sea Scrolls. Here it is taken for granted that the Christological sense should have been visible even to a neutral observer.

Food and Flood (Chapter 6)

As in Mark, John couples a miraculous provision of food with a gravity-defying stroll on the waves. One interesting difference is the surprising note that the crowd, so enthused by Jesus multiplying the food (or just providing so much food for free?), start making noise about what a great king of the Jews Jesus would make. John says they wanted or tried to "take him by force" to sweep him into power. But does this mean they were going to try it *against Jesus' will?* As if they already knew he disdained the whole idea?[614] That seems odd. I have always suspected

---

[612]Quoted in Bultmann, *Gospel of John*, p. 259, note 2
[613]Quoted in Bultmann, *Gospel of John*, p. 259, note 2.

there has been some garbling of an intended statement that they wanted to "make him king by force" *of arms*, assuming he'd agree to it. But of course, like the fan-mobbed Beatles in A *Hard Day's Night*, Jesus had to contrive a hasty exit.

Lena Einhorn[615] makes a pretty striking case that the feeding of the crowd in the wilderness, especially as a prelude to messianic revolution, is a retelling of Josephus' accounts of Theudas and the Egyptian prophet whipping up their followers, leading them into the desert, and promising them miracles as a catalyst for the expulsion of the Roman occupation (cf., Acts 5:36-37; 21:38; Matt. 24:23-26; Rev. 12:13-14).

The simple statement that "they saw Jesus walking on the sea and drawing near to the boat" (verse 19) conveys a proper chill despite, or even because of, its reticent simplicity. But then we read that, as soon as he climbs into the boat with the terrified disciples, they at once find themselves at their destination. It is as if they had awakened from a dream. Quite eerie.

But the crowd are up for a return visit to the buffet and meet Jesus on shore, hoping for more chow. Jesus calls them on it. He knows they only want a handout and rebukes them. It is not quite clear whether they are supposed to realize the supernatural origin of the food. Maybe, like the old Protestant Rationalists, they thought Jesus had a bunch of Keebler Elves baking the stuff in a hidden kitchen. In any case, Jesus goes on to compare and contrast the provision of manna in the desert with his feeding of the multitude, treating the latter as an allegory for his soon-coming donation of his flesh as a "medicine of immortality" (as the Ignatian Epistle to the Ephesians 20 called it).

The Ecclesiastical Redactor has been at work again. The original point of the Bread of Life discourse seems to have been much like that in Proverbs 9:1-6:

> Wisdom has built her house,
> she has set up her seven pillars.
> She has slaughtered her beasts, she has mixed her wine,

"Think you that I came down the years to rule an ant-hill for a day? [...] Dare you tempt me with a crown of dross, when my forehead seeks the Pleiades, or else your thorns?" Gibran, *Jesus the Son of Man*, p. 3.

615 Lena Einhorn, *The Jesus Mystery: Astonishing Clues to the True Identities of Jesus and Paul* (Guilford, CT: Lyons Press, 2007); Einhorn, *A Shift in Time: How Historical Documents Reveal the Surprising Truth about Jesus* (New York: Yucca Publishing, 2016).

she has also set her table.
She has sent out her maids to call
  from the highest places in the town,
  "Whoever is simple, let him turn in here!"
To him who is without sense she says,
"Come, eat of my bread
  and drink of the wine I have mixed.
Leave simpleness, and live,
  and walk in the way of insight."

But the Ecclesiastical Redactor has applied a heavy-duty sacramentalism, rewriting the text as a profound Eucharistic meditation. Only those who partake of the flesh of the Son of Man will find salvation. It is a bit difficult to square this with verse 63, "It is the spirit that gives life, the flesh is of no avail; the words that I have spoken to you are spirit and life," which must be a vestige of the original discourse, in which the true bread from heaven was divine wisdom or gnosis.

The chapter closes with John's version of the Caesarea Philippi confession of Peter (John 6:66-71). We saw the first half of the confession scene back in John 1:19-21, where it was reapplied to John the Baptist. Here in chapter 6, we do not run through the list of guesses again, but there is still a contrast between the wrong opinion of the crowd and the correct opinion of Peter. The crowd, baffled by the Bread of Life discourse, begin drifting away, their hopes for Jesus extinguished. And Jesus, as in Mark, has a "well, then" question for the disciples, not "Who do *you* say that I am?" but "What about you? Will you go, too?" Again, it is Peter who pipes up: "Lord, to whom shall we go? You have the words of eternal life; and we have believed, and have come to know, that you are the Holy One of God" (John 6:68-69). Mark had "the Christ," Luke "the Christ of God," and Matthew "the Son of the living God."

I Am the Way, the Fib, and the Lie (7:1-13)

Jesus' brothers are portrayed here as sneeringly cynical toward Jesus, whose public career they seem to regard with amused contempt. One imagines they are getting ready for the journey to Jerusalem for the Feast of Tabernacles and notice that Jesus is not doing the same. They express mock surprise: since he's obviously trying to make a reputation for himself, it's not like him to let an opportunity for public exposure ("photo ops") pass by. Jesus replies that the time is not right for him to make the trip. This sounds like he is planning his schedule according to his horoscope, and it says, "Don't travel today." But it's not just a question of timing; he says he is going to *skip* the feast this time. But as soon as they depart, snickering and making the finger-rotating "crazy" sign, Jesus grabs his valise and sneaks out, traveling the road incognito. So Jesus was lying. Some Christian scribes just could not bear this and added the word "yet." "I am not *yet* going up to the Feast." But this is a prime case where the more problematic reading has to be judged the original. It is impossible to imagine anyone chopping the "yet" if it stood so in the original. But if the original had "I'm skipping it this time, fellas," you can well imagine a scribe, trying to be more scriptural than scripture, adding the word "yet."

So why the fib? Did he just not want the company of these jerks? That seems pretty trivial. And once he got there and started his soapbox preaching, didn't he realize his brothers would know about it? "Hey Jude, *look!* That lying son of a *bitch!*" That's a great way to win his brothers over!

Well, we need not ask why Jesus would lie to his brothers (depicted like Cinderella's evil step-sisters). The whole scene is fiction. So the real question is what *John* was driving at. And the answer is that he just wanted an excuse to vilify the Heirs,[616] the Christian leadership faction who claimed to be part of Jesus' messianic dynasty.[617]It is a matter of ecclesiastical politics

Not Bad for a Hick! (7:14-24)

Jesus is expounding on something or other, maybe fine points of the Torah or the likelihood of extraterrestrial life, and his hearers somehow know he never studied with the rabbis. "How is it that this man has learning when he has never studied?" (John 7:15). Jesus overhears them and replies: "My teaching is not mine but his who sent me"[618] (7:16).

---

[616] Mack, *Myth of Innocence*, pp. 90-91.

[617] Ethelbert Stauffer, "The Caliphate of James." Trans, Darrell J. Doughty. *Journal of Higher Criticism* 4/2 (Fall 1997), pp. 120-143; James Tabor, *The Jesus Dynasty: His Hidden History, his Royal Dynasty, and the Birth of Christianity* (New York: Simon & Schuster, 2007).

[618] The evangelist might as well be defending his own position as the Paraclete who (ostensibly) shares no original teaching of his own, but merely passes along whatever the glorified Jesus imparts through him. Hmmm... come to think of it, maybe that *is* the point here.

This is a classic theme, to accentuate your prophet's lack of formal education in order to claim, "It comes from God! You're right: this guy could never have come up with it by himself!" The same is said of Peter and his colleagues in Acts4:13, not to mention Joseph Smith and the Prophet Muhammad. Furthermore, this pair of verses (plus verse 27: "Yet we know where this man comes from; and when the Christ appears, no one will know where he comes from") looks like John's version of Mark 6:1-3a (i.e., up to and excluding "And they took offense at him"). This is also why the brothers of Jesus are mentioned earlier in the chapter: because they are listed in the Mark 6 passage. Note that John places it in Jerusalem, not in Galilee as in Mark. Even more puzzling is the use of the proverb "a prophet has no honor in his own country" back in John 4:44 when Jesus is leaving a successful campaign in Samaria and returning to Galilee where he is *welcomed* (verse 45).

In verse 17, where Jesus is getting started on an insulting rant worthy of Don Rickles, he provides an *ad hominem* that Christian evangelists have never ceased to employ: "If any man's will is to do his [i.e., God's] will, he shall know whether the teaching is from God or whether I am speaking on my own authority." Let me get this straight. You mean, if I don't agree with you it's only because I'm unwilling to do the will of God? I'm refusing to part with some favorite sin, or I'd think you were right? Of course, the Gospel of John is a dogmatic tract written to promote a species of religious zealotry. There is no interest here in fostering the disinterested search for truth. Christianity is not about that.

Jesus winds up and lets fly another scorcher: "Did not Moses give you the law? Yet none of you keeps the law. Why do you seek to kill me?" (7:19). *None* of these Jews bothers to keep the Torah commandments? This is so patently absurd that it hardly counts as an insult. One must sympathize with the Pharisees: "You are a demoniac! Who is trying to kill you?" Jesus comes across as a paranoid schizophrenic. It is pretty obvious he had never read *How to Win Friends and Influence People*.[619]

What can Jesus (i.e., John) mean? In what sense could these Jews be said to have repudiated the Torah? In verses 22-23 we find the closest thing we're going to get to an answer: "Moses gave you circumcision (not that it is from Moses, but from the fathers [i.e., the Genesis Patriarchs], and you circumcise a man upon the Sabbath. If on the

---

[619] He *could* have, right? So *what* if Dale Carnegie wouldn't be writing it for another couple of millennia? Jesus was omniscient, wasn't he (John 21:17)?

Sabbath a man receives circumcision, so that the law of Moses may not be broken, are you angry with me because on the Sabbath I made a man's whole *body* well?" The reference goes back to the healing of the crippled man at Bethsaida in chapter 5. Jesus is shown here using standard rabbinical exegesis, reasoning from a lesser case to a greater. What applies to foreskin-snipping must surely hold good for healing the whole darn body! This is typical of intra-rabbinical debates. The difference of opinion is over the proper application of the commandments. It is ridiculous to say that, if you do not accept Jesus' opinion, you are "not keeping the law."

Whence and Whither? (5:25-44)

This gospel knows nothing of Jesus' birth in Bethlehem. In 7:28 Jesus admits that the Jews of Jerusalem "know where I am from." And where is that? Galilee: "But some said, 'Is the Christ to come from Galilee? Has not the scripture said that the Christ is descended from David, and comes from Bethlehem, the village where David was?'" (7:41b-42). "Are you [Nicodemus] from Galilee, too? Search [the scriptures] and you will see that no prophet is to rise from Galilee" (John 7:52).[620] Apparently Jesus saw nothing here to refute. It just didn't matter. Interesting.

But even more interesting is the speculation overheard in verses 35-36:"The Jews said to one another, 'Where does this man intend to go that we shall not find him? Does he intend to go to the Dispersion among the Greeks and teach the Greeks? What does he mean by saying, "You will seek me and you will not find me," and, "Where I am you cannot come"'?" I think this originally had something to do with John 12:20-23:

> Now among those who went up to worship at the feast were some Greeks. So these came to Philip, who was from Bethsaida in Galilee, and said to him, "Sir, we wish to see Jesus." Philip went and told Andrew; Andrew went with Philip and they told

---

[620] This condescension reminds me of an amusing moment at the Jesus Seminar when one of the Fellows was patiently explaining to Darrell Doughty just why his opinion on something was obviously false. Doughty smiled and replied, "You're talking to me as if I were a grad student, but that's okay." He then defended his view, the novelty of which had made it seem automatically far-fetched to the man who had kindly sought to set him straight.

Jesus. And Jesus answered them, "The hour has come for the Son of man to be glorified."

Come again? How is that a response? Call me crazy, but I would bet we have here traces of the original version of the story told in Eusebius (*Ecclesiastical History* 1.13.5 and 22.) according to which King Abgarus of Edessa, ill and hoping Jesus might cure him, sent emissaries to invite Jesus to take refuge from his persecutors by fleeing to Edessa, where he should be given a hearty welcome. Jesus, Eusebius said, sent a letter in reply to the effect that he could not accept the king's kind invitation because he had to press on to the cross to atone for mankind's sins. But after that he would dispatch a disciple to heal the ailing king. I believe the proto-Johannine version was pretty much the same, adding that some of Jesus' critics heard the exchange and wondered if Jesus would take the "Greeks" up on their offer and flee to safety. Jesus' otherwise abrupt reply makes sense if these "Greeks" had made Abgarus' offer and Jesus declined it in favor of his saving destiny.

Verses 37-39 are surely one of the high points of this gospel.

On the last day of the feast, the great day, Jesus stood up and proclaimed, "If any one thirst, let him come to me and drink. He who believes in me, as the scripture has said, 'Out of his heart shall flow rivers of living water.'" Now this he said about the Spirit, which those who believed in him were to receive; for as yet the Spirit had not been given, because Jesus was not yet glorified.[621]

Or perhaps we should translate, as we legitimately could, "If anyone thirst, let him come to me; and let him drink, who believes in me," followed by the narrator's comment, "As the scripture has said, 'Out of

---

[621]Compare this from the Odes of Solomon 11:6-8:
> Speaking water came to my lips
> abundantly from the spring of the Lord.
> I drank and became drunk
> from the spring of immortality;
> Yet my drunkenness was not that of ignorance,
> but I departed from vanity.

Quoted in Bultmann, *Gospel of John*, p. 185.

his heart shall flow rivers of living water.'" In either case, it isn't clear what scripture is being referred to.

The next sentence really should be translated, "This he said about the Spirit which those who believed in him should receive. For the Spirit was not yet, because Jesus was not yet glorified" (verse 39). It doesn't actually say "was not *given;*" that is a harmonizing gloss added by translators. Here is another one of those Luke-John parallels. Acts 19:2 has Paul ask a monastic community if they have received the Holy Spirit (because, like Pentecostals, they'd know it if they had), and they respond with puzzlement: "We have never even heard that there *is* a Holy Spirit!" *Not,* mind you, that the Holy Spirit *has been given.* That's more harmonization. One wonders if biblical authors writing such things could have had anything like Trinitarianism in mind.

The Word Is Mightier Than the Sword (7:45-52)

The Sanhedrin has had enough. They send a party of soldiers to arrest Jesus, but they come back empty-handed. Their masters demand to know why. It seems the soldiers were so entranced by Jesus' words that they just couldn't bring themselves to arrest him! The priests and Pharisees are, needless to say, not pleased. The scene reminds me of that in Acts 5:21-26 where the guards assigned to bring the apostles out of their cells to face the Sanhedrin come back empty-handed because an angel has sprung the Twelve in the wee hours. I think also of Matthew 28:11-15, when the guards posted at Jesus' tomb sheepishly report to the Sanhedrin that the body is gone. Are these different oral tradition variants of the same original story (whatever that may have been)?

The irritated Pharisees are disgusted and indignant at the stupid populace, willing to be taken in by this small-town charlatan: "This crowd, who are ignorant of the law, are accursed!" (John 7:49). This awful sentence forever stands as a conscience and a condemnation of self-important academics who believe their education makes them better than the common people.

That Adulterating Pericope (7:53-8:11)

The famous story of the woman taken in adultery did not originally belong to this or any other canonical gospel.[622] It is missing from the earliest manuscripts, and it pops up in various places, in late copies of Luke, right after 21:38, and just after John 7:36 or 21:24. And it is easy to see why some scribes felt it was just too good to let it vanish into the stream of oral tradition. Good thing they did, so that now it finds shelter in the deutero-canonical umbra of marginal notes.

So what is it about? The woman has been caught in the act. Presumably her husband is a member of the mob. They want to know whether Jesus agrees with the Torah regulation that she (and her partner in crime, who is conspicuously absent from this scene!) should be stoned to death. Uh, why *wouldn't* he? Or why would people *think* he might not? Their challenge functions as a set-up for Jesus' pronouncement, and that narrative motivation is much more plausible than any imaginable motive in real life. It is possible that the story began as a "hypothetical" in early Christian legal debates. "What would Jesus do?"

Is Jesus pictured as denying that any human being has the right to condemn another, since there really is no standpoint of moral superiority? "No one is good but God alone" (Mark 10:18). "Judge not that you be not judged" (Matt. 7:1). That is the logic, I think, but don't count Jesus as an anarchist yet! Since his reply does not actually condemn the capital punishment commandment as barbaric or excessive, the point would seem to be that your knowledge of your own sins should make you reconsider *pressing charges*. When Joseph believes his pregnant fiancé has cheated on him, he decides to spare her the public disgrace (and possible execution!) by quietly breaking the engagement and cutting his losses (Matt. 1:19). Jesus does not deny one has the right to invoke the *lex talionis*; it would just be the higher road to turn the other cheek (Matt. 5:38-39).

The Illuminating Man (8:12-30)

The chapter opens with a powerful initial declaration by Jesus of himself as a shining beacon, and in terms redolent of the Baptist/Mandaean background from which this gospel emerged:

---

[622] "As per George T. Zervos, this story was originally about Jesus' mother's reputation of adultery. I believe William Petersen shows good evidence that this pericope is original, but was early on deleted out of prudishness and shock on the part of church leaders" (Samuel Zinner, e-mail to the present author, July 21, 2016).

Whoever is enlightened and instructed by me
rises and beholds the place of life.
Whoever is not enlightened and instructed by me
is cut off (from the light), and falls into the great ocean of Suf.

(John-Book 214:1)[623]

But then the chapter declines into another turgid exchange between Jesus and his critics. By whose authority does he speak? How many references ("witnesses") can he provide on his own behalf? If he lists himself as one of them, does it count? Why are his critics so thickheaded? Isn't it because they are, to use H.P. Lovecraft's[624] term, "self-blinded earth-gazers"? *Yada yada yada.* Wake me when it's over! Doesn't this kind of argument miss the point of Jesus' declaration being a *revelation*? If you can, and if you have to, "authorize" it by invoking established authorities, it can't be much of a revelation, can it? Nothing new. Checking the scriptures (John 5:39; 7:52) is merely to make sure the so-called revelation falls within the safe parameters of familiar orthodoxy. What happened to simply hearing the voice of the Good Shepherd and responding to it?[625]

Limited Time Offer (8:21-30)

Jesus keeps hectoring his opponents, hurling threats of damnation unless they capitulate to his demand to believe in him. But there is a surprising note. Jesus tells them they're going to be sorry they didn't get on board while they had the chance, because one day soon, the welcome mat will be withdrawn, and they will realize their error too late. "I go away, and you will seek me and die in your sins; where I am going, you cannot come" (John 8:21). "When you have lifted up the Son of man, then you will know that I am he" (8:28a). This amounts to vindictive

---

[623] In Foerster, *Gnosis*, p. 233.

[624] H.P. Lovecraft, letter to Frank Belknap Long of Feb. 27, 1931, in H.P. Lovecraft, *Selected Letters* Vol. III, (Sauk City: Arkham House, 1971), p. 295. My thanks to S.T. Joshi for tracking down this quote for me.

[625] Bultmann, *Gospel of John*, pp. 263-264.

taunting. Doesn't it imply that Jesus thinks they will eventually realize that he is the savior and even seek to be included in his flock? And that they will hear the loving Father and the gentle Savior reply in unison, "Tough luck, bastards! You should have believed when you had the chance!" Hmmm, come to think of it, isn't that precisely the scenario made explicit in Matthew 25:10-12 and Luke 13:23-28? It is what Freud called a "childish revenge-fantasy."[626] Can a religious doctrine predicated on emotional immaturity be accepted as divine truth? And, besides, why would God be restricted by a deadline? As I read it, 2 Peter 3:8-9 says he isn't.

Honest Abe and the Father of Satan (8:31-59)

There are some pretty strange things in the rest of the chapter. For one thing, Jesus is supposed to be talking with a group of fellow Jews who had "believed in him," yet what he says must qualify as the single most vituperative rant in this gospel. You wish you could understand the dialogue as a Johannine polemic against some unnamed faction of late first, early second-century Christians, as Brown suggests,[627] but the language seems to me to go way beyond that. If the opponents were this awful, would John even have said they "believed in" Jesus? Some mix up?

But Brown may be right after all. Suppose John is addressing a group of Jewish Christians who insist on the need for keeping the Torah. If they do not, they fear, they will lose their primacy as Abraham's heirs. Galatians 3:10-18 rejects such a position, insisting that all Christ-believing Gentiles are Abraham's children, too. Galatians 3:23-29; 4:1-11 warns that those who embrace the Torah's commandments are renouncing mature sonship and submitting to slavery, and this might be the point of John's Jesus telling these "Jews who believed in him" that they are slaves, not sons. But sons of the devil? Galatians comes within range of that one when it says legalist Jewish-Christians were, from birth, enslaved to the "elemental spirits" (Gal. 4:9) whom he seems to equate with the demonic Principalities and Powers.[628]

---

[626] Sigmund Freud, *Psychopathology of Everyday Life*. Trans. A.A. Brill (New York: Macmillan, 1914), p. 77.

[627] Brown, *Community of the Beloved Disciple*, pp. 76-78.

[628] Dodd, *Historical Tradition*, pp. 379-380.

The great line, "The truth shall make you free," is a Stoic maxim,[629] not a Jesus original, though it's hard to see why that should matter. The response to Jesus' remark makes superficial sense, but would Jews in Roman Palestine really claim they had "never been in bondage to anyone"? This shows a historical amnesia on a par with American high school students who can't tell you what century the Civil War happened.

In 8:37 Jesus grants that these Jews are descended from Abraham, but in verse 39 he denies it, apparently intending something like Romans 2:28, "He is not a Jew who is one outwardly"[630] or Luke 3:8, "Bear fruits that befit repentance, and do not begin to say to yourselves, 'We have Abraham as our father'; for I tell you, God is able from these stones to raise up children to Abraham." But then he launches into this wild spiel, reminiscent of Sethian Gnosticism: these Jews are not really descended from Abraham, but from the devil, as evidenced by their essential, genetic inability to agree to true statements even when they recognize them as such. As Satan's spawn, they can produce only lies and murder, since that's all, like Their Father Below, they have to offer.

We usually take verse 44 as meaning "You are of your father, the devil," which is bad enough, but Bultmann[631] insists that "your father the devil" is grammatically impossible in the original Greek, and that it has to be rendered "You are of the father of the devil"![632] This was a common Gnostic mytheme[633] appearing, for example, in the Acts of Thomas 32. Islamic mythology tells of Khabis, the father of Iblis (an Arabized form of the Greek *diabolos*, "devil.")[634]

What are we to make of John 8:51 ("If anyone keeps my word, he will never see death")? It is tempting to write it off as another "spiritual"

---

[629] Dodd, *Historical Tradition*, p. 380.

[630]In fact one wonders if John is not actually borrowing from Romans here. Compare John 8:34 with Romans 6:20.

[631]Bultmann, *Gospel of John*, p. 318. In the dualistic heresies of Eastern Europe, the father of the devil is God himself. Mircea Eliade, *The Two and the One.* Trans. J.M. Cohen. Harper Torchbooks (New York: Harper & Row, 1965), pp. 82-88.

[632] "The reference is to Cain, that is Cain is the devil; Cain is the murderer from the beginning ['Genesis']; who is Cain's father? The serpent!" (Samuel Zinner, e-mail to tis author, July 21, 2016).

[633]Bultmann, *Gospel of John*, p. 318, note 2.

[634] See the fascinating use of the "Father of Satan" idea in John Carpenter's 1987 film, *Prince of Darkness.*

statement by Jesus/John but grossly misunderstood by Jesus' bone-headed opponents (cf., John 6:52: "How can this man give us his flesh to eat?"). But he will say *that* in 11:25-26; *this* sounds different. "Will never see death"? This is more naturally understood (outrageous as it sounds) in either an apocalyptic or a Gnostic framework. In the first case, the point would be along the lines of Mark 9:1, "There are some standing here who will not taste death before they see the kingdom of God come with power." This, of course, was a belief current in the evangelist's (or the redactor's) own day, as witness John 21:23a, "The saying spread abroad among the brethren that this disciple was not to die." Again, think of the slightly over-optimistic Jehovah's Witnesses bumper sticker, "Millions now living will never die."

Irenaeus informs us that the Gnostic teacher Menander taught that his initiates would not die, a belief still held by radical New Thought teachers today: immortality in the flesh. (Needless to say, their track record is not so good.) I have long wondered if, whatever early Christian tradition this saying came from, that is after all what the original intent was. When you think of it, this claim is hardly less likely to be true than that in John 15:16, 24-25; Mark 11:24. Since Menander was a disciple of Simon Magus, might that be why Jesus' opponents say Jesus is a Samaritan in verse 48?

This saying is quoted back at Jesus by his opponents in John 8:52, but with a slight difference: "If anyone keeps my word, he will never *taste* death." Isn't that interesting? A Jesus saying is already being altered in the process of oral transmission, and that after only a few seconds! And the Bible, not Bultmann, tells us so!

Jesus says he is as high on the Great Chain of Being as his opponents are low. In verse 42, we hear the words of a dubiously human divine hypostasis: "I proceeded and came forth from God." In my *Pre-Nicene New Testament*, I render the sentence as "I came forth from the Godhead and have appeared." These are the accents of one of the Aions of the Pleroma of Light. Verse 58 is another in the same vein, even though it is conventionally mistranslated as an allusion to the Exodus story of the Burning Bush, "Before Abraham was, I am." But, as Jason BeDuhn has shown, the Greek must be translated "I have been since before Abraham came to be."[635] Don't get me wrong: Jesus' words certainly amount to a claim of otherworldly pre-existence (cf., John

---

[635] Jason David BeDuhn, *Truth in Translation: Accuracy and Bias in English Translations of the New Testament* (New York: University Press of America, 2003), Chapter Ten, "Tampering with Tenses," pp. 103-112.

17:24). This is not an inspired carpenter from Nazareth; this is an entity who remembers igniting the stars.

> I am the Jokabar-Kusta
> who went out from the house of my father and came hither.
> I came with concealed glory
> and with light without end.
> (Ginza 318:29 ff.)[636]

Blind Man's Bluff (Chapter 9)

Mark did not hesitate to show Jesus employing healing techniques that led some to call him a magician (Mark 7:32-37; 8:22-26; 3:22). Matthew and Luke omitted both of these magical healings, but, surprisingly, John tells an equivalent tale of Jesus healing a congenitally blind man in chapter 9. He spits on a smear of dirt and applies the mix to the sightless eyes, commanding the fellow to go wash it off in the Pool of Siloam, which John reminds us means "sent." And this is why he includes the story. Though John's Jesus, of all the gospel versions, is the one least likely to have to use gimmicks, methods, or means of any kind, our evangelist finds the story worthwhile because of the allegorical potential (surprisingly undeveloped here) of the "sending" element, a recurrent theme throughout the gospel.

Obviously, the point of the story is the play between spiritual and physical blindness, but another topic of (perhaps unintended) interest is *reincarnation*. Does the question of the disciples imply that they believed in it? "Rabbi, who sinned, this man or his parents, that he was born blind?" (verse 2). I think it does. What else could it mean? Consider a striking modern parallel.

> In Jaipur I met in December 1892 an old Pandit, almost naked, who approached me groping his way. They told me that he was completely blind. Not knowing that he had been blind from birth, I sympathized with him, and asked by what unfortunate accident the loss of sight had come upon him. Immediately and without showing any sign whatever of bitterness, the answer was ready to his lips:-*kenac'idaparadhenapurvasminjanmanikritena*, "by some crime committed in a former birth."[637]

---

[636]Quoted in Bultmann, *Gospel of John*, p. 68, note 1.

The only alternative suggestion I have ever heard seems pretty remote to me: A rabbinical commentary on the Song of Solomon somehow raises the question of whether a fetus whose mother eats some nonkosher food incurs his mom's ritual impurity. If so, there you are: a sinful fetus! Could the disciples have had something like this in mind? (Plus, can you imagine even the most stringent legalist thinking God would blind the baby for some dietary lapse of his mother? Are pickles and ice cream nonkosher?)

But is it any more plausible that the disciples could have entertained the doctrine of reincarnation? Sure it is. Don't forget the permeation of the Near East by cosmopolitan Hellenism. The very institution of rabbis with circles of disciples, the hermeneutical rules for scripture, Greek translations of scripture, and various syncretistic borrowings, Josephus' descriptions of the Essenes as Pythagoreans and Pharisees as Stoics, Philo's claim that Plato cribbed everything from the Pentateuch—none of this allows us to suppose Judaism was hermetically sealed off from omnipresent Hellenistic influences. And reincarnationism was a Gnostic doctrine and was later on full display in Jewish mysticism. So why not?

Did the Johannine Jesus accept the doctrine? He doesn't say. John might have had Jesus explicitly repudiate both of the alternatives posed by the disciples: sins left over from a previous life as well as the notion that God was punishing the sins of the man's parents by blinding their son. But he doesn't. He simply sweeps these aside. We don't know if either guess might be true in other instances, but he happens to know that they do not apply to the case at hand. Then why? God had let the poor bastard grope along blindly for decades so he could star in an object lesson today. Well, he *was* rewarded with considerably more than fifteen minutes of fame.

Apparently the Pharisees shared the views of the disciples. They tell the former blind man, "You were born in utter sin!" (verse 34).

And, as noted earlier, there is a major anachronism here in that the synagogue ban on Christians, predicted as a future event relative to Jesus (John 16:2), is depicted here as already having been decreed (9:22). The evangelist's narrative bounces back and forth between his own time and the ostensible time of Jesus, something he scarcely tries to hide (John 16:12-15).

---

[631] Paul Deussen, *The Philosophy of the Upanishads*. Trans. A.S. Geden (Edinburgh: T&T Clark, 1906), p. 313.

A Christig with a Crook (Chapter 10)[638]

Jesus proclaims himself the Good Shepherd, i.e., as opposed to a mere hired hand who has no real commitment to the flock of which he has been put in charge. Jesus, by contrast, is like David who, as a shepherd boy, did not fear to risk his life driving away fierce predators (1 Sam. 17:34-35). The hired hand runs for the hills at the first lion's or wolf's growl he thinks he hears. Think of the Synoptic parables of servants placed in charge of running the estate in their master's absence (Mark 13:34-37; Matt. 25:14-30). John's Jesus compares himself to the faithful servant in charge of the flock. And in doing so, he leagues himself with the Mandaean Revealers.[639]

> I am a shepherd, who loves his sheep. (John-Book 42:27 ff.)[640]

> No wolf jumps near our fold, and they need have no fear of the fierce lion... No thief penetrates into the fold, and they need not worry about an iron knife. (John-Book 45:11 ff.) [641]

> And understand my knowledge,
> Ye who know me in truth;
> Love me with affection,

---

[638] Once when I was serving as a Eucharistic minister on Easter Sunday at Saint Stephen's Episcopal Church in Goldsboro, North Carolina, I had the pleasure of standing next to Bishop Sidney Sanders as we waited to process down the nave. I asked him if he carried his shepherd's crook to use as a Vaudeville hook in case the priest's sermon was going on too long. But he wouldn't admit it.

[639] C.H. Dodd, *Interpretation of the Fourth Gospel*, p. 130, rejects Bultmann's understanding of Mandaeanism as a major influence on John's gospel, suggesting that the influence is in the opposite direction. Of course he could be right, but I have sided with Bultmann. The Mandaean texts use the shared language and imagery in a way that seems original and natural in its context. The same could be said for John's use of the same language and images, but in view of the clear tendency of John's gospel to distance itself from Baptist rivals, it seems to me Bultmann's theory of a Baptist Gnostic switching over to Jesus-Gnosticism and bringing his favorite elements with him, makes the most sense of the evidence.

[640] Quoted in Bultmann, *Gospel of John*, p. 368.

[641] Quoted in Bultmann, *Gospel of John*, p. 368.

Ye who love.
For I do not turn away my face
From them that are mine.
For I know them.
(Odes of Solomon 8:12 ff)[642]

I carry the sheep thence, and give them water to drink out of my cupped hand... I bring them to the good fold, and they graze near me. (John-Book 45:3 ff.) [643]

My little sheep! My little sheep, come! Follow my call! ... Everyone who has heard my call and taken heed of my voice and turned his gaze on me I will seize with both hands.... Everyone who did not hear my call sank. (John-Book 48:1 ff.) [644]

Have confidence in Manda d'Haiye. Like a good shepherd who keeps watch, he will keep far from you all spirit of apostasy. Like a good shepherd who leads his sheep to their fold, he will set you down and plant you down before him. (John-Book 42:19 ff.)[645]

There are significant theological hints here and there in the chapter. Verse 16 ("other sheep not of this fold," etc.), in a somewhat contrived fashion, anticipates the Gentile Mission, even as John 4:35-38 looks forward to the Samaritan Mission.

John 10:18 is the only place in the canonical New Testament where Jesus is said to raise *himself* from the dead. Elsewhere he is depicted as purely passive.

Verse 26 seems to imply predestination: those hostile to Jesus, to whom his message sounds like the ravings of a demoniac, not merely *do* not hear him but *cannot* hear him. And why? Because they are not members of his flock. You might expect it to be the other way around.

John 10:30 is one of the clearest declarations in the gospel, hell, even in the New Testament, of the Godhood of Jesus: "I and the Father are one!"[646] No wonder Jesus' hearers go into theological shock!

---

[642]J. Rendel Harris, *The Odes and Psalms of Solomon* (London: Cambridge University Press, 1911), p. 101.

[643]Quoted in Bultmann, *Gospel of John*, pp. 368.

[644]Quoted in Bultmann, *Gospel of John*, pp. 368.

[645]Quoted in Bultmann, *Gospel of John*, pp. 367-368.

Nothing cagey about this! No mere implications, as in Mark 2:7, "Hey, *wait* a minute! Who can forgive sins but God alone? This guy's a friggin' *blas*phemer!"

Nor was it only monotheistic Jews who thought so; in the second century there were Christian schools of thought, variously called Sebellians[647] and Patripassians,[648] who directly equated Jesus and the Father. Bart Ehrman[649] has demonstrated how such early Christological disputes led to scribal alterations of the New Testament text in order to yank the rug out from under "heretics" by sabotaging their trump-card proof-texts. I think verses 33-38 provide us a clear example. These verses seem to contradict the bold claims to Godhood Jesus made in verse 30. In verses 33-38, Jesus' critics again accuse him of blasphemy: "You, being a man, make yourself God!" The logic of Jesus' reply would seem to be this: scripture itself uses such language of common Israelites to whom scripture was first given. So Jesus should be allowed to use it of himself, right? But he doesn't! He says only that he is God's *son*. So what's the big deal? Why would John/Jesus, having made such a powerful declaration, try to wriggle out of it in this manner, like some craven politician trying to "walk back" a statement that has gotten him into trouble? He wouldn't have. The conniving squeamishness on

---

[646] "There's a lot going on here as far as rabbinic parallels are concerned; 10:27, 'hear my voice' + 10:30, 'are one,' this is an allusion to the Shema', 'Hear, O Israel the Lord God, the Lord is one,' which Jewish mysticism interprets as implying three modalities of God which are nevertheless one, given three divine names in the Shema''s opening line. Jewish rabbinic tradition forms the word 'ed, 'witness' from the *ayin* of Hear and the *dalet* of One in the Shema', and this explains John 10:25's trope of 'bear witness.' Verse 34 then refers to the *matantorah* where the Hebrews became gods according to rabbinic sources. Verse 38, 'the Father is in me and I am in the Father' is also alluding to the two tetragrammatons, the two Lords of the Shema'—we have the two Powers doctrine, a doctrine of Rabbi Akiva who proclaimed Bar Kokhba the messiah. John 5:43 probably alludes to Bar Kokhba, whom the Jewish Christians accepted, 'if another comes in his own name, him you will receive'" (Samuel Zinner, e-mail to this author, July 21, 2016).

[647]Named for Sabellius, one of those who taught this doctrine.

[648]So called because their theology seemed to imply that the *Father* himself *suffered* on the cross.

[649]Ehrman, *Orthodox Corruption of Scripture*, p. 263, estimates that controversies over Patripassianism were not a major occasion for text-tampering, but he does give a couple of instances. Please note that he is trying to explain extant variant manuscript readings, while I am speculating on possible textual funny business at a stage pre-dating our earliest manuscripts.

display here is that of theologically timid Christian copyists[650] eager to do an end run around the pesky Patripassians.

The Mummy Returns (Chapter 11)

The resurrection of Lazarus occurs only in John's gospel. It is by far the most spectacular of the gospel resurrections, and its absence from the Synoptics suggests it is fiction, as if the narrated events did not already make that obvious. Where did it come from? Critics point to a pair of likely sources, whether we prefer to consider them as complementary or as alternatives. But it is hard to deny that they both are involved in some way. The first is Luke's story of Lazarus and the Rich Man (Luke 16:19-31). Note the similarities, as if you hadn't already. In both a man named Lazarus dies, though in Luke he is a destitute beggar hoping in vain for help from the Rich Man, while in John, Lazarus implicitly *is* the rich man. In Luke, the Rich Man, now in hell, pleads for Lazarus to be sent back to this world to turn the Rich Man's brothers from their evil ways. In John the sisters hint that they want Jesus to restore Lazarus from the dead. In Luke the request is refused because a Jacob Marley-like visitation from Lazarus would not be enough to dissuade sinners from their accustomed course. In John Lazarus does return, and, while some are convinced to believe in Jesus, the miracle only hardens the resolve of his enemies to kill him. The parallels are not complete, but even the differences tend to confirm the larger parallel since they make sense as intentional alterations.

Second, the Lazarus story resembles the myth of the resurrection of Osiris to a degree that makes apologists squirm. I cannot improve on Randel Helms's summary of the striking parallels.

> In the Egyptian myth, Osiris, who dies, has two sisters, Isis and Nephthys. Osiris lies dead at Annu, the Egyptian necropolis, known in Greek as Heliopolis and in the Old Testament as Beth-shemesh (Jer. 43:13) –"City of the Sun" and "House of the Sun" respectively. This necropolis had a variety of formulaic names in Egypt: "the mansion of the Prince in On," "the House of the Aged Prince who dwelleth in An," the "great house of Anu." Just as Heliopolis was readily semitized as Beth-shemesh, the House of Anu is readily semitized as Beth-anu. Likewise

---

[650] See Bultmann, *Gospel of John*, p. 389, for a similar view.

"Lazarus" (the Greek form of the Hebrew name "Eleazer") readily associates itself with the name of the god Osiris (semitized as El-Osiris)...

According to Wallis-Budge, the "body of the Aged One, a name of Osiris, reposed in Annu." Lazarus lies in his tomb at Bethany. The dead one is bewailed by his sisters. According to Utterance 670 of the Pyramid texts, "they come to Osiris the king at the sound of the weeping of Isis, at the cry of Nephthys, at the wailing of these two spirits." At Bethany, Jesus saw "Mary weeping and the Jews her companions weeping" (John 11:33). Of the dead god in Annu it is said: "O Osiris the King, you have gone, but you will return; you have slept, [but you will awake]; you have died, but you will live" (Utterance 670). On learning of the death of Lazarus, Jesus says, "Our friend Lazarus has fallen asleep, but I shall go and wake him" (John 11:11). Jesus approaches the tomb and says "Take away the stone" (John 11:39). To Osiris it is said, "The tomb is opened for you, the doors of the tomb-chamber are thrown open for you" (Utterance 665A). Objecting to Jesus' demand, Martha says, "Sir, by now there will be a stench; he has been there four days" (John 11:39). After Osiris is resurrected, we are told in Utterance 670, "Osiris speaks to Horus, for he has removed the evil [which was on the King] on his fourth day." Moreover, according to Utterance 412, Osiris is told, as he lies dead in the House of Annu, "O flesh of the king, do not decay, do not rot, do not smell unpleasant." The dead one in Annu/Bethany is then told to arise: "I am Horus, O Osiris the King, I will not let you suffer. Go forth, wake up" (Utterance 620); "Then he raised his voice in a great cry: 'Lazarus, come forth'" (John 11:43). The wrappings of the dead must be removed: "O King, live for you are not dead. Horus must come to you that he may cut your cords and throw off your bonds; Horus has removed your hindrance" (Utterance 703); "The dead man came out, his head and feet swathed in linen bands, his face wrapped in a cloth. Jesus said, 'Loose him; let him go'" (John 11:44).[651]

But I would like to float a third possibility, namely that John has hybridized the Lukan Lazarus story with another Synoptic story he does not otherwise reproduce. It was the story of an exorcism, the *big*

[651]Helms, *Gospel Fictions*, pp. 98-99.

exorcism, but John does not like exorcisms; there are none in his gospel. You may wind up thinking I am a Samaritan and have a demon, but here goes.

Lazarus is the Gadarene Demoniac. It's perfectly simple, really. The Demoniac dwells amid the tombs; Lazarus is in a tomb. The Demoniac has been bound in fetters but always escapes them, while Lazarus is bound in linen wrappings but is released from them. Jesus commands the Legion of demons to "come out" of the man, while Jesus commands Lazarus to "come out" of the tomb. And, as for the name Lazarus, again, John borrowed it from Luke. What do you think?

Dare I say it? Nikos Kazantzakis's version[652] of this story is even better than John's.

> "Bring him back from Hades, Rabbi! Call him and he'll come!"
>
> Jesus took them both by the hand and lifted them up. "Let us go," he said. We all ran behind them until we came to the grave. There Jesus stopped. All the blood went to his head, his eyes rolled and disappeared, only the whites remained. He brought forth such a bellow you'd have thought there was a bull inside him, and we all got scared. Then suddenly while he stood there, trembling all over, he uttered a wild cry, a strange cry, something from another world. The archangels must shout in the same way when they're angry. ... "Lazarus," he cried, "come out!" And all at once we hear the earth in the tomb stir and crack. The tombstone begins to move; someone is gradually pushing it up. Fear and trembling... Never in my life have I feared death as much as I feared that resurrection. I swear that if I was asked what I wanted to see more, a lion or a resurrection, I would say a lion. [...]
>
> The women shrieked, many of the men hid themselves behind rocks, and we who remained trembled. The tombstone rose little by little. We saw two yellow arms and then a head all green, cracked and full of dirt; finally the skeleton like body wrapped in the shroud. It put forward one foot, then the other, and came out. It was Lazarus.

---

[652] Nikos Kazantzakis, *The Last Temptation of Christ.* Trans. P.A. Bien (New York: Bantam Books, 1961), p. 362.

In the film version,[653] Jesus crouches down in front of the tomb to help Lazarus climb out, and the first we see of him is his arms, as he grabs Jesus and attempts to pull him in! A great foreshadowing of Jesus' own eventual destiny.

Okay, now back to theology. John's story of Lazarus is the great object lesson of realized eschatology. The "fact" that Lazarus need not wait for the apocalyptic End of the age to rise is a way of saying that the *real* resurrection, spiritual rebirth, is something that happens *here and now*.

Jesus' climactic saying (for me, even more climactic than Lazarus' emergence from the tomb), "I am the resurrection and the life" (verse 25), appears in some manuscripts simply as "I am the resurrection," which strikes me as even more powerful.

The raising of Lazarus has a huge impact, convincing many to sign up with Jesus. The Sanhedrin begins to panic, fearing that Jesus' following will gain sufficient numbers to spark some gesture of defiance against Rome, and if that should happen, it would mean the demolition of the Jerusalem Temple and the dissolution of the Jewish nation. Caiaphas the high priest ("for that year," as if the high priestly office was limited to a one-year term)[654] says the problem is genuine but that the solution is no mystery. Kill Jesus, and the problem will solve itself (cf., Acts 5:36-37). Caiaphas, John says, had a prophetic gift as one of the perks of his office and was predicting the future (*ex opera operatum*), that "one man should die for the people, and that the whole nation should not perish" (verse 50). Of course, he is speaking more truly than he knows. An equal irony is that this sacrifice will *not* avert the destruction of the Temple and the exile of the people; indeed, ultimately it will prove the cause of it.

It must be admitted that John's literary acumen fails him when he feels the need to "correct" himself when he fears some reader might get the wrong idea. In verse 42, he has Jesus explain to his Father that he only said a prayer of thankfulness for the benefit of the bystanders. "Not that I had any doubt you'd come through with the miracle, of course! I just wanted to go through with the charade of praying so they wouldn't

---

[653]Screenplay by Paul Schraeder.

[654]Dodd, *Historical Tradition*, p. 94, note 3. The evangelist must have been thinking of the high priests of pagan religions in Syria and Asia Minor, who served a single year, whereas the Jewish high priests remained in office till they died. Bruce, *New Testament Documents*, p. 50, suggests that John knew that but merely meant to refer to that "fateful year." Nice try.

think I was taking it for granted, even though, as I just said, I *was!*" What? God doesn't *know* this already? He needs to be *told?* Of course, the "bystanders" in question are the readers, *us.* Pretty clumsy, huh?

Smear Campaign (12:1-8)

John's anointing scene has much in common with other anointing scenes (and still other scenes, as we will shortly see) in the gospels, but it is by no means simply the same event as described by a different witness. Strauss[655] laid out a striking pattern of inter-gospel borrowing to explain the similarities and differences between all these texts.

We begin with Mark's anointing story (14:3-9) set in Bethany. In it an unnamed woman anoints the head of Jesus and receives criticism for it from some unspecified bystanders. Jesus defends her. Matthew 26:6-13 just repeats Mark's story, narrowing down the identity of the nay-sayers as "the disciples."

Unrelated to this episode is another preserved in two sources: the interpolated story of the woman caught in adultery (at John 7:53-8:11) and what seems to be a slightly different version in the Gospel according to the Hebrews in which the accused woman is said to be guilty of "many sins." The woman is dragged before Jesus and dumped at his feet by a group of scribes and Pharisees, who denounce her, but Jesus defends her and tells her to go free.

These two stories have been combined, either redactionally or inadvertently in oral transmission. The result is the story in Luke 7:36-50, in which a sinful woman anoints, not the head, but the feet of Jesus (instead of simply being dropped at his feet as before). A Pharisee condemns her, and Jesus defends her, finally telling her, too, to go free.

There is another Lukan story (10:38-42), also featuring a woman at Jesus' feet. She is Mary who sits listening to Jesus' discourse. This might seem innocent enough, but her sister Martha criticizes her for leaving her to get dinner ready all by herself. Jesus defends Mary.

---

[655] David Friedrich Strauss, *The Life of Jesus Critically Examined.* Trans. George Eliot (May Ann Evans). Lives of Jesus Series (Philadelphia: Fortress Press, 1972), pp. 410-412. C.H. Dodd suggests a slightly different view of the matter: "I suggest that this kind of cross-combination is more easily carried out in the course of oral transmission than in composition from literary sources." (*Historical Tradition*, p. 170; cf., pp. 172-173.

John's anointing scene combines features of all these stories. Jesus is again a guest at a dinner in the home of Mary and Martha (plus Lazarus, borrowed from Luke 16:20). Mary is the central actor again, but she is not merely listening at Jesus' feet; this time she is anointing Jesus' feet and wiping them with her hair, like her counterpart in Luke 7, and she, too, receives criticism, this time from Judas Iscariot (one of "the disciples" in Matthew). She is not criticized for previous sinfulness, as the sinner of Luke 7 and the adulteress in John 8:4 are, but rather for the extravagant waste of ointment, as in Mark and Matthew.

Hey! Remember That Time Jesus Rode That Donkey? (12:9-19)

We are quite familiar with the Triumphal Entry from the Synoptics. The major distinctive aspect in John's version is the frank admission that no one on the scene thought he was witnessing a prophesied messianic entry, not the crowds, not even the disciples! "His disciples did not understand this at first; but when Jesus was glorified, *then* they remembered that this had been written of him and had been done to him" (John 12:16). So why were Jesus' fans acclaiming him the "king of Israel" (verse 13)? This is especially odd since the phrase "even the King of Israel" reads like a parenthetical explanatory phrase for the benefit of the reader. Did our evangelist think those present at the time *did* or did *not* believe they were seeing God's long-awaited Messiah? He says not, but he goes out of his way to make it clear he intends the crowd to be acclaiming Jesus king. It may be a candid admission that he has rewritten the scene in retrospect and no doubt does so elsewhere.

No Second Thoughts (12:27-29)

Here is a John-versus-Synoptics contradiction so sharp that we must conclude John does not like what he read, specifically in Luke 22:42-44:

> "Father, if thou art willing, remove this cup from me; nevertheless not my will, but thine, be done." And there appeared to him an angel from heaven, strengthening him. And being in an agony he prayed more earnestly; and his sweat became like great drops of blood falling down upon the ground.

Many pious readers have long been troubled over the Synoptic Gethsemane scene, as it strikes them as unseemly for a Jesus whom they imagine as unflappably Stoic even in the face of crucifixion. John apparently felt the same way, so he omitted and obliquely criticized the scene. Jesus is not in Gethsemane when he says the following, but it's pretty obvious what John has in mind.

> "Now is my soul troubled. And what shall I say? 'Father, save me from this hour'? No, for this purpose I have come to this hour. Father, glorify thy name." Then a voice came from heaven, "I have glorified it, and I will glorify it again." The crowd standing by heard it and said that it had thundered. Others said, "An angel has spoken to him."

Jesus raises the question, "I am distressed, but do you think I would try to evade the destiny that lies before me, as Luke says I did? God forbid!" We know John had Luke's version in mind because he also ridicules the notion of an angel appearing to Jesus, a la Luke, with some encouraging words. "If you think an angel spoke to him, you're as sadly mistaken as the fools in the crowd!"[656] Not all manuscripts of Luke contain the verses about the angel and the bloody sweat, but John was reading one that did.

We have already seen how the request of certain Greeks for an audience with Jesus might originally have been part of a story parallel to that told by Eusebius of the emissaries of King Abgarus. I believe that this indignant repudiation of the very idea of escaping the cross is the natural continuation of that story, just as Jesus thanks Abgarus' messengers but says he is determined to go through with the crucifixion. This would seem the solution to a long-standing exegetical puzzle.

Splinters of Glory (12:23-24, 32-34; cf., 3:14-15)

---

[656] Notice how easy even John thought it was for bystanders to hear something said to or by Jesus (John 21:23) and get it wrong? So much for the value of eyewitness testimony (as if we had any). "I think it was 'Blessed are the cheese makers.'" (Graham Chapman, John Cleese, Terry Gilliam, Eric Idle, Terry Jones, and Michael Palin, *Monty Python's The Life of Brian (of Nazareth)* [New York: Ace Books, 1979], p. 14).

Strange as it might seem, Artemidorus' *Oneirocritica*, an ancient dictionary of dream symbolism, tells us that dreaming of one's own crucifixion signified that one should soon experience great success![657] The basis of the signification was that "lifted up" could mean either physical elevation on the cross or social elevation. I don't think Freud would find fault with this interpretation. Often the subconscious taps the conscious mind on the shoulder with dream puns like this. The very same association underlies the usage of John's gospel whereby Jesus' being "lifted up from the earth" denotes both his physical elevation on the cross and his victorious return to heavenly glory.

The Acts of John recounts how, during the crucifixion, John fled to a cave in the nearby Mount of Olives, where the spiritual Christ, the *real* Christ, an apparition of incandescent light, informed him that the fools at Golgotha only *thought* he was being crucified and in the years to come would perpetuate that error, though in fact he was neither suffering nor dying.

> You hear that I suffered, yet I did not suffer; that I did not suffer, yet I did suffer; that I was pierced, yet I was not struck; hanged, yet I was not hanged; that blood issued from me, and it did not issue forth. In sum, what they say about me did not happen to me, but what they do not say, that I did suffer! (101)[658]

This notion also occurs in the Koran, Surah 4:156-158.

> They denied the truth and uttered a monstrous falsehood against Mary. They declared: "We have put to death the Messiah Jesus the Son of Mary, the apostle of Allah." They did not kill him, nor did they crucify him, but he was made to resemble another for them. Those that disagreed about him were in doubt concerning his death, for what they knew about

---

[657] Dodd, *Interpretation of the Fourth Gospel*, pp. 377-378; Justin J. Meggitt, "Artemidorus and the Johannine Crucifixion" *Journal of Higher Criticism* 5/2 (Fall 1998), pp. 203-208.

[658] Price, *Pre-Nicene New Testament*, pp. 728-729. "As I explain in my forthcoming Thomas commentary, this whole tradition stems from Wisdom 3:2, 'In the eyes of the foolish they *seemed* to have died, and their departure *was thought to be* an affliction'" (Samuel Zinner, e-mail to this author, July 212, 2016).

it was sheer conjecture; they were not sure that they had slain him. Allah lifted him up to His presence.[659]

It seems an intriguing possibility that the Gospel of John has some such understanding in mind with its talk about Jesus being "lifted up" on (or from?) the cross (or at least the gospel might have before the Ecclesiastical Redactor got his mitts on it).

Zen Master Jesus (12:44-45)

In John 12:44 Jesus announces "He who believes in me believes not in me, but in him who sent me!" This profound theological point reverberates through centuries of Eucharistic theology all the way to Paul Tillich's doctrine of religious symbols: a symbol *is* not the Holy but *participates* in the Holy to which it *points*.[660] A Zen saying provides a perfect parallel. "If a man asks me where the moon is located, and I point my finger up to the starry sky, and the inquirer thinks my hand is the moon, he is no better off than before he asked."[661] Thus Jesus *is* not the Father but *points the way* to the Father (John 14:6).

And yet look what he says in the very next verse! "And he who sees me sees him who sent me!" That saying sure looks like the very opposite of the one that precedes it: the gap is closed; Son and Father are identified, precisely as in John 14:9, "He who has seen me has seen the Father." It looks to me like verse 44 is a scribal "correction" to verse 45 with its Patripassian Christology (see the discussion of John 14:9, below).

Verse 44 strikes me as a perfect little cameo of Reader-Response criticism, which tries to understand a text through a fresh reader's eyes. The impression one receives reading one part of a text remains even when reading further would seem to contradict or undermine that first impression, producing a kind of dialectical loop.

---

[659] *The Koran.* Trans. N.J. Dawood. Penguin Classics (Baltimore: Penguin Books, 1974), p. 382, marginal alternate translation.

[660] Paul Tillich, *Dynamics of Faith.* World Perspectives Series. Harper Torchbooks Cloister Library (New York: Harper & Row, 1958), pp. 41-45; Tillich, "Religious Symbols and our Knowledge of God," in Robert M. Price, ed., *The Ground of Being: Neglected Essays of Paul Tillich* (Selma, NC: Mindvendor Publications, 20115), pp. 298-311.

[661] My memory quote.

> Whereas most traditional holistic interpretations of texts neglect the sequential interpretations and effects upon the reader in favor of the final holistic interpretation, reader-response critics believe that the series of interpretations and effects which lead up to the final synthesis are also important and have value.[662]

The first perception of John 12:44 is "whoever believes in me." Are you going to drop that once you read the next part of the sentence, "believes not in me, but in him who sent me"? Are you supposed to say to yourself, "Yikes! I guess I was going wrong when I thought Jesus was the object of faith! I guess I should worship his Father, period!"[663] No, the two are balanced in tension. The full saying presupposes you are to be in the state of believing in Jesus but at the same time seeing further on, to the Father whom Jesus represents. You can see Patripassianism in the process of morphing into Trinitarianism in the space of this single verse.[664]

All-You-Can-Understand Buffet (chapters 13-14)

As James M. Robinson[665] lucidly explains, a wide range of early Christian literature draws a dividing line between the public teaching of

---

[662] James Resseguie, "Reader-Response Criticism and the Synoptic Gospels" *Journal of the American Academy of Religion* 52 (1984), p. 317, quoted in Stephen D. Moore, *Literary Criticism and the Gospels: The Theoretical Challenge* (New Haven: Yale University Press, 1989), p. 79.

[663] I guess Wolfgang Iser (*The Act of Reading: A Theory of Aesthetic Response* [Baltimore: Johns Hopkins University Press, 1980], e.g., p. 186) would say you should abandon first impressions as you would discard a tentative hypothesis in light of new evidence, but I can't see it that way in this case.

[664] Arthur W. Wainwright, *The Trinity in the New Testament* (London: SPCK, 1969), pp.264-267, understands it is not a question of whether the New Testament, or even just the Gospel of John, "teaches" the Trinity doctrine. Instead we can observe in the texts various first steps toward answering the questions implicit in early Christian adoration of Jesus Christ while trying to remain monotheistic. This is a prime example of what Tillich discusses, the Bible implicitly raising ontological questions, but leaving it to readers to attempt to answer them. See Paul Tillich, *Biblical Religion and the Search for Ultimate Reality.* James W. Richard Lectures in the Christian Religion, University of Virginia, 1951-52 (Chicago: University of Chicago Press, 1955), pp. 82-85.

[665] James M. Robinson, "On the *Gattung* of Mark (and John)," in David G.

Jesus and the advanced course. In light of the latter, the former is said to be figurative, parabolic, usually and inevitably misunderstood. But, as I have suggested earlier, what we really have here is a kind of allegorization of a simpler, self-sufficient earlier teaching, in which parables were told, as they are today, to make things *simpler* to understand.[666] The earlier, public version is said in retrospect to have been the "kid stuff" version propounded by the first of a pair of revealers, the Proclaimer, while the new, deeper stuff, is the needful interpretation by the second revealer, the Foundation. The whole business is just another instance of the age-old process of ventriloquism whereby later teachers pretend to decode the familiar scriptures so as to disclose hitherto "hidden" secrets for the illuminati. The original scriptures, teachings, parables, etc., were obscure in the sense that they "hid" what is now supposed to be their secret teaching. And it is the latter which the allegorizers father onto the older material in order to claim the pedigree of scripture, Jesus, the Buddha, Muhammad, etc., for their own, more sophisticated, abstruse doctrines. We must seriously doubt that the original teachers/writers would have recognized the new teaching as having anything to do with them. An old rabbinical tale[667] has God send Moses to earth to observe (invisibly) a classroom in which students are feverishly debating biblical interpretation. Moses, baffled, goes back up to heaven and demands of an amused Jehovah, "Well, what on earth was *that?*" God wryly replies, "Why, Moses! Don't tell me you don't recognize your own Torah!"

Robinson shows how the dividing line might be moved like a slide rule from its presumably original position at the resurrection either forward or backward in the narrative sequence.[668] In Mark, for example, the parables of chapter 4 are made into duds that do not explode into truth till the illuminati light the fuse with their superior intellect or their doctrinal decoder key. The disciples sheepishly ask Jesus just what the hell he is talking about. He is disappointed: "You have to *ask?*" He takes it for granted that the common fools and dolts, an accursed multitude that knoweth not the law, do not understand his meaning. It's not for them anyway. Then, one must ask, why did he bother with

Buttrick, ed., *Jesus and Man's Hope.* Volume I. A Perspective Book (Pittsburgh: Pittsburgh Theological Seminary, 1970), pp. 108, 112-113.

[666]Archibald M. Hunter, *Interpreting the Parables* (Philadelphia: Westminster Press, 1960), p. 13, 110-112.

[667] Thanks to my beloved mentor Michael S. Kogan for this wonderful tale.

[668]Cf., Dodd, *Interpretation of the Fourth Gospel*, p. 291, note 1.

them? Why not spend his time in private instruction with his inner circle? Obviously because the earlier tradition envisioned Jesus teaching the common people in common terms. Gnostics had to piggyback on this tradition in order to claim Jesus' authority for their speculations, so, rather than present it de novo, they had to go back to the earlier version and do their ventriloquism on it. Right, Jesus?

Acts has Jesus spill the beans during forty days after Easter. But later Gnostic texts like Pistis Sophia and the Apocryphon of James push the line to a still later point, when Jesus, after his ascension to heaven, returns to impart even more esoteric revelations to the disciples. The ascended Jesus became a goose with an endless supply of golden eggs. You might say Catholic and Gnostic types of Christianity divided at the point when Catholics killed that goose because they were sick of the eggs. Every time a new one hatched, one had to go back to the theological drawing board. Gnostics, by contrast, liked the novelty and could afford to like it, since they did not have the same institutional concerns. There were Gnostic theories and speculations but no Gnostic creeds. They attended study groups, not churches.[669]

The Last Supper in John is essentially a Resurrection Dialogue[670] pushed back into the Passion narrative. Here we begin to hear the "inside stuff," even though it contains numerous predictions, after the fact, of yet further revelations to come. But the trick is "The hour is coming and now is!"

All God's Chilluns Got Feet (13:1-17)

The original Johannine Last Supper dialogue was done at the end of chapter 14. Let's consider that first. Chapter 13 opens with the foot-washing scene. It is self-evidently a lesson in humility, a safeguard against the sort of pretention on display in Acts 6:2. But there are more aspects to it. Bultmann[671] theorizes that John is elaborating an original pronouncement story issuing in something like Luke's parallel saying, "Which is the greater? One who sits at table, or one who serves? Is it not

---

[669] Peter Brown, *The Body and Society: Men, Women, and Sexual Renunciation in Early Christianity.* Lectures on the History of Religions, Number 13 (New York: Columbia University Press, 1988), pp. 118-119.

[670] Pheme Perkins, *The Gnostic Dialogue: The Early Church and the Crisis of Gnosticism.* Theological Inquiries (New York: Paulist Press, 1980).

[671] Bultmann, *Gospel of John*, p. 462, note 3.

the one who sits at table? But I am among you as one who serves" (Luke 22:27). That is an almost irresistible suggestion.

But then we come to the cringe-inducing exchange between Peter and Jesus (John 13:8-11). Peter feels it grossly improper for Jesus to lower himself to such menial service, but once Jesus tells him he *has* to let Jesus wash him, he changes his tune: "Well, in that case, why stop at the feet? How about a total-body sponge bath?" Jesus: "Uh, let's not go *overboard* here! You're already clean. You're like a man fresh from a bath and on his way to a dinner appointment. When he gets there his feet *do* need to be washed again because of the road dust he picked up on his way. But that's *all* he needs." This almost *has* to refer to some kind of penance rite. What else *could* it mean? If, as some, e.g., Oscar Cullmann,[672] suggest, the reference is to regular participation in Holy Communion, that would make sense of it, true, but then you'd expect some other metaphor, something suggesting eating and drinking. The case is closed, in my opinion, when we get to what sound like words of institution: "I have given you an example, that you also should do as I have done to you" (13:15). Bultmann[673] considered the evidence for such a ceremony too late (third century), but J. Ramsey Michaels[674] considers it likely enough that John knows of one and wants to see it continue. In that case, Michaels says, it would have been a ritual of humility, but not a sacrament, presumably of penance. But surely penance *would* have to be the point.

Deniers and Betrayers (13:18-30)

The next section, 13:18-30, is devoted to Jesus predicting his imminent betrayal. There is a surprising suggestion that Judas was not up to this point intending to collude with the authorities, nor even to eliminate Jesus. It is only once Judas chances to dip his bread (or chunk of meat) into the dish simultaneously with Jesus that the devil possesses him. But Jesus already knew who it would be (John 6:64, 70-71; 13:17). Jesus tells Judas to get up and go about his nefarious business (verse 27), but the disciples, unaware of what is really going on in front of them, suppose

---

[672] Oscar Cullmann, *Early Christian Worship*. Studies in Biblical Theology No. 10 (London: SCM Press, 1953), pp. 105-109.

[673] Bultmann, *Gospel of John*, p. 469-470, note 2.

[674] J. Ramsey Michaels, *John*. Understanding the Bible Commentary Series (Grand Rapids: Baker Books, 1989), p. 247.

that Judas is being sent to purchase supplies for the upcoming Passover seder (verse 29), which means *this isn't it*. For John, the Last Supper is *not* a Passover meal.

In verses 37-38 Jesus practically scoffs at Peter's affirmation of undying loyalty: "Yeah? Then how come you're going to deny me three times this very night?" This is reminiscent of Oedipus kicking against the goads of Fate. In order to avoid the shameful act Jesus has predicted, Peter follows Jesus as far as he can: the high priest's courtyard. But this very effort steers him into the dangerous situation which will occasion his cowardice!

The Sword of the Planets (13:31-14:6)

Jesus has announced his imminent departure. Bags packed, he has his ticket to heaven, but the disciples don't realize this. Where is he going? And can't they go with him? No, not yet, he says. But he will at some point return for them and take them back with him. This sounds like the eschatology on display in 1 Thessalonians 4:17, "then we who are alive, who are left, shall be caught up together with them in the clouds to meet the Lord in the air; and so we shall always be with the Lord." Nothing about a millennial kingdom here on earth (as in Revelation 21:9-22:5). No, Jesus returns just long enough (hovering in the air) to welcome his saints, then returns to his heavenly abode with them in tow. They shall meet him in the air and forever live with him *there*.

And can Jesus give them directions? He answers, as it were: "You already know the way there, because you know me. I am the way, as well as the truth and the life.[675] The Gnostic reverberations of all this are pronounced.

> I will go to assign a place to Hibil [Abel] in the new abode, and then I will come quickly to you. Do not be afraid of the sword of the planets [i.e., the threatening Archons trying to bar the way of the ascending soul], and let there be no fear of anxiety

---

[675] James Moffatt, *A New Translation of the New Testament* (New York: Harper & Brothers, 1935), translates "the true and living way" (Herbert Dennett, *A Guide to Modern Versions of the New Testament: How to Understand and Use Them* (Chicago: Moody Press, 1966), p. 118.

among you. Afterwards, certainly, I come to you... Truly I am with you. Every time that you seek me you will find me; every time that you call me I will answer you. I am not far from you. (Ginza 235:33)[676] (cf., John 14:1-3, 13, 27)

Everyone who... hears and believes me,
For him is a dwelling prepared in the place of light. (cf., John 14:2-3)
Whoever... hears me not,
His dwelling will be removed from the place of light,
His name will be excised from my roll.
(John-Book 244:18 ff.)[677](cf., Rev. 3:5)

Do not be afraid or anxious; and do not say, "They have left me behind in this world of evil," for I am coming to you soon. (Manda d'Haiye to Anos [Enosh], Ginza 261:15)[678] (cf., John 14:1-3; Rev. 22:20)

Behold, I am going to the house of life now, and then I will come and free you from the evils and sins of this world... I will lead you up on the way on which Hibil [Abel] the righteous and Sitil [Seth-el] and Manda d'Haiye are ascending, away from this world of evils. (Ginza 268:4 ff.)[679] (cf., John 14:1-4)

Continue steadfast in thy assurance,
Until thy lot is complete.
When thy lot is complete,
I myself will come to thee.
I will bring thee robes of brilliance...
I will free thee from the evils,
I will rescue thee from the sinners.
I will let thee live in thy Skina (dwelling),
In a pure place I will rescue thee.
(Mandaean Liturgy 226)[680] (cf., John 14:1-3)

---

[676]Quoted in Bultmann, *Gospel of John*, pp. 598-599.

[677]Quoted in Bultmann, *Gospel of John*, p. 156, note 4.

[678]Quoted in Bultmann, *Gospel of John*, pp. 598-599, note 6.

[679]Quoted in Bultmann, *Gospel of John*, pp. 598-599, note 6.

[680]Quoted in Bultmann, *Gospel of John*, pp. 598-599, note 6.

Thou hast shown us the way, along which thou hast come out of the house of life. Along it we want to make the journey of true, believing men, so that our soul and our spirit abide in the Skina [dwelling] of life. (Mandaean Liturgy 38).[681] (cf., John 14:6)

I have leveled a way from darkness to the bright dwelling. (John-Book 198:20 f.)[682](cf., John 14:6)

[The Kusta is the] way of the perfect, the path that ascends to the place of light. (Ginza 95)[683]

Thou hast brought us out of death. Thou hast shown us the way of life, and hast made us walk the path of truth and faith. (Mandaean Liturgy 77)[684] (cf., John 14:6)

Thou art the way of the perfect, the path that ascends to the place of light. Thou art the life from eternity... Thou art the truth without error. (Ginza 271:26 ff.)[685] (cf., John 14:6)

(Behold) the house of my acquaintances,
who know of me,
that among them I dwell,
In the hearts of my friends,
in the mind of my disciples.
(Mandaean Liturgy, 198)[686] (cf., John 14:23)

(The Helper comes to the Soul and says:)
Thou shalt dwell with me,
and in thy heart will we find a place.
(Ginza 461:15 ff.)[687] (cf., John 14:23)

---

[681]Quoted in Bultmann, *Gospel of John*, pp. 603-604, note5.

[682]Quoted in Bultmann, *Gospel of John*, pp. 603-604, note5.

[683]Quoted in Bultmann, *Gospel of John*, pp. 603-604, note5.

[684]Quoted in Bultmann, *Gospel of John*, pp. 606, note 3.

[685]Quoted in Bultmann, *Gospel of John*, pp. 606, note 3.

[686]Quoted in Bultmann, *Gospel of John*, pp

[687]Quoted in Bultmann, *Gospel of John*, pp

Forgive a bit of theological hair-splitting, but does John 14:6 necessarily imply what we always hear that it means, that one must believe in Jesus in order to be saved? Indeed it might. That is a wholly natural reading of it. But technically that's not exactly what it *says*, is it? Jesus is the way to the Father, and no other path will get you there. But do you have to consciously believe in Jesus? Do you have to have seen the street sign? It is worth noting that a number of theologians have suggested that one may indeed be treading the way of Jesus even without knowing it. Roman Catholic Karl Rahner speaks of "Anonymous Christians" who seek the saving grace of whatever god they know, being unaware of the Christian Jesus (or perhaps culturally indoctrinated against him). C.S. Lewis seemed to hold a belief much like this as well. Perhaps the most important thinker along these lines is Raymond Panikkar,[688] a Roman Catholic with an Indian background, who theorizes that, though no one is saved except by the grace of God in Christ, members of other faiths may find salvation not *despite* but *through* their religions. The piety and sacraments of Hinduism, Judaism, Islam, Buddhism, etc., become conduits for the unrecognized grace of Christ.

Christian Universalists likewise hold that the atonement of Christ saves all people whether or not they repent and believe. This blanket amnesty, they teach, is the result of the atonement wrought by Christ. The conscious acceptance of it, while desirable, cannot be required; otherwise it would become a saving work in its own right. Jesus did not die *trying* to save everyone; his death *did* in fact save them. And this satisfies John 14:6 because there is no alternate means of salvation.

If John meant to say that one must believe in Jesus to be saved, to reach the Father, it could be taken as another sign of the gospel's Marcionite-Gnostic character. Robert Eisler[689] quotes a neglected fragment from Papias, preserved by Fortunatian, early fourth-century Bishop of Aquileia, in his anti-Marcionite preface to John's gospel:

> The Gospel of John was revealed and given to the Churches by John whilst he was still alive in his body, as Papias, called the Hieropolitan, the beloved disciple of John, has reported in his five books of "Exegetics." But (he who) wrote down the Gospel, John dictating correctly the true (evangel), (was) Marcion the

---

[688] Raymond Panikkar, *The Unknown Christ of Hinduism* (London: Darton, Longman & Todd, 1964).

[689] Robert Eisler, *The Enigma of the Fourth Gospel: Its Author and its Writer* (London: Methuen, 1938), p. 156.

heretic. Having been disapproved by him for holding contrary views, he was expelled by John. He had, however, brought him writings, or letters, from the brethren who were in the Pontus.

What is the point of this odd story? If this had actually happened, of course, John would have burnt the tainted text and dictated a new version to a new secretary. As I read the story, it must be an excuse for Marcionite elements in the finished and published gospel. Many who read it rejected it as Marcionite (just as the Alogoi rejected it and the Roman presbyter Gaius ascribed it to the Gnostic Cerinthus). The rejoinder, the story Eisler sets forth, is a qualified concession to these detractors, pleading that it was not John's fault.

Why would John 14:6 imply Marcionism? Because its assertion would seem to leave out of account the righteous of pre-Jesus Israel, wouldn't it? It is safe to say the ancient Israelites knew nothing about Jesus. Granted, John does say that both Abraham (John 8:56) and Isaiah (John 12:41) happily foresaw Jesus' advent, but this claim may be viewed as a piece of polemic, turning the opponents' authorities against them, rather than evidence of a comprehensive theology.

Johannine Recognitions (14:7-11)

Here is another Christological shocker: "Have I been with you so long, and yet you do not know me, Philip? He who has seen me has seen the Father!" *Wait* a second—*what* did I just hear? Yes, that's right: anyone who has seen Jesus was seeing God, they just didn't realize it, though maybe they should have. As much of a jolt as this seems, and *is*, the motif is certainly not new in the Bible. Abraham put on a fancy supper for Jehovah and his bodyguards without the slightest clue who it was. He finds out only later. God lingered with Abraham, but his attendants went on into Sodom on their fact-finding mission. They are angels, but the surly Sodom mob does not know that (though Jude thought they did, Jude verse 7). Abraham and Lot are already among the halo-sporting sheep envisioned in Matthew 25:34-40, while the members of the Sodom Men's Club have joined the herd of Baphomet goats. The Emmaus disciples, too, were probably glad in retrospect they had not been trading dirty jokes while sharing the company of a mysterious Stranger on the way home. The Writer to the Hebrews warns (13:2) his (or her) readers not to turn away visitors seeking shelter, since there's always the possibility they are angels going Trick or Treat. But of course, we're not talking about angels here. He who sees Jesus beholds God Almighty!

Or *does* he? Verses 10-11a have Jesus back-pedaling. "Had you going there, didn't I, Phil?" No, the truth is much less Patripassian: Jesus is "only" indwelt by the Father, and in the same way Jesus indwells the Father, whatever the hell *that* might mean! But it doesn't matter *what* it means. What counts is what it does *not* mean, namely that Jesus is the Father incarnate.[690] Surely what we have here is another scribal interpolation like that in John 10:34-36.

Are You Greater Than Jesus? (14:12-14)

Christians have long had their hands full trying to explain away Jesus' promise that his believers should one day perform greater works than his. One of the most popular lame reinterpretations is that Jesus' "works" are his teachings (but would that really be any better?). Or maybe he is talking about the wider arena of evangelism that will be open to his disciples. That's about as bad as the lame-ass Calvinist redefinition of the 1 Corinthians "gift of prophecy" as if it denoted nothing more than "preaching the gospel."

But no: the Pentecostals are right. They have to be. Jesus is portraying himself as Elijah, about to ascend into heaven and ready to impart his miracle-working Spirit to his successor, Elisha, who does in fact perform twice the miracles recorded of Elijah. Here it will be helpful to think of what Jesus says in John 17:26, "I have made known to them thy Name," a phrase with striking parallels in the Greek magical papyri.[691] In these Hellenistic magic books (cf., Acts 19:19) we read invocations to various great deities from whom magical powers are

---

[690] Dodd, *Interpretation of the Fourth Gospel*, pp. 194-195, makes a valiant attempt to make sense of the whole thing (verses 9-10) as an original unit teaching the unity of Jesus with the Father in a kind of proto-Trinitarian interpenetration. But when you look at the gospel's own explanations of these terms, the statement (as Dodd understands it) seems like overblown rhetoric. Jesus is "in" the Father insofar as he perfectly carries out his will (John 15:10a). The Father is "in" Jesus in that he energizes Jesus' miracles, like a battery in a flashlight (John 14:0-11). Christians "abide in" Jesus insofar as they obey his commandments (John 15:10b). That's *it*? I see this mystification of language precisely as a redactional attempt to obfuscate the plain meaning of "He who has seen me has seen the Father."

[691] Morton Smith, *Jesus the Magician* (New York: Harper & Row, 1978), p. 132.

sought. To Osiris one says, "Glorify me as I have glorified the Name of your son Horus!" (*Papyri graecae magicae* VII. 504). To Thoth, likewise: "in heaven before Phre, I will glorify thee before the moon, I will glorify thee on Earth. [...] I am he whom you met under the holy mountain[692] and to whom you gave the knowledge of your greatest Name, which I shall keep holy, communicating it to none save to [my] fellow initiates in your holy rites" (*Papyri graecaemagicae* XII. 92ff.) This is perhaps how Jesus can expect his apprentices to exceed his own thaumaturgical feats, by bequeathing to them the powerful Name of God which enabled him to do what he did. That is how the Jewish anti-gospel Toledoth Jeschu accounts for Jesus' powers.[693]And this would fit pretty well with the fact that this gospel does not mind showing us Jesus using the old spit-and-polish technique to heal the blind man, another bit of ancient magic. I realize such speculations will be out of the question for those who find it theologically odious. But what can you do?

Verses 16-17, 25-26 predict the sending of the Paraclete, which we have already discussed.

Closed-Circuit Parousia (14:21-23)

Originally the futuristic eschatology of early Christianity stipulated that, when Jesus should return as the sky-filling Son of Man, every set of eyes would witness the sight: "Behold, he is coming with the clouds, and every eye will see him, every one who pierced him; and all tribes of the earth will wail on account of him" (Rev. 1:7; cf., Matt.14:27, 30).[694] What "that other" Judas says in John 14:22, "Lord, how is it that you will manifest yourself to us, and not to the world?" expresses the difficulty some Johannine Christians felt at the introduction of (Gnostic) realized eschatology.[695]

---

[692]Godfré Ray King [Guy Ballard], *Unveiled Mysteries* (Chicago: Saint Germaine Press, 1939), Chapter III, "The Royal Teton," pp. 72-108; Chapter IV, "Mysteries of the Yellowstone," pp. 109-125, recounts similar initiatory revelations deep underground. I'm not vouching for their truth, you understand.

[693]This text is included in my *Pre-Nicene New Testament*. See especially 2:1-8.

[694] Norman Perrin, *A Modern Pilgrimage in New Testament Christology* (Philadelphia: Fortress Press, 1974), Chapter II, "Mark 14:62: The End Product of a Christian Pesher Tradition?" pp. 10-22.

Verse 28 ("You heard me say to you, 'I go away, and I will come to you.' If you loved me, you would have rejoiced, because I go to the Father; for the Father is greater than I.") is in gross contradiction to the "Patripassian" verses in 8:58; 10:30; 14:9. Even orthodox Trinitarians flinch when they read this verse, since their system posits that the Father and the Son are "separate but equal," but John 14:28 is clearly subordinationist (like 1 Corinthians 11:3), I don't care *what* you say! Some try to harmonize, positing that what Jesus means is simply that he is about to leave behind this vale of tears and return to the celestial glory from which he had descended for the vexing duration of a tedious incarnation (cf., Phil. 2:6-8; 2 Cor. 8:9; Mark 9:19). In other words, "You should be happy for me, since it is a far, far better place I go to!" But Jesus doesn't say that. And pretending that's what he meant is just to write your own *Living Bible*. So why the contradiction? Again, I have to think our gospel text embodies readings from competing versions of the text made by competing factions and subsequently harmonized by later scribes who, like all ancient Christian copyists, did not want to risk leaving out anything that might be inspired text.

The Last Supper discourse, as it originally stood, ended right here: "I will no longer talk much with you... Rise, let us go hence" (verses 30, 31). But then Jesus won't shut up! What follows in the next three chapters are additions to the discourse. We seem to be looking at a case similar to that of the two juxtaposed versions of the chain of Markan miracle stories (compare Mark 6:30-52; 7:24-37 with 8:1-26). Thus there are in effect two versions of the Last Supper discourse.[696] Chapter 15:1-17 and chapter 17 are distinctive, self-contained pieces, while 15:18 through the end of chapter 16 pretty much rehashes the contents of chapters 13-14, especially the imminent departure of Jesus and his replacement by the Paraclete. Little if anything essentially new is added. Again, we read the text on two levels: a prediction of future events side by side with their retrojection into the time of Jesus. For example, compare 16:25 with 16:29. Jesus predicts that *one day* he will speak clearly without veiling the truth in figurative form, but this has already come to pass seconds later! "The hour is coming—and now is!" Because, as with apocalyptic literature, the "predictions" have been made after the fact.

---

[695] I imagine that converts to today's "Preterist" movement, with its realized eschatology, at first feel the same disappointment.

[696] Gerd Lüdemann, *What Jesus Didn't Say* (Salem, OR: Polebridge Press, 2011), pp. 69-72.

Branch Offices (15:1-5)

Chapter 15:1-5 gives us the famous True Vine discourse, a pivotal text for Christian devotionalism. Right off the bat, we must note not only that the only parallel to the Synoptics is the metaphor of chopping down unfruitful trees or pruning away unfruitful branches (Matt. 3:10; Luke 3:9; 13:6-9), but also that this Johannine discourse is plainly cut from the same cloth as similar Mandaean Gnostic texts.

> A vine am I, a vine of life,
> a tree in which there is no falsehood.
> The tree of praise,
> from which every one who smells at it comes alive.
> Whoever hears his word,
> his eyes are filled with light.
> (Right Ginza 2:3)[697] (cf., John 15:1)

> I am a tender vine...
> And the great (life) was my planter.
> (Ginza 301:10 ff.)[698] (cf., John 15:1)

> The vine which bears (fruit) ascends,
> (The vine) which bears nothing is cut off here (from the light)
> (Right Ginza 5:2)[699] (cf., John 15:2, 6)

> And thy pure shoots are to thrive excellently... they are to be untied with thee, and not to
> be cut off. (Mandaean Liturgy 252 f.)[700] (cf., John 15:5-6)

> Abide strong and steadfast in me, you who know me... my friends.. do not change the discourse of my mouth...
> (Mandaean Liturgy 217)[701] (cf., John 15:4-5,7)

---

[697] Foerster, *Gnosis*, p. 229.

[698] Quoted in Bultmann, *Gospel of John*, pp. 531-532, note 3.

[699] Foerster, *Gnosis*, p. 233.

[700] Quoted in Bultmann, *Gospel of John*, pp. 533, note 1.

[701] Quoted in Bultmann, *Gospel of John*, p. 536, note 5.

> Abide in the love of the Lord,
> Ye beloved ones in the Beloved;
> Ye who are kept, in Him that liveth:
> Ye who are saved in Him that was saved.
> (Odes of Solomon 8:23)[702] (cf., John 15:9)

Does the True Vine discourse describe a "personal relationship with Christ" as, e.g., Andrew Murray assumed?[703] Such a devotional idiom is certainly one way of applying the passage, though there are others, such as the old Liberal Protestant technique of meditating on the "picture"(of the personality) of the (supposedly) historical Jesus on display in the gospels.[704]

Divine Debriefing (chapter 17)

I have long wondered whether this prayer was (or was based on) the farewell prayer of the Beloved Disciple, the Paraclete himself, shortly before his death and the crisis it caused among his disciples (John 21:23). At any rate, the Gnostic echoes are loud and clear.

> Thereupon I fulfilled in order the works which my Father had set me. (John-Book 224:17)[705] (cf., John 17:4)

> If it is thy wish... let the measure of my disciples be made full,

---

[702] Quoted in Bultmann, *Gospel of John*, p. 546.

[703] Andrew Murray, *Abide in Christ: Thoughts on the Blessed Life of Fellowship with the Son of God* (Old Tappan, NJ: Spire Books, 1900). Bultmann (*Gospel of John*, p. 535) understands the abiding in Christ much as Murray does, insofar as it primarily denotes *receptivity*, though he thinks John definitely does not imply a personal interaction or mystical relationship between God / Christ and the individual (pp. 526, 536; cf., p. 614).

[704]Wilhelm Herrmann, *The Communion of the Christian with God Described on the Basis of Luther's Statements.* Trans. J. Standish Stanyon, rev. R.W. Stewart. Second English Edition. Crown Theological Library (New York: G.P. Putnam's Sons, 1906), pp. 61-78; Harry Emerson Fosdick, *The Personality of Jesus: The Soul of Christianity.* A Sermon Preached at Temple Beth-el, New York, Sunday, April 13, 1930. By "old Liberal theology," I refer to a time when there *was* Liberal theology, before it all degenerated into Green Politics and Stalinist Political Correctness.

[705] Quoted in Bultmann, *Gospel of John*, p.495, note 8.

and so may my disciples arise to the place of light. (John-Book 236:26 ff.)[706] (cf., John 17:12)

The brightness of life rests on me,
It rests on my disciples,
Whom the Seven in this world persecute.
(Mandaean Liturgy 208)[707] (cf., John 17:14-15)

The great (life) called and commissioned me,
and laid his wisdom over me.
(He laid over me) the well-guarded form,
which is kept for me in the hidden places.
He laid over me love,
which shall be given to my friends.
(Ginza 333:27ff)[708] (cf., John 17:23)

Coming Along Quietly (18:1-11)

The arrest in Gethsemane does not follow a prayer of agony as in the Synoptics. John has dispensed with all that back in chapter 12. Here he snipes at the cowardly-seeming Synoptic accounts again. "Shall I not drink the cup the Father has given me?" It is a rhetorical question only, as if to say the very idea is absurd and offensive.

Judas' presence seems superfluous. In Mark 14:44 and Matthew 26:4, Judas says he will indicate whom to arrest by giving Jesus a friendly kiss. That is why he has accompanied the arresting party. Luke 23:47 has Judas lead the mob, implying he alone knew where to find Jesus at this time of night, though why not simply tell them where to find him? So the kiss, which he nonetheless plants on Jesus, must be a vestige of the Markan original. But in John, Judas seems just to be along for the ride, since Jesus first asks the soldiers, "Whom do you seek?" They answer, "Jesus of Nazareth," and Jesus fesses up: "That's me." At this the whole arresting party collapses to the ground like a bunch of bowling pins! They regain their feet, brush themselves off, and things take their course as if nothing untoward had happened! Of course, nothing *did*. The

---

[706] Quoted in Bultmann, *Gospel of John*, p. 519, note 1.

[707] Quoted in Bultmann, *Gospel of John*, pp. 499-500, note 9.

[708] Quoted in Bultmann, *Gospel of John*, pp. 165.

gospel writers frequently have Jesus say things over the heads of the characters in the scene, right to the readers. This time it is not a saying, but an event that goes right by the characters, direct to the readers. The point is to assure the reader that, despite appearances, Jesus has things under control.[709] No one can take him against his will (John 10:17-18).

The story is closely parallel to 2 Kings 1:9-15, where Elijah's roasting of two groups of fifty sent to arrest him makes it clear that, when he finally does go back with a third (terrified) fifty, he isn't doing it because he's being forced to. But there is a gospel parallel, too: the overwhelming of the soldiers like enemy ninjas flattened by Bruce Lee is exactly analogous to Jesus' reassurance to the disciples in Matthew 26:53-54, "Do you not think I cannot appeal to my Father, and he will at once send me more than twelve legions of angels? But how then should the scriptures be fulfilled, that it must be so?"

A similar tale is told of the sage Apollonius of Tyana, imprisoned by Domitian's goons. In the gloomy cell, Apollonius reassures his disciple Damis.

> "No one will kill us."
>
> "And who is so invulnerable as that?" asked Damis. "And when will you be freed?"
>
> "As far as my judge is concerned, today" was the reply, "but as far as I am, immediately."
>
> So saying, he took his leg out of its shackle and said to Damis: "I have given you proof of my freedom. Be courageous."
>
> At that moment, says Damis, he first understood clearly that Apollonius's nature was godlike and more than human. (Philostratus, *Life of Apollonius*, VII:39)[710]

The abortive sword fight familiar from the Synoptics here is embellished with specificity, for we learn that it wasn't some also-ran disciple like Bartholomew or Lebbaeus who sliced the high priest's servant's ear off (when of course he meant to split his skull); it was Peter. Maybe the evangelist inferred his identity by connecting the dots with John 13:37, where Peter affirmed, "I will lay down my life for you!" And who lost the ear? Now we know! His name was "Malchus." As Bultmann (whom I would nominate as the Paraclete!), noted, these names represent the "novelistic and legendary character of the development"[711] of the

---

[709] Bultmann, *Gospel of John*, p.637.

[710] Philostratus, *Life of Apollonius*, p. 195.

tradition, the same tendency that we can observe in later, apocryphal gospels where, e.g. the two men crucified with Jesus are given the names "Demas" and "Gestas" and the centurion who stabs Jesus is named "Longinus."

Another Jesus (18:12-38-19:24)

This much of the story is not remarkably different from the Synoptic versions, but all four are remarkably reminiscent of the story of another Jesus, told by Josephus, one Jesus ben-Ananias.

> An incident more alarming still had occurred four years before the war at a time of exceptional peace and prosperity for the City. One Jeshua, son of Ananias, a very ordinary yokel, came to the feast at which every Jew is supposed to set up a tabernacle for God. As he stood in the temple he suddenly began to shout: "A voice from the east, a voice from the west, a voice from the four winds, a voice against Jerusalem and the Sanctuary, a voice against bridegrooms and brides, a voice against the whole people." Day and night he uttered this cry as he went through all the streets. Some of the more prominent citizens, very annoyed at these ominous words, laid hold of the fellow and beat him savagely. Without saying a word in his own defence or for the private information of his persecutors, he persisted in shouting the same warning as before. The Jewish authorities, rightly concluding that some supernatural force was responsible for the man's behaviour, took him before the Roman procurator. There, though scourged till his flesh hung in ribbons, he neither begged for mercy nor shed a tear, but lowering his voice to the most mournful of tones, answered every blow with "Woe to Jerusalem!" When Albinus -for that was the procurator's name- demanded to know who he was, where he came from and why he uttered such cries, he made no reply whatever to the questions but endlessly repeated his lament over the City, till Albinus decided he was a madman and released him. (*The Jewish War* VI, 302)[712]

---

[711] Bultmann, *Gospel of John*, p. 641, note 2.
[712] Josephus, *The Jewish War*. Trans. G.A. Williamson. Penguin Classics (Baltimore: Penguin Books, 1970), pp. 349-340.)

Four years after this incident, the wild-eyed prophet's prediction came true. It happened during the Roman siege, and it brought with it Jesus ben-Ananias' death. He was crushed by a catapulted stone. The gospel parallels are pretty striking. Both prophets named Jesus arrive in Jerusalem for one of the great feasts. Both instigate disturbances in the Temple. Both proclaim imminent doom and the destruction of the Temple. Both warn the crisis will mean the end of ordinary life, e.g., marriages (Matt. 24:38). The elders drag each Jesus before the Roman procurator. When this man tries to question him, he receives in reply only silence. The Roman, baffled, asks him where he is from (John 19:9). Finally he has the prophet of doom flogged and lets him go (Luke 23:22b).

Theodore J. Weeden[713] argues quite effectively that the Passion narrative of Jesus ben-Ananias (at least the general memory of the story/events, but very likely the specific Josephus passage) has formed the basis for all four of the gospel Passion narratives of Jesus. I concur. And the clincher is the detail of the Procurator (Pilate in the one case, Albinus in the other), mystified at the stubborn reticence of the accused, asking where the prophet hails from, scarcely a necessary or expected element of the plot structure. What an irony! Apologists try to persuade themselves that Josephus mentioned Jesus (in the flagrantly spurious *Testimonium Flavianum*), but they're righter than they want to be: he *did!* His story of Jesus ben Ananias became part of the gospel. The gospels are post-Josephus.

John makes the intriguing statement that Peter managed to get past the bouncer because he was with "another disciple," "who was known to the high priest." Huh? The high priest was acquainted with some Galilean hick? But of course it does not specify that this disciple was one of the Twelve.[714] John was probably thinking of Nicodemus or Joseph of Arimathea.

Another memorable detail in John's special version of the Passion is the exchange between Jesus and Pilate, culminating in Pilate's jaded dismissal, "What is truth?" It is a rhetorical question indicating that Pilate is a hard-nosed pragmatist with no patience for metaphysical abstractions. Truth, he implies, is one more empty illusion. To him,

[713] Theodore J. Weeden, "The Two Jesuses" *Facets and Foundations Forum*. New Series 6, 2 Fall 2003.
[714] Bultmann, *Gospel of John*, p. 483.

Jesus is merely a harmless bore, which is no crime. The scene is reminiscent of Acts 18:14-15.

We have already observed John's editing of items in the Synoptic accounts of which he disapproves. For this evangelist, Jesus was not baptized by John. John's Jesus scoffed at the very idea that he might seek to evade crucifixion. And now John eliminates Simon of Cyrene carrying the cross-arm to Golgotha in place of Jesus. Why? He must be thinking of Jesus' discipleship challenge in Mark 8:34: "If any man would come after me, let him deny himself and take up his cross and follow me." And a man who says this does *not* carry his own cross? John will not have it.

Live (but not for Long) from Golgotha (19:17-37)

Does verse 25 mean to list three women or four? Is "Mary the wife of Clopas" supposed to modify "his mother's sister"? Or is that the name of a third woman, with the second left anonymous (like "Jesus' mother")? If the former, then we have the anomaly of two sisters with the same name. ("This is my brother Darryl, and this is my other brother Darryl." Yikes!). But then John never actually refers to Jesus' mom by name (cf., John 2:1, 3, 5, 12), does he? If we are supposed to know Jesus' mother is named "Mary," then I think we have to go with Robert Eisenman[715] and suppose that Mary the mother of Jesus has been cloned in order to avoid calling *her* "the wife of Clopas," this last name being a Greek equivalent of and substitute for "Cleopas" (Luke 24:18), which is in turn a variant of "Alphaeus" and the Semitic root that also appears in the word "*caliph*," "substitute," the vicar of Muhammad. Thus the disciple "James of Alphaeus" (Mark 3:18) might originally have been the same as James the Just, "the brother of the Lord" (Gal. 1:19) who was the caliph of Jesus and head of the Jerusalem Church.

"Substitute" is the key term here, because people were already promulgating a doctrine of the Perpetual Virginity of Mary, in which case Mary cannot really have been the wife of any mortal, and James cannot be the biological brother of Jesus nor the son of Jesus' mother!

---

[715] Eisenman, *James the Brother of Jesus*, pp. XVIII, 118, 199, 592, 782, 821, 840, 842, 844-845, 848.

Likewise in Luke 24:10, "Mary the mother of James" must be a *different* Mary who *could* have been the mother of James the Just. Whew!

> Jesus' brothers are slowly turning into 'cousins', finally made into a general doctrine by Jerome two centuries later. Mothers become aunts and finally even their *own* sisters! Fathers *turn into uncles*, all having something to do with the growing doctrine of Jesus' divine birth and the concomitant 'perpetual virginity' of Mary, as concretized in the second century in the Protevangelium, ascribed to James as well. This Infancy Gospel also excludes all other births on Mary's part, thereby contradicting the Gospels [Mark 3:31-32; 6:3; John 7:3-5; Acts 1:14] even as we have them.[716]

At any rate, the business about the crucified Jesus directing the Beloved Disciple henceforth to take Jesus' mother into his care is a bit of narrative scaffolding erected over a substructure of ecclesiastical politics. What? Why? Ask yourself, "Wouldn't Jesus' surviving brothers have been the ones to look after their mother?" Not a chance, because, as we saw back in John 7:3-5, the evangelist vilifies them as unbelievers and thus hardly fit caretakers for the Blessed Mother. The issue is not "Who should have custody of Mother Mary?" That issue is long moot, if it was ever real to begin with. The question is fairly obvious code for "Which Christian figurehead's present-day faction should have authority over Mother Church?" And the answer is, of course, the Johannine sect should have the primacy.

Getting crucified "is thirsty work,"[717] and Jesus' case was no exception—or *was* it? John has Jesus say, "I thirst," but he prefaces the exclamation with the words "to fulfil the scripture," or in other words, "but verily he was just kidding." This implies, at the very least, what Käsemann called "naïve docetism,"[718] and maybe not so naïve at that. Jesus was *not* actually parched; the script just required him to say so. The idea is much the same as the Buddhist belief[719] that Gautama, like all

---

[716] Eisenman, *James the Brother of Jesus*, p. 844.

[717] Remember the quoted part from *The Wicker Man?*

[718] Ernst Käsemann, *Testament of Jesus*, p. 26. "In what sense is he flesh, who walks on the water and through closed doors, who cannot be captured by his enemies, who at the well of Samaria is tired and desires a drink, yet has no need of drink and has food different from that which his disciples seek?" (p. 9).

subsequent bodhisattvas, was not really incarnated at all but only gave off the appearance of flesh and blood. Everything he did was a pre-set charade, including his ostensible enlightenment in the shade of the Bodhi Tree.

The attending soldiers had enough pity for Jesus to try to assuage his thirst, so they hoisted up to him a sponge dipped in vinegar (sour wine). How'd they get it to him? Our manuscripts have them putting the sponge on the tip of a hyssop reed. Uh... good luck with *that*. "Hyssop" has to be a very early copyist error, substituting *ussōpō* ("on a hyssop stem") for *ussō* ("on a lance").[720]

Verses 31-33, 36 offer us another contrived fulfillment of scripture (either Psalm 34:20; Exod. 12:46; or Num. 9:12). We read that the Roman troops had to concede to Jewish sensibilities by breaking (clubbing) the legs of the crucified men, hastening their lingering death by preventing them from lifting their chests to inhale, killing them by suffocation. Jesus, however, they found already dead, so they didn't bother. Or did they? Our friend the Ecclesiastical Redactor has inserted a contradictory patch (verses 34-35, 37) according to which the soldiers were by no means so sure Jesus had already expired and essayed to find out (or to finish him off) by harpooning him in the rib cage, whereupon both water and blood gushed out, like water from the rock.[721] The point of the insertion? The goal is to "nail" the sacraments of water baptism and Holy Communion onto the crucifixion scene.[722]

And the claim that the prodigy was attested by a sworn witness is part of the interpolation and does not imply eye-witness authorship of the whole gospel,[723] though the interpolator may have wanted to create that impression, as he seems to do again in his appendix to the gospel (chapter 21:24).

---

[719] Edward J. Thomas, *The History of Buddhist Thought* (London: Routledge & Kegan Paul, 1951), pp. 174, and Chapter XVI, "The Career of the Bodhisattva," pp. 198-211; Har Dayal, *The Bodhisattva Doctrine in Buddhist Sanskrit Literature* (New York: Samuel Weiser, 1978), Chapter VII, "The Last Life and Enlightenment," pp. 292-317.

[720] Bultmann, *Gospel of John*, p. 674, note 2; Dodd, *Historical Tradition*, p. 124, note 2 continued from p. 123.

[721] The action described is an "allegory of reading" (Paul de Man) for the procedure of the interpolator, stabbing the extant text in the side with new, contradictory material.

[722] Bultmann, *Gospel of John*, pp. 677-678.

[723] Contra Bruce, *New Testament Documents*, p. 59.

Stashing the Savior (19:38-42)

From gospel to gospel, Joseph of Arimathea gets progressively more sanctified. Mark depicts him as a pious man, a Sanhedrinist, "looking for the kingdom of God" to appear (Mark 15:33), just like the devout Jerusalemites in Luke 2:25, 38; 24:21. Matthew 27:57 neglects to tell us Joseph belonged to the Sanhedrin because he didn't like Mark 14:64's implication that Joseph must have voted to condemn Jesus. Matthew also tells us Joseph was wealthy, perhaps implied in Mark as well, since he is said to have a private tomb. And Matthew's Joseph is also characterized as "a disciple of Jesus." Luke 23:50-51 does make Joseph a member of the council but hastens to exempt him from voting against Jesus, an obvious piece of white washing. John's gospel explains how Joseph could have been both a disciple and a Sanhedrinist: he was a closet disciple (John 19:38) like Nicodemus (John 3:2; 7:50-52) who dared stick up for Jesus only in carefully chosen words because he did not want to lose his position (cf., John 5:44). Joseph and Nicodemus act together in seeing to Jesus' burial. One wonders if we are to understand this action as finally coming out of the closet to "confess Jesus before men," rather like Antigone risking her life by retrieving the corpse of her brother to give him a decent burial.

In this gospel Joseph pointedly does *not* take the body directly to his own tomb. There is no time for that; the Day of Preparation is about to begin. So they stash the corpse in a convenient tomb near Golgotha, planning to return as soon as the coast is clear. When Mary Magdalene arrives at this tomb and finds it unoccupied, she naturally infers that she has just missed Joseph and Nicodemus transferring Jesus' body somewhere else. But she doesn't know where. (Maybe his own tomb, which would certainly not have been located near Golgotha.)

Tell Them Goodbye for Me (20:1, 11-18)

Unlike the Synoptics, nothing is said here of a *group* of women visiting the tomb, or of their plans to anoint the body. Joseph and Nicodemus have already seen to that, which Mary must know if she knows where they placed the body. This episode absolutely must have originally continued directly with verse 11, before either the evangelist or the redactor interrupted it with the visit of Peter and the Beloved Disciple (verses 2-10). She looks into the tomb and finds it not quite empty after all: a pair of angels are sitting like bookends on the rock-shelf where the corpse had been laid out. Apparently she had no inkling who they were, any more than Abraham recognized the celestial nature of his visitors in Genesis 19. No haloes, no wings. They ask her what the trouble is, just as Jesus incognito asks the two Emmaus disciples in Luke 24. She explains her grief, then hears another man ask her the same question. She explains again. It is Jesus, though she does not recognize him, not too surprising in the circumstances, until he calls her by name. Overjoyed, she goes to embrace him, but he tells her not to. Why?

Randel Helms[724] solved a longstanding problem when he discerned how this story borrows the self-disclosure of the angel Raphael at the climax of the Old Testament Book of Tobit. When Tobias first saw Raphael, he "did not know" he was really an angel (Tobit 5:5); likewise, when Mary, weeping outside the tomb, first saw Jesus there, she "did not know" who he really was (20:14). Having delivered Sarah from her curse, Raphael reveals himself to Tobit and his son Tobias and announces, his mission complete, that "I am ascending to him who sent me" (Tobit 12:20), just as Jesus tells Mary, "I am ascending to my father and your father, to my God and your God" (John 20:17).

So why does the risen Jesus warn Mary "Touch/hold me not, for I have not yet ascended to the father" (20:17a)? This is probably an indication of docetism, that Jesus (at least the risen Jesus) cannot be touched, not having (any longer?) a fleshly body. Why docetism? It would nicely complete the parallel between John 20 and the Raphael revelation/ascension scene, where the angel explains (Tobit 12:19):

"I am Raphael, one of the seven angels who enter and serve before the glory of the Lord." Stricken with fear, the two men fell to the ground. But Raphael said to them, "No need to fear; you are safe. Thank God now and forever. As for me, when I came to you it was not out of any favor on my part, but because it was God's will. So continue to thank him every day; praise him with song. Even though you watched me eat and drink, I did not really do so; what you were seeing was a vision. So now get up from the ground and praise God. Behold, I am about to ascend to him who sent me; write down all these things that have happened to you." When Raphael ascended, they rose to their feet and could no longer see him. They kept thanking God and singing his praises; and they continued to acknowledge

---

[724] Helms, Gospel Fictions, pp. 146-147.

these marvelous deeds which he had done when the angel of God appeared to them. (Tobit 12:15-22, New American Bible)

The Johannine episode must originally have circulated independently of the famous Doubting Thomas story with its tactile proofs, hence need not be consistent with it; note that in 20:17b Jesus seems to anticipate *not seeing the disciples again*. He pointedly does *not* tell her to instruct the disciples to meet him shortly, as in Mark. Instead, he says, essentially, "Tell them goodbye for me, okay?"

Last One to the Tomb Is a Rotten Egg! (20:2-10)

The inserted episode of Peter and his companion must originally have been introduced with the arrival of Mary Magdalene *and others* ("*we* do not know where they have laid him"), as in the Lukan parallel (Luke 24:10-12). In Luke's version (at least in the Western Text), no other disciple accompanied Peter when he ran to see for himself, which suggests the ideal or fictional character of the Beloved Disciple. In John, the Beloved Disciple beats Peter to the tomb but halts there, allowing Peter to go past him and enter first. Why include such a detail? Raymond E. Brown[725] cogently proposes that what we are seeing here is a tactful tip of the mitre to Petrine seniority by a writer who owed allegiance to the Johannine sect but with no hostility toward Petrine sectarians. He depicts the Beloved Disciple in subtly superior terms, first by making him the first to reach the empty tomb, and, second, by having him suddenly realize what has happened: Jesus has risen. Peter, by contrast, returns home baffled. In the same way, the evangelist thought, Johannine Christians are more advanced than their Petrinist "weaker brethren."

Apologists[726] have contended that this scene must stem from eye-witness testimony because of the vividly detailed description. But such vividness is hardly unknown to fictional narrative, as witness a similar scene from the second-century C.E. novel *Chaireas and Kallirroe* by Chariton.

---

[725] Brown, *Community of the Beloved Disciple*, pp. 82-85.

[726] J.N.D. Anderson, *Christianity: The Witness of History: A Lawyer's Approach* (London: Tyndale Press, 1969), pp. 96-97; John R.W. Stott, *Basic Christianity* (Grand Rapids: Eerdmans, 1958), p. 51; F.F. Bruce, *New Testament Documents*, p. 49.

The grave robbers closed the tomb carelessly; they were careless in the night. Chaireas was guarding and toward dawn he approached the tomb, supposedly to bring crowns and jewels, but really he had in mind to kill himself. For he did not admit that he was unbetrothed from Kallirroe, and he considered death to be the only healer of grief. When he came close, however, he found the stones moved away and the entrance open. He looked in and was shocked, seized by a great perplexity at what had happened. Rumor made an immediate report to the Syracusans about the miracle. All then ran to the tomb; no one dared to enter until Hermocrates ordered it. One was sent in, and he reported everything accurately. It seemed incredible~the dead girl was not there. Then Chaireas thought he ought to see again the dead Kallirroe; but when he searched the tomb he was able to find nothing. Many came in after him, disbelieving. Amazement seized everyone, and some said as they stood there, "The shroud has been stripped off, this is the work of grave-robbers; but where is the body?" Many gossips and rumor-mongers were busy in the multitude. But Chaireas looked up to heaven and stretched forth his hands, "Who of the gods, being my rival, has carried off Kallirroe and now has her with him?" (Chaireas and Kallirroe, 3:3)[727]

We have to wonder whether the Beloved Disciple really understood that Jesus had arisen, i.e., whether the evangelist meant to say so. For one thing, he comments, "For as yet they did not know the scripture that said he must rise from the dead" (verse 9), which, by itself, would seem to mean they *still* did not know it.[728] Second, the disciples turn around and head back, *not to the other disciples*, but *to their individual homes*, i.e., back in Galilee, which is just where we find them in the Johannine Appendix (21:2-3). From this I must infer that the insertion John 20:2-9 was originally the beginning of the section we call the Johannine Appendix. I think John 20:1, 11-18 was an independent story.[729] So was

---

[727] Dungan and Cartlidge, eds., *Sourcebook of Texts*, pp. 157-158.

[728] What about previous predictions by Jesus that he should rise? This verse seems to be a tacit admission that the belief in Jesus' resurrection arose on the basis of esoteric scripture exegesis, not from anyone's memories of seeing a risen Jesus.

[729] The author of the Gospel of Mary Magdalene seems to have known it as such, as the whole book seems to take up right as John 20:18 leaves off. The

John 20:19-23, another version of the scene in Luke 24:36-43. John 20:24:-29 was yet another insertion, as we will shortly see.

You Kinda Had to Be There (20:19-23)

In the Lukan version of the scene, Jesus displays his hands and feet, presumably to prove he was the same man they had seen crucified, since his extremities still bore nail wounds. I say "presumably" because, though victims were often nailed to their crosses, sometimes they were simply tied with rope, and no gospel crucifixion account says one way or the other (though of course John 20:25, a resurrection story, says he had been nailed up). Anyway, John says he showed them his hands and *side*. Why the change? We can thank the Ecclesiastical Redactor who had Jesus stabbed in the side. He changed "feet" (as I suggest the story, like Luke's parallel, originally read) to "side" in order to adjust it to his previous insertion into the crucifixion account. Ditto in the upcoming Doubting Thomas pericope, which must originally have lacked "and place my hand in his side," which sounds like an add-on anyway after the two previous clauses, which mention "the print of the nails" and "the mark of the nails" but leaves it at that.

I suspect that John did not like the possible implication of Luke's version, that Jesus' demonstration of his wounds was meant to prove his fleshly corporeality, that he was no ghostly apparition but rather a man who had *escaped* death, not *returned from* it. No, John must make it clear that Jesus had really and truly died and thus really and truly risen from the dead. He had not escaped Judea and Galilee to go teach among the Jews of the Diaspora,[730] as apparently some believed, but ascended to heaven, which is why no one in Palestine ever saw him again.

Verses 21-23 give us John's version of both the Great Commission and Pentecost, the equipping of the apostles for their evangelistic mission. This important feature makes it impossible for the Doubting Thomas episode to have been organically connected to this one. For in John 20:24 we suddenly learn that Thomas had more important business elsewhere when the resurrected Jesus came a-calling. Jesus, we

---

male disciples have not seen the risen Jesus and are not going to, so they have to ask Mary what he said to her.

[730] The Acts of Thomas, which has Thomas, the *identical twin* of Jesus (*ahem*), preach the gospel in far-off India, may well have originally assumed this, with later redaction substituting Thomas for the look-alike Jesus.

would have to assume, either did not notice Tom was absent or didn't have time to wait for him to get back, so he imparted the Spirit to the others and split. Absurd. The 20:19-23 episode plainly presupposes all eleven were present.

For All You Skeptics out There (20:20-29)

Haven't you felt that God is asking a lot more from you than he did from those "lucky, lucky bastards,"[731] the disciples? Not much trouble believing in the resurrection of Jesus *if you saw it with your own eyes*, right? But if you didn't (and that's *all* subsequent Christians), you're at one heck of a disadvantage. But you have to believe it anyway, or you're in serious trouble. Well, that is the point of the Doubting Thomas tale. At the end of it, Jesus pretty much just turns to the audience and addresses the reader: "Blessed are those who have not seen yet believe" (verse 29). The reader is supposed to identify vicariously with Thomas, but that's a cheat. In case you haven't noticed, *you still haven't seen the risen Jesus for yourself!* This is no less a mere piece of narrative than the resurrection stories before it. Snap out of it! You're still just as bad off. Anyway, this device was by no means unique to John. Here is another specimen.

> This young boy would never agree to the immortality of the soul. "I, my friends, am completing the tenth month of praying to Apollonius to reveal to me the nature of the soul. But he is completely dead so as never to respond to my begging, nor will I believe he is not dead." Such were the things he said then, but on the fifth day after that they were busy with these things and he suddenly fell into a deep sleep right where he had been talking. Now, the rest of the youths studying with him were reading books and busily incising geometric shapes on the earth, when he, as if insane, suddenly leaped to his feet, still seeming to be asleep, the perspiration running off him, and cried out, "I believe you!" When those present asked him what was wrong, he said, "Do you not see Apollonius the sage, how he stands here among us, listening to the argument and singing wonderful verses concerning the soul?" "Where is he?" they said, "for he has not appeared to us, even though we wish this more than to have all mortal wealth." But the youth replied, "It seems

---

[731]Chapman, Cleese, Gilliam, Idle, Jones, and Palin, *Life of Brian*, p. 61. Some manuscripts read "jammy bastards" (p. 151).

he came to discuss with me alone concerning the things which I would not believe." (Philostratus, *Life of Apollonius of Tyana*, VIII:31)[732]

It Is (Almost) Finished (20:30-31)

This brief bit must have originally served as the conclusion of the Signs Source, the list of miracle stories John incorporated, amplifying the wonder-stories into theological lessons. And the evangelist figured it would make a good ending to his own book.[733]

Post-Credits Scene (chapter 21)

This chapter pretends to offer us the very first resurrection appearance. The disciples, as anticipated in John 20:10, have given up the dream that occupied them for some three years (in this gospel anyway), like the disillusioned disciples from Emmaus in Luke 24. They have returned to their homes and their worldly jobs, only to be rudely jolted back into the waking dream by a dim figure hailing them from the shore of the Lake of Tiberias (= Sea of Galilee). The question is innocent enough: "Caught anything yet?" Something seems familiar, and one squinting disciple (presumably intended as the Beloved Disciple, but who knows?) recognizes him. If the disciple is the Beloved Disciple, it would make sense for him to be the one to recognize the risen Jesus, harking back to John 20:8, where he also shows similar perceptiveness. Peter, hearing it is Jesus, whom they all had given up for dead, cannot wait for the boat to come to shore and springs into the water. Perhaps his urgency stems from his loyal devotion, earlier professed but betrayed. Perhaps he wants to ask forgiveness, especially in view of the direction his conversation with Jesus will shortly take.

Did this much of the story become the Walking on Water episode? In Mark 6:47-50 the disciples are out on the Sea of Galilee without Jesus, whom they suddenly spy from the boat. The sight of him walking "on" the sea terrifies them. Why? Mark takes the preposition *epi* to mean "on top of," implying that Jesus is defying gravity, striding on the

---

[732] Trans. Dungan. Dungan and Cartlidge, eds., *Sourcebook of Texts*, pp.295-296.
[733] Bultmann, *Gospel of John*, p. 698.

surface of the lake. But it might as easily be taken in the sense of "on the verge of." That would be terrifying if the one you saw walking on the shore was *dead* the last time you saw him! And that is the case in John 21.

The miraculous catch of fish, already discussed in connection with Luke chapter 5, must have been borrowed from this story of the sage Pythagoras, son of Apollo.

> At that time he [Pythagoras] was going from Sybaris to Krotona. At the shore, he stood with men fishing with nets; they were still hauling the nets weighed down [with fish] from the depths. He said he knew the number of fish that they had hauled in. The men agreed to do what he ordered, if the number of fish was as he said. He ordered the fish to be set free, living, after they were counted accurately. What is more astonishing, in the time they were out of the water, none of them died while he stood there. He paid them the price of the fish and went to Krotona. They announced the deed everywhere, having learned his name from some children. (Iamblichus, *Life of Pythagoras* 36:60 f, 134-136)[734]

The specific number of the fish, 153,[735] "happens" to be one of the numbers sacred to Pythagoreans. No coincidence if you ask me. But the number business no longer makes sense in a non-Pythagorean story. Imagine the absurdity entailed in taking the Johannine story as a record of real events. Who's going to bother counting fish when you're in the company of the resurrected Son of God?

The dialogue between Jesus and Peter seems to signify, as all readers can see, the forgiveness and reinstatement of Peter as the prime apostle, excusing his shameful denials. But another widely accepted reading of the text is groundless: Jesus first asks Peter if he "loves" (*agapaō*) him, and Peter answers that he does "love" (*phileō*) him. Ditto the second time: Peter again answers with the word *phileō*. The third time, Jesus asks Peter if he loves him, using *phileō*. Sermons tell us that there is a big difference between the two Greek words, *agapaō* denoting selfless commitment, *phileō* implying "mere" friendly affection. But this is to read too much into the text, since the two words are synonyms. Is there supposed to be some meaningful difference between the

---

[734] Trans. Cartlidge. Dungan and Cartlidge, eds., *Sourcebook of Texts*, p. 55.

[735] George J. Brooke, *The Dead Sea Scrolls and the New Testament* (Minneapolis: Fortress Press, 2005), pp. 282-297.

alternation of synonyms between "Feed my lambs" in verse 15, "Tend my sheep" in verse 16, and "Feed my sheep" in verse 17? Not likely.

Jesus kills the mood in verses 18-19 when he predicts that in future years, the aged Peter will be led off to crucifixion. Why does the writer bring this up? In order to pave the way for Peter to ask what fate awaits his rival, the Beloved Disciple, because what all this is leading up to is the implication that the position of Peter will, upon his death, pass to the unnamed Beloved Disciple.[736]

Originally, the Ecclesiastical Redactor seems to have thought the Beloved Disciple would hold his supremacy till the Parousia, assuming it was a few decades away (allowing time for Peter to have grown old before his martyrdom). And since the Beloved Disciple is never named, but seems to be another epithet for the Paraclete, it is possible the redactor was thinking of a succession of Paracletes spanning the time till the Parousia. In fact, this is what happened, as we have seen, with several individuals sequentially announcing themselves as the channeler for the Paraclete, including Montanus, Mani, and Muhammad.

But whoever wrote verse 23, which attempts to reinterpret the saying in verse 22, did not read it that way, inferring that the Beloved Disciple to whom Jesus referred was one specific individual who, however, had died in the meantime. As Bultmann[737] suggested, verse 23 looks like a "correction" by this subsequent writer after the Ecclesiastical Redactor's death, trying to solve a problem inadvertently created by his own misunderstanding of the passage. If the Ecclesiastical Redactor himself had considered the Beloved Disciple/Paraclete to be a single, specific individual and already seen the problem of his dying too soon, while the world still stood, wouldn't he have incorporated the reinterpretation of the "tarry till I come" saying as purely hypothetical into his account in the first place? Instead, it looks like someone found himself stuck with a text he dared not strike out or rewrite, but could only reinterpret by means of an explanatory gloss.

Seems Like a Seam (21:25)

The Ecclesiastical Redactor attempts here to simulate the original ending of the gospel, paraphrasing it to create the same effect. It is a

---

[736] Bultmann, *Gospel of John*, p. 706.
[737] Bultmann, *Gospel of* John, p. 715.

classic redactional seam whereby an interpolator attempts to reproduce the hook from which the original narrative depended. Interestingly, the wording here ("the world itself could not contain the books that would be written") balances off that of the opening of Luke's gospel ("many have undertaken to compile a narrative of the things which have been accomplished among us").

Robert M. Price is one of the chief advocates for the controversial Christ Myth theory. He has debated Bart Ehrman, William Lane Craig, Craig Blomberg, James White, and many others. He holds two Ph.D. degrees, in Systematic Theology and New Testament. He hosts two podcasts, The Bible Geek and The Human Bible. He has written many books and academic articles and was a Fellow of the Jesus Seminar for some two decades. He is the founding editor of the *Journal of Higher Criticism*. Among his books is *The Case Against "The Case for Christ": A New Testament Scholar Refutes the Reverend Lee Strobel*. (Upon hearing that Price was to speak at a conference, Strobel hastily withdrew.) Price no longer even seeks employment in universities and seminaries, where his opinions are unwelcome, preferring to impart his knowledge on the internet and in his writing. He rejoices to be married to Carol and to have two brilliant daughters, Victoria and Veronica. He can be contacted at criticus@aol.com.

Printed in Great Britain
by Amazon